*The Destruction of the
Medieval Chinese Aristocracy*

HARVARD-YENCHING INSTITUTE MONOGRAPH SERIES 93

The Destruction of the Medieval Chinese Aristocracy

Nicolas Tackett

Published by the Harvard University Asia Center
Distributed by Harvard University Press
Cambridge (Massachusetts) and London 2014

© 2014, 2016 by the President and Fellows of Harvard College

Printed in the United States of America

The Harvard-Yenching Institute, founded in 1928, is an independent foundation dedicated to the advancement of higher education in the humanities and social sciences in Asia. Headquartered on the campus of Harvard University, the Institute provides fellowships for advanced research, training, and graduate studies at Harvard by competitively selected faculty and graduate students from Asia. The Institute also supports a range of academic activities at its fifty partner universities and research institutes across Asia. At Harvard, the Institute promotes East Asian studies through annual contributions to the Harvard-Yenching Library and publication of the *Harvard Journal of Asiatic Studies* and the Harvard-Yenching Institute Monograph Series.

Publication of this book was partially underwritten by the Mr. and Mrs. Stephen C. M. King Publishing and Communications Fund, established by Stephen C. M. King to further the cause of international understanding and cooperation, especially between China and the United States, by enhancing cross-cultural education and the exchange of ideas across national boundaries through publications of the Harvard University Asia Center.

Library of Congress Cataloging-in-Publication Data

Tackett, Nicolas, 1975–
 The destruction of the medieval Chinese aristocracy / by Nicolas Tackett.
  pages cm. — (Harvard-Yenching Institute monograph series ; 93)
 Includes bibliographical references and indexes.
 ISBN 978-0-674-49205-9 (hardcover : alk paper)
 ISBN 978-0-674-97065-6 (pbk : alk paper) 1. China—History—Tang dynasty, 618-907. 2. China—History—Tang dynasty, 618–907—Sources. 3. Aristocracy (Social class)—China—History—To 1500. 4. Elite (Social sciences)—China—History—To 1500. 5. Power (Social sciences)—China—History—To 1500. 6. Social change—China—History—To 1500. 7. Adjustment (Psychology)—Social aspects—China—History—To 1500. 8. China—Social life and customs—221 B.C.–960 A.D. 9. China—Social conditions—221 B.C.–960 A.D. I. Title.
 DS749.35.T33 2014
 951'.01708621—dc23
                         2013038080

Index by the author

∞ Printed on acid-free paper

First paperback edition 2016

Last figure below indicates year of this printing
25 24 23 22 21 20 19 18 17 16

for Liu Kan

Contents

List of Figures   ix
Acknowledgments   xi
Conventions   xiii
Map of Tang China   xv

Introduction   1
    The Transformation of Medieval Elites   3
    Tomb Epitaphs as a Historical Source   13

1 *The Bureaucratic Aristocracy of Medieval China*   27
    Clan Lists and the Classification of the Great Clans   29
    The Demographic Expansion of the Medieval Aristocracy   36
    The Geographic Dispersal of Great Clan Descendants   44
    Bureaucratized Aristocrats   61
    Conclusion   67

2 *The Geography of Power*   70
    Localizing Elites   72
    Capital Elites   82
    National Elites in the Provinces   88
    Other Elite Migratory Pathways   98
    Conclusion   105

3 *The Capital Elite Marriage Network*   107
    Reconstructing Patrilines   108
    Localizing Patrilines   113
    Geographic Distribution and Size of the Late Tang Political Elite   119
    The Social Landscape of the Capitals   122
    Marriage Networks and Social Capital   129
    Conclusion   141

4 *The Late Tang Provinces*   146
    The Late Tang Provincial System and the Hebei Autonomous Provinces   149
    Recentralization after the Xianzong Restoration   155

The Tang Political Oligarchy and the Provinces   160
　　　Social Mobility in Provincial Governments   170
　　　Provincial Cultures   178
　　　Conclusion   185

5　*Huang Chao and the Destruction of the Medieval Aristocracy*   187
　　　Chang'an under Huang Chao   191
　　　Devastation in Luoyang and the Provinces   206
　　　The Demise of the Tang Elite   218
　　　The Survivors and the New Structure of Power   231

Conclusion   235

Appendix A: Guide to the Accompanying Database   243
Appendix B: Estimating the Total Size of the Late
　　Tang Capital Elite   248
Appendix C: Sources of Ninth-Century Excavated Epitaphs   250

Bibliography   253
Personal Name Index   265
General Index   275

Figures

0.1. Epitaph of Li Gao   14
1.1. Forty-four eminent clans not included in extant clan lists   34
1.2. Frequency of attribution of great clan status in ninth-century epitaphs (by region)   37
1.3. Relative prestige of clan attributions in ninth-century epitaphs (by region)   39
1.4. Incidence of elites residing in the same prefecture or province as choronym place of clan origin (by region)   47
1.5. Choronym places of origin of elites from four select prefectures   48
1.6. Incidence of elites residing in the same prefecture or province as choronym place of clan origin (by select prefectures)   53
1.7. Core versus periphery localization of native and nonnative clans in the Lower Yangzi region   54
2.1. Percentage of individuals who died in prefecture/province of burial (by region) (800–880 CE)   77
2.2. Site of death of individuals buried in the capital region (800–880 CE)   78
2.3. Length of epitaph texts in different regions of China   83
2.4. Family traditions of officeholding among elites (by region) (800–880 CE)   85
2.5. National versus local prominence of officeholding elite (by region) (800–880 CE)   86
2.6. Private residences in the provinces belonging to Luoyang or Chang'an elites   89
2.7. Places of provincial burial of individuals with national ancestries   92
3.1. Places of burial of members of select patrilines   115
3.2. Suburbs of burial of branches of two Luoyang-based patrilines   117
3.3. Places of burial of the top seventy-five officeholding patrilines   120

3.4. Major types of capital elites (Chang'an versus Luoyang)   121
3.5. Percentage of burials for kinsmen or kinswomen of chief ministers (by region)   121
3.6. Marriage network of late Tang elite families   123
3.7. Composition of capital-based marriage cliques   126
3.8. Elite residency patterns in Chang'an   128
3.9. Top ninth-century officials by patriline home base and marriage network   134
4.1. Office rotations of two ninth-century Youzhou officials   153
4.2. Methods by which governors of select provinces acceded to office (by year and province)   163
4.3. Backgrounds (civilian or military) of governors of select provinces (by year and province)   164
4.4. Governors with family history of bureaucratic service (by year and province)   165
4.5. Governors based in the capital or with ties to the capital marriage network (by year and province)   166
4.6. Types of service in provincial bureaucracies (by home region and class of officials)   177
4.7. Places of county and prefectural service of capital-based officials   180
4.8. Places of county and prefectural service of provincial officials serving in their home provinces   181
5.1. Consolidation of post-Tang regimes in North China (875–920 CE) (by province and year)   216
5.2. Consolidation of post-Tang regimes in the Middle/Lower Yangzi (875–920 CE) (by prefecture and year)   217
5.3. Number of excavated epitaphs in the capital region and in Hebei/Hedong (by decade)   225
5.4. Number of excavated epitaphs from the capital region (by period)   226
5.5. Military battles and campaigns with more than ten thousand reported casualties in the period 750 to 919   229

Acknowledgments

First and foremost, I would like to express my thanks to my graduate advisor, Robert Hymes, for his extensive help and encouragement during the decade I spent writing my dissertation and its prequel, this present study. During my student years, I also had the good fortune of attending seminars taught by many others who have also made a mark on my development as a historian, and to whom I am grateful: Robert Harrist, Li Feng, Martin Kern, Ellen Neskar, Richard Bulliet, Zhang Xiqing, Sarah Schneewind, Hal Kahn, Valerie Hansen, Christian de Pee, and Christian Lamouroux. Thanks also to Paul Smith for participating in my dissertation defense. For his insightful comments to my presentations at conferences over the past few years and for inspiring all of us doing GIS and prosopography, I extend my gratitude to Peter Bol.

My research time in China was made possible by a Columbia University Traveling Fellowship and a grant from the Fulbright-Hays Doctoral Dissertation Research Abroad Program. I also benefited from a year at the Getty Research Institute and in the Stanford Introduction to the Humanities program. Thanks to all who made those fellowships possible. Charles Salas and Ellen Woods were particularly supportive. I would also like to thank all who helped me obtain access to research material: Wang Xiaomeng and Li Jugang of the Shaanxi Provincial Archaeological Institute; Li Chaoyuan of the Shanghai Museum; Meng Fanfeng of the Hebei Institute of Archaeology; as well as the staffs of the Changshu Museum, the Changzhou Museum, the Yangzhou Museum, the Shanghai Library, the Shandong Museum of Stone Carvings, and the various libraries at Peking University.

While writing this book, I have benefited from long conversations with Miranda Brown, Al Dien, Huang Yijun, Ye Wa, Tim Davis, Alex Cook, Linda Feng, Tom Mullaney, Brian Vivier, Tony DeBlasi, Lu Yang, Jessey Choo, Zhang Cong, Sukhee Lee, Lewis Mayo, Zhang Tianhong, and Iiyama Tomoyasu. Since arriving at Berkeley, I have also enjoyed countless wonderful and inspiring discussions with numerous of my department colleagues, including several (somewhat grueling) ones on Lomas Cantadas (aka El Toyonal!). Special thanks to David Johnson and Geoffrey Koziol for their particularly detailed comments to my manuscript, and to Kristen Wanner, editor at the Harvard University Asia Center. I have also received invaluable feedback over the years from Rong Xinjiang, Li Hongbin, Patricia Ebrey, Lau Nap-yin, Ch'en Jo-shui, and many others. In addition, Liu Kan has consistently provided me with the invaluable practical perspective of a peasant turned cultural geographer.

Finally, I would like to extend special thanks to my father, Timothy Tackett, who first exposed me to the historical profession (in the archives of the French provinces some three decades ago), and who has been a constant source of encouragement, as well as of constructive comments and criticism of my written work.

—N. T.

Conventions

1. The bulk of the primary source material used for this study consists of tomb epitaphs and other funerary biographies. A personal name index at the back of the book provides database epitaph numbers for all individuals with inscriptions mentioned by name in the text. In the main text (but not in footnotes), an asterisk (*) following a personal name indicates that an inscription exists for the individual in question. For full citation information, readers are invited to obtain the epitaph number from the personal name index and consult the full Microsoft Access database (or the abridged Microsoft Excel spreadsheet). See Appendix A for download instructions.
2. The raw data for most calculations in this study are available in the accompanying Access database. This database is described in appendix A. It includes information about far more epitaphs (over 3,000) and individuals (over 30,000) than those mentioned in the personal name index. The calculations for most (but not all) of the figures are available in the database. They can be found among the "queries" listed in the navigation pane. They are clearly labeled; the calculations for figure 1.1, for example, appear in the query "Fig I_1 Forty-four excluded eminent clans." In addition, a few footnotes refer to additional database queries. For example, note 14 in chapter 1 invites readers to consult "Fig I_note14 9th c choronyms" in the database, a query that can also be found listed in the navigation pane.
3. Years are identified using the Western calendar. In order to minimize confusion, any single Chinese year is converted into a single Western year, even though the Chinese new year begins several weeks after the Western new year. Thus, most events dated in this monograph to the twelfth month of a given year would, in fact, have occurred in January or February of the following year in the Western calendar.
4. In maps of China, the coastline (with the exception of portions of the coast between Shanghai and the Bohai Sea), rivers (with the

exception of the lower reaches of the Yellow River), and latitude and longitude coordinates of most counties in the southeast and some counties elsewhere were obtained from "CHGIS, Version 4" (Cambridge, MA: Harvard-Yenching Institute, January 2007). Some additional coordinates of counties were obtained from Ruth Mostern and Elijah Meeks, "Digital Gazetteer of Song Dynasty China v.1.1" (2010). Much of the remaining geographic data, including Tang era coastlines and river courses, accords with Tan Qixiang, *Zhongguo lishi ditu ji*, volume 5. The boundaries of Tang China appearing on the map of Tang China on the facing page represent the approximate limits of direct Tang political control in the ninth century. The Tang regime did not actually demarcate its borders in such clear terms. Situating Tang China within the modern borders of the People's Republic of China is done for reference only in order to help orient the reader.

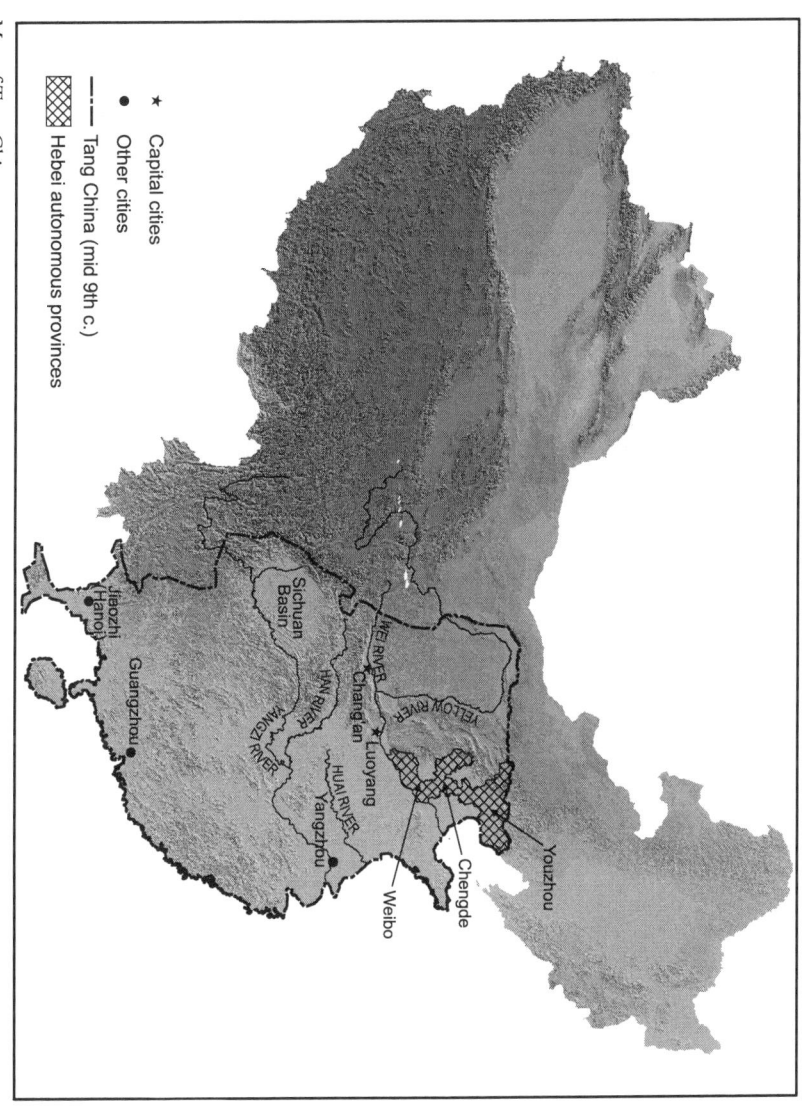

Map of Tang China

Introduction

Born into one of the most famous aristocratic families of ninth-century China, Ms. Lu possessed a pedigree of unquestionable eminence. Although her family was originally from Fanyang in the northeast, it had relocated to the great capital city of Luoyang at least two centuries earlier. There, Ms. Lu's forebears joined a social circle that came to dominate society and, through its influence over the state bureaucracy, political power. Not atypical of a woman of her station, Ms. Lu could trace her ancestry through an unbroken line of officeholders going back to the Han dynasty, some seven centuries earlier; several hundred of her clansmen had served in the governments of the successive post-Han dynasties, including the Tang (618–907). When she was fourteen, mindful of the importance of pedigree, Ms. Lu's family found a suitable match for her in a young man from another great Luoyang-based clan. Unfortunately, her husband died when she was still quite young. Nevertheless, she maintained her high status in society, looking after her children's education and arranging their marriages. She must have felt enormous pride when her son earned the prestigious *jinshi* civil service examination degree and when, in 878, her son-in-law—scion of yet another eminent Luoyang family—became chief minister and one of the most powerful men in China. Three years later, however, Ms. Lu's life and the whole world she had known came to an abrupt end.[1]

---

1. Accounts of the life of Ms. Lu 盧氏 (818–81) and her husband, Li Shu 李杼 (802–50), can be reconstructed from the three epitaphs discovered in her tomb; for transcriptions of the epitaphs and a description of the tomb in question (a tomb referred to as "M9112" in the report), see *Yanshi Xingyuan Tang mu*, pp. 168–252, 361–69. For a reconstruction of the genealogy of Ms. Lu's branch of the Fanyang Lus, see *XTS* 73 上:2885–2912; her great-grandfather appears on p. 2907 of the table. Chapter 3 of the present monograph provides more information on her clan (which I identify as patri-

At first, the threat must have seemed remote to the residents of the capital cities of Chang'an and Luoyang. Although a series of uprisings had broken out in central China in the mid-870s, imperial armies had succeeded by the end of the decade in routing the rebels, pushing them far back toward the deep south. Suddenly, however, in the seventh month of the year 880, the rebel Huang Chao (d. 884) took advantage of a weakness in the empire's defenses to cross the Yangzi River. It took him only four more months to capture Luoyang, and, before the end of the year, his army marched into Chang'an. Then began one of the most infamous massacres in the annals of Chinese history. Ms. Lu's daughter and son-in-law, the chief minister, were victims of the bloodshed. She, herself, was a bit more fortunate, escaping with her two sons to a family-owned villa in the countryside some one hundred kilometers east of Luoyang. But her good luck did not last. Perhaps because of an epidemic that accompanied the warfare and chaos, both she and one of her sons died of illness less than a month apart in the late spring of 881. With the surrounding region in turmoil, it was not until a year and a half later that it became safe enough for her youngest son to return her remains to Luoyang for burial alongside her husband. By then, four of Ms. Lu's five children had died without heirs, and the mood among surviving family members was grim. Scrawled unevenly onto the side of one of the epitaph stones buried in her tomb was a note written by her nephew: "Another year has passed since the Son of Heaven went to Sichuan. The great bandit Huang Chao has not yet been captured and killed. With the ravages of war overtaking Luoyang and Gong County, the people have no means by which to survive" 天子幸蜀，歲再周矣，巨寇黃巢，尚稽誅擒．鞏、洛兵荒，人無生理．[2]

Although the emperor did, in fact, return from Sichuan to recapture the throne, the once mighty Tang dynasty lived on in name alone. Imperial legitimacy collapsed as warlords seized control of the provinces, ushering in nearly three decades of upheaval, during which dozens of independent regimes all across the country battled for preeminence.[3] By the middle

---

line 5485). The earliest known clansman buried in Luoyang was Lu Chisong 盧赤松 (569–625); see *Mang Luo beizhi sanbai zhong*, p. 67, for an image of his epitaph. The chief minister in question was Cui Hang 崔沆 (d. 880).

2. See epitaphs from Ms. Lu's tomb. For more on the Huang Chao Rebellion, see chapter 5.

3. For a description of the warlords who battled each other for preeminence in the

of the first decade of the tenth century, most of the smaller regimes had been subsumed into larger states. At this point, in the fourth month of the year 907, the warlord controlling the Yellow River Basin and much of North China ordered the execution of the last Tang emperor, by then merely his puppet, thus bringing the dynasty to its final demise. What emerged from the Tang's collapse—first the so-called Five Dynasties and then the great Song empire (960–1279)—was not merely a sequence of different political regimes. The tenth century witnessed the coalescing of an entirely new social order. The great medieval families that had maintained their prestige for most of the first millennium CE, across multiple dynastic transitions, vanished entirely from the scene. Under the Song dynasty, a culture of merit came to eclipse the aristocratic ethos of earlier times, largely precluding any resurgence of the old order.

The present book seeks to explain this dramatic societal and cultural transformation. It focuses on the final century of Tang rule. Although generations of scholars have explored the profoundly different characteristics of the Tang and Song elites, a vast corpus of new epigraphic material now allows us to elucidate the precise sociocultural processes that led from one social order to the next. On the basis of a collective biography involving tens of thousands of women and men, this volume examines both how the bureaucratic aristocracy of medieval China managed to maintain its influence despite important political and institutional developments in the mid-Tang and why the great clans disappeared so completely with the fall of the dynasty. In the process, it explores in great detail the inner workings of an elite society living well over a thousand years ago. A subsequent study will address the cultural transformation during the post-Tang period whereby a new elite self-identity emerged that discarded many of the ideals and values held by Ms. Lu and the old aristocracy to which she belonged.

The Transformation of Medieval Elites

In fact, between the late Tang and the early Song dynasties, China underwent a series of dramatic changes that utterly transformed society.[4]

---

north after Huang Chao's rebellion, see chapter 4 as well as Wang Gungwu, *Structure of Power*, pp. 6–84.

4. The Japanese journalist and historian Naitō Torajirō 内藤虎次郎 (1866–1934)

A commercial revolution brought about a significant monetization of the economy, the expansion in certain regions of marketing networks deep into the countryside, and the development and spread of urban centers.⁵ Following a concomitant demographic transformation, the center of gravity of China's population shifted to the south, thrusting the Yangzi River valley and the southeast coast to a prominence they had never before held.⁶ Simultaneously, remarkable technological innovations increased agricultural productivity, while the greatly expanded use of the printing press substantially enlarged the literate population.⁷ During this same period, China would also witness a number of major developments in thought and religion, with the emergence of Neo-Confucianism—a fundamentally new approach to understanding Classical texts—and the popularization of new religious cults and practices.⁸ So fundamental were these changes that many Chinese of later times imagined that the Song regime itself had ushered in an entirely new era. Writing several hundred years later, the historian Chen Bangzhan 陳邦瞻 (d. 1623) asked rhetorically, "The state system of today, the customs of the populace, the administration of the bureaucracy, the dogma of scholars, did any of these not first emerge during the Song?" 今國家之制, 民間之俗, 官司之所行, 儒者之所守, 有一不與宋近乎?⁹

---

is credited with first describing this great transformation. The Naitō thesis became influential among Japanese scholars of China in the mid-twentieth century, and among American scholars during the 1960s and 1970s (although Naitō's claim that the Song marked the beginning of the "early modern period" is no longer taken seriously). For an overview of the thesis and a more recent critique, see Miyakawa, "Outline" and Lau Nap-yin, "He wei 'Tang Song bianqe.'" More recently, there has been a flurry of publications on the thesis in Mainland China. See, for example, Li Huarui, "Ershi shiji zhong ri 'Tang Song bianqe' guan"; volume 11 (2005) of the journal *Tang yan jiu*, especially the introduction by Zhang Guangda; and Li Huarui, ed., *"Tang Song bianqe"lun*.

5. Shiba, "Urbanization"; Shiba, *Commerce and Society*; Twitchett, "T'ang Market System"; Twitchett, "Merchant, Trade, and Government"; Skinner, "Introduction: Urban Development in Imperial China"; Shiba, "Sōdai no toshika o kangaeru."

6. Hartwell, "Demographic, Political, and Social Transformations," pp. 365–94.

7. Elvin, *Pattern*; Cherniack, "Book Culture and Textual Transmission."

8. Bol, *"This Culture"*; Hansen, *Changing Gods*.

9. Chen Bangzhan, *Songshi jishi benmo*, pp. 1191–92. Chen argues that the Tang-Song transition constituted the third of three great historical transformations, the first two being the initial establishment of civilization in antiquity followed by the establishment of a unified empire at the end of the third century BCE.

But perhaps the most dramatic of the changes associated with this so-called Tang-Song transition was the transformation in the nature and composition of the Chinese sociopolitical elite. The twelfth-century scholar Zheng Qiao 鄭樵 (1104–62) succinctly described its essence: "Up until the Sui and Tang dynasties, officials had dossiers [identifying the offices of their ancestors], and families had genealogies. The appointment of officials relied upon the dossiers; marriages between families relied upon genealogies. . . . Ever since the Five Dynasties, one no longer asks about family background when selecting officials, and one no longer asks about family prestige when arranging marriages" 自隋唐而上, 官有簿狀, 家有譜系, 官之選舉, 必由於簿狀, 家之婚姻, 必由於譜系. . . . 自五季以來, 取士不問家世, 婚姻不問閥閱.[10] In other words, whereas one's pedigree was critical in the Tang, by the Song, people no longer felt that it mattered. Over the past several decades, historical scholarship has made enormous strides in elaborating upon the nature of both the Tang and the Song elites. David Johnson, Patricia Ebrey, Mao Hanguang, Sun Guodong, and others have characterized the relatively circumscribed medieval aristocracy that defined its status on the basis of blood.[11] Robert Hartwell, Robert Hymes, Peter Bol, and Beverly Bossler have all described the new, more diffuse collective of elite families who first emerged in the early Song, families who justified their dominance of society and politics on the basis of talent and education.[12] They represented the core element of what has sometimes been called the "Chinese meritocracy" and would constitute one of the most striking distinctions between Chinese and Western societies over the course of the subsequent millennium.

But beyond this general account of the sharp distinction between the two elites, disagreement remains as to how this transformation actually

---

10. Zheng Qiao, *Tongzhi*, 25:439. Shen Gua 沈括 (1031–95) made a similar observation. He concluded an essay describing the medieval custom of ranking clans by observing that "this custom gradually fizzled out at the end of the Tang" 其俗至唐末方漸衰息. See Shen, *Mengxi bitan*, pp. 772–73.

11. Ebrey, *Aristocratic Families*; Johnson, *Medieval Chinese Oligarchy*; Johnson, "Last Years"; Mao Hanguang, "Tangdai tongzhi jieceng shehui biandong"; Sun Guodong, "Tang Song zhi ji shehui mendi."

12. Hartwell, "Demographic, Political, and Social Transformations," pp. 405–25; Hymes, *Statesmen and Gentlemen*; Bol, "*This Culture*," pp. 32–75; Bossler, *Powerful Relations*.

transpired. Most important for the present volume, there is no consensus on what brought about the aristocracy's decline or even on when the process began. For some—including Yang Yunru 楊筠如 (1903–46), Tang Zhangru 唐長孺 (1911–94), and many other influential historians of the Six Dynasties Period—the aristocracy had already gone into decline by the founding of the Sui dynasty (581–618), when China was reunified following hundreds of years of post-Han disunity. According to this view, warfare and uprisings dealt a blow to the aristocracy, while its base of power was further weakened as the newly strengthened central government extended its control into provincial society. Simultaneously, the systems in place that granted ranked families the hereditary right to serve in government were effectively dismantled, preventing the old elite from maintaining its monopoly on political power.[13]

More commonly, however, scholars situate the transformation within the Tang dynasty itself. Yet there is no consensus as to when precisely or why the changes took place. The great early-twentieth-century Chinese historian Chen Yinke 陳寅恪 (1890–1969), for example, underscored the effects of the expanded civil service examination instituted under Empress Wu (r. 690–705). According to Chen, factionalism and violence during the last two centuries of Tang rule often pitted scions of the aristocracy against a new class of elites composed of civil service examination graduates.[14] By contrast, others, notably Denis Twitchett and Tonami Mamoru 礪波護, have emphasized the institutional and political innovations implemented in the aftermath of the An Lushan Rebellion of the mid-eighth century.[15] According to this thesis, the breakdown of the "equal field" system—which had once mandated the regular redistribution of land—and the deregulation of commerce created an environ-

---

13. Yang Yunru, *Jiupin zhongzheng*; Tang Zhangru, "Menfa," esp. pp. 11–20. For an overview of more recent perspectives on the rise and fall of the great families of the Six Dynasties, see Chen Shuang, "Jin ershi nian Zhongguo Dalu diqu," pp. 17–18.

14. Chen Yinke, *Tangdai zhengzhi shi*, esp. pp. 20–24. Yoshioka Makoto has taken a similar position, stressing that the "new elite" emerged from among prominent local elite families; see "Hasseiki zenhan ni okeru Tōchō kanryō kikō."

15. Twitchett, "Introduction," esp. pp. 20–21, 24–31; Twitchett, "Merchant, Trade, and Government," esp. p. 93; Twitchett, "Composition," esp. p. 79; Tonami, "Sōdai shitaifu," pp. 193–203; Tonami, "Chūsei kizokusei." See also Otagi Hajime, "Tōdai kōhan ni okeru shakai henshitsu," which argues that the exams and the post-An Lushan provincial order together spurred the emergence of a new elite.

ment favorable to the development of new landed and commercial elites. Simultaneously, financial commissions set up to tap into these commercial profits as well as provincial governments established to bring order to the countryside after the rebellion were said to have preferred men of talent to scions of the aristocracy. These commissions, it is argued, began recruiting the sons of merchants and other recent parvenus, providing the "newly risen" 新興 elite with unprecedented opportunities to enter officialdom and, over time, to acquire political influence.

However, empirical evidence suggests that all of these influential theories have underestimated the ability of the old elite to withstand changes in institutional and societal structures. In fact, several important studies have shown that the old families managed quite successfully to perpetuate their grip on political power until the very end of the Tang dynasty. David Johnson demonstrated that, even in the post–An Lushan period, the majority of Tang chief ministers came from aristocratic family backgrounds.[16] Sun Guodong came to similar conclusions by examining a somewhat larger sample of Tang bureaucrats.[17] And Mao Hanguang, in a study of all levels of the Tang bureaucracy, confirmed that a small number of families actually increased their influence over time and came to represent by the final three decades of the dynasty close to half of all known officeholders.[18] Several chapters in the present volume will provide abundant additional evidence in support of these conclusions.

But if the old clans indeed continued to dominate political life in the second half of the ninth century, how exactly did they manage to survive for such a long period? And why did they disappear so abruptly in the tenth century? The fact that both Ms. Lu and her husband—like so much of the Tang political elite—came from unbroken lines of officeholders going back centuries is remarkable and requires an explanation. It is equally striking that few, if any, of her or her husband's clansmen are even mentioned in sources after the ninth century.[19] On the basis of a

---

16. Johnson, *Medieval Chinese Oligarchy*, pp. 131–41.
17. Sun Guodong, "Tang Song zhi ji shehui mendi," pp. 213–18. For a critique of Sun's definitions and categories, see Johnson, *Medieval Chinese Oligarchy*, pp. 145–46.
18. Mao Hanguang, "Tangdai tongzhi jieceng shehui biandong," pp. 223–24; Tackett, "Transformation," pp. 63, 101.
19. For descriptions of the total disappearance of the old aristocratic clans after

few telling anecdotes, David Johnson has hypothesized that "class wars" at the end of the Tang dynasty fueled by "violently anti-aristocratic feeling" played an important role—a hypothesis that my own research shows to be not far from the mark.[20] But even Johnson has argued that, by the ninth century, the aristocracy was "no more than an idea," an elite that was "not founded . . . on genuine social or political realities."[21] Similarly, according to Patricia Ebrey, it constituted merely a "status group" whose survival "rested on a . . . precarious balance."[22] But could an obsolete class that had outlived its place in society really maintain its status and power for so long? Was its domination of the bureaucracy to the end of the ninth century not evidence enough that it had adapted well to institutional and socioeconomic developments occurring during the dynasty?

These questions point to one final problem with current discussions of the Tang elite and its demise. As it turns out, not all scholars define the Tang elite in the same way. Were the great families of the Tang dynasty first and foremost members of a status elite, represented by the lists of eminent clans described in the following chapter? Or were they essentially a socioeconomic elite, whose rise and fall paralleled changes in China's land tenure system?[23] Or were they ultimately a political power elite defined by their ability to dominate the bureaucracy? In other words, in our consideration of elite society, how can we best assess the configuration among the Weberian classic trinity of status, wealth, and power? One of the goals of this monograph is to sort through this problem by first exploring Tang China's status elite (chapter 1) and socioeconomic elite (chapter 2), before proceeding to a careful discussion of the bureaucratic aristocracy that maintained, I will argue, both high status and dominant political power.

Tang historians have been hampered in their exploration of these questions by the relative sparsity of source material, especially by comparison

---

the fall of the Tang, see Johnson, "Last Years," pp. 48–59; Johnson, *Medieval Chinese Oligarchy*, pp. 141–48; Ebrey, *Aristocratic Families*, pp. 112–13.

20. Johnson, "Last Years," pp. 68, 100.
21. Johnson, *Medieval Chinese Oligarchy*, p. 48.
22. Ebrey, *Aristocratic Families*, pp. 32, 113–14.
23. For an overview of Japanese scholarship on land tenure across the Tang-Song transition, see McDermott, "Charting Blank Spaces," pp. 13–16.

with the voluminous documentation available to scholars of the Song period. After a flurry of studies in the 1960s and 1970s that mined traditional sources for anecdotes and isolated examples assumed to be typical, research into Tang society largely reached an impasse. This situation has changed dramatically with the availability of new sources. An astonishing abundance of new epigraphic data—notably the excavated tomb epitaphs described in detail below—has the potential of entirely revitalizing the study of Tang history. With the availability of such material, it is possible to reexamine late Tang society in finer detail than would have been possible just a decade ago and to resolve definitively a number of unanswered questions. Whereas earlier historians have had to limit their purview to a small number of the most powerful and highly educated men whose biographies grace the pages of traditional dynastic histories, it is now possible to place these men in the context of an elite society defined far more broadly. Epigraphic materials allow us to re-create the lives of women and men not only in the lower echelons of the bureaucracy, the military, and the corps of eunuchs, but also among merchants and major landowners who, though wealthy and influential at the local level, did not necessarily hold government titles. By examining the margins of the upper class, it is possible to clarify substantially the relationship between status elites, economic elites, and political elites, and to understand better how some families remained influential for centuries only to disappear suddenly with the fall of the Tang.

While exploiting new sources of data, this study also seeks to reconceptualize the late Tang elite in three important ways. First, it moves away from the notion that the transformation from the Tang to the Song involved a single socioeconomic trajectory whereby the great clans of the Tang were displaced by a new elite. The Tang upper class—like most successful elites in world history—was highly adaptable to new situations.[24] There is, in fact, little evidence from the eighth or ninth centuries suggesting that a cohesive new class of women and men had begun to threaten the old social order. Attempts to interpret late Tang

---

24. For another example of elites adapting to changing political circumstances, one might turn to the Roman senatorial aristocracy and the landowning elite of the Aegean and Anatolia, who "changed identity" instead of "declining to extinction" after the demise of the Roman Empire. See Wickham, *Framing the Early Middle Ages*, pp. 206–7, 238–39.

factionalism at court as a manifestation of class struggle have largely failed.²⁵ It seems clear that, rather than catalyzing the demise of the old elite through a competition for dominance during the Tang, new elites rose to prominence only after the fact, filling a vacuum left behind by the destruction of the great medieval clans at the end of the dynasty. Thus, the fall of the aristocracy and the rise of a new order should be treated as separate sociocultural phenomena.

Second, the present study is based fundamentally on a multiregional perspective. Most historians of Tang China have concentrated on developments they believe to have affected China as a whole, drawing at the most a distinction between the north and the south. But there are other ways of conceptualizing the geography of the empire that permit a clearer understanding of the sociopolitical structure of power. For example, when exploring the nature of the Tang elite, it is essential to distinguish the capital region—that is, the Tang's two capital cities and the corridor linking them—from the provinces in general, a distinction to be developed in some detail in chapter 2. It is also important to pay attention to the unique characteristics of the three autonomous Hebei provinces in China's northeast, which were in many respects politically and culturally isolated from the rest of Tang China. There is good reason to believe that, as a result of its cultural isolation, Hebei would be the initial source of the new meritocratic culture that would rise to dominance in subsequent centuries.

Third, this study develops techniques for better analyzing kin and marriage networks, based, once again, on the epigraphic materials. As Robert Hymes has argued in his local study of the Fuzhou elite during the Song dynasty, it is impossible to understand an individual's place in society without considering the place of the individual's close relatives.²⁶ However, there have been almost no attempts to date to analyze in systematic fashion an entire elite social network. As we shall see, digital techniques permit the reconstruction of a surprisingly large portion of the late Tang aristocracy and its marriage ties. One goal of this monograph is to assess the explanatory power of a social network of this type,

---

25. Wechsler, "Factionalism"; Dalby, "Court Politics," pp. 652–54; Tonami, "Chūsei kizokusei."

26. Hymes, *Statesmen and Gentlemen*, pp. 35–38.

with the assumption that such networks constitute an important asset of "social capital" that can help an elite reproduce itself in power.²⁷ Chapter 3 will examine how the aristocracy's marriage network served as a concrete resource, as important as its status and prestige, a resource that all but guaranteed its long-term political survival. Besides shedding light on the nature of power, networks can also explain the dynamics of cultural change. Networks, by definition, consist of individuals and families who interact with each other on a regular basis and who are likely, therefore, to share common beliefs and ritual practices. As the embodiment of particular subcultures, networks can thus be thought of as one of the fundamental elements of a culture. In principle, then, it is possible to explore the elite's changing sense of identity from the perspective of the shifting composition of its social networks.

In order to treat effectively the large amounts of biographical, geographic, and network data compiled for this study, it has been necessary to make use of a variety of quantitative techniques. Since the 1980s, the use of quantification in historical research has declined quite significantly. The fiascos of an earlier period of quantitative hubris have taught us that statistics and other forms of data manipulation must be deployed with great care and responsibility. There is always the danger that tables and graphs can "flatten" data, dissimulating the potential significance of unique and aberrant characteristics of individual cases. Unfortunately, moreover, readers do not always have access to the raw data, so they cannot effectively evaluate methodological details. Nevertheless, if the historian proceeds with great care, there is the potential to revolutionize the field of medieval Chinese history by exploiting the range of new digital resources presently available, notably the Chinese Historical Geographic Information System (CHGIS) and the Chinese Biographical Database (CBDB). Whenever possible, in order to give readers the opportunity fully to evaluate the graphs and tables used in this study, the original data has been made available on the web sites of both the author and the publisher (see appendix A). In addition, a portion of the data has already been integrated into CBDB.

Finally, a few words on the use of the term "aristocracy."²⁸ The Tang

---

27. Bourdieu, "Capital social."
28. I am not alone in making use of a rather inclusive definition of the term "aristocracy." See also Wickham, *Framing the Early Middle Ages*, pp. 153–54. Wickham

elite that constitutes the subject of this study shared a number of features with the later European aristocracy. It maintained an ethos of superior education, manners, and moral standards based on the notion of good breeding, a notion that led to an insistence on good marriages. Its claim to superiority was rooted in ancient pedigrees (real or fictive) that were recorded in genealogies that went back hundreds of years. This elite held de facto (albeit not de jure) hereditary rights to political power based on a principle of accumulated merit, described in the following chapter. In sum, this elite maintained both moral and political domination. Finally, its power and prestige were essentially independent of the regime, and, indeed, they had been maintained across multiple dynastic transitions.

But it is important to stress that, although it was a cultural analog to the European aristocracy, the Chinese aristocracy described in this monograph was by no means identical. Unlike the European case, it was not a juridical category after the sixth century, and its members did not hold hereditary titles of nobility.[29] It did not pride itself on its military valor, thus in many ways resembling the Roman senatorial aristocracy more than later European "nobles of the sword."[30] The great families of Tang China also did not maintain large landed estates over multiple generations.[31] Moreover, in China, as previously emphasized, the aristocracy cannot properly be conceptualized as having formed an obstacle to the development of either an absolute monarchy or the bourgeoisie. Finally, because of the system of concubinage, the meaning of heredity was somewhat different in China as compared to Europe.[32]

---

depends on a similarly inclusive definition for a proper comparative study of the very different societies emerging in Europe and the Mediterranean after the decline of the Roman Empire.

29. Johnson, *Medieval Chinese Oligarchy*, pp. 5–17.

30. See Wickham, *Framing the Early Middle Ages*, pp. 155–65, for a good description of the Roman senatorial aristocracy. Like Tang great clans, Roman senatorial elites derived their prestige from officeholding and from a cultured, literary lifestyle. Unlike the Tang great clans, however, the high status of Roman senators also depended on their immense landed estates.

31. See the section of chapter 1 titled "The Geographic Dispersal of Great Clan Descendants" for more on why landownership played a relatively minor role in defining the Tang aristocracy.

32. It is difficult to understand how sons of concubines often had the same status as their brothers born of the principal wife since good marriages were deemed so important to preserving the aristocracy. The key to this problem is that, besides inheriting the

Tomb Epitaphs as a Historical Source

Tomb epitaphs (*muzhiming* 墓誌銘) in the Tang period consisted of square slabs of limestone (or, in some cases, of brick or even porcelain), usually between a foot and a half and two feet in width, on which were inscribed biographies of the deceased that were generally from several hundred to several thousand words in length.[33] These objects were placed flat on the floor of the tomb chamber, alongside the coffin of the deceased and other grave goods. The inscription was usually protected by a decoratively carved limestone cover. Because, by the ninth century, the *muzhiming* was deemed a literary genre, the texts of some two hundred of them survive in the collected works of late Tang writers.[34] In recent decades, thousands of additional Tang era tomb epitaphs have come to light, unearthed by archaeologists and grave robbers alike.[35] Figure 0.1 depicts a rubbing of one such epitaph. Along with a limited quantity of other epigraphic material—notably the several dozen surviving spirit-path steles 神道碑 and other monuments erected outside of tombs—it is this vast corpus of new biographical material that has permitted a comprehensive reexamination of the Tang aristocracy and its demise.

The texts of tomb inscriptions are rich with information of interest to historians, often information unavailable in any other historical source. They contain lengthy eulogistic passages that express the values and ideals of the society of the time. They record the dates and places of death and burial of the deceased, and they also usually identify the father, grandfather, great-grandfather, husband or wife, as well as, on occasion,

---

blood of the father, sons of concubines were educated and brought up by the principal wife. Upbringing played as important a role as blood in the Chinese concept of heredity. See Bray, *Technology and Gender*, pp. 353–54; Ebrey, *Inner Quarters*, pp. 230–31.

33. There exists an abundant literature on tomb epitaphs. For a comprehensive description by the foremost Chinese authority on Tang epitaphs, see Zhao Chao, *Gudai muzhi*. For an account of epitaphs as religious objects and their development as a literary genre, see Davis, "Potent Stone."

34. All epitaphs from surviving collected works are included in the Qing dynasty collectanea *Quan Tang wen* 全唐文 (Complete Tang prose). A few of them may actually not have been intended for the tomb. Han Yu's 韓愈 (768–824) epitaph for Li Yu 李于 (776–823) seems to be more of an exhortation against the medicinal use of cinnabar than a eulogy for the deceased. For a discussion of this epitaph, see Davis, "Entombed Epigraphy."

35. See appendix C for more information on sources of excavated epitaphs.

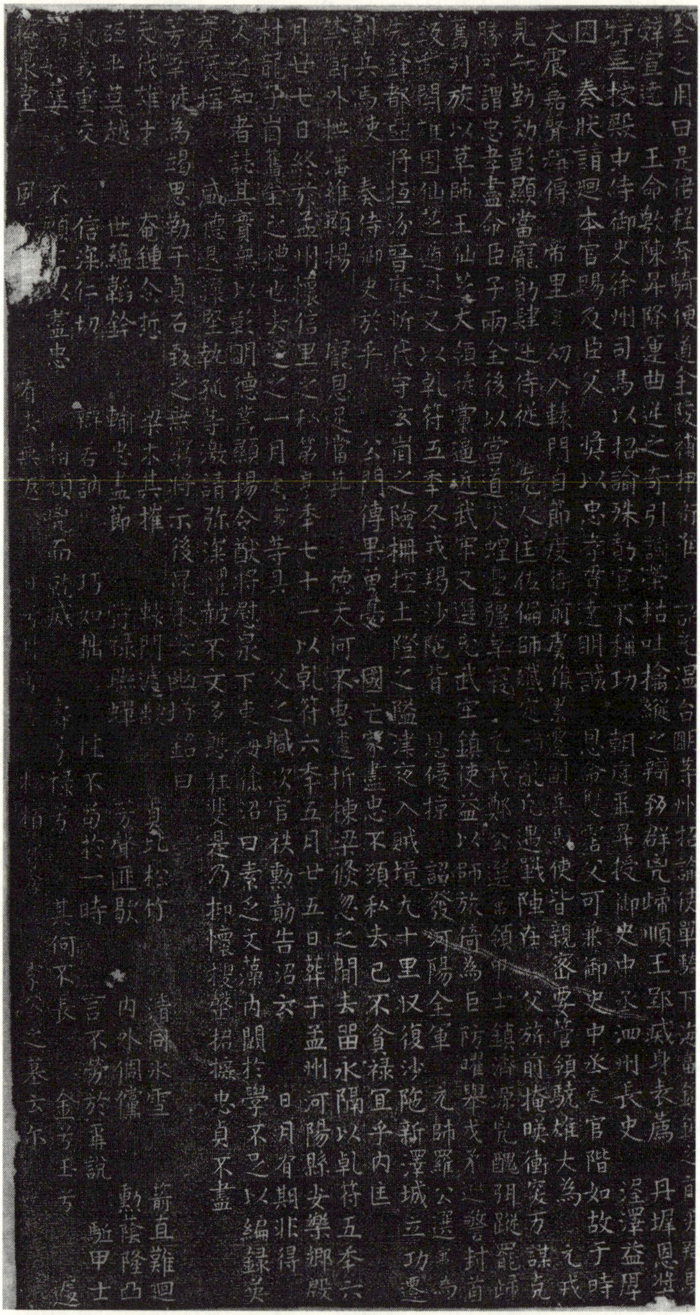

FIGURE 0.1. Epitaph of Li Gao 李皋 (808–78). Photograph of epitaph rubbing has been divided onto two pages for the sake of readability; the original epitaph stone is square.

唐故河陽軍節度押衙左廂馬步都虞候銀青光祿大夫檢校國子祭酒兼御史中丞上柱國隴西郡李公墓誌銘

八諱鼻字子□隴西狄道人也其先歷國太奏漢□□□聖代文武勳台輔芊芊河山綿統為世所聞
□□□□□□□□□□□□□□□□□□□□□□□□□□□皇河陽軍節度押衙馬公即先府君之次子前夫人張氏
□□□□□□□□□□□□□□□□□□□□公河陽軍節度押衙右廂馬步都虞候兼監察御史盛莒次曰盛□又□□□□
□□□□□□□□□□□□□□□□□□夫人撐哀充東都久水趙氏夫人曰盛兒方呻青重□□女二人長曰未適□季□□□□
□□□□□□□□□□□□□□□□□□□□大和九年夏五月廿七日奄忽以二嗣孤幼續娶文已□夫人兼監察御史盛
□□□□□□□□□□□□□□□□□□公戒之曰公之婚娶皆勳舊雲時賀蹄□□□□□□□
□□□□□□□□□□其童持書□向延軍□□女之藩□進躍進□□□□□
□□□□□□□□□一抆公士之初□賞□蘭木□取其長奴□□□□□□
□□一抆賊可□越酒□□所謂莫非瘀而□□皆□□□□□□□□
□□□□鞴□□□□詐欢武通□□□□□□□□□□□□
□□□□□□□□□□□□□□□□□□□□□□□□
□□□□□□□□□□□□□□□□□□□□□□□□
□□□□□□□□□□□□□□□□□□□□□□

the maternal grandfather, father-in-law, and sons-in-law. Chapters 2 and 3 will explore the uses of such data for analyzing geographic variations in elite composition and for reconstructing kin and marriage networks. Tomb epitaphs also provide an abundance of data useful for analyzing demographic patterns, including age at marriage and at death, numbers of sons and daughters, and records of migration. They describe, usually in considerable detail, the bureaucratic career of the deceased (or of her husband). And, finally, many incorporate fascinating anecdotes that bring to life women and men who lived well over a thousand years in the past.

In the context of the present study, one particular value of tomb inscriptions involves their function as an identifying marker of members of the wealthier strata of society. Epitaphs were both necessary elements of elite burials and elements generally restricted to those who could afford more elaborate funerary rites.[36] Many of these inscriptions articulate a deep concern about leaving a grave site unmarked. A frequent refrain noted that, over the passing eons, geological forces would transform the landscape in such a way that "grave tumuli will perhaps be leveled" 陵谷恐平 and "the pine and cypress trees [traditionally planted beside the tomb] will disintegrate into broken sticks" 松柏摧爲折薪.[37] According to one epitaph:

> Mountains become fields, fields become oceans;
> Of that which survives from antiquity, what has not been transformed?
> Young pines and new tumuli, we know them to be ephemeral;
> In a thousand years, all that will remain is the epitaph marking the site.
>
> 山作田兮田作海，萬古存兮誰不改，
> 青松新隴曉無年，千載惟留銘記在.[38]

As anecdotal literature makes clear, numerous ancient graves were stumbled upon by accident in the Tang, just as many historical tombs excavated today were first uncovered by farmers plowing their fields or by

---

36. For a similar argument regarding Song era epitaphs, see Bossler, *Powerful Relations*, p. 10.
37. Epitaphs of Wang Qi 王岐 (747–803) and Fu Cun 傅存 (d. 860).
38. Epitaph of Chen Huan 陳環 (780–842). For other similar examples, see Tackett, "Transformation," p. 12.

men digging cellars or wells.³⁹ How were families to know that someone in the distant future would not uncover their own tombs? In case of this eventuality, it was essential to explain to the women and men of the future that the human remains in the tomb were worthy of the utmost respect. Thus, those families with sufficient means made sure to place in the grave the "true account of the facts" 事實 of the deceased's life, carved onto the one material known never to perish—stone.⁴⁰ In one inscription, the author explained that, "by recording this here, we can hope that later generations will appreciate [the deceased]" 今斯記者, 欲異代識焉.⁴¹ According to another, "The tomb must have an epitaph: how else would others grasp the virtuous conduct of the former gentleman?" 墓宜有誌, 豈他人可以詳先君之德之行.⁴²

But the preparation of an epitaph was only one of the many steps critical to an ideal burial, all of which could cost substantial sums. One had to hire a diviner to select an auspicious day for the funeral.⁴³ If a good day could not be found, it was not uncommon to place the deceased in a temporary grave near the clan cemetery while awaiting a more favorable moment.⁴⁴ In such a case, there would be additional reburial expenses at a later date. One also had to hire a geomancer

---

39. Davis, "Potent Stone," p. 266; Li Fang, *Taiping guang ji*, 369:2937, 386:3083, 390:3119, 391:3124, 391:3126.

40. Epitaph of Chen Shishang 陳師上 (779–839). Innumerable epitaphs explicitly state that stone is a material that does not perish. For example, according to the epitaph of Wang Zhen 王振 (768–833), "stone is that which does not decay" 石可不朽.

41. Epitaph of Fan Mengrong 范孟容 (791–831). Several epitaphs refer to themselves as "veritable records" 實錄 of the life of the deceased.

42. Epitaph of Li Gongdu 李公度 (784–852). For another articulation of the notion that "a burial must have an epitaph" 葬宜有銘, see Han Yu's epitaph for Du Jian 杜兼 (750–809).

43. For an interesting account of a diviner at work, see the epitaph of Ms. Luo 駱氏 (746–808). That divination was taken very seriously is clear from the fact that certain days were evidently more popular for burials. For example, according to my data, 12 of 37 epitaphs (32 percent) dating to the year 834 involved burials on one of only three days: the twenty-fourth day of the eighth month, and the fourteenth and twentieth days of the eleventh month. There is some evidence that the selection of the day depended partly on the surname of the deceased. See epitaph of Wei Yu 韋齡 (d. 859).

44. Epitaphs of Cui Zhi 崔植 (791–856), Ms. Cui 崔氏 (784–858), Yu Ruxi 于汝錫 (791–847), and Ms. Li 李氏 (771–822). See also epitaph of Zhang Guan 張觀 (803–63) in conjunction with that of his uncle, Zhang Xin 張信 (782–850), which confirms the site as that of the clan cemetery.

to select a suitable site for the tomb so as to assure that the spirit of the deceased remained at ease.⁴⁵ If the tomb were poorly situated, the family might later discover that "the fengshui was not balanced," a situation undoubtedly "ill-fated for the surviving descendants" 不福遺嗣 that necessitated an immediate relocation of the tomb at additional cost.⁴⁶ Then, after selecting a choice spot, families sometimes needed to buy the land. Especially in the Yangzi Delta region, epitaphs frequently alluded to the purchase of burial land, often incorporating language reminiscent of land contracts.⁴⁷

In terms of expenses, this was only the beginning. Elite tombs were not simple pits into which coffins were deposited. They consisted of an underground chamber, often built of brick and sealed with a stone door, on top of which was erected a large dirt mound. A variety of objects were placed within the tomb, some of substantial value, including bronze mirrors, ornamental objects of jade and lacquer, and glazed ceramics.⁴⁸ Some of these items were auspicious symbols; others were of use to the deceased post mortem, as explained in one inscription: "Today, those of us gathered in the tomb have all brought inside models of objects that the lady customarily used for adornment or for enjoyment; her spirit will certainly be pleased to use these" 今於兆中，皆取夫人平昔服玩之物樣製，致于其內，神道固當喜用之.⁴⁹ Besides preparing the grave, there were also expenses associated with mortuary rituals, including both the encoffinment ceremony and the funerary procession.⁵⁰ For both of these,

---

45. Numerous epitaphs, especially from Luzhou 潞州 and southern Hebei, describe in geomantic terms the landscape surrounding the tomb in the four cardinal directions.

46. Epitaphs of Li Gao 李皋 (733–92) and his wife Ms. Cui 崔氏 (742–97), who were reburied 103 paces away from their original tomb; of Liu Song 柳鞏 (751–813); and of Ms. Zheng 鄭氏 (780–838).

47. For thirteen such epitaphs, see Tackett, "Transformation," p. 52. In addition, see epitaphs of Ms. Gong 龔氏 (744–804), Liu Gongzhi 劉公制 (792–836), Wang Xiting 王希庭 (762–841), Gong Zuzhen 龔祖真 (772–847), Shen Xian 申憲 (d. c. 850), Ms. Shi 石氏 (774–853), Xu Taiqing 許太清 (770–857), and Niu Yanzong 牛延宗 (834–77). For two additional examples, see Hansen, *Negotiating Daily Life*, pp. 57–58.

48. For a thorough account of the tomb structures and burial goods of an elite cemetery near Luoyang, see Ye Wa, "Mortuary Practice," esp. pp. 109–277. For an account of Chinese tombs as an entire cultural universe, albeit with a focus on an earlier period in China's history, see Wu Hung, *Art of the Yellow Springs*.

49. Epitaph of (Ms.) Wang Taizhen 王太真 (840–62).

50. Ye Wa describes how archaeologists can distinguish grave goods associated with

one normally had to hire musicians and officiants, including someone to intone the text of the epitaph stone.⁵¹

Lastly, there was the question of the epitaph, itself. First, it was necessary to purchase two slabs of limestone, one for the main inscription and one for the epitaph cover. These stones were sometimes cut from the rock of a famous mountain elsewhere in the empire, to be transported, probably at considerable expense, to the grave site.⁵² Then one had to recruit individuals to compose the text, to pen the calligraphy (initially with ink), and, finally, to carve the ink impression into the stone. Especially in the provinces, specialized workshops may have been commissioned for these tasks. Some of the cruder epitaphs reveal obvious signs of having been produced in shops. These types of inscriptions rarely record the names of the authors and calligraphers, but they do sometimes take note of the total word count, undoubtedly an accounting technique used to calculate the final price of the work.⁵³ And there are even a few cases in which two epitaphs appear to have been manufactured by the same individuals. For example, significant portions of the inscriptions for Zheng Shuyi* 鄭恕己 (d. 851) and Lü Jianchu* 呂建初 (826–69) are verbatim

---

the encoffinment ceremony from those associated with the funerary procession. See Ye Wa, "Mortuary Practice," p. 153.

51. That the epitaphs were read aloud is clear from the occasional pronunciation instructions that appear as in-line commentaries carved onto the stone. For examples, see epitaphs of (Ms.) Cui Chengjian 崔成簡 (753–819), Ms. Du 杜氏 (752–829), Ms. Li 李氏 (774–839), Zhao Wenxin 趙文信 (763–845), Wang Yun 王惲 (789–845), Li Dan 李眈 (d. 857), (Ms.) Liu Bing 劉冰 (826–68), and Ms. Pei 裴氏 (852–77). In five of these nine cases, the pronunciation instructions appear in the rhymed verse at the end, perhaps suggesting that these portions were more likely to be intoned during the burial ceremonies. One might expect the highly educated literati of the capital—the subjects of most of the epitaphs in question—not to have required pronunciation assistance, suggesting that it was a hired officiant rather than a family member who read the epitaph aloud.

52. For explicit references to the purchase of stones for the epitaph, see epitaphs of Shi Shimian 施士丏 (734–802), Ms. Zhao 趙氏 (d. 819), Cui Yuanli 崔元立 (806–26), and Guo Wenggui 郭翁歸 (784–845). For reference to a stone cut from a famous mountain, see epitaph of Lei Kuang 雷況 (d. 870).

53. For examples, see epitaphs of Ms. Zhang 張氏 (795–855), Ms. Song 宋氏 (759–819), Lai Zuoben 來佐本 (d. c. 873), Yang Jian 楊釰 (833–79), and Fei Fu 費俯 (856–77). See Tackett, "Transformation," p. 22, for images of the character count tally carved onto the epitaph stone.

copies of each other.⁵⁴ Even the calligraphy seems to have been produced by the same hand.⁵⁵

In the two capital cities of Luoyang and Chang'an, families were spared some of these costs. Authors and calligraphers were often kinsmen, relatives by marriage, or men who had once depended on the patronage of the deceased.⁵⁶ For example, when a certain Cui Yuanli* 崔元立 (806–86) died at a young age, his eldest brother purchased a stone and then commanded a second brother to compose the text of the inscription. In the case of Sun Bei* 孫備 (832–70), his mother traveled four hundred kilometers to ask Sun's beloved cousin to write the epitaph.⁵⁷ In these cases, the signatures of the authors and calligraphers—which generally included these men's full bureaucratic titles—probably served partly to highlight the prestige of the deceased's social network.⁵⁸ It is for this reason that, when Lu Chu* 盧初 (732–75) was reburied fifty-four years after his death, his descendants did not replace the older epitaph, composed by his uncle the chief minister. Instead, they simply affixed an addendum.⁵⁹ But whereas capital elites might not be required to hire

---

54. In particular, the eulogistic passages are essentially identical in these two epitaphs; the relevant dates and names, however, are customized for the individual in question.

55. For other examples, see Tackett, "Transformation," pp. 14–15, 24; epitaphs of Ms. Xun 荀氏 (809–54) and of Ms. Su 蘇氏 (824–78), paying particular attention to the last three columns of each; and epitaphs of Mr. Jia 賈公 (779–817) and of Ms. Lü 呂氏 (764–816).

56. Authors and calligraphers who were relatives by blood or marriage are usually identified as such in their signature lines. Ties of patronage, by contrast, are difficult to identify. In the case of the epitaph of Lu Zhan 盧占 (d. 866), for example, there is no explanation of the deceased's relationship to the author, Yuan Wei 源蔚. In the epitaph of Lu's brother, Lu Pan 盧槃 (d. 879), however, one discovers that Lu Pan was Yuan's patron. Thus, Yuan presumably composed Lu Zhan's epitaph on behalf of his patron as well.

57. In another case, the brother of the deceased wrote the text of the inscription and then ordered his subordinate to pen the calligraphy; and, in another, a son was ordered by a family elder to produce the calligraphy for his father's epitaph. See epitaphs of Wei Zhouji 魏舟濟 (790–849) and Ma Jing 馬儆 (d. 832).

58. Han Yu makes clear the prestige conveyed by the author of an inscription in his epitaph for Shi Hong 石洪 (771–812), in which he goes so far as to identify the eminent individual who had composed Shi's father's epitaph.

59. The original calligraphy was apparently deemed less valuable: the text of the inscription composed by the uncle was rewritten onto a new stone along with the addendum.

an author or calligrapher, they did need to pay men to inscribe the text into the stone, men who were sometimes also charged with filling in details left out by the calligrapher.[60] These carvers were lower in status, craftsmen rather than highly educated literati, and so were almost never relatives of the deceased.[61] They rarely signed their names; those that did often held low-level positions as stone workers in the employ of the central government.[62] Interestingly, many extant carvers' signatures belonged to men from a small number of families.[63] It is possible that the families in question were renowned for the quality of their carvings. Thus, they may have been asked to sign their names on the stones to make it clear that a premium had been paid for their services.

It is not possible to ascertain the cost of each element of the funerary preparations. However, a few epitaphs do reveal the price of the land. Thus, we know that the family of the eunuch Tong Guozheng* 同國政 (787–851) expended 113.35 strings of cash to purchase a 7.56 *mu* graveyard

---

60. Numerous epitaphs have a blank space in lieu of the given names of one or more of the deceased's ancestors, suggesting that these names were sometimes filled in later. In some cases, one or more of the names indeed appear to have been carved by a different hand. See, for example, epitaphs of Cui Wu 崔俉 (795–871), paying particular attention to the given names of the deceased and his father; and of Ma Zhiling 馬直令 (831–74), paying particular attention to the father's name. In some cases, characters for death and burial dates do not adhere to the regular gridlike spacing of the other characters in the text, suggesting that dates were also sometimes added later. See, for example, epitaph of (Ms.) Zhang Jing 張婧 (825–66). It was presumably quite often the carver who added this information, as made explicitly clear in the carver's signature on the last line of the epitaph of Miao Zhen 苗縝 (786–844).

61. The one exception that I am aware of involves the epitaph of Guo Liang 郭良 (770–841), authored by his nephew Han Shifu 韓師復, a member of a Luoyang family of carvers. This is an interesting case because Guo was a low-level military official, a type of person one rarely encounters in Luoyang epitaphs. It is possible that this man's family would not have had the resources to commission an epitaph but were able to obtain one at bargain prices through Han Shifu's intervention.

62. Several of these men held the title of Carver of the Jade Slips 鐫玉册官, an office apparently attached to the Department of State Affairs.

63. Specifically, according to my data, one-third (15/45) of Luoyang epitaphs with a carver's signature were carved by men surnamed Han 韓; approximately the same proportion (24/65) of Chang'an epitaphs were carved by men surnamed either Shao 邵 or Qiang 強. The fact that many of these men were craftsmen attached to the Department of State Affairs suggests that their work was probably deemed of high quality.

in the outskirts of Chang'an.[64] And we know that the cost of this prime real estate near the imperial capital (15 strings per *mu*) was over twice as high as land in the vicinity of Yangzhou in the Yangzi Delta region.[65] But there is no information on the expenses associated with the other components of the burial. Fortunately for the historian, however, a few epitaphs do disclose the total price of the entire mortuary process. In fact, the cost could be staggering. When Feng Shenzhong* 馮審中 (810–52) died while serving as chief of staff 節度押衙 to the provincial governor of Hedong, the governor sent a subordinate to accompany his remains back home to Chang'an, offering the family an additional 200 strings of cash to allay other expenses.[66] The brother of Wei Jinghong* 衛景弘 (812–55) provided an equal sum of money when Wei died away from home; in this case, the money was also intended to help support his widow and orphan son. Some burials apparently could cost even more. When Li Xun* 李潯 (803–60) died in the Han River valley, a friend provided over 300 strings of cash to pay for the coffin and for the return of his body to Chang'an. And when the eldest daughter of Ms. Zhang* 張氏 (761–817) sought help in moving her mother's body from Chang'an to Luoyang for reburial, one son-in-law felt obliged to donate 300 strings of cash. It is likely that a part of these costs was associated with the expense of transporting remains long distances, a procedure that probably necessitated the organization of special rituals to ensure that the soul of the deceased did not separate from the body. However, the cost of transport was by no means the only major expense. One provincial governor provided 500 strings of cash and 50 rolls of silk for a military officer in the provincial army who had died locally and was to be buried locally as well.[67] By means of comparison, 200 to 500 strings of cash was enough to feed from

---

64. This land seems to have included one guard house 營一所 and 1.56 *mu* of land to support the guards 管地. In calculating the price of a *mu*, I have used the approximate conversions 1 *mu* = 240 square *bu* and 1 string of cash = 1,000 cash.

65. Two Yangzhou epitaphs, those of Xu Ji 徐及 (751–834) and Mr. Zhang 張公 (789–859), allude to land purchased at rates of 4.1 and 6.4 strings per *mu*, respectively.

66. Probably because of the extra expense of returning a body home for burial, there are other examples of provincial governors making the arrangements and financing the return of a subordinate's remains to the capital for interment. See, for instance, epitaph of Yuan Gun 元袞 (758–809).

67. Epitaph of Wang Dajian 王大劍 (743–809).

fifty to a hundred adult males for an entire year.⁶⁸ Little wonder, then, that families frequently complained that they had "exhausted the wealth of the household in order to prepare for the funeral in accordance with ritual" 罄家內之資財備遷葬同禮.⁶⁹

To be sure, there were a variety of ways to cut costs. One could rent rather than buy the land for the graveyard.⁷⁰ Or one could convert one's own farmland into a burial site for one's kinsmen.⁷¹ In lieu of purchasing a new slab of limestone for an epitaph, one could even recycle an older stone. The funerary inscription of Wang Shiyong* 王時邕 (799–845), for example, was carved onto the back of a block cut from a Buddhist stele dating to a century earlier. That of Zhao Gongliang* 趙公亮 (842–84) shows traces of an earlier epitaph for another man, named Yang Xishi 楊希適, which had been partly polished off.⁷² It was also common for a family to save money by not commissioning a new stone for a man's wife. In the case of Fu Cun's* 傅存 (801–60) epitaph, an addendum announcing his wife's demise was awkwardly squeezed between the title and the first line of text.⁷³ And one boy who died at a young age was interred within his father's tomb with a small note carved onto the side of the father's epitaph.⁷⁴

However, although there were ways of cutting costs, the mortuary practices of the late Tang upper class were, without doubt, expensive. Empirical evidence generally confirms that tomb epitaphs were characteristic of only the more sophisticated tombs and were limited to families

---

68. It cost about 4 strings of cash to feed an adult male for an entire year. See Huang Zhengjian, "Han Yu richang shenghuo," p. 256.

69. Epitaph of Liu Hui 劉惠 (772–848). For other examples of widows turning to friends or relatives to finance burials, see epitaphs of Ms. Li 李氏 (812–69) and of Meng Jiao 孟郊 (751–814).

70. Epitaphs of Ms. Wang 王氏 (836–49) and of (Ms.) Zhu Siniang 朱四娘 (d. 850).

71. Epitaph of Cai Zhi 蔡賨 (807–45). Before the demise of the land registration system, tombs seem often to have been placed on mulberry land (which, unlike grain land, remained in the family generation after generation); the "statement of purpose" at the end of an epitaph frequently makes reference to "mulberry land."

72. For an image of one corner of Zhao's epitaph, see Tackett, "Transformation," 23. For more similar examples, see epitaphs of Yu Yan 于偃 (710–50), Qiao Shixi 喬師錫 (785–848), Ms. Li 李氏 (823–56), and Wang Xun 王詢 (c. 808–77).

73. For an image, see Tackett, "Transformation," p. 23.

74. Epitaph of Gu Chongxi 顧崇傃 (765–847).

who had the resources to fund more elaborate burials.⁷⁵ Sumptuary laws did apply to certain elements of the burial rituals, but these laws seem not to have affected the epitaph itself.⁷⁶ Thus, it is fair to say that any individual with a tomb inscription was by definition a member of the wealthier strata of society. That is not to say that these individuals came from a homogeneous socioeconomic class. Moreover, the corpus of excavated epitaphs discovered at any one locale represents a roughly random cross-section of elite society in that one region alone.⁷⁷ Compared to the dynastic histories, tomb epitaphs provide data on a much greater range of elites, from the most powerful court bureaucrats to landowners of more modest means. Thus, in the case of a series of tombs from the late Tang that were excavated in the vicinity of Zhenjiang (in Jiangsu Province), the simpler tombs contained brick epitaphs, while the more elaborate ones had inscriptions carved onto limestone.⁷⁸ Presumably, this discrep-

---

75. A series of regional studies seems to confirm this generalization. To list two examples, in Anhui, vertical shaft tombs 豎穴墓 and pit tombs 土坑墓 of the Tang period had few grave goods at all; by contrast, double-chambered brick tombs always contained epitaphs. In Tang and Song Hubei, there was a direct correlation between tomb size, quality of grave goods, and presence of a tomb inscription. See Fang Chengjun, "Anhui Sui Tang zhi Song muzang," p. 51; Yang Baocheng, ed., *Hubei kaogu faxian*, pp. 304–6, 319–25.

76. Spirit-path steles and other stones placed in front of the tomb, for example, seem to have been subject to sumptuary regulations. See stele of Yang Ning 楊凝 (773–803), which explains these regulations. But these regulations did not apply to epitaphs. See Tackett, "Great Clansmen," pp. 109–10. Indeed, Ye Wa has convincingly argued that the state's enforcement efforts targeted the visible aspects of mortuary practice rather than what was actually placed within the tomb. See Ye Wa, "Mortuary Practice," esp. pp. 296–98. Thus, there were restrictions on the transportation of epitaph stones by carriage during the funerary procession but not specifically on the placement of epitaphs within the tomb. Perhaps for this reason, it is possible that some epitaphs were actually carved in advance at the site of the tomb. See epitaph of Ms. Xue 薛氏 (805–48), which explains that the author "carved a stone inscription at the tomb" 刻石誌于墓.

77. Archaeological efforts dedicated to excavating Tang era tombs differ substantially by region. Thus, although one can compare the percentages of epitaphs from different regions that share a particular characteristic, one should avoid comparing total numbers of epitaphs from different regions.

78. Liu Jianguo, "Jiangsu Zhenjiang Tang mu," p. 146. One might argue that individuals with brick epitaphs should not be treated as members of the upper classes. It should be noted, however, that brick epitaphs constitute a very small percentage of the corpus of inscriptions used in this study.

ancy reflected two rather different socioeconomic groups. The epitaphs are all the more valuable for the social historian in that they demarcate a range of economic levels within the elite strata of society.

This study is divided into five chapters. Chapter 1 explores the usefulness and limitations of the most common means used by scholars today to identify members of the Tang aristocracy: their clan names. Abundant evidence confirms that surnames and places of origin were frequently deployed in texts of the period to designate "great clans." But although these clans remained an important status group, I argue that their situation had changed substantially by the ninth century. The vast majority of such families (with the exception of those residing in the peripheral regions of the southeast) no longer had direct links with their places of ancestral origin. Moreover, the fecundity of such families—facilitated by the presence of concubines—resulted in large numbers of individuals who could claim descent from famous families, so that the prestige of the names was substantially diluted. Thus, it is clear that the political elite of the ninth century that actually held major positions in the bureaucracy consisted of only a very small subgroup of the biological descendants of these old families.

If the clan name is insufficient for identifying members of the dominant sociopolitical elite, how does the historian go about doing so? The subsequent two chapters discuss first residence patterns and then marriage networks as alternative indicators for identifying and describing its members. Chapter 2 approaches this issue by comparing the composition of the wealthiest families (i.e., the subjects of excavated epitaphs) residing in different parts of the empire. This comparison reveals a clear divide between a national elite based in the capital cities of Chang'an and Luoyang (and their surrounding regions) and a local elite based in the provinces. Such a pattern, I will argue, created a "colonial" relationship between center and periphery that sharply distinguished the Tang empire from the Late Imperial state.

Chapter 3 describes how the geographic concentration of the dominant political elite in the two imperial capitals both reinforced and was reinforced by a tightly knit and highly circumscribed marriage network consisting of a small subgroup of the pre-Tang great families. This network was composed of two cliques—one organized around the imperial clan and one around the most eminent of the old families. It was the members of these two cliques who constituted the dominant political elite that essentially monopolized power during the late Tang. The social capital embedded in the capital-based elite marriage network allowed this elite to control both recruitment into the bureaucracy and appointments to the highest posts in the bureaucratic hierarchy.

Chapter 4 then reevaluates the functioning of the provincial commissions, bureaucratic structures established in the wake of the great An Lushan Rebellion of the mid-eighth century that took over many of the administrative responsibilities once managed by the central government. Historians have often argued that these provincial governments constituted both a centrifugal force obstructing the power of the central government and an important avenue of new upward social mobility. In fact, I show that the central government and the long dominant bureaucratic elite both adapted well to the new circumstances and largely maintained their hold on power. By the second half of the ninth century, the capital-based social network of national elites had managed to coopt all potential avenues of upward mobility.

But how then did this elite—which had survived several earlier dynastic transitions and rebellions—disappear suddenly and completely with the fall of the Tang? This question is resolved in chapter 5. Although the An Lushan Rebellion has attracted far more attention among Chinese historians, chapter 5 demonstrates that the Huang Chao Rebellion of the late ninth century was far more destructive to the old families. When the rebels all but annihilated the two capital cities of Chang'an and Luoyang, they physically eliminated a large percentage of the political elite, whose permanent residences and property holdings were overwhelmingly concentrated in these two cities. It was their physical elimination that—more than anything else—brought about their near immediate demise.

I

The Bureaucratic Aristocracy of Medieval China

In the year 822, the family of the "lady" Liu Neize* 柳內則 (749–821), a distant cousin of Liu Zongyuan 柳宗元 (773–819), commissioned an epitaph that was conceived both as a tribute to the woman in question and as an encapsulation of the aristocratic values prevailing in the last century of the Tang dynasty:[1]

> When ranking [clans] from around the empire, there are distinctions between those who lead and those who follow; when assessing them, it is unambiguous which are important and which are not. There are those [individuals] who receive the teachings of righteousness and harmony, and who respect the importance of inherited achievements. These individuals have deep esteem for their ancestries and do not take lightly their family relations. Thus, they inevitably marry people of their own station: the men are granted fitting consorts, and the women are matched to [husbands] to whom they submit. With law and morality in perfect agreement, distant and near kin are not at odds with each other. The caps and sashes [of their elegant clothing] are displayed in profusion; their descendants prosper and flourish. This is the way to preserve one's family while respecting one's origins. [One can, thus,] hope never to decline for one hundred generations. Then there are those [individuals] who abandon their families and forget their origins, who go against their duties in order to pursue their own interests. They debase their ancestries while

---

1. Liu Zongyuan was her fourth cousin once removed.

esteeming other [lesser] families; they value wealth, while breaking up the [proper] order of the ranks. Thus, they inevitably associate themselves with those who are [socially] remote and distance themselves from those who are [socially] akin. They look toward their own livelihood without understanding the virtue of proper marriage ties; they look for shortcuts without understanding the [more onerous] path of righteousness. This is called the dilution of one's customs and the severe tarnishing of one's family heritage.

國朝差敍, 則先後有別; 品藻, 則輕重甚明. 其有本仁義雍和之教, 稟閥閱相承之重. 深敬祖始, 不忘吾耦. 則必慕族類而婚, 依族類而嫁. 使男得其配, 女適其歸. 法教無二途, 疏戚無間言. 纓緌紛綸, 枝葉蕃昌. 是爲克家敬本之道, 冀不失於百代也. 其有捨族忘本, 異尚封己, 卑祖始而尊他門, 厚幣財而分甲乙, 則必親其所疏, 疏其所親. 顧衣食而不知配耦之端, 視步武而不知仁義之塗. 斯風俗之澆薄, 保家之甚病.

The author of the epitaph articulated in unambiguous terms an aristocratic worldview typical of his era. He imagined a hierarchy of clans in which some were unquestionably superior to others. These great families were characterized by appropriate breeding, behavior, and beliefs, built on the accumulated achievements of a long continuous line of eminent forebears. The widely held belief in inherited virtue meant that good marriages were critical to avoid watering down the accomplishments of the past generations. Those who married beneath their station would diminish the worth and status of their families.

Although Liu Neize's tomb inscription was perhaps atypical in the length at which it discussed the great clans of medieval China, the thousands of extant ninth-century epitaphs suggest that this aristocratic vision was in no way unusual. Time and time again, in praising a woman's or a man's ancestry, the inscriptions referred to the deceased's family as a "top-ranked house" 甲門, an "eminent clan" 令族, a "famous surname" 著姓, or "the foremost among the hundred lineages" 百氏之首.[2] Members of these preeminent families were praised repeatedly for their education and their proper comportment. In the case of one clan, "its sons and daughters heeded what they were taught and possessed the virtue of gentility" 其子女聞教訓, 有幽閒之德; the scions of another

---

2. See, for example, epitaphs of Ms. Lu 盧氏 (750–805), Ms. Li 李氏 (828–59), Ms. Lu 盧氏 (818–81), Shi Xiaozhang 史孝章 (800–838), and Wang Zhengyan 王正言 (755–818).

"adhered to frugality and morality as their norm, thus securing eminence and fame for generations" 率儉德爲常, 故世世有令聞.³ Family members were commended for choosing spouses wisely: "for generations, through their ritual practice and their marriage ties, they constituted a paramount clan 'East of the Mountains'" 代以禮樂婚媾爲山東之盛族.⁴ They were also extolled for their service to the emperor, holding bureaucratic posts generation after generation, so that their "officeholding and marriages were both exquisite" 官婚具美.⁵ In the context of a culture marked by a strong aristocratic ethos, achievement and merit were built up over time: "among people in general, each inherits the essence of their family; . . . if they are able to cultivate this essence, then they will not diminish the endeavors of their ancestors" 大凡人物中, 各世其家實 . . . 苟能修其實, 則無墜祖先之業也.⁶ One could only acquire prestige through birth, though if one failed to live up to one's ancestry, one's family might easily decline in status.

But who were the families in question? Did the nature of these aristocratic clans change over time? And what were the links between political power and the status acquired through family background? This chapter will discuss the commonly employed strategies for identifying membership in the great clans. I will then reassess the significance of claims to particular ancestries on the basis of data contained in the rich troves of extant tomb inscriptions. By the ninth century, I will argue, a claim of descent from an old pre-Tang clan had lost some of its luster, as such claims became increasingly commonplace; only a small subgroup of the old families continued to dominate political power.

Clan Lists and the Classification of the Great Clans

One approach to distinguishing members of the great families of Tang China, still sometimes used by historians today, is to focus on surnames alone. This was essentially the approach used by Liu Neize's family,

---

3. Epitaphs of Ms. Lu 盧氏 (767–812) and Li Shihua 李士華 (754–816).
4. Epitaph of (Ms.) Cui Qi 崔琪 (815–60).
5. Epitaph of Lu Chu 盧初 (732–75).
6. Epitaph of Li Shihua 李士華 (754–816). Beverly Bossler has suggested that this sort of accumulated virtue may have been tied to Buddhist notions of karma. See Bossler, *Powerful Relations*, p. 21.

in which the only important distinction was an individual clan's relative proximity to Chang'an: "On the whole, as for the great clans and their illustrious marriage partners, beyond the passes [in Hebei and Henan] there are the Li, Lu, Zheng, and Cui clans; within the passes [in Shaanxi] there are the Pei, Wei, Liu, and Xue clans" 大凡族氏之大, 婚媾之貴, 關外則曰李、曰盧、曰鄭、曰崔, 關中則曰裴、曰韋、曰柳、曰薛. Other ninth-century discussions of elite society present similar lists of distinctive clan names, albeit sometimes with variations in the particular families included.[7] However, such names alone are generally of limited value to the historian. Indeed, the relative sparsity of surnames in circulation meant that a very large number of individuals shared the eight or nine family names in question.

In fact, most medieval texts identify aristocratic families with greater precision, preceding the surname with the clan's place of origin, a component of clan appellation referred to by David Johnson as the "choronym."[8] Clan choronyms generally consisted of old commandery names that predated the systematic renaming of prefectures undertaken during the reign of the first Tang emperor.[9] By the ninth century, because they no longer referred to existing place-names, choronyms were inherently claims to a family history that extended far into the past, before the founding of the dynasty. Moreover, from a methodological perspective, they are readily distinguishable from other toponyms. In the epitaph of a certain Ms. Cui* "of Qinghe" 清河崔氏 (793–843), for example, we are told that "from the time that the Northern Wei [386–534] began recognizing the great households, promoting the Four Surnames as clans of the top rank, up until the present day, the 'small branch' of the Qinghe Cui family has been [ranked] number one" 自元魏重門戶推四姓爲甲族至今, 崔氏清河小房爲第一. In this case, the choronym "Qinghe" refers to Qinghe Commandery in Hebei, which during most of the Tang dynasty was actually known as Beizhou, or Bei Prefecture. Although, as in this example, the subbranch of a given family

---

7. For an alternate list, see epitaph of Ms. Zhang 張氏 (807–69), which replaces the surname Liu found in Liu Neize's epitaph with the surname Xiao 蕭 and also adds eight southern surnames.

8. See Johnson, *Medieval Chinese Oligarchy*, p. 165 (n. 46) for an explanation of the coining of the term "choronym."

9. For more, see ibid., p. 63.

was sometimes important to the family's sense of identity, the focus of this chapter is on the larger "clan," defined on the basis of a particular choronym-surname combination.

But how does the historian determine which families were deemed most eminent by ninth-century contemporaries? Fortunately, two lists of clans—both dating to the tenth century—have been discovered among the stash of paper manuscripts found at the turn of the twentieth century in a cave near Dunhuang, in China's Far West. Following the lead of David Johnson and Ikeda On, I refer to these two lists as "A" and "C." A third list of great clans (called "E") has been reconstructed by Ikeda on the basis of data contained in an early Song geographic text.[10] List C is the most extensive of the three, containing the names of 791 clans; lists A and E include the names of only 258 and 362 clans, respectively.[11] After careful analysis, Johnson has concluded that the latter two lists—which are generally similar in content—are both versions of a state-sponsored catalog of great clans compiled in 749 under the direction of the powerful mid-eighth-century chief minister Li Linfu 李林甫 (683–752). The longer C list combines Li Linfu's catalog with a second, unknown source. There is good reason to believe, as Johnson suggests, that these lists largely defined the preeminent clans of the mid- and late Tang. However, the lists are not without problems; in particular, their accuracy and reliability can be put into question. Johnson found evidence, for example, that list E was derived from a "bad text"; and, in general, a number of Dunhuang manuscript editions are known to be error-prone.[12] On the basis of new data from epigraphic material, it is

---

10. For an introduction to these lists of great clans, see ibid., pp. 62–70; Ikeda, "Tōdai no gunbō hyō"; Twitchett, "Composition." A high-resolution digital version of list C is available at the International Dunhuang Project (http://idp.bl.uk), under the pressmark "S.2052"; although not yet digitized, list A should eventually be available under the pressmark "BD08418." Transcriptions of all three lists appear in appendix 4 of Johnson's monograph.

11. For the number of clans appearing on each list, see Johnson, *Medieval Chinese Oligarchy*, pp. 64, 67, 68.

12. Ibid., p. 74; Nugent, *Manifest in Words*, pp. 27–71. Although Nugent—looking at Dunhuang documents from a literary perspective—insists that manuscript editions containing substantial textual variants constituted more than merely "flawed embodiments of an imagined original" (p. 27), variants in lists of prestigious clans would surely have been deemed "errors" by members of the dominant social elite. Besides the problem of errors in the manuscripts, one should remember that, after the mid-eighth

now possible to reevaluate Johnson's lists on an empirical basis. Tomb epitaphs typically identify the choronym and surname of the deceased as well as those of a certain number of the deceased's relatives by marriage.[13] In total, known epitaphs dating to the period 800 to 880 identify 6,255 different individuals by surname, of which 4,311 are identified by both choronym and surname. To be sure, claims made by some individuals to eminent choronyms could have been fictive—a possibility discussed in more detail below. But one could argue that even fictive claims reveal which clans were considered by contemporaries to be most prestigious. In any case, the 606 distinct choronym-surname combinations used by these 4,311 individuals can complement Johnson's three lists, thereby producing a more accurate enumeration of those clans that possessed the greatest status and prestige in ninth-century society.

This empirically derived enumeration helps us to revise the previously mentioned lists in two respects. First, it is now clear that Johnson's lists contained far more clan names than are actually encountered in ninth-century epitaphs. Only about two-fifths of the clans on the A and E lists (107/258 and 149/362, respectively) and one-quarter of the clans on the C list (204/791) ever appear in the epigraphic record of the period.[14] Moreover, of those names that one does encounter, about two-fifths (96/254) are mentioned only once in the entire corpus of ninth-century inscriptions.[15] If one assumes—as noted in the introduction—that extant epitaphs represent a roughly random sample of the elite population, then one can conclude that most of the clans appearing on Johnson's clan lists had an insignificant presence in

---

century, Dunhuang was no longer under Tang control; thus, the Dunhuang lists (A and C) were not necessarily representative of the situation in China in the ninth century. In addition, it is not certain to what degree Li Linfu's lists (A and E), prescribed by the central government, accurately described the clans deemed most prestigious in the society at large.

13. In most cases, the choronym appears before the deceased's surname in the title line of the epitaph; in some cases, the choronym appears as the deceased's place of origin or place of ancestral origin.

14. See "Fig 1_note14 9th c choronyms" in database. In addition, list C contains a total of sixty-nine clans that appear in the epigraphic record but that do not appear on lists A and E.

15. See "Fig 1_note15 9th c chor appearing only once" and "Fig 1_note14 9th c choronyms" in database.

ninth-century elite society. Presumably, by the late Tang, many families once deemed eminent had dropped out of the upper classes and remained on lists of eminent clans only as historical relics.[16] Second, the empirically derived enumeration of clans can help fill lacunae in our current understanding of which families were deemed eminent in the late Tang. Of all individuals identified by surname and choronym in ninth-century epitaphs, 87 percent (3752/4311) belonged to or claimed to belong to clans that appear on one or more of Johnson's lists, thus demonstrating on empirical grounds the importance of these lists.[17] But who were the 13 percent of individuals who belonged to clans not appearing on the lists? Johnson and others have already noted that the extant clan lists are incomplete; both the A and E lists, for example, are dozens of names short of the 398 names their prefaces claim that they contain.[18] I would hypothesize, then, that the 13 percent represented families that were among those excluded names. In order to test this hypothesis, one can examine a sample, namely, the 44 excluded clan names that one encounters three or more times in ninth-century epitaphs. It turns out that 35 of these 44 can be shown to have been politically prominent families on the basis of other documentary evidence (fig. 1.1).[19] But even in the case of those among the 14

---

16. The Dunhuang clan lists should probably be thought of as exhaustive attempts to include all families from particular prefectures that were ever famous at any time. Traditional Chinese reference works tend to prefer exhaustive treatment of their subjects, a tendency that can mislead readers into treating as significant phenomena that are in fact relatively minor. The madman in Lu Xun's famous short story overemphasized the significance of cannibalism in traditional China by misunderstanding in precisely this way a pharmaceutical encyclopedia.

17. See "Fig 1_note17 chor on Johnson lists" in database. In some cases, the choronym is a known pre-Tang commandery name but does not appear associated with any surnames on the lists; in some cases, the choronym appears on the lists, but the surname in question does not appear as an eminent clan from that particular commandery. Place names appended to surnames that are not pre-Tang commandery names were excluded from these statistics.

18. Johnson, *Medieval Chinese Oligarchy*, pp. 70–71.

19. Note that some of these forty-four clans may have been subbranches of other clans. For example, the Fuchun Sun 富春孫 clan is not cataloged in clan lists A, C, and E; however, the genealogical tables in *Xin Tang shu* clarify that one branch of the Sun family of Le'an 樂安, a family that does appear on the clan lists, fled south from its place of origin and reestablished itself in Fuchun. See *XTS* 73 下:2945.

Clan	n	Reference	Clan	n	Reference
長樂馮	17	M 172; L 1:7; G66	新野庾	5	L 6:892; G50
燉煌張	14	M 160; G78	河內張	4	G11
河南于	14	M 152; L 2:230	丹陽陶	4	G62
上黨苗	13	M 165	汝南譚	4	
北平田	11	G99	廣平劉	4	M 160; L 5:683
昌黎韓	11	M 156; L 4:487	河南長孫	4	M 162; L 7:1071
南陽樊	10	M 167; L 4:445; G84	河南源	4	M 155
富春孫	10		中山劉	4	M 187; L 5:681; G63
太原白	9	M 158	平陽敬	4	L 9:1340; G95
馮翊嚴	8	L 5:779	北平陽	3	M 179, 181; L 5:590
武威段	8	L 9:1284; G90	陳郡謝	3	G67
常山張	8	M 166	蒼梧瞿	3	
高陽齊	7	M 194	張掖烏	3	
京兆王	7	M163; G22	順陽范	3	L 7:1152
陳郡袁	6	M 154; L 4:435; G67	高平李	3	
陳郡殷	6	M 169; L 4:395; G67	北海唐	3	G97
安定張	6	M 158; G1	金城申屠	3	
沛國武	6	L 6:882	金城申	3	M 192
燉煌令狐	5	M 152; L 5:632; G78	晉昌唐	3	G49
頓丘李	5	M 173; G77	長城陳	3	L 3:338
上谷張	5		長樂賈	3	M 160; L 7:1044
琅琊支	5		中山張	3	
			Total: 267		

FIGURE 1.1. Forty-four eminent clans not included in extant clan lists

Includes clans encountered three or more times among agnates and affines mentioned in epitaphs empirewide dating to the period 800–880. Key to references: G = *Guangyun* list, as reconstructed in Ikeda, "Tōdai no gunbō hyō," pp. 94–95; M = Mao Hanguang, "Tangdai tongzhi jieceng shehui biandong," pp. 147–99; L = Lin Bao, *Yuanhe xingzuan fu si jiaoji*.

percent who cannot be shown to have been from prominent families, it is surely significant that they appended a pre-Tang commandery name to their surnames. Why would they identify a place-name that was no longer valid as their place of origin? The only plausible explanation is that, by doing so, they were exploiting what had become by then the standard means to lay claim to a prestigious ancestry—using a defunct commandery name as one's site of ancestral origin. Consequently, in the subsequent discussion, I will treat all individuals identified by both choronym and surname as members of a status group that claimed an ancient aristocratic pedigree.

Nevertheless, there can be little doubt that some clans were more prominent than others. The most eminent of all were the so-called marriage-ban clans.[20] Emperor Gaozong (r. 649–83) had forbidden these families to intermarry, hoping thereby to weaken their social prestige. In fact, the ban was entirely ineffective, serving only to elevate their status. Sun Guodong and Yoshioka Makoto have defined a slightly larger group of twenty-eight clans derived from a list of famous families produced by Liu Fang 柳芳, the great Tang expert on genealogy.[21] Yoshioka has gone on to equate these twenty-eight clans with a "national aristocracy" 門閥 of extremely powerful clans, hypothesizing that the remaining clans on the Dunhuang clan lists constituted a lower tier of elites prominent at the prefectural level only.[22] Finally, one can define empirically the most prominent clans. Mao Hanguang has organized all clans according to their total number of known Tang era officeholders. On the basis of Mao's list, one can identify unambiguously the top sixteen officeholding

---

20. These seven clans were the Zhaojun Lis 趙郡李, Longxi Lis 隴西李, Taiyuan Wangs 太原王, Xingyang Zhengs 滎陽鄭, Fanyang Lus 范陽盧, Qinghe Cuis 清河崔, and Boling Cuis 博陵崔. See Johnson, *Medieval Chinese Oligarchy*, pp. 50–51.

21. Liu Fang additionally classifies these clans into five regional groups. Besides the seven marriage-ban clans (all from Shandong, except the Longxi Li family from Guanzhong), they are as follows: the Jingzhao Du 京兆杜, Hedong Liu 河東柳, Hedong Pei 河東裴, Hedong Xue 河東薛, Jingzhao Wei 京兆韋, and Hongnong Yang 弘農楊 clans from Guanzhong; the Henan Lu 河南陸, Henan Yuan 河南元, Henan Yuwen 河南宇文, Fufeng Dou 扶風竇, Henan Yu 河南于, Henan Yuan 河南源, and Henan Changsun 河南長孫 clans from Daibei, who migrated south to the capital region during the Northern Wei; the Chenjun Xie 陳郡謝, Langya Wang 瑯琊王, Lanling Xiao 蘭陵蕭, Chenjun Yuan 陳郡袁 "émigré clans" 僑姓, who migrated south to serve the southern dynasties in the pre-Tang period; and the Wujun Zhu 吳郡朱, Wujun Lu 吳郡陸, Wujun Zhang 吳郡張, and Wujun Gu 吳郡顧 clans from the Suzhou region in the southeast. See Sun Guodong, "Tang Song zhi ji shehui mendi," pp. 213–15; Yoshioka, "Hasseiki zenhan ni okeru Tōchō kanryō kikō"; Yoshioka, "Zui Tō zenki ni okeru shihai kaisō."

22. Note that Twitchett draws a similar distinction between a "super-elite of extremely powerful clans" and a "very much larger group of locally prominent lineages." See Twitchett, "Composition," pp. 56–57, 76.

clans.²³ Needless to say, Mao's lists are helpful for clarifying the relationship between the great clans as a status group and political power.

The Demographic Expansion of the Medieval Aristocracy

Any broad reading of Tang era tomb epitaphs makes readily apparent the prevalence of claims to aristocratic descent. Using the full list of 6,255 individuals—of which the 4,311 described above constitute the subset identified by both choronym and surname—figure 1.2 tabulates the frequency of claims to great clan descent in late Tang inscriptions from several regions where epitaphs have been discovered in particular abundance, including the Western Capital of Chang'an, the Eastern Capital of Luoyang, the "capital corridor" linking these two metropolises (a zone whose importance will be discussed in more detail in the following chapter), the Lower Yangzi (including both Suzhou and the southern economic nexus of Yangzhou), Zhaoyi Province (which spanned southeastern Hedong and southwestern Hebei), and the three autonomous Hebei provinces. In the table, all attributions of pre-Tang commanderies as places of clan origin are considered evidence of a claim to aristocratic descent. It is assumed that individuals mentioned in epitaphs resided near where their epitaphs were discovered; the correlations between places of death and burial will be discussed in more detail in chapter 2.

As the leftmost column of figure 1.2 indicates, in all regions of the empire, from three-fourths to over 90 percent of the subjects of epitaphs were said to be of aristocratic descent. If one assumes that epitaphs from any given region constitute a relatively random sample of individuals with the most wealth and status in that region (as discussed in the introduction), then one can conclude that the overwhelming majority of late Tang socioeconomic elites either descended from the great aristocratic clans or accepted the notion that it was prestigious to assert descent

---

23. Mao Hanguang, "Tangdai tongzhi jieceng shehui biandong," pp. 147–50. Besides the seven marriage-ban clans, these included the Langya Wangs 瑯琊王, Hongnong Yangs 弘農楊, Jingzhao Weis 京兆韋, Hedong Peis 河東裴, Nanyang Zhangs 南陽張, Qinghe Zhangs 清河張, Pengcheng Lius 彭城劉, Bohai Gaos 渤海高, and Tianshui Zhaos 天水趙. All of these clans produced over one hundred known officeholders based on data Mao collected from 2,647 individuals mentioned in *Jiu Tang shu* and *Xin Tang shu* and 5,222 individuals mentioned in Tang period tomb epitaphs. Mao does not himself create a category for the top sixteen officeholding clans.

Region	Deceased	Deceased or agnate	Deceased, affine, or agnate	Spouse	Affine
Chang'an	75% (464/620)	85% (529/620)	90% (557/620)	49% (247/502)	48% (395/830)
Luoyang	87% (871/998)	94% (938/998)	97% (964/998)	72% (584/810)	71% (1,143/1,621)
Capital Corridor	82% (108/131)	92% (121/131)	95% (125/131)	80% (106/132)	66% (155/235)
Zhaoyi	92% (120/130)	92% (120/130)	95% (123/130)	63% (81/129)	43% (118/274)
Auton. Hebei	83% (111/134)	86% (115/134)	91% (122/134)	60% (77/128)	53% (108/203)
Lower Yangzi	91% (129/141)	91% (129/141)	95% (134/141)	56% (75/133)	53% (123/232)
Elsewhere	87% (193/223)	88% (197/223)	95% (212/223)	65% (142/218)	56% (211/380)

FIGURE 1.2. Frequency of attribution of great clan status in ninth-century epitaphs (by region) Includes all relatives of deceased mentioned in epitaphs dating to the period 800–880. "Great clan status" means place of clan origin is a pre-Tang commandery (appearing either as a choronym appended to a surname or within a discussion of an individual's ancestry). For practical reasons, percentages in the first three columns are calculated per total number of epitaphs, whereas percentages in the last two columns (which deal with affines, whose numbers vary per epitaph) are calculated per total number of individuals. Under consideration are the deceased (subject of the epitaph), agnates (family members of the same surname), spouses, and affines (relatives by marriage, including spouses, sons-in-law, and so forth). Only great clan claims made within the text of epitaphs are considered, except in case of agnates, where great clan attribution is considered for any member of the "patriline" (as defined in chapter 3).

from such families. It should be noted, however, that some families deemed their pedigrees to be so well established that it was not necessary to identify explicitly their places of ancestral origin. Thus, a number of individuals whose epitaphs do not mention their choronyms can be shown (using techniques described in chapter 3) to have belonged to a patriline some of whose members did profess great clan descent in their own epitaphs.[24] Including this group as well (column 2 of figure 1.2), then one finds that 85 percent or more of elites from all regions either were or could claim to be of aristocratic descent. The figure rises to over 9 in 10 for all regions if one includes individuals who, though not themselves of such prestigious origins, had marriage ties with purported aristocrats (column 3).[25] Without doubt, attributions of great clan descent were prevalent in all regions of China.

Figure 1.3 categorizes attributions of aristocratic descent according to the relative prestige and exclusivity of the great clans in question. Categories include (1) all families appearing on Johnson's lists (A, C, or E); (2) the sixteen clans that produced the largest number of officeholders over the course of the Tang; (3) Liu Fang's twenty-eight famous families; and, most eminent of all, (4) the seven "marriage-ban" clans. Not surprisingly, in all regions, well over four-fifths of purported aristocrats claimed descent from a clan on one of Johnson's lists. More remarkable, however, is the disproportionate number of claims to ties with the much smaller, more exclusive groups of clans. In most regions, over half of the elites mentioned in tomb inscriptions purportedly descended from one of the sixteen top officeholding clans; a quarter to a third in most regions (over half in Luoyang) claimed descent from one of the seven marriage-ban clans.[26] In other words, even in regions far from the choronym places of origin of the families in question, a substantial propor-

---

24. For example, the epitaph of Yang Hao 楊晧 (840–58) never mentions his choronym. But the epitaphs of his uncle Yang Sili 楊思立 (d. 875) and of several other close relatives identify him as a member of the Hongnong Yang family. It seems to have been particularly common for the imperial clan not to mention the clan's purported choronym of Longxi 隴西.

25. To be sure, choronyms were less consistently mentioned in the case of spouses and other in-laws (columns 4 and 5). But this tendency is not entirely unexpected given that epitaphs generally provided far less information about relatives by marriage.

26. Moreover, three-quarters (76 percent) of Luoyang elites claimed descent from one of just twenty-five families. See "Fig 1.3 Prestige of Clan Attributions" in database.

Region	Clan lists	Marriage ban	Liu Fang's top 28	Officeholding top 16	n
Chang'an	87%	30%	50%	57%	862
Luoyang	89%	51%	65%	68%	2,014
Capital Corridor	84%	37%	50%	59%	263
Zhaoyi	86%	30%	31%	50%	238
Auton. Hebei	87%	27%	33%	60%	219
Lower Yangzi	81%	10%	25%	35%	252
Elsewhere	85%	24%	30%	49%	404

FIGURE 1.3. Relative prestige of clan attributions in ninth-century epitaphs (by region)
Includes only individuals with great clan status, as defined in figure 1.2. As an example, "30%" at the top of column 2 means 30 percent of the 862 individuals mentioned in Chang'an epitaphs who have a pre-Tang commandery as their place of clan origin claimed membership in one of the seven marriage-ban clans.

tion of elites claimed descent from the small number of most prestigious families.

Although the majority of epitaphs from most regions of China were composed on behalf of officeholders or their immediate relatives—a trend discussed in detail in chapter 2—officeholders were by no means the only group to assert family ties to the most prominent clans. Even among individuals with no known ties to the political bureaucracy, a large proportion claimed great clan descent. One such man, the Qingzhou merchant Zhao Cong* 趙琮 (d. 875), was said to be a scion of the Tianshui Zhao clan, one of the top sixteen officeholding families.[27] Both his mother and his wife were members of one of the marriage-ban clans, the Taiyuan Wangs.[28] Similarly, the Hebei landowner Mr. Xu* 許公 (d. 867), a man also with no known family connections to government, supposedly belonged to the Yingchuan Xu clan.[29] So too Zhang Wu* 張武 (826–83), from Zhaoyi, whose epitaph does not even

---

27. Although it is sometimes difficult to identify merchants in epitaphs because of a propensity to avoid mentioning one's involvement in commerce, Zhao's epitaph is quite clear that he "went north and south to trade" 南北貿賈.

28. For a similar example, see the epitaph of Sun Sui 孫綏 (798–878) of the Le'an Sun clan.

29. The Yingchuan Xu clan appears on clan lists A and E. Mr. Xu had no known family ties to the government; his epitaph, however, provides an extensive account of his land and mulberry tree holdings. See Tackett, "Transformation," p. 51.

mention his occupation, yet who was purportedly a descendant of one of the top sixteen clans. Of his three wives and three sons-in-law, five claimed membership in a clan appearing on Johnson's lists; moreover, his second wife was a Tianshui Zhao and his second son-in-law was a Hedong Pei, both among the top sixteen clans. In those regions of China with relatively large populations of non-officeholding elites—notably Zhaoyi Province and the Lower Yangzi region—one encounters dozens of similar cases. In sum, across the empire, a wide range of elites, some with political power and some without, claimed aristocratic descent.

But how accurate were such claims? There are, in fact, a few cases that are highly suspect, involving contradictory attributions of choronyms. According to his own inscription, Dong Tangzhi* 董唐之 (804–58) descended from the Longxi Dong family. But the epitaph of his wife, Ms. Wang* 王氏 (824–70), asserts he was from a certain Dong family of Jiyin.[30] Contradictions occasionally even appear within the same epitaph. Thus, the title line of one epitaph dating to 834, discovered in the vicinity of Luoyang, identifies the deceased as the "Gentleman Cui of Qinghe Commandery" 清河郡崔府君; the text of the epitaph, however, asserts that "his ancestors came from Boling" 其先出于博陵.[31] The Qinghe Cuis and Boling Cuis were two different marriage-ban clans; it is not possible that the individual in question was a descendant of both.[32] Yet suspect claims of this sort are quite rare. More problematic are the general trends implied in figures 1.2 and 1.3. Is it really possible that so many individuals all over the empire, including people with no family members in government, could legitimately claim such prestigious ancestries? And, if so, is it likely that so many of

---

30. Similarly, according to his epitaph, Song Zaichu 宋再初 (777–858) is said to be from the Song family of Guangping, an attribution confirmed in his wife's epitaph. Yet an inscription composed for Song's uncle Song Ti 宋遏 (735–85), discovered some dozen miles away, explains that the Song family hailed from Julu Commandery.

31. Epitaph of Cui Xu 崔勗 (c. 786–c. 834).

32. Another epitaph, for a certain Liu Hui 劉惠 (772–848), asserts, "The ancestors of the Liu clan . . . were eminent in Pengcheng, Hejian, and Hongnong; the gentleman was an esteemed descendant of these three eminent clans" 劉氏之先 . . . 望彭城河間弘農, 府君即是三望之崇裔). The Pengcheng Lius, Hejian Lius, and Hongnong Lius are all clans that appear on the Dunhuang clan lists; yet cursory inspection of extant genealogical records makes clear that it was not possible to descend simultaneously from all three families.

them descended from the small group of very eminent clans? Why did so many use choronyms that asserted blood ties to a few particularly famous families rather than to locally based clans?

In fact, there are indications that the vast majority of such claims may indeed have been accurate. Occasionally, in the same epitaph, one affine (daughter-in-law or son-in-law) is said to be a member of a great clan (i.e., she or he is identified by surname and choronym), whereas another is not (i.e., she or he is identified by surname alone).[33] If great clan attributions were fabricated by the family of the deceased or by the author of the epitaph, why would choronyms not have been assigned to all affines mentioned in the epitaph? The plausibility of a number of claims to prestigious choronyms is further bolstered by the relatively frequent references to extant clan genealogies. Consider Ms. Dou* 竇氏 (d. 879), buried in Hebei but allegedly descended from the Dou family of Fufeng (west of Chang'an). Her epitaph explicitly asserts that her eminent ancestors grace the pages of both the historical records 史載 and, more significantly, the family genealogy 家諜.[34] In the case of Yan Haowen* 閻好問 (810–73), of the Henan Yan family, we are told that his thirty-fourth-generation ancestor, named Zhi 芝, had served as governor in Sichuan and that his twenty-third-generation ancestor, named Ding 鼎, had once been prefect of Jizhou.[35] Such specific details of distant ancestry strongly suggest the existence at that time of a genealogy, a document that would have substantiated credible claims to great clan descent.

But the strongest evidence that most claims to great clan descent may have been accurate stems from basic demographic principles. In a society without primogeniture and where the sons born to concubines had the same legal privileges as those born to a wife, scions of prominent families

---

33. See epitaphs of Li Rang 李讓 (793–850), He Fu 何俛 (801–66), Huang Gongjun 黃公俊 (803–78), and Ma Liang 馬良 (810–83).

34. For other similar examples, see epitaphs of Xu Zhi 許贄 (809–52), Ms. Chen 陳氏 (832–56), Yao Jixian 姚季仙 (787–863), Zhao Congyi 趙從一 (792–868), Ren Xuan 任玄 (812–68), Gu Qian 顧謙 (806–72), Yue Bangsui 樂邦穗 (827–77), Luo Qian 駱潛 (848–84), and Ms. Wei 衛氏 (844–86).

35. For other examples of inscriptions that reveal knowledge of ancestry beyond the fourth generation, see epitaphs of Tao Daiqian 陶待虔 (d. 849), Ms. Zhang 張氏 (795–855), Zhou Yu 周璵 (787–856), He Hongjing 何弘敬 (806–65), Daxi Ge 達奚革 (795–866), Wen Lingshou 溫令綬 (806–74), and Cui Yisun 崔貽孫 (859–80).

had the potential for expanding exponentially.[36] One way of assessing the fecundity of the upper class is to average the numbers of the deceased's sons, numbers often provided by the epitaphs.[37] There is good evidence that, in many cases, only surviving children were noted in the inscriptions and that children dying in infancy were excluded.[38] If one focuses only on men over sixty years old at their deaths, one can calculate the average number of sons surviving into their twenties. Thus, a sample of epitaphs from Chang'an and Luoyang reveals that the typical elite male had about 3.3 sons, most of whom would have survived to adulthood.[39] More specifically, 18 percent had one son, 20 percent had two sons, 16 percent had three sons, and 42 percent had four or more sons. Only 3 percent of men had no male offspring.[40] It is worth noting that military

---

36. The practice of concubinage has widespread implications for the study of premodern demographics in China. For example, unlike in the study of premodern demographics in Europe, it makes more sense to focus on a man's offspring than on a woman's offspring.

37. Epitaphs often identify the total number of sons and of daughters before identifying each individually by name and office (in the case of sons), or by husband's name and office (in the case of daughters).

38. It is my sense that epitaphs either note explicitly that an offspring has died in childhood or—far more commonly—do not mention the dead offspring at all. For example, we know from the epitaph of Wei Yuan 韋媛 (810–81), wife of Yang Hangong 楊漢公 (785–861), that Yang had twenty one children (thirteen sons and eight daughters), three born of his first wife, five of his second wife, and thirteen of concubines. At the time of Wei's death, two sons and one daughter had died in adulthood, two sons had died in their teens, and one son and two daughters had died very young. Based on a calculation of their approximate ages, it appears that Yang outlived one son and three daughters. Yang's epitaph only mentions twelve sons and five daughters; apparently, the epitaph entirely avoids mentioning the offspring who had died. For similar examples, compare epitaphs of Zheng Juan 鄭娟 (821–65) and her husband Cui Xinggui 崔行規 (817–67), of Ms. Cai 蔡氏 (775–850) and her husband Xie Shaoqing 解少卿 (770–835), of Ms. Cui 崔氏 (790–826) and her husband Lu Boqing 盧伯卿 (774–840), and of Ms. Lu 路氏 (751–804) and her husband Pei Zha 裴札 (728–84).

39. See "Fig_L_note39_avg sons at capital" in database. This figure is based on a sample of 159 epitaphs from Chang'an or Luoyang composed for men over the age of fifty-nine. Only epitaphs that state both the total number of sons and the total number of daughters have been considered. Cf. Yao Ping, *Tangdai funü*, pp. 326–35, which proposes a slightly lower average. Yao's figures, however, include provincial elites as well.

40. To be sure, a certain number of men without male offspring would have adopted a son and may appear in these statistics as having one son. As sons are usually adopted within the patriline, this phenomenon should not affect the average.

men in the sample—especially those of high rank—were generally more prolific, perhaps indicative of a family strategy to compensate for war-related deaths in early adulthood. Military men, however, constituted a relatively small percentage of the elite population under consideration here.[41] A second means of estimating the number of sons per elite male is to consider the deceased's order of birth among his siblings—a detail also frequently indicated in the epitaphs. Among epitaphs for males at least thirty years of age from Chang'an and Luoyang, it turns out that 39.7 percent of the males were first sons, 22.6 percent were second sons, 15.4 percent were third sons, and 10.5 percent were fourth sons.[42] Extrapolating from these figures, one can calculate that approximately 17 percent of elite men would have had only one son, 14 percent two sons, 15 percent three sons, and as many as half or more would have had four or more sons. Although this approach does not allow one to calculate averages, this distribution is certainly in line with an average of over three sons per male.[43]

This impressive fecundity of the Chinese elites—linked in part to the role of concubines—has important implications. One thousand clan scions reproducing at a rate of three surviving males per generation could theoretically expand to twenty million over a three-hundred-year period.[44]

---

41. For example, according to their epitaphs, the military men Linghu Mei 令狐梅 (793–854) and He Wenzhe 何文哲 (764–830) had, respectively, 20 children (12 of whom were sons) and 10 children (6 of whom were sons). In the sample of 158 capital elites, only 14 are classified as military men. See appendix A for a description of how military men are distinguished from civilian bureaucrats.

42. See "Fig_L_note42 order in sib seq" in database. These statistics are based on 305 epitaphs from Chang'an or Luoyang for men over the age of 29 for whom the position in the sibling sequence is identified. Owing to the small number of fifth and later sons, their percentages are not statistically significant.

43. Let $a1$ be the proportion of men with one son, $a2$ the proportion with two sons, $a3$ the proportion with three sons, and so on. Let $x1$ be the percentage of males who are first sons, $x2$ be the percentage of males who are second sons, $x3$ be the percentage of males who are third sons. Then $x1 = a1 + (1/2)a2 + (1/3)a3 + \ldots$; $x2 = (1/2)a2 + (1/3)a3 + \ldots$; $x3 = (1/3)a3 + \ldots$ Thus, $x1 = a1 + x2$, $x2 = (1/2)a2 + x3$, $x3 = (1/3)a3 + x4$, and so forth. So, $a1 = x1 - x2 = 39.7\% - 22.6\% = 17.1\%$, $a2 = (x2 - x3)*2 = (22.6\% - 15.4\%)*2 = 14.4\%$, $a3 = (x3 - x4)*3 = (15.4\% - 10.5\%)*3 = 14.7\%$. If one assumes that 3 percent of males had zero sons, then all of these percentages should be reduced by approximately $(100*16\%) - (97*16\%) = 0.5\%$.

44. This figure is based on an interval between generations of thirty-five years; see chapter 3 for more on average intervals between generations. For a graphical depiction

However, this rate of expansion assumes that all descendants could afford to support several concubines, an implausible assumption in the case of descendants who fell from the ranks of the upper class. Nevertheless, if we then consider the large numbers of aristocratic clans present in the mid-eighth century—791 appeared on the longest Dunhuang list—it is perfectly plausible that so many elites could claim to be descendants of great clans. Moreover, wealthier elites reproduced faster than less wealthy elites because they both could afford more concubines and could support a larger number of children. The result was a snowball effect whereby the most successful clans reproduced faster, allowing them to occupy an ever greater share of government positions. Indeed, Mao Hanguang has shown that, over the course of the Tang dynasty, the top thirty-nine clans gained ground in their overall political prominence.[45]

Thus, although not all claims made by provincial elites to great clan descent may have been true, the evidence suggests that the vast majority were probably perfectly accurate. Indeed, the very existence in the provinces of so many genuine descendants of great clans made it plausible for a minority of dubious social climbers to concoct such prestigious connections. In the context of the aristocratic ethos of the era, descent from a great family remained the sine qua non for pretensions to upper-class status. But the old aristocracy was being watered down all across the empire by an ever increasing number of claimants. By the ninth century, great clan status was no longer sufficient in itself to define the highest levels of the sociopolitical elite.

The Geographic Dispersal of Great Clan Descendants

David Johnson and Patricia Ebrey have shown that two of the most prestigious Hebei clans had largely abandoned their old homes, reestablishing themselves in Luoyang, by the middle of the Tang dynasty.[46] In a more recent study of a larger sample of thirteen of the most prominent clans, Mao Hanguang has documented the "centralization of

---

of the exponential growth of three prominent clans, see Ebrey, *Aristocratic Families*, p. 171.

45. Mao Hanguang, "Tangdai tongzhi jieceng shehui biandong," pp. 223–24; Tackett, "Transformation," pp. 63, 101.

46. Johnson, "Last Years," pp. 32–40; Ebrey, *Aristocratic Families*, pp. 91–93.

the Tang civil bureaucratic clans" 唐代士族之中央化.⁴⁷ The epigraphic record further corroborates these findings, suggesting more specifically that prominent branches of the great clans arrived in the capital in several waves. Some, like the Guzang branch of the Longxi Lis, were probably already entrenched in Luoyang at the beginning of the sixth century.⁴⁸ By contrast, many of the important Hebei families, including the Fanyang Lus, the Zhaojun Lis, and the Boling Cuis, do not seem to have relocated until the seventh century.⁴⁹ Finally, as we shall see, some of the clans based closest to the capital may not have left their places of clan origin until the eighth century or later.

But to what extent did this "centralization" process affect the medieval elite as a whole? Were there other prominent migratory pathways for scions of the old families? And, most important for understanding the nature of the medieval aristocracy during the Tang, did lesser branches of the great families preserve their high status at the clan's place of origin even while their more prominent cousins relocated to the capital? If this were the case, it is possible that a landed elite in the provinces might have maintained an independent power base that could have stood up to and resisted the authority of the state. The early Qing scholar Gu

---

47. Mao Hanguang, "Cong shizu jiguan."

48. For Luoyang epitaphs for Guzang Lis dating to 505 and 649, respectively, see epitaphs of Li Rui 李蕤 (464–505) and Li Xuan 李絢 (558–622).

49. The "second house" of the "northern branch" of the Fanyang Lus was in Fanyang as late as 625 but in Henan by 680. See epitaphs of (Ms.) Li Yuexiang 李月相 (535–618)—wife of Lu Wengou 盧文構—and of Lu Pude 盧普德 (611–80). The "eastern branch" of the Zhaojun Lis was in Zhaojun from the 530s to the 570s but in Luoyang by no later than the first half of the eighth century. See epitaphs of Li Bi 李弼 (479–526), Li Xian 李憲 (c. 480–c. 537), Li Xizong 李希宗 (501–40), Li Xili 李希禮 (511–56), Li Junying 李君穎 (540–73), Li Zumu 李祖牧 (511–69), Li Jiong 李迥 (689–730), and Li Di 李迪 (c. 683–c. 747). The "southern branch" of the Zhaojun Lis was in Zhaojun as of 574 but in Luoyang by 787. See epitaphs of Li Zhilian 李稚廉 (508–74) and of Li Xie 李澥 (718–60). And the "western branch" of the Zhaojun Lis was in Luoyang at least by the mid-seventh century; see epitaph of Li Daosu 李道素 (623–39). The "second branch" of the Boling Cuis was in Boling as late as the first half of the seventh century but in Chang'an by 650. See epitaphs of Cui Ang 崔昂 (508–65), Cui Dashan 崔大善 (571–87), Cui Zhongfang 崔仲方 (539–614), and Cui Gan 崔幹 (d. c. 650). Finally, the "great branch" of the Boling Cuis was in Luoyang by the second half of the seventh century. See epitaphs of Cui Tai 崔泰 (576–636), Cui Wujing 崔無競 (631–90), and Cui Xuanliang 崔玄亮 (608–49). For a discussion of the correlation between place of burial and place of residence, see chapter 2.

Yanwu 顧炎武 (1613–82)—who located over a hundred medieval tombs of the Hedong Pei clan in Wenxi 聞喜 County at the site of the pre-Tang Hedong Commandery—seems not to have doubted that medieval aristocratic families indeed remained entrenched at their old home bases. In an essay titled "A Record of Pei Village" 裴村記, Gu praised "powerful lineages" like the Peis on the grounds that they constituted—in his view—a "solid foundation upon which to erect the state."[50] For Gu, it was the presence of great families in the provinces that had helped stabilize the Tang empire, making it one of the greatest of China's dynasties.

But, as it turns out, Gu was wrong in seeing the Hedong Pei clan as typical of Tang provincial society. In reality, Hedong Commandery (located in the southwestern corner of the region later known as Hedong Province) was somewhat unique because it was situated relatively close to both of the two great capital cities. Moreover, Gu's assessment of the Pei clan was based for the most part on tombs from the earliest period of the Tang. There is good evidence that most survivors of this family had relocated to either Chang'an or Luoyang by the late eighth century. Unfortunately, most of the Tang era tombs once littering the countryside of southwestern Hedong were systematically destroyed in the 1960s and 1970s as part of an effort to clear up land for farming.[51] However, a Qing era gazetteer of Wenxi County preserves a list of most of the tombs encountered by Gu Yanwu.[52] All seem to date to the fifth through eighth centuries.[53] Such findings are confirmed, moreover, by the epitaph record. An examination of the fifty-two individual Hedong Peis for whom inscriptions survive reveals that clan members did live primarily in Hedong in the seventh century but that they moved progressively to either Chang'an or Luoyang during the course of the eighth century.[54] As late as the mid-ninth century, the epitaph for the spouse of a clansman still described the old clan cemetery near a mountain in Hedong, where

---

50. Twitchett, "Composition," pp. 52–54.

51. Personal conversation on 23 March 2011 with Li Baiqin 李百勤, director of the Yuncheng Bureau of Culture.

52. Li Zuntang, ed., *(Qianlong) Wenxi xian zhi* 9.13a–18a.

53. I was able to find in my database, in some cases tentatively, 42 of the 93 individuals listed in the gazetteer. See "Fig 1_note53 Pei clan in Wenxi" in database. All of these individuals seem to have died in the eighth century or earlier.

54. See "Fig 1_note54 Pei clan home base over time" in database.

	Place of clan origin	
Region of burial	Same prefecture	Same province
Chang'an	10% (82/800)	10% (82/800)
Luoyang	3% (49/1,918)	3% (49/1,918)
Lower Yangzi	6% (13/222)	13% (29/222)
Capital Corridor	4% (9/246)	6% (15/246)
Auton. Hebei	1% (3/201)	8% (17/201)
Zhaoyi	1% (2/218)	5% (10/218)
Elsewhere	1% (4/364)	3% (10/364)

FIGURE 1.4. Incidence of elites residing in the same prefecture or province as choronym place of clan origin (by region)

Place of residence defined as the place of burial (as explained in chapter 2). Included are the subjects of epitaphs dating to the period 800–880 as well as their relatives by marriage.

"ancient graves protruded from the mountain, and pine and cypress trees [which traditionally marked tombs] spread out over a hundred *li*" 山突古墳, 松檟百里.[55] It is significant, however, that the epitaph in question was discovered in the vicinity of Chang'an.

Figure 1.4 assesses in a more systematic fashion the places of clan origin of individuals mentioned in ninth-century epitaphs from multiple regions. Once again, the basis for the statistics is the group of 4,311 individuals described previously. One can assume that this sample of clan names roughly reflects the composition of the wealthier strata residing in each particular area. The regions included are those where epitaphs have been discovered in particular abundance. The evidence is patently clear. Across the empire, by the ninth century, it was extremely unusual to find an aristocrat who still resided in the prefecture or province of the clan's home base while maintaining the economic resources necessary for a burial that included an epitaph. Figure 1.5 presents cartographically the places of clan origin of ninth-century elites residing in four select prefectures. There are some notable variations in the four maps. Suzhou epitaphs (fig. 1.5a), for example, mention a number of individuals with clan origins in the Lower Yangzi region, whereas the Lower Yangzi is poorly represented in epitaphs from the other three prefectures. By

---

55. Epitaph of Ms. Du 杜氏 (799–835).

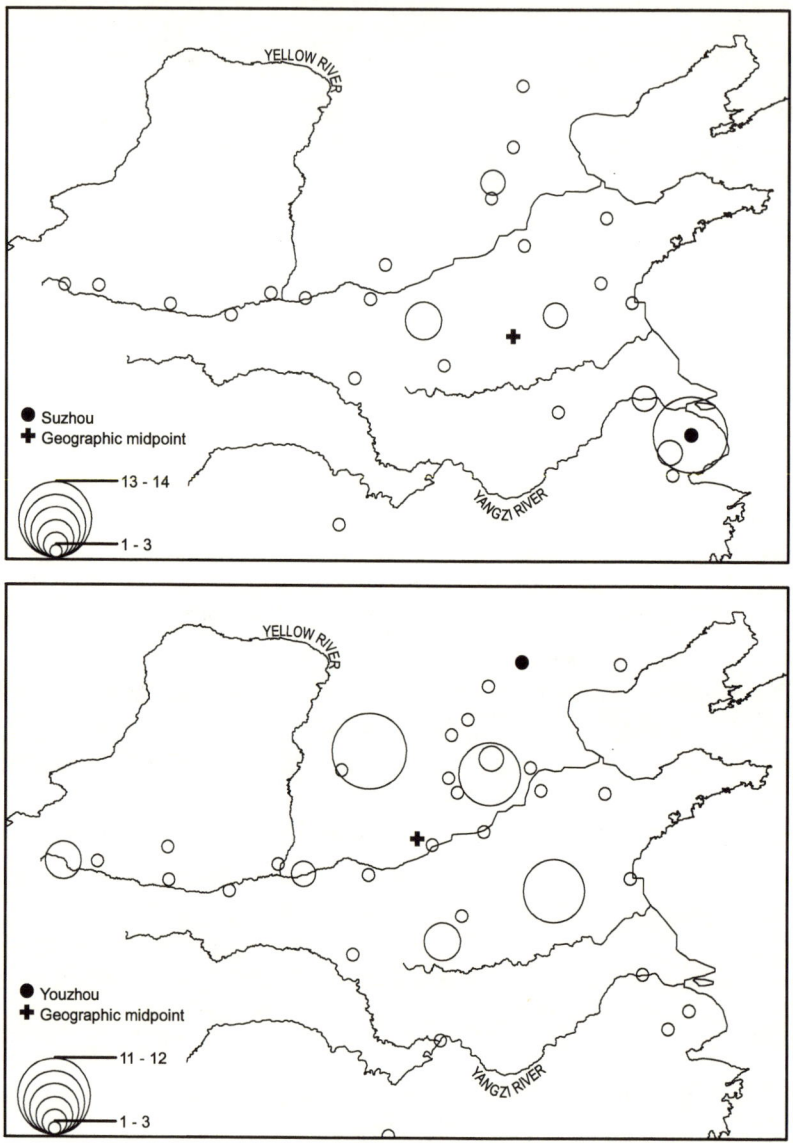

FIGURE 1.5. Choronym places of origin of elites from four select prefectures. (a) Suzhou elites. (b) Youzhou elites. (c) Luzhou elites. (d) Luoyang elites.

Each map considers only epitaphs from the prefecture in question. Includes choronym places of origin (i.e., pre-Tang commanderies claimed as family place of origin) of all subjects of epitaphs and their relatives by marriage. Geographic midpoint is equivalent to averages of latitudes and longitudes of all choronym places of origin.

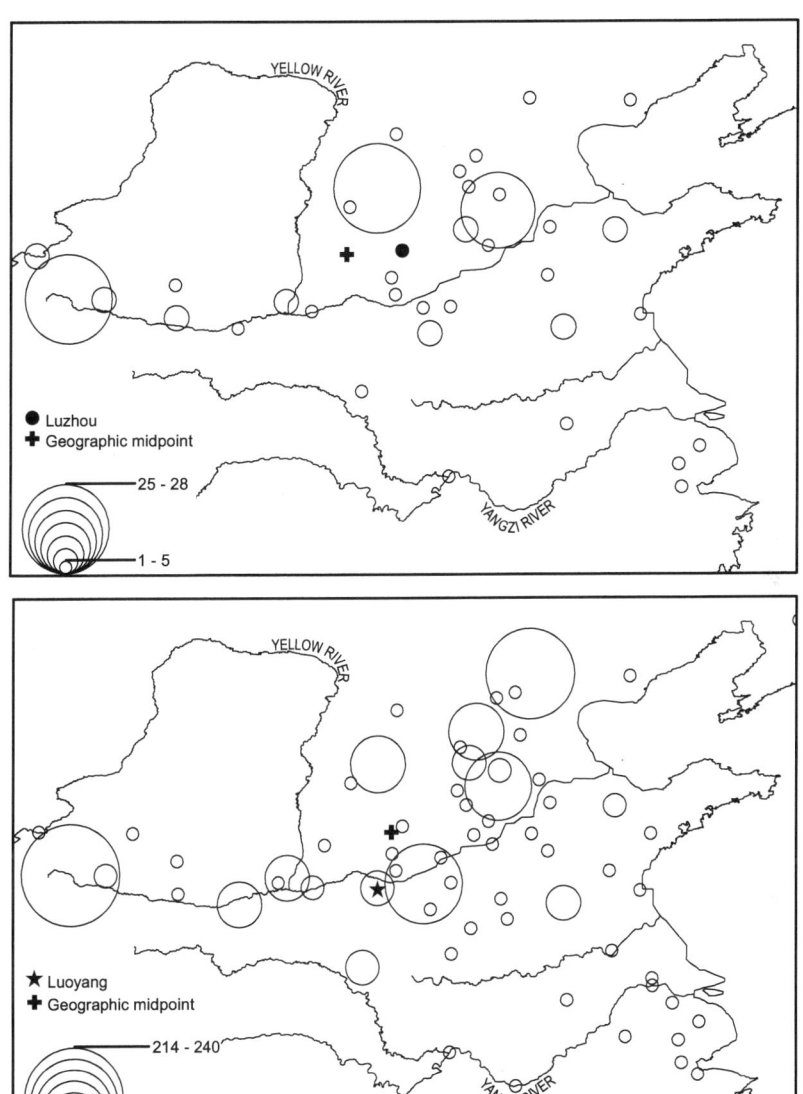

contrast, Suzhou epitaphs rarely refer to clans from modern-day Shanxi Province, the region east of the Yellow River, whereas these clans were prevalent in epitaphs elsewhere. What is most striking, however, is the degree to which elites residing in all four of these prefectures claimed descent from clans whose places of origin were scattered empirewide, often many hundreds of kilometers away. Although a certain number of claims may have been fictive, if one assumes that most were not, then the four maps present convincing evidence that the medieval elite lineages, each once based in a single prefecture, had been thoroughly shuffled and redistributed from their sites of origin to new locales all across the empire.

Before seeking to explain this wholesale geographic mobility of the old aristocracy, it is worth investigating those exceptional cases of native elites who still remained in their ancestral homelands as late as the ninth century. Among the regions defined in figure 1.4, Chang'an had the largest percentage of native elites (10 percent). This relatively higher proportion is largely attributable to the fact that one of the top sixteen officeholding clans, the Jingzhao Weis, and one of Liu Fang's top twenty-eight clans, the Jingzhao Dus, were both entrenched in the southern suburbs of this great city. In the words of one contemporary adage, "The Weis and Dus south of the city are only five feet away from Heaven and comparable [to each other] in prestige" 城南韋杜，去天尺五，望之比也.[56] In absolute numbers, Luoyang had the next largest number of native elites, about two-fifths of whom were members of the Henan Yuan clan. But the overall percentage of native elites in the Eastern Capital was substantially less than in Chang'an, probably because they were overwhelmed in numbers by the marriage-ban clans that—as we shall see in chapter 3—came to dominate Luoyang society.

By the ninth century, there were still a few native clans living in the capital corridor surrounding Chang'an and Luoyang. One still encountered individuals in Zhengzhou claiming descent from the local and very prestigious Xingyang Zheng 滎陽鄭 clan. Moreover, as previously discussed, branches of the Hedong Pei clan continued to inhabit their homeland in large numbers well into the eighth century. The Hedong

---

56. Epitaph of (Ms.) Wei Yuan 韋媛 (810–81). For a description of one cluster of Wei clan tombs, see Zhang Yun, "Guanyu Xi'an nanjiao Biyuan chutu."

Xue clan had an equally significant presence there as well. According to the Song epigrapher Chen Si 陳思 (fl. 1225–64), steles for this family were "particularly numerous" 尤多 in the region.⁵⁷ A few of these steles have survived to this day, including the early-eighth-century spirit-path inscriptions of Xue Baoji 薛寶積 and of his grandfather Xue Daoshi 薛道實, which now stand amid the apple orchards of Linyi 臨猗 County on a plateau overlooking modern-day Yuncheng and the Zhongtiao 中條 range separating the plains of southwestern Shanxi from the Yellow River valley (see cover photo). By the ninth century, however, most of the prominent Peis and Xues had gone to the capital, with only a few stragglers remaining behind.⁵⁸

The cases discussed thus far all adhere to a fairly predictable pattern. If one assumes a link between elite status and political power—a link explored in more detail in chapter 2—one would anticipate a certain number of native clans in and around the two imperial capitals of Chang'an and Luoyang. There, they might have maintained property and exerted influence locally while still retaining a presence at the capital. But figure 1.4 suggests that, in one other region much farther removed from the capital—the Lower Yangzi—one may have encountered an even greater number of clans residing near their places of origin.⁵⁹ More precisely, some 13 percent of individuals mentioned in epitaphs from this region had family roots in their province of residence, a substantially higher percentage than in other parts of Tang China. The statistics are even more striking if one includes another group of families with a long-standing presence in the southeast, the so-called émigré clans 僑姓 that had accompanied the Jin regime in its flight south in 316 CE and that

---

57. Chen Si, *Baoke congbian* 10.47a.

58. For examples of stragglers, see epitaphs of Xue Jian 薛謇 (749–815), Xue Ping 薛苹 (746–819), Xue Ping 薛平 (757–836), and Xue Yiju 薛貽矩 (850–912).

59. In addition, there is the case of autonomous Hebei. Although few descendants of the great families from Hebei lived in their prefectures of clan origin, some did live in the larger administrative unit of their provinces of origin. But these statistics are probably misleading. Hebei was the homeland of several of the marriage-ban clans, clans whose descendants were encountered all over the empire in large numbers. As figure 1.3 makes clear, the marriage ban-clans were no more frequently found in Hebei than in many other parts of the empire. Much like the case of Cui Fangjian discussed below, the ancestors of most of these individuals had probably relocated to their present homes because of their office and lived only by coincidence near their places of clan origin.

had later taken advantage of their political clout at the Eastern Jin court to garner large tracts of land.[60] Indeed, several of the top officeholding families of the Eastern Jin, including the Chenjun Xies, the Chenjun Yuans, the Yingchuan Yus, the Runan Zhous, and, especially, the Langya Wangs—who dominated the government in the fourth and fifth centuries—were all originally from Huaibei in the north.[61] Many descendants of these clans appear to have remained in the south well after the Sui-Tang reunification. According to the epitaph record, no less than 12 percent (27/222) of individual elites from the Lower Yangzi region were from these émigré clans.[62] Adding this percentage to that in figure 1.4, one finds that a full quarter of individuals with choronyms mentioned in southeastern epitaphs made a claim of descent from families already entrenched in the region centuries before the founding of the Tang.

Figure 1.6 is similar to figure 1.4 but with data presented for selected prefectures for which a relatively large number of epitaphs are preserved. Once again, one finds that, in the ninth century, most elite clans were living nowhere near their places of clan origin. One exception was Zhengzhou, in the capital corridor near the center of political power. But more striking were the elites in Suzhou, in the Yangzi Delta region, a third of whom lived either in their prefecture of clan origin or in a neighboring prefecture within Zhexi Province. Unlike the situation in most parts of China, a sizable population of great clan descendants in the Suzhou region had apparently never left their original power base.[63] For example, Gu Qian* 顧謙 (806–72), who had once served as a county

---

60. Ebrey, *Aristocratic Families*, pp. 20–21.

61. For the list of top officeholding families during the Southern Dynasties, see Mao Hanguang, *Liang Jin Nanbeichao shizu zhengzhi*, pp. 17–22. According to Hua Guorong, "Nanjing Liuchao ," p. 285, many of these families intermarried with each other and were buried not far away from each other in the vicinity of modern-day Nanjing.

62. See "Fig 1_4 Still at place of clan origin (by province)" in database.

63. Although too few late Tang epitaphs survive from northern Zhejiang to draw conclusions based on statistical evidence, there are anecdotal indications that this region may also have had a number of natal great clans. Ms. Sun 孫氏 (794–850) of the Fuchun Sun clan (a branch of the Le'an Sun family that reestablished itself in the south) was buried alongside her natal clan cemetery, in the Fuchun region. Luo Xiang 羅珦 (736–809) of the Kuaiji Luo clan was buried in Yuezhou (formerly Kuaiji Commandery). And the epitaph of Luo Qian 駱潛 (848–84) of the Kuaiji Luo clan, who was buried in Yangzhou, refers to a clan cemetery in Kuaiji.

Prefecture of burial	Same prefecture	Same province
Luzhou 潞州	2% (3/188)	6% (11/188)
Mengzhou 孟州	0% (0/124)	4% (5/124)
Yangzhou 揚州	1% (1/120)	2% (2/120)
Youzhou 幽州	2% (2/90)	4% (4/90)
Suzhou 蘇州	20% (14/71)	34% (24/71)
Qingzhou 青州	4% (2/55)	4% (2/55)
Mingzhou 洺州	3% (1/34)	6% (2/34)
Zhengzhou 鄭州	18% (6/33)	18% (6/33)

FIGURE 1.6. Incidence of elites residing in the same prefecture or province as choronym place of clan origin (by select prefectures)

Based on the same data as figure 1.4.

magistrate in the north, chose to retire and then die at his home in Huating County, Suzhou Prefecture. Whereas he himself was a member of the Wujun Gu family, his mother was a Wujun Lu, one son-in-law was a Wujun Zhang, and another son-in-law a Wuxing Yao. In other words, Gu Qian's close relatives included three of the four Wujun (i.e., Suzhou) great clans appearing on Johnson's lists as well as one of the two prominent families from Wuxing (i.e., Huzhou) on the opposite banks of Lake Tai. Another epitaph reveals that the Wujun Lu clan, perhaps as might be expected, also had an extensive cemetery nearby, on a mountain northwest of Huating.[64]

The survival in the Lower Yangzi region of large numbers of native elites affords the possibility of exploring in somewhat more detail the process by which one group of elites came to replace another. In this region, the impact of great clan scions from elsewhere is particularly noticeable when one pays attention to the distinction between "core" and "peripheral" areas. As proposed by William Skinner and later applied to the Tang-Song period by Robert Hartwell, each of China's seven or eight "macroregions" contained "core" areas—where ease of communication and transport spurred the development of administrative, commercial, and population centers—and "peripheral" areas that were less developed

---

64. Epitaph of Ms. He 何氏 (778–845).

Region	Core	Periphery
Suzhou native clans	2	19
Regional native clans	5	30
Émigré clans	19	6
Clans from elsewhere	203	90

FIGURE 1.7. Core versus periphery localization of native and nonnative clans in the Lower Yangzi region

Based on a subset of figure 1.4 data from epitaphs from the Lower Yangzi region (i.e., Yangzhou, Runzhou, Changzhou, or Suzhou Prefectures). "Suzhou native clans" refers to clans with the Wujun choronym; "regional native clans" refers to clans with choronyms in Yangzhou, Runzhou, Changzhou, Suzhou, Huzhou, or Hangzhou; "émigré clans" refers to the Langya Wangs 琅邪王, Ru'nan Zhous 汝南周, Yingchuan Xuns 潁川荀, Hedong Weis 河東衛, Gaoyang Xus 高陽許, Lujiang Hes 盧江何, Jiyang Jiangs 濟陽江, Chenjun Yuans 陳郡袁, Chenjun Xies 陳郡謝, and Chenjun Yins 陳郡殷; "clans from elsewhere" refers to clans from outside the region and includes the émigré clans. "Core" counties (i.e., in the vicinity of modern-day Nanjing as well as along the Grand Canal) include Jinling 晉陵 and Wuxi 無錫 Counties in Changzhou 常州; Dantu 丹徒 and Shangyuan 上元 Counties in Runzhou 潤州 (representing modern-day Zhenjiang and Nanjing, respectively); Changzhou 長洲, Wu 吳, and Jiaxing 嘉興 Counties in Suzhou 蘇州; and Jiangdu 江都, Jiangyang 江陽, and Yangzi 揚子 Counties in Yangzhou 揚州. "Periphery" counties include Jiangyin 江陰 and Yixing 義興 Counties in Changzhou; Jintan 金壇 and Jurong 句容 Counties in Runzhou; Changshu 常熟, Haiyan 海鹽, Huating 華亭, and Kunshan 崑山 Counties in Suzhou; and Hailing 海陵 in Yangzhou. List of émigré clans compiled from Hua Guorong, "Nanjing Liuchao de Wangshi, Xieshi, Gaoshi muzang," p. 285, and Mao Hanguang, *Liang Jin Nanbeichao shizu zhengzhi zhi yanjiu*, p. 17, but excluding clans that remained prominent in the north as well as clans that never once appear in ninth-century epitaphs from the south.

and less desirable as places of residence.⁶⁵ Figure 1.7 reclassifies the Lower Yangzi region data from figure 1.4 according to this distinction, defining the core as consisting of the counties immediately adjacent to the Grand Canal as well as those adjoining Jinling, the site of modern-day Nanjing.⁶⁶ As the figure reveals, native southern great clans (specifically families claiming the Lower Yangzi choronyms such as Wujun and Wuxing) are disproportionately (30/35 = 86%) encountered in epitaphs from peripheral counties. By contrast, émigré clans (19/25 = 76%) and clans from other parts of the empire (203/293 = 69%) are both dispro-

---

65. Skinner, "Regional Urbanization"; Hartwell, "Demographic, Political, and Social Transformations." Skinner explicitly distinguishes administrative from commercial centers; it is not necessary to draw such a distinction for the purposes of the present discussion.

66. For a previous classification of the counties of the Lower Yangzi on this basis, see Hartwell, "Demographic, Political, and Social Transformations," p. 391.

portionately found mentioned in epitaphs from core counties. This data suggests the possibility that, as newer clans arrived in the region, they settled in more desirable core regions, displacing native elites and forcing them into peripheral areas.

What might account for these observed patterns of migration, both involving the Lower Yangzi and other parts of the empire? Many epitaphs make note of their clan's movements without offering any explanation of motivation. Thus, Zhang Shiji* 張仕濟 (789–810), from the Zhang clan of Qinghe (in central Hebei), was buried in Yangzhou, about five hundred miles to the southeast. His epitaph notes simply that he lived in the Lower Yangzi region because his ancestors had relocated there sometime in the past. But not all epitaphs were as laconic. When inscriptions do provide more details, political turmoil is often cited as the cause. Typical is the case of Wang Rui* 王睿 (810–72), from the Taiyuan Wang clan, which once lorded over central Hedong Province. To account for Wang's residence in southern Hebei at the time of his death, his epitaph explains that "with the turmoil of the An Lushan Rebellion, [his clansmen] scattered to the north and the south" 以安史亂離分派南北. (Ms.) Hou Luoniang* 侯羅娘 (778–852), apparently from an old clan from Shanggu in northern Hebei, was buried in the vicinity of modern-day Nanjing, far to the south of Shanggu. According to her epitaph, her ancestors fled there when the Jin evacuated North China in 316, over a half millennium before her death. It is impossible to know whether the author of this inscription had textual evidence of family migration so far in the past or was relying on an oral tradition. But it is undeniable that people from all classes were sometimes compelled to flee from turmoil and warfare. There is substantial evidence, for example, that the An Lushan Rebellion of the mid-eighth century altered in significant ways the provincial structures of power in China's northeast.[67] Although some accounts of ancestral flight might have been fabricated, most were almost certainly accurate.

Even more common than stories of escape from turmoil, however, were claims that a family had relocated after an ancestor was appointed

---

67. In particular, especially in Hebei, the descendants of numerous former comrades-in-arms of An Lushan and his successor Shi Siming remained influential in provincial society well into the ninth century. See Tackett, "Great Clansmen," pp. 126–27.

elsewhere to serve in office. For example, the ancestors of Ms. Zhang* 張氏 (759–820), from the Qinghe Zhang clan, had moved from Hebei to Chang'an, where she was buried. According to her epitaph, "generation after generation served near the Hao River [i.e., in Chang'an], so her family relocated to 'within the passes'" 代累仕鎬, 家徙關中. Indeed, as we have seen, many families migrated to the capital region as part of the process of centralization of Tang civil bureaucratic clans. Thus, there is little reason to doubt Ms. Zhang's story. But the capital was not the only destination of migrating ancestors. All over the empire, officeholding was probably the most common stated reason for a family's relocation far from its choronym place. Ma Zhiling* 馬直令 (831–74), who was buried in Luzhou, provides a good example. Ma was a member of the Fufeng Ma clan, once based west of Chang'an. However, his ancestors had relocated to Luzhou several hundred miles to the east "because of office" 因官. So too the ancestors of Ms. An* 安氏 (800–851), also a resident of Luzhou, had arrived from Wuwei 武威, some six hundred miles to the west, after being enfeoffed in the region several centuries earlier. In this case, the fact that, by the ninth century, enfeoffments of this sort had not been granted by the central government for hundreds of years adds credibility to this account of ancient migration. According to the epitaph of Liu Ruyuan* 劉如元 (724–98), from the Pengcheng Liu clan, his distant forebears had first migrated to Hebei. Later, his fifth-generation ancestor served as a border general on the northern frontier, whereupon he relocated his family to a site near modern-day Horinger, in Inner Mongolia, well over five hundred miles north of Pengcheng Commandery. Hundreds of ninth-century epitaphs provide similar accounts of the peregrinations of an individual's family.

The example of Cui Fangjian* 崔方揀 (779–861) of the Boling Cui family is particularly revealing. Although he lived in Jingjing 井陘 County (in northwestern Hebei), only fifty or so miles to the southwest of the defunct Boling Commandery, it was, nevertheless, in a separate administrative region. The family's movements are clarified by the biography of an earlier Cui from Jingjing, undoubtedly a relative, named Cui Xinggong 崔行功 (d. 674).[68] We learn that his great-grandfather Borang

---

68. Cui Xinggong's biographies, preserved in the standard histories of the Tang, clarify the ancestry of this branch of the family. See *JTS* 190上:4996 and *XTS* 201:5734.

伯讓 moved away from Boling in the late sixth century as a result of a bureaucratic appointment farther south. It is significant that even such a relatively short move from the family's home base was thought to require an explanation and that this explanation involved officeholding. Thus, family relocation following government appointment to a particular location—a phenomenon described in more detail in chapter 2—seems to have been a widespread phenomenon and must have accounted for much of the geographic reshuffling of the old clans.

All of these explanations provided in the epitaphs—whereby powerful individuals or families from one region relocated elsewhere in multiple waves to serve in office or to flee political turmoil—account very well for the data presented in figures 1.4 to 1.6. After centuries of migration according to such patterns, the great clans eventually disappeared from their native places nearly everywhere, although their descendants did survive as members of the elite in other locations scattered all about the empire. Some native clans persisted in the Yangzi Delta region. One possible reason was that this area was at considerable distance from the geographic center of political power around the two capital cities in the north. It is also possible that it was a wealthier region—as would be the case in subsequent centuries—so that even families inhabiting less desirable land might have maintained the economic resources to afford burials with tomb epitaphs.

As a result of the survival of native families in the southeast, one can gain a sense of the migratory processes that gradually transformed society. More than likely, the great southeastern clans were diluted or displaced in the Nanjing–Grand Canal region beginning with the appearance of the émigré clans of the Eastern Jin, who probably settled in the vicinity of the new capital city of Jinling. Indeed, descendants of the most powerful of all émigré clans, the Langya Wangs, are believed to have been buried in the northern outskirts of Jinling continuously for a half millennium after their initial arrival in the fourth century.[69] With the appearance of a new wave of immigrants in the Tang, some settling

---

69. The epitaph and tomb of Ms. Hou Luoniang 侯羅娘 (778–852), wife of a Langya Wang, was found in a region north of Jinling where numerous Langya Wang tombs of the Six Dynasties Period have been found. See Li Xuelai, "Jiangsu Nanjing shi," p. 479. For more on the Wang clan tombs of the Southern Dynasties period, see Hua Guorong, "Nanjing Liuchao."

down after serving there in office and others fleeing the chaos brought about by the An Lushan Rebellion, the old entrenched clans were often able to survive only by relocating to the Lower Yangzi macroregional periphery, where, remarkably, they did manage to continue dominating local society nearly a millennium after first establishing their influence in the region.

At this point, we can return to the question, to what extent did the old aristocracy maintain a provincial power base that might have stood up to and resisted the authority of the state? Although most late Tang elites claimed descent from great clans first established centuries earlier, they did not constitute an intact pre-Tang provincial power structure. Although still influential at court and in China generally, the great families were rarely dominant political and social forces at their original home bases. One might argue that those members of the old aristocracy known to have relocated to the Tang capital cities of Luoyang or Chang'an could have maintained estates in their home locales, managed by agents who would forward revenue to the capital. Comparative examples far removed in both time and space illustrate just such a possibility. The Marquis de Lafayette, one of the most powerful men in eighteenth-century France, lived in Paris and rarely returned to his native Auvergne (perhaps 250 miles away); yet he did own land there as well as in several other provinces of France.[70] Perhaps even more striking, in much earlier times, Roman senatorial aristocrats possessed estates as far away as Egypt.[71]

But a similar arrangement was implausible in Tang China for several reasons. To begin with, in the context of Chinese social norms, the most likely means for managing far-flung estates would have been to rely on trusted kinsmen.[72] The virtual absence of any clansmen at the original

---

70. Gottschalk and Maddox, *Lafayette*, pp. 19, 20. In contrast, when the Roncherolles family, originally from Normandy, began to spend more time in Paris over the course of the eighteenth century, they ended up selling most of their provincial estates, investing instead in the resources and social connections available only in the capital. See Dewald, *Pont-St-Pierre*, pp. 166–67.

71. For a description of the empirewide estates of Rome-based aristocrats, see Wickham, *Framing the Early Middle Ages*, pp. 163–65.

72. In Rome, by contrast, managers were often privileged slaves whose loyalties lay more with their masters than with the less privileged slaves whom they managed. See Aubert, *Business Managers*, p. 161.

home base of the family, however, precludes this possibility. Equally significant were issues of logistics. Tang China did not possess a particularly well developed system of monetary transfer; rents would have had to be paid in kind.[73] Yet, the Chinese empire was far larger in size than France or any other Western European state. Moreover, unlike Rome, China had no Mediterranean Sea offering the possibility of relatively cheap water-borne transport.[74] The Grand Canal, first constructed in the Sui dynasty, was used to ship tax grain from the south to the Yellow River valley, but this riverine transport system by no means resolved all of the logistical difficulties of bringing grain to the capital.[75] In brief, it would have been enormously difficult for a capital-based family to maintain a distant provincial estate.

Cultural factors also played a role. Roman senatorial elites as well as later European noble families derived tremendous social prestige from the extensiveness of their landholdings. Moreover, because landowners were often perceived to be more politically reliable, landownership was oftentimes a precondition for political office. Finally, land was widely deemed the safest vehicle for storing family wealth.[76] Tang China differed from its Western counterparts on all of these counts. Amid the social milieu of top political and social elites, owning extensive tracts of land was anything but a source of prestige.[77] Possession of a large estate

---

73. There is no evidence that financial mechanisms existed permitting large-scale absentee or managerial landlordism until the late Ming or Qing; even then, it occurred only in some regions of China. See Elvin, *Pattern*, pp. 250–54; Esherick and Rankin, "Introduction," pp. 17–21.

74. Water-borne transport was much cheaper and more efficient than overland transport in preindustrial times. It has been estimated that a single horse attached to a barge can pull a boat weighing 250 times what the horse could carry on its back. Consequently, in preindustrial times, the transport of bulk commodities by sea was on the order of fifty times cheaper than transport by land. See Roth, *Logistics*, pp. 190 (n. 256), 197.

75. For an extensive account of the insufficiencies of the riverine transport system, see Twitchett, *Financial Administration*, pp. 84–96.

76. Aubert, *Business Managers*, p. 161; Kehoe, *Investment, Profit, and Tenancy*, pp. 71–75; Treggiari, "Sentiment and Property"; Nicolet, *Censeurs et publicains*, pp. 163–87.

77. The example of the epitaph of Mr. Xu (d. 867), described earlier in this chapter, which describes his property holdings in incredible detail, is a noteworthy exception. In general, epitaphs rarely say anything at all about an individual's land. Mr. Xu, from Hebei, likely belonged to a provincial elite culture that defined prestige and status in very different ways.

was often considered suspect, even constituting evidence of ill-gotten gains accrued during a tenure in office.⁷⁸ Furthermore, in order to maximize tax revenue, the state actively sought throughout the first half of the Tang dynasty to limit property size through the regular redistribution of land.⁷⁹ Even after the "equal-field" system was dismantled in the post–An Lushan period, land remained in principle the property of the emperor.⁸⁰ To be sure, a strong tradition of the inviolability of private property rights would develop by Song times; but one should not assume that such a tradition had emerged as early as the ninth century. Put simply, land was by no means the safest of investments. It was far better for safeguarding the long-term prosperity of one's family to expend extra resources raising numerous sons, hiring tutors to educate them, and maintaining libraries of classical texts. Successful families also spent money building political connections, perhaps by entertaining powerful ministers or even by directly donating excess wealth to the court. The occasional discovery by archaeologists of hordes of treasures suggests that burying portable wealth constituted one final means of storing wealth, especially in times of upheaval.⁸¹ In sum, though many of the medieval great families survived intact through the Tang dynasty, they did not control significant estates in distant provinces, estates that might otherwise have provided them with an alternative base of power. Chapter 2 will reveal that some capital-based elites did accumulate land in the provinces while serving there in office. But they likely did not maintain

---

78. In the first half of the eighth century, there were numerous laws designed to limit estate size, including a 737 statute requiring that "land held in perpetuity" (i.e., mulberry tree land) revert to the state after the death of the second generation. See Twitchett, *Financial Administration*, pp. 4, 16–18. In fact, all forms of wealth were deemed suspect when held by government bureaucrats. Provincial governors were the targets of particular scrutiny when they accrued large fortunes while in office. See Peterson, "Court and Province," pp. 521–22. A large number of epitaphs sought to praise their subjects' honesty by noting that their families were penniless upon their retirement from office; for one example, see the epitaph of Bi Jiong 畢坰 (751–811).

79. For a good overview of the equal-field system and its dismantling, including an extensive discussion of seminal Japanese scholarship, see Twitchett, *Land Tenure*, pp. 16–25.

80. Twitchett, *Financial Administration*, p. 22.

81. Qi Dongfang, "Burial Location," pp. 20–24; Rong Xinjiang, *Sui Tang Chang'an*, pp. 48–65. For allusions by Tang contemporaries to the discovery of hordes of treasures in the post–Huang Chao period, see chapter 5, p. 222–23.

these lands after the family had returned to the capital. The epitaph of Wang Xiuben* 王修本 (d. 837) provides a telling example. Wang died at a family estate in Yangzhou, although an earlier eighth-century epitaph for his fourth-generation ancestor confirms that the Wang clan cemetery lay far away, in the Beimang hills north of Luoyang.[82] Wang's final request to his wife was to sell their Yangzhou residence and bring his remains and those of seven clansmen back north. Although part of his motivation for divesting of the property was to secure the funds necessary to bring several bodies back to Luoyang for burial, he undoubtedly also realized there was little sense in maintaining a property in the south once his family had returned to the capital.[83] All things considered, the scions of the old aristocracy are probably well represented by the great mid-ninth-century minister Li Deyu 李德裕 (787–849) and his family. It is known that, despite hailing from a Hebei great clan, Li had never set foot in his place of origin, and neither he nor his father owned property outside of the Chang'an-Luoyang region.[84]

Bureaucratized Aristocrats

For the great aristocratic families, as we have seen, family prestige depended in large measure on generations of bureaucratic service,[85]

---

82. The fourth-generation ancestor was Wang Xuanqi 王玄起 (649–96). Although this ancestor is not mentioned in Wang Xiuben's epitaph, the link between the two men is nearly certain: the name of Xuanqi's third son is the same as the name of Xiuben's great-grandfather; the difference in years between the two men accords perfectly with typical age differences between generations; and both epitaphs are listed in a Republican era catalog (see Guo Peiyu and Guo Peizhi, eds., *Luoyang chutu shike*, pp. 228–29, 356), suggesting that they were excavated at a similar time, probably in the 1920s. Although Xiuben's epitaph only identifies his place of burial as Henan County, its place of excavation in 1925, according to the Guo brothers' catalog, was Boyue'ao Village 伯樂凹村, which is consistent with the place of excavation of epitaphs from Heyin Canton 河陰鄉, where Xuanqi was buried. See Yu Fuwei and Zhang Jian, eds., *Luoyang chutu muzhi*, pp. 361–63.
83. See epitaphs of both Wang Xiuben and his wife Ms. Wei 韋氏 (802–57).
84. Johnson, "Last Years," pp. 39–40, 60.
85. For an earlier discussion of a "bureaucratized aristocracy" 官僚貴族, see Tonami, "Sōdai shitaifu," pp. 197–201. Tonami used the term to refer to the aristocracy's cooption of the civil service exams and the central government rather than specifically to the transformation in the way prestige was defined. See also Watanabe, "Chū Tō ki ni okeru 'monbatsu.'"

reinforced through marriage with other families with similar traditions of officeholding—a situation, as seen in Lu Chu's* 盧初 (732–75) epitaph, in which "officeholding and marriages were both exquisite." It is little surprise then that families in their epitaphs placed great emphasis on the government service of their ancestors. All but the shortest tomb inscriptions began with what might be termed their "distant genealogy," an account of some of the more famous officeholders among the deceased's distant forebears. The "distant genealogy" was then followed by the "near genealogy," which identified the name and position of all of the deceased's immediate ancestors: usually the father, grandfather, and great-grandfather, and sometimes also the fourth-, fifth-, and even sixth-generation ancestors. The "distant genealogy" in the epitaph of Huangfu Pi* 皇甫鉟 (799–862) is particularly elaborate but not atypical in its themes and underlying structure:

> His ancestry begins with Chongshi, son of Duke Dai of Song [8th c. BCE], who had the courtesy name Huangfu and served as the Song minister of education. He begot Zhong; Zhong begot Fa. Fa named his clan after his grandfather's courtesy name. With the rise of the Han dynasty, [the character for] *fu* [in "Huangfu"] was changed, and this became their surname. At the beginning of the reign of [Han] Wudi [156–87 BCE], Luan, prefect of Yongzhou, first relocated from Luguo to Maoling [near Chang'an], so Luan is considered the first ancestor [of the clan]. Luan begot Pou, who earned [the title of] "most filial" and was made district magistrate of Pengcheng, whereupon he relocated to Anding [Commandery] in the north, establishing his home in Sanshui [County]. Pou begot Jun, who twice served as Commandant of Anding during the Eastern Han. Jun begot Leng, general of the Trans-Liao, who, at the beginning of the Yongping era [58–75 CE], relocated to Chaona County in Anding, where [the clan] became a famous surname of the commandery. Leng had eight sons, who became the Eight Ancestors and whose tombs were all at the opening of Stone Tiger Valley west of Anding City. . . . The Gentleman [i.e., the deceased] was the descendant of Qi, sixth son of the Trans-Liao [general]. Qi begot Jie, governor of Yanmen; Jie begot Song, who was defender-in-chief [of the entire empire] and received the posthumous name Yuan. Song's great-grandson was Mi, whose courtesy name was Shi'an and who was Mentor to the Heir Apparent during the [Western] Jin dynasty [265–316 CE]; later, he refused repeated requests to serve and gave himself the name Master of Dark Tranquility. The Gentleman was the seventeenth-generation descendant of Dark Tranquility. His sixth-generation ancestor was Decan, investigating censor during the Sui.

其先自宋戴公之子充石字皇父, 爲宋司徒. 生仲. 仲生發. 發以王父字
爲族. 漢興, 改父爲甫, 因氏焉. 至武帝初, 雍州牧鸞, 始自魯國徙茂陵,
故起鸞爲始祖. 鸞生衮, 舉至孝, 爲彭城相, 北徙安定, 家三水. 衮生儁,
東漢復爲安定都尉. 儁生稜, 渡遼將軍, 以永平初徙居安定朝那, 爲郡著
姓. 稜有八子, 爲八祖, 墳墓皆在安定郡城之西石虎谷口.... 公即渡遼第
六子旗之後也. 旗生節, 爲雁門太守. 節生嵩, 爲太尉, 謚元. 嵩曾孫謐,
字士安, 晉中庶子, 後累徵不起, 號玄晏先生. 公即玄晏十七世孫. 六代祖
德參, 隋監察御史.

This distant genealogy adheres to a conventional formula. It begins with an account of how and when the clan first acquired its surname.[86] Next, after skipping ahead six hundred years to the Western Han period, it identifies by name the "first ancestor" of the clan, who was probably the earliest ancestor to appear in the comprehensive genealogical tables preserved by individual families.[87] Although it was often the "first ancestor" who established the clan at its place of origin, in the case of the Huangfu family, it was instead the man's son who first moved to Anding Commandery, the choronym place of the clan. The distant genealogy then concludes by identifying the particular branch of the Anding Huangfus to which the deceased, himself, belonged. With the naming of the sixth-generation ancestor, the epitaph shifts to the near genealogy, subsequently identifying the names and offices of each of the next five ancestors, including those of the deceased's own father. Besides contain-

---

86. Some epitaphs begin with much earlier ancestors, even pushing as far back as the mythical Five Emperors of antiquity. But most Tang genealogists seem to have agreed that surnames were first acquired sometime during the Western Zhou dynasty.

87. Although no Tang great clan genealogy is extant, such "distant genealogies" provide some clues regarding the underlying structures that such genealogies would have had. They seem to have resembled in basic format the clan genealogies of the Ming and Qing period. Genealogical tables in the Late Imperial period were divided into two parts: (1) an account of the single line of forebears beginning in antiquity and culminating in the founding ancestor of the clan in question (often an individual who had lived in the Song dynasty, close to a millennium earlier in the case of early-twentieth-century clan genealogies); and (2) the descendants of multiple branches and subbranches of the family beginning with this founding ancestor. The "distant genealogy" of Huangfu Pi seems to suggest that the Huangfu family possessed in the ninth century a clan genealogy tracing the family's very distant ancestors along a single patriline through the Trans-Liao general—who had lived in the Western Han, nearly a millennium earlier—before providing more detailed accounts of the descendants of the various branches and subbranches descended from the general's eight sons.

ing all of the characteristic narrative elements of the archetypal distant genealogy, Huangfu Pi's epitaph is also typical in its repeated emphasis on the family's tradition of bureaucratic service. Nearly all named ancestors are said to have held government offices, many of them ranking among the most prestigious posts in the empire. Thus, the distant genealogy served above all to provide evidence of the accumulated talent and political achievements of the family.

There was an obvious problem with basing prestige on the accomplishments of distant forebears. By the ninth century, a large number of individuals could have professed descent from the sixth son of the Trans-Liao general, Huangfu Pi's twenty-second-generation ancestor; even more individuals could have claimed as a forefather Huangfu Pou, the man who had first established the clan at Anding. Although Anding Huangfu was a prestigious clan name, the value of the name would have been gradually watered down through the generations. One way to deal with this problem was to focus on a more recent tradition of officeholding as a source of prestige. The epitaph of Lu Xian* 盧峴 (720–74) is typical of a large number of inscriptions composed for descendants of the most prestigious families. As a scion of one of the marriage-ban clans, Lu had impeccable credentials as a member of the old aristocracy. But his epitaph does not dwell on his distant genealogy, stating merely that, "ever since the Wei dynasty, [the clan's] offices, marriage partners, and own members, all [ranked] among the pure and top grade of the realm; all of this is written in brief in the national histories; detailed accounts are available in the family genealogy" 自魏已降, 官婚人物, 爲天下清甲, 大略書於國史, 詳言在乎家牒. The epitaph does, however, name Lu's three most recent ancestors, all of whom served in respectable provincial-level posts. Whereas there were certainly countless Fanyang Lus scattered all over the empire, relatively few of these individuals could claim the prestige of continuous government service through several recent generations. More, therefore, than his status as a Fanyang Lu, it was the officeholding tradition documented in his near genealogy that constituted his claim to honor and prestige.

Invariably, there were enormous pressures on young aristocrats to obtain positions of government service. One generation's failure in this pursuit might permanently tarnish the prestige of that branch of the family, making it all the more difficult for successors to enter officialdom in the future. Epitaphs, such as that of Lu Guang* 盧廣 (c. 738–c. 775), occasionally articulate in explicit terms concerns about a family's potential decline. Lu had been recommended for office by numerous capital grandees, all but guaranteeing him a long and distinguished career. At first, as a student of the Daoist classics, he had considered rejecting officeholding since it involved "acquiring an empty name in order to adorn oneself" 得虛名以自飾. Yet, in the end, for the sake of his family, he disregarded his personal disinterest in worldly concerns, choosing to "adorn" himself with a provincial appointment in China's southeast. In part, as he explained it, he needed a salary to support his aging parents. More important, however, he felt obliged to maintain the prestige of his lineage. "I am by good fortune from an eminent clan from East of the Mountains," he asserted. "Only by holding official rank can I avoid diminishing my family's reputation" 某幸爲山東望族, 纔有班序, 則爲不墜家聲.

Although prestige stemmed primarily from the achievements of one's own patriline, epitaphs occasionally mentioned other eminent relatives among collateral branches of an individual's family. Members of the great officeholding clans seldom included named cousins, uncles, or great-uncles unless they had served in a particularly prominent office, especially that of chief minister. But some of the less eminent provincial families—who, as we shall see in the following chapter, typically had not held office over successive generations—took pains to identify even a single officeholder among their collateral lines. Because of the emphasis on good marriages, eminent relatives by marriage also appear in some inscriptions. Thus, fathers-in-law or maternal grandfathers might well be mentioned whenever they held a respectable government position. On the whole, however, epitaphs usually mention only the most famous among the more distant agnates and affines.[88] A particularly elaborate example of references to multiple relatives by marriage can be found in the inscription of a certain Ms. Li* 李氏 (813–63), from the eminent Longxi Li clan. Besides her own father, grandfather, and great-grandfather, her epitaph identifies several of her mother's immediate forebears,

---

88. In the case of affines, besides distant ties to chief ministers, distant ties to emperors and to provincial governors also seem to have been worthy of mention.

two of whom had been chief ministers. It also makes note of the father of one son-in-law and the grandfather of another, both of whom had also once served as chief minister. Far from merely asserting that she was the scion of one of the seven marriage-ban clans, the eulogy for Ms. Li took great care to situate her within a dense network of prominent kinsmen and relatives by birth and by marriage.

In addition to the genealogical sections of epitaphs, there are other clues that suggest that, by the ninth century, a legacy of officeholding surpassed the choronyms and the early clan history as the chief marker of status. There seems to have been a tendency in the ninth century for authors and calligraphers of epitaphs to signify their identity by reference to their officeholding positions and to exclude their choronyms altogether. The latter seem to have been mentioned primarily in cases where the individuals held no office. Thus, among signatures on epitaphs from Chang'an and Luoyang, 80 percent (1,063/1,321) identified themselves with an office alone, but only 8 percent (111/1,321) specified a choronym alone, and 5 percent (62/1,321) used both a choronym and an office.[89] As nearly all of these capital-based authors were great clansmen, it is significant that official titles were deemed more impressive than mere choronyms.[90] A similar pattern can be observed, moreover, among sons-in-law mentioned in epitaphs. They too were generally identified by choronym and surname only if they had not yet entered officialdom.[91]

---

89. Only 6 percent (85/1,321) mentioned neither choronym nor office. See "Fig 1_note89 author chor vs surname" in database. The infrequency with which authors and calligraphers were given neither a choronym nor an office may suggest that names appeared in some sense naked if unmodified by a praiseworthy attribute.

90. The use of choronyms in signature lines in extant collected works from the Tang may suggest that choronyms alone were sometimes used in more intimate documents, such as letters, whereas the full official titles were used in texts that were more formal in nature.

91. For example, in Ge Juyuan's 蓋巨源 (811–73) epitaph, two sons-in-law have official titles and no choronyms, whereas the third son-in-law has a choronym but no title. Similarly, in the epitaph of Ms. Zheng Xiushi 鄭秀實 (784–856), the only one of four sons-in-law whose surname is not preceded by a choronym is the son-in-law who held the title of prefect of Yizhou.

Conclusion

There can be no doubt that the aristocratic great clans, defined on the basis of choronyms and surnames, held enormous prestige in Tang society. Choronyms appeared in abundance as attributes to surnames. The "distant genealogies" of epitaphs often elaborated on the early background of a clan in considerable detail. The existence of multiple copies of Tang era lists of famous clans—even in the remote, far western town of Dunhuang—suggests that individuals felt a need throughout the empire for reference works that identified the realm's most eminent families. It is clear, however, that aristocratic status, as it was transmitted over time, could be shaped by a multiplicity of factors.

Despite a pervasive sense that a choronym was important to a clan's eminence, by the ninth century, such designations no longer carried the preeminent distinction of former times. The extraordinary demographic expansion of great clan descendants—facilitated by the inclusion of the offspring of multiple concubines—inevitably diluted the status of the choronyms alone. What had become increasingly important was, first, an officeholding tradition among one's most recent forebears; and, second, one's position within networks of kinship that included a number of men of great eminence. It is for this reason that many epitaphs for scions of the greatest families emphasized the deceased's "near genealogy" rather than the "distant genealogy."

This chapter has also sought to demonstrate the extent to which descendants of the great clans had dispersed from their ancestral homelands over the centuries. Although historians have long known that many aristocrats had relocated to the capital region by the mid-Tang, by studying the vast corpus of provincial epitaphs, one can determine whether or not kinsmen still ranked among the local elite at the places of clan origin. As it turns out, by the ninth century, outside of the immediate vicinity of the imperial capitals, the only significant concentration of native clans at their original territorial bases was in the macroregional periphery of the Lower Yangzi Basin. Simultaneously, the pattern of displacement of native elites to peripheral regions also provides clues for understanding the geography of power during the late Tang, a topic that will be explored in considerable depth in the next chapter.

Two important points should be emphasized. First, although it was ultimately officeholding that determined status, this fact does not mean that prestige was defined by the successes of the individual alone. Rather, typical of a mentality that can be described only as "aristocratic," lengthy genealogical discussions in the epitaphs indicate that it was *descent* from officeholders that was critical to the self-identity of the status group. Unlike the situation in Song times, when there existed the widespread notion that talent might exist irrespective of birth and when rags-to-riches stories were heralded, in the Tang, pedigree remained the most significant marker of prestige.[92] Of course, the notion that a clan could accumulate achievements over the generations provided a perfect ideological justification for nepotism. From the perspective of the present day, the *yin* privilege—whereby the close relatives of a high official could automatically obtain a bureaucratic position—has often been portrayed in contemporary scholarship as some sort of legally sanctioned corruption. In the Tang, however, when composing epitaphs eulogizing deceased relatives, a family readily admitted to having activated this privilege because the use of *yin* was in itself a marker of distinction, indicative of the presence of eminent bureaucrats among the close kinsmen. The emperors, themselves, fully embraced this ideology. They were known and praised for "seeking out [for office] the sons and grandsons of the former ministers of past emperors in order to reward their merits and achievements" 追先帝舊臣子孫以答功績.[93]

Second, though the most eminent ninth-century lineages were defined by their service to the state, the aristocrats in question were not the mere pawns of the Tang regime. In principle, their officeholding traditions long predated the founding of the dynasty. A landed aristocracy on the European model had the capacity to assert its independence from the state and the monarchy on the basis of its wealth in land. The bureaucratic aristocracy of the Tang was not a landed aristocracy, but the merit it accumulated after generations of service had the potential to facilitate greatly its survival across a political transition. As long as its core members survived the change of regime and the new political order accepted the ideology of the aristocracy, these families could distinguish themselves from social strivers by laying claim to an accumulated merit that no other families possessed.

---

92. For a discussion of the praise of poverty under the Song, see Bossler, *Powerful Relations*, pp. 17–18.

93. Epitaph of Zhang Xun 張曛 (747–813).

The following two chapters will largely set aside the issue of choronyms in order to assess alternate ways of defining the late Tang upper class. Chapter 2 will explore in considerable detail how geography defined the power structure by ascertaining the geographic distribution of elites and the relationship between geographic mobility and social mobility. Chapter 3 will then propose a new way of analyzing clans on the basis of reconstructed networks. By analyzing elites from the perspective of their social networks, it will become more apparent how the old aristocracy adapted so remarkably well to political change in the Tang, largely succeeding in monopolizing top positions in the bureaucracy until the very end of the dynasty. The analysis in the following two chapters will also help clarify why the old aristocracy disappeared so completely after the fall of the dynasty at the turn of the tenth century.

2

The Geography of Power

In the hills southeast of Tengzhou 滕州, Shandong Province, a Jin dynasty stele dating to the year 1193 purportedly marks the tomb of the famed early Tang general and statesman Li Ji 李勣 (594–669).[1] According to the inscription, commissioned by a man claiming to be his nineteenth-generation descendant, Li was first buried next to Emperor Taizong's 太宗 (597–649) mausoleum at Zhaoling, near the Tang capital city of Chang'an. Li's tomb and coffin were desecrated, however, when his grandson Jingye 敬業 rebelled in 684 after Empress Wu began to usurp imperial authority. When Wu fell in 705, Li's descendants transported his remains to the site of the 1193 stele.

Elements of this story are plausible. Other sources confirm that Li Ji was indeed buried near Zhaoling, that his tomb was defiled, and that the family was later rehabilitated in 705. But the 1193 stele also diverges from established accounts in important ways. According to the standard histories, Jingye was captured while attempting to flee by boat across the Bohai Sea to Korea, and he was then executed along with many of his relatives. The stele, by contrast, asserts that he escaped with his wife and sons, reestablishing roots near modern-day Tengzhou. Far more problematic is that the standard histories recount that Emperor Zhongzong

---

1. For the location of this tomb on a map and a description of the tomb and stele, see *Zhongguo wenwu ditu ji: Shandong fence* 1:179, 2:204. For a transcript of the stele, see Wang Zheng et al., eds., *(Daoguang) Tengxian zhi* 14.17a–18b. The earliest reference I have found to this stele is in a late-sixteenth-century gazetteer; see Yang Chengfu et al., eds., *(Wanli) Tengxian zhi* 5.17a.

restored Li Ji's tomb to all its former glory in 705, precluding any need to relocate his remains elsewhere.²

As it turns out, archaeology has largely confirmed the official version of the story. A second tomb purporting to be that of the great general was excavated near the Zhaoling site in 1971. This tomb was enormous in size, with a lengthy entry ramp leading down to a chamber buried beneath three mounds, each over a dozen meters in height. Fragments of red and black painted scenes of dancers and musicians suggest that it was once splendidly decorated. And, although the tomb had been robbed in later centuries, it nevertheless still contained over thirty burial objects, including Tang era painted ceramics, an intricate war helmet, a gold-plated bronze scabbard with a ceremonial wooden sword, and a large seventh-century epitaph recounting Li's life and career.³ It is simply implausible that early-eighth-century descendants would have removed their ancestor's remains from such a splendid mausoleum, especially without the accompanying grave goods. Moreover, a careful analysis of the text of the 1193 stele proves that it was based on an eleventh-century history of the Tang rather than on any genealogical information that might have been preserved independently by the family.⁴

But there is one more reason to doubt the account of the Jin era stele. In this chapter, I will explore the geographic localization of Tang elites as an alternative means of understanding the relationship between wealth, status, and power. Whereas wealthy families (i.e., families who commissioned epitaphs for their dead) and great clansmen could be found all

---

2. *JTS* 67:2490–92; *XTS* 93:3820, 3822–24.

3. For descriptions of the tomb, see *Zhongguo wenwu ditu ji: Shaanxi fence* 2:377; Li Haoyang, ed., *Zhaoling wenshi baodian*, 111; *Zhaoling Tangmu bihua*, 145. The three mounds confirm historical sources, which note that Li Ji's tomb was surmounted by mounds representing three mountains in the distant lands where Li had once defeated Turkish armies. See *ZZTJ* 201:6361.

4. Specifically, the stele quotes one of the commentaries concluding the *XTS* chapter containing Li Ji's biography. Compare the passages "公之孫敬業, 因民不忍, 起兵覆宗, 至掘公之冢而暴其骨" (from the stele, p. 17b) with "及其孫, 因民不忍, 舉兵覆宗, 至掘冢而暴其骨" (from *XTS* 93:3824). *XTS* chapter conclusions consist of original editorial commentaries, rather than text lifted from earlier historical material, so the stele text was almost certainly copied from *XTS*. Moreover, both the stele (p. 17b) and *XTS* 93:3820 (in the biography of Li Ji) erroneously state that Li died at the age of eighty-six. By contrast, the contemporaneous seventh-century epitaph from his tomb, undoubtedly more reliable, says he died at the age of seventy-six.

over the empire, the dominant political elite was heavily concentrated in the two capital cities of Chang'an and Luoyang as well as in the zone between the two cities. Thus, it would have been exceedingly unlikely for an eighth-century descendant of Li Ji to have sought to diminish the prestige of Li's name by relocating his remains to Shandong, quite some distance from the capital region.[5] The stele's claim, however, does make sense in the context of a later era. As Robert Hymes and others have shown, over the course of the Song and subsequent centuries, there was a fundamental reorientation of imperial power such that the predominant political elite came increasingly to inhabit the provinces rather than the capital.[6] By 1193, society had changed to the point that the fictive relocation of Li Ji's bones by eighth-century kinsmen was imagined to be plausible. Historians today, however, should not project onto the Tang a model of society inspired by our understanding of the Late Imperial period. In the Tang, there existed both a provincial elite, whose power and influence did not extend beyond the local arena, and a very different capital-based elite that all but monopolized the upper echelons of imperial power across the whole empire.

Localizing Elites

In order to explore the geographic distribution of political power in the late Tang, one must first deal with the vexing problem of determining an individual's home base. Tang officials frequently traveled all over the empire for the sake of their careers. Sun Dang* 孫讜 (809–68), a typical example, variously served in Chang'an, in Henan, in northern Hebei, as well as in Sichuan. Despite this remarkable geographic mobility, however, it would be incorrect to conclude that Sun had no home.

---

5. In the Tang, the right to burial next to an imperial tomb was a privilege granted to individuals, not families. Unfortunately, I have thus far encountered nearly no epitaphs for ancestors or descendants of Li Ji that can confirm the Li family was, in fact, based in the Chang'an-Luoyang region. There does exist an epitaph for a grandson buried near Luoyang in 688 (four years after the family was purged); this grandson, Wu Qindai 武欽戴 (665–79), had been granted Empress Wu's surname because of the loyalty to her of his branch of the family. There is also an epitaph dating to 717 for one of Li Ji's granddaughters, Ms. Li 李氏 (654–716), also buried near Luoyang.

6. Hymes, *Statesmen and Gentlemen*. For a good overview of Late Imperial local elites, see Esherick and Rankin, "Introduction," 1–24.

Because bureaucratic appointments typically involved tenures of no more than three years, men like Sun often spent long periods of time out of office. Even when in office, they did not always bring their families along with them.[7] They also needed to return somewhere at the end of their careers. The problem is that epitaphs and other traditional biographies rarely identify in explicit terms the location of an individual's home base. When they identify an individual's "place of origin," it is usually the pre-Tang commandery corresponding to the clan choronym.[8] But, as we have seen, choronyms referred not to the places where individuals, themselves, resided, but rather to the place where their forebears had lived, often centuries earlier.

How then does one identify a family's home base? In her study of the Song elite, Beverly Bossler hypothesized that the "primary geographic attachment" of Chinese elites was generally speaking not far from the family cemetery.[9] This hypothesis is, in fact, well suited to the use of epitaphs as a source, since epitaphs usually specify with considerable precision the place of burial of the deceased. Even in cases where the burial location is unstated in the text of the epitaph, it can be deduced if the excavation site of the epitaph is known. In chapter 1, I took more or less for granted that the provincial descendants of the great clans resided where they were buried. However, because equating place of residence with place of burial is fundamental to the analysis in this chapter, it is important to test the validity of Bossler's hypothesis for the Tang period.

There is ample evidence that, in the ninth century, family relationships were thought to continue even after death. Dead kinsmen were commonly believed to interact with one another in the family cemetery. Thus, in an epitaph for a four-year-old girl composed by her father in the year 818, the father expressed the hope that his daughter might find comfort in the presence of her deceased relatives: "The [surrounding] earth adjoins the tomb of your deceased uncle; the wind [above] adjoins

---

7. Although it seems that officials often brought their families along, they were less likely to do so if sent out to particularly remote sites. As noted by Han Yu, in his epitaph for Han Na 韓挐 (808–19), it was only when an official was sent to a distant post as punishment for a crime that he was required to bring his family along.

8. For a comparison of places of origin in epitaphs to those in Tang dynastic history biographies, see Takeda, "Tōdai shijin," pp. 466–93.

9. Bossler, *Powerful Relations*, pp. 42–43.

the pine trees of the western cemetery. May your young soul not fear the darkness below" 土接亡叔之墓, 風接西塋之松, 冀爾孩魂, 不怕幽壤. In a similar inscription, this time composed by a father for his four-year-old boy, the author imagines the delight of his own father upon discovering a grandson alongside him in the netherworld of the clan burial ground: "The day after tomorrow, I will bury you alongside the tomb of the former gentleman [i.e., my father]. As such, I will return your bones next to [his] great tomb. When he gets to know you, he will play with you like any grandson. Take my place at his side, and serve him below ground. How happy he will be!" 越翌日合祔上先府君之塋, 是用歸爾骨于大墓之側, 爾其有知, 當爲弄孫, 代吾左右, 承顏泉隧, 其樂如何![10] Even the most mundane elements of family life transcended death; deceased kinsmen provided each other with an escape from boredom, fear, and loneliness.

Relationships between living kinsmen and the dead were equally important. During the three-year mourning period, one was expected to remain near the tombs of one's parents in order to provide regular sacrifices. Thus, according to the epitaph of Ms. Zhai* 翟氏 (d. 819), who was buried in the hills north of Luoyang, her son Han Gongwu 韓公武 (d. 822) "adhered to his integrity and left government service, residing in the Eastern Capital in order to offer mourning sacrifices" 委節去位, 奉喪以居東都.[11] Bossler has also emphasized the importance of regular sacrifices performed even well after the mourning period was over. It was probably for this reason that Lu Congya* 盧從雅 (767–834), from a Luoyang-based clan, "could not bear to distance himself from the [clan] tombs, so he ardently sought an appointment at a branch office in Luoyang" 不忍遠違墳墓, 懇求分職洛下. Similarly, Zhao Junzhi* 趙君旨 (776–834), after leaving a provincial post as prefect of Lianzhou 連州, "had the fervent wish to return home to make offerings at the tombs" 浩然有歸故鄉奉墳墓之志. And there is the case of the grandson of a couple buried in Shandong decades earlier: "Recently, the younger grandson, Kai, who long missed them with an inexhaustible heart, each time thinking of them with thoughts of filiality, was pained by the fact

---

10. Epitaphs of Li Desun 李德孫 (815–18) and Zheng Xingzhe 鄭行者 (805–8).
11. For other examples, see the epitaphs of He Fu 何撫 (783–823), who lived in Luoyang for a full seven years after retiring to mourn his father, and of Cui Fu 崔俌 (754–805).

that the deceased grandfather's tomb had been adrift for so long" 今次孫揩, 長懷罔極之心, 每軫人子之思, 痛先祖墳域漂泊時久. After receiving an appointment near their place of burial, he took advantage of the opportunity to move their remains to the family burial ground in Mengzhou, north of Luoyang.[12]

Needless to say, then, people insisted on being laid to rest with their kin. In some cases, they would rush home when seriously ill to facilitate the logistics of burial. For example, when Mr. Peng* 彭公 (c. 780–c. 831)—a eunuch serving as army supervisor 監軍 in Jiangling on the Middle Yangzi—fell ill, he returned right away to Chang'an, where he died in his private residence in the city's Yongxing 永興 Ward. Hou Ji* 侯績 (770–835) was serving as a county magistrate in Shanzhou in the capital corridor until his health began to decline, whereupon he returned home to Luoyang to die. Epitaphs preserve accounts of many similar cases.[13] In situations when it was not possible to return home right away, individuals might make a special request to family members to escort their bodies back post mortem. In fact, in epitaphs for individuals who died far from home, it became almost a trope to incorporate a deathbed scene featuring the deceased making a final request of this sort. For example, both Yuan Xian* 苑咸 (710–58) and his wife had died in the south in the midst of the turmoil brought about by An Lushan's rebellion. The epitaph—composed a half century later at the time of reburial in Luoyang—quotes the wife's final words: "Return us to our home cemetery for burial" 歸祔鄉園.

But, as is clear from this last example, transporting remains back home was not always immediately possible. In some cases, the costs were prohibitive and money needed to be raised first; in other cases, it was necessary to await a ritually auspicious moment for moving bodies.[14] Consequently, families often resorted to "temporary burials" 權葬 near the place of death. Because elites often died while serving or accompany-

---

12. Epitaph of Yan Yuanzhen 顏元貞 (d. c. 745). For a similar example, see epitaph of Feng Sui 封隨 (778–835).
13. For examples of individuals returning home to Chang'an or Luoyang after falling ill, see epitaphs of Ms. Zheng 鄭氏 (d. 871), Cui Qi 崔芑 (788–851), Wang Xun 王訓 (727–67), and Wang Shi 王適 (771–814).
14. Moving bodies was dangerous as well as expensive, as there was the risk that the soul might separate from the body.

ing somebody serving in an office far from home, the bodies of numerous kinsmen might accumulate in temporary graves at several sites of government service around the empire. Several kinsmen might then be brought home for burial all at once, perhaps after a descendant attained a high-salaried post in the bureaucracy. A certain Yang Tong 楊彤, for example, who served in an important position in the Jiangxi provincial government, organized the reburial of three of his brothers in 826 and then of his father in 828. The four men had been buried temporarily at several locations around the empire, including Chang'an and Hangzhou; all were laid to rest in Luoyang near the tombs of Yang's grandfather and the grandfather's two brothers.[15]

Given the aforementioned beliefs about the afterlife and the responsibilities of the living to their dead ancestors, the ideal situation was for a family to live in one place, not far from their burial ground. However, for a variety of reasons, individuals did sometimes migrate away from home permanently. In these cases, the family may have continued to send its first-generation of dead back to the old clan cemetery if possible. Eventually, however, once it was clear that the family would not return to its former place of residence, the difficult decision was made to establish a burial ground at the new home. In such cases, there seems to have been a preference initially to bury or rebury several family members together, presumably so that no deceased kinsman would be in the ground all alone.[16] Alternatively, a relative buried nearby—even a relative by marriage—might provide companionship for the recent dead. An interesting example involves Chen Xuanlu* 陳宣魯 (808–40), whose grandparents were buried in Yangzhou in Huainan, where his two brothers lived as well. In a relatively rare example of a late Tang relocation to the capital, Chen's father purchased land near Luoyang, where Chen was buried. Although Chen was all alone in the new cemetery, the author of the inscription noted: "The tomb . . . of his maternal grandfather is situated in the north field of Goushi County. . . . Today, the Gentleman's solitary tomb lies here [in Luoyang]. As it is within eyesight of the tombs of his mother's clansmen, one cannot say he will

---

15. See the epitaph Yang composed for a loyal family servant, Wang Wan 王綰 (d. 797).

16. For a good example, see the account below of the Zhi family's relocation to Luoyang.

Region of burial	Died in same prefecture	Died in same province
Chang'an	75.8 (391/516)	75.8 (391/516)
Luoyang	47.1 (410/870)	47.1 (410/870)
Chang'an–Luoyang Corridor	52.6 (51/97)	53.6 (52/97)
Autonomous Hebei	81.8 (72/88)	96.6 (85/88)
Elsewhere	85.5 (247/289)	89.6 (259/289)

FIGURE 2.1. Percentage of individuals who died in prefecture/province of burial (by region) (800–880 CE)

Includes all epitaphs dating to 800–880 CE for which prefectures of death and burial are both known. Provincial boundaries are generally defined as they stood during the Yuanhe era (806–820). Prefectures of death and burial are usually identified explicitly in the epitaphs, though, in the case of provincial epitaphs stating only that the deceased died "at home," the prefecture of death is assumed from context (generally where the deceased is said to be from, when this place is not the choronym place of clan origin).

not remain in contact [with the mother's clansmen's spirits]" 外祖... 松檟在綾氏縣北原.... 今君之獨墓於此, 與外族塋域遠若相望, 不爲無素矣. Although it was a big deal to establish a new cemetery far from one's old home, doing so was the only practical option to ensure the proper sacrifices.

Besides ascertaining religious motivations, one can also turn to empirical evidence to assess Bossler's hypothesis. Epitaphs rarely identify the deceased's place of residence per se, but they do note the location of death, which in most cases would have been at the individual's home. Figure 2.1 compares places of burial and death, excluding cases of "temporary" burials. According to the figure, in most regions of China outside of the capital region, people tended to die in the same prefecture and province as their place of interment. Very often, the burial sites in question were identified explicitly as the clan cemetery (usually 先塋). Thus, one can surmise that most people living in the provinces indeed resided near the sites of their ancestral tombs.

Burials in the capital region—including Chang'an, the capital corridor, and especially Luoyang—were unusual in that a relatively significant percentage of the individuals in question died away from their places of burial. As it turns out, however, most deaths away from the capital occurred while traveling or while serving in office in the provinces. Figure 2.2 refines the data from figure 2.1, classifying the precise site of death—when specified in the epitaph—as either a private residence,

	Region of death			
Site of death	Same province	Chang'an	Luoyang	Elsewhere
private residence	33 (87%)	2 (100%)		6 (21%)
office/government apartment	3 (8%)			21 (72%)
inn/while traveling	2 (5%)			2 (7%)
Total	38 (100%)	2 (100%)	0	29 (100%)

	Region of death			
Site of death	Chang'an	Luoyang	Corridor	Elsewhere
private residence	215 (88%)	3 (50%)	7 (23%)	9 (13%)
office/government apartment	9 (4%)	1 (17%)	17 (57%)	48 (72%)
inn/while traveling	2 (1%)	1 (17%)	5 (17%)	5 (7%)
other	17 (7%)	1 (17%)	1 (3%)	5 (7%)
Total	243 (100%)	6 (100%)	30 (100%)	67 (100%)

	Region of death			
Site of death	Luoyang	Chang'an	Corridor	Elsewhere
private residence	212 (83%)	35 (58%)	33 (50%)	52 (21%)
office/government apartment	15 (6%)	11 (18%)	25 (38%)	159 (63%)
inn/while traveling	4 (2%)	9 (15%)	4 (6%)	27 (11%)
other	23 (9%)	5 (8%)	4 (6%)	15 (6%)
Total	254 (100%)	60 (100%)	66 (100%)	253 (100%)

FIGURE 2.2. Site of death of individuals buried in the capital region (800–880 CE). (a) Burials in capital corridor. (b) Burials in Chang'an. (c) Burials in Luoyang.

Private residences are identified by a number of terms, most frequently 私第, 私舍, 別業, and 別墅. Official residences are identified by terms such as 官舍, 公館, 廨宅, and 郡舍; included also are individuals who died at their "place of office" (e.g., "位"), with no further details on the site of death, or at the place of office of their husband, father, or other close relative. "Other" places include temples, palaces (in Chang'an), rented properties, and other temporary lodgings. Temporary burials are excluded, as are cases where the place of death is unspecified—including cases of individuals dying in residences (第, 宅, 舍) that are not identified as public or private.

a government apartment (or the site of a bureaucratic appointment), or an inn (or other temporary accommodation used while traveling). As shown in the figure, in the capital region, between 83 and 88 percent of individuals dying in the vicinity of their place of burial died in a private residence, a residence that had sometimes been in a family's possession for decades.[17] By contrast, between 75 and 85 percent of capital elites dying outside of the capital region died in temporary lodgings, such as government apartments, travel inns, or temples. The strong tendency for families buried in the capital to possess houses in the capital region but not elsewhere implies that the capital region was where they resided and, consequently, where they felt it worth their time and money to obtain permanent lodgings.

There is additional incidental evidence to corroborate this point. Although epitaphs typically say very little about the deceased's land

---

17. The fact that houses remained in the possession of a family for decades is extrapolated from the observation that, as attested by their epitaphs, it was common for several family members or two spouses to die several years or decades apart in private residences in the same ward of either Chang'an or Luoyang. For instance, Chen Shidong 陳士棟 (786–839) and his wife died twenty-three years apart, both in a "residence" 第 in Chang'an's Xiude 修德 Ward. There are also a number of cases of family members dying over an even longer span of time in the same ward of one of the capitals. Wei Zhongfu 魏仲俛 (782–825), his brother Wei Zhonglian 魏仲連 (780–848), and Zhonglian's grandson Wei Chou 魏儔 (819–65) all died over a forty-year period in a private residence in Luoyang's Qinghua 清化 Ward. Liu Honggui 劉弘規 (775–826) and his grandson Liu Zunli 劉遵禮 (816–68) died forty-two years apart in a private residence in Chang'an's Laiting 來庭 Ward. Cui Zhen 崔鎮 (819–75) and his first cousin Cui Shu 崔鉥 (801–20) died fifty-five years apart in a private residence in Chang'an's Tongyi 通義 Ward. Lu Zhi 盧直 (771–823), his son Lu Zonghe 盧宗和 (789–832), his cousin Lu Fang 盧方 (768–830), and Fang's granddaughter Lu Leniang 盧樂娘 (858–78) died over a fifty-five-year period in a residence in Luoyang's Kangsu 康俗 Ward. Yang Ning 楊寧 (744–817), his grandson Yang Sili 楊思立 (d. 875), and his great-grandson Yang Hao 楊晧 (840–58) all died over a fifty-eight-year period in a private residence in Chang'an's Jinggong 靖恭 Ward. Zhao Teng 趙藤 (756–810) and his son Zhao Tu 趙途 (811–70) died sixty years apart in a country villa in Hu County. Sun Jiazhi 孫嘉之 (657–739) and his grandson Sun Ying 孫嬰 (745–801) died sixty-two years apart in a private residence in Luoyang's Jixian 集賢 Ward. Cui Yong 崔泳 (746–88) and his grandnephew Cui Xinggui 崔行規 (817–67) died seventy-nine years apart in a "multigenerational residence" 世第 in Luoyang's Yude 毓德 Ward. Finally, the epitaph of Yao You 姚侑 (747–802) notes explicitly that he retired (and later died) in a mansion in Luoyang's Cihui 慈惠 Ward that had been first established by his great-grandfather a century earlier.

and property except when identifying the deceased's site of death, a few epitaphs do reveal a bit more about where families owned houses. For example, the epitaph of Wei Xiang* 韋祥 (d. 812), who died in Chenzhou 陳州—probably where he was serving in office—notes that Wei's wife had died fourteen years earlier in a "private residence" in Luoyang, where both were buried.[18] There are also examples of individuals brought back to the capital to lay in wake in a "private residence" before burial.[19] In the case of Liu Tanjing* 劉談經 (748–804), who died in a government residence in Ningzhou 寧州, his epitaph notes incidentally that "his home was in Luoyang" 家在東洛. And there is the example of Lu Zixian* 盧子獻 (842–69), who died during an uprising in Ezhou 鄂州, where his father was serving in office; his epitaph reveals that he was born in a "private residence" in Luoyang. Finally, a few epitaphs note explicitly that capital elites dying in the provinces were on their way home to the capital region. A certain Ms. Fan* 范氏 (821–75) was "about to return to Luo[yang]" when she died unexpectedly while visiting her daughter in Yangzhou, where her son-in-law was undoubtedly serving in office. If she was "returning" to Luoyang, one can presume that Luoyang was her home. Wei Dushi* 韋都師 (d. 856) offers a similar example. Although she died on a boat in the south, she was at that time accompanying her uncle back to Luoyang after the completion of his term as prefect of Luzhou.[20]

In sum, because of the importance of the enduring relations between clansmen, both living and dead, individuals were usually buried near their homes, at the place where their family lived most of the time. Capital elites proved to be an exception, largely because they seem to have been far more mobile than provincial elites. However, although they traveled to other parts of the empire and they were assigned to

---

18. For similar examples, see epitaph of Lu Jifang 盧季方 (782–848) in conjunction with that of his wife Ms. Zheng 鄭氏 (808–64), as well as epitaphs of Cui Liang 崔亮 (772–828), Li Huai 李懷 (730–801), Liu Yan 劉沇 (727–99), and Ms. Lu 盧氏 (795–860).

19. Epitaphs of Wang Zhiyong 王志用 (787–837), Ms. Zheng 鄭氏 (784–833), Cui E 崔鍔 (804–22), Liang Chengzheng 梁承政 (807–70), and Mr. Wang 王公 (780–829).

20. For other examples of elites buried in Luoyang who also returned there while between posts, see epitaphs of Sun Ju 孫筥 (788–860) and Ms. Zhang Liuke 張留客 (842–71).

offices sometimes far away, they came back to the capital region at other times in their lives to tend to an ill relative,[21] when biding their time between official appointments,[22] or after retirement.[23]

Methodologically, this means that, owing to the patrilineal structure of Chinese families, a clan's home base can be identified on the basis of the places of burial of male kinsmen, their wives, or unmarried kinswomen. The most common exceptions to this rule involved "temporary" 權 burials—usually explicitly identified as such in the inscriptions—where it was understood that the deceased was to be reburied elsewhere at a later date. A less common exception involved permanent migration elsewhere, a phenomenon discussed in more detail below. In most cases, "temporary" burials involved individuals who died far from home while traveling or serving in office, and who could not be brought home for burial right away.[24] Because these burials cannot be used to identify an

---

21. According to epitaphs of Ms. Cui 崔氏 (812–57) and her husband Lu Jian 盧 緘 (804–61), Lu abandoned his post to return to Luoyang to tend to his elder brother, who had fallen ill.

22. Among men buried in Luoyang, one encounters Li Ping 李評 (787–831), who, according to his epitaph, had died while in office in the far north but had earlier in his life "for a full twenty years led a carefree existence between Luoyang and [nearby] Zhengzhou" 凡廿年優游鄭洛之間; Lu Pan 盧槃 (d. 879), who, according to his epitaph, lived in semiretirement in a country villa at Longmen, just south of Luoyang, before his appointment to office in Shenzhou 申州, where he died; and Li Zhao 李釗 (826–79), who, according to his epitaph, died while in office in the west but had previously "returned to Luo[yang] after dismissal from [another] office" 罷職歸洛.

23. For example, according to his epitaph, Li Qun 李群 (778–826) "returned to a leisured life in Luoyang" 歸閑於洛陽 after retirement; he died there later that year and was then buried there in the "ancestral cemetery." For additional examples of individuals "returning" to Luoyang after retiring, see epitaphs of Chen Shishang 陳師上 (779–839), Sun Jingyu 孫景裕 (d. 870), Tao Ying 陶英 (737–801), Sun Dang 孫讜 (809–68), Shangguan Zheng 上官政 (765–829), and Yao You 姚侑 (747–802). For examples of Chang'an-based elites returning to Chang'an, see epitaphs of Wei Wendu 韋文度 (789–844), Wang Jin 王瑾 (826–47), and Wei Fang 韋方 (800–30).

24. In other cases—as discussed below—"temporary" burials are indicators of migration elsewhere; the first generations at the new site may have planned to return to the ancestral home, but subsequent generations would take root at the new location. Finally, in some cases, "temporary" burials involved burials that were very near the ancestral cemetery but that, for reasons of cost or of ritual protocol, did not incorporate all of the essentials of a proper final burial. For examples of this last phenomenon, see epitaphs of Cui Zhi 崔植 (791–856), Zhang Guan 張觀 (803–63), Ms. Cui 崔氏 (784–858), Yu Ruxi 于汝錫 (791–847), and Ms. Li 李氏 (771–822).

individual's home base, they have been excluded from many of the statistical calculations in this chapter.

Capital Elites

An analysis of data from late Tang epitaphs makes clear that there was a sharp distinction between elites based in the capital regions and those based elsewhere. In the context of this chapter, "capital elites" designates the elite residents of either the Western Capital of Chang'an or the Eastern Capital of Luoyang. Given a number of shared characteristics described below, this group also includes many of the officeholding families based in the zone in between these two cities, a region I have been referring to as the "capital corridor." Communication routes in this zone seem to have been quite good. Travel between the two capitals took ten days or less.[25] By contrast, it might have taken four months or more to travel back to the capital from Hunan or Jiangxi, south of the Yangzi.[26] Thus, the families inhabiting the capital region shared in the advantage of relatively easy access to the imperial court.

One somewhat impressionistic way to compare capital and provincial elites is to evaluate the size and quality of their respective epitaphs, a

---

25. One way of assessing travel times using epitaphs is to look at how long it took to transport bodies back to the capital from elsewhere in the empire, data that epitaphs occasionally provide. According to the epitaph of (Ms.) Wang Taizhen 王太眞 (840–62), who died in Hezhong midway between the two capitals, her body arrived in Chang'an ten days after her death. According to the epitaph of Wei Bing 韋冰 (774–827), his spouse's remains, initially buried in Hezhong, arrived in Chang'an eighteen days after her temporary tomb was opened. And in the case of (Ms.) Zheng Zizhang 鄭子章 (831–53), it took eleven days to move her body from Chang'an to Luoyang. In all three cases, some time would have been expended performing necessary rituals. In addition, one would imagine that individuals not accompanied by their relatives' corpses could have traveled at slightly faster speeds. The Japanese monk Ennin, however, who seems to have been in no hurry to leave China, spent fifteen days traveling between the two capitals while on his way home to Japan. See Reischauer, *Ennin's Diary*, pp. 368–69.

26. According to the epitaph of Ms. Yu 于氏 (840–71), it took her husband just under four months to bring her remains back to Luoyang from her place of death in Hongzhou 洪州 (modern-day Nanchang, in central Jiangxi). It took slightly longer—six months—for the husband of Ms. Zheng 鄭氏 (784–833) to bring her remains back to Luoyang from Hunan in the south. Finally, it took over a year to move the body of Li Pu 李璞 (811–55) from Liuzhou 柳州 (in the deep south) back to Luoyang, a period of time that included a stop at a villa the family owned along the Han River.

Region	n	Size index
Chang'an	314	649
Luoyang	470	645
Autonomous Hebei	101	583
Chengde	15	637
Youzhou	46	599
Weibo	40	545
Capital Corridor	70	573
Lower Yangzi	91	311
Elsewhere	225	425

FIGURE 2.3. Length of epitaph texts in different regions of China

Size index, illustrated by black bars, was determined by squaring the total number of columns of text. In general, this index is directly proportional to the total character count.

conceivable indicator of relative wealth.[27] Figure 2.3 compares epitaphs from different regions of China on the basis of the square of the average number of columns of text, an index roughly proportional to the total number of characters in the text.[28] If, as suggested in the introduction, epitaphs were priced according to total character count, then this index provides a basis for assessing the cost of producing the inscription. According to figure 2.3, epitaphs from the capital region and from the autonomous provinces in Hebei tended to be larger than epitaphs from other parts of the empire. In addition, although not without exceptions, the quality of the calligraphy carved onto the stones tended to be substantially better in the case of inscriptions from the capital cities.[29]

---

27. Epitaph size is certainly not a definitive indicator of wealth. Some archaeologists have argued that overall energy expenditure is a more reliable determinant of vertical social status than the presence, absence, or elaborateness of any single grave good or tomb feature. See Carr, "Mortuary Practices," esp. pp. 178–81. Other archaeologists warn against drawing a link even between total energy expenditure and vertical social status. For example, in Victorian England, the less affluent often built gaudier funeral monuments, whereas wealthier families built increasingly restrained monuments as a sign of their distinction. See Cannon, "Historical Dimension."

28. The number of columns was tabulated rather than total character count for reasons of convenience.

29. This distinction is readily apparent when visually inspecting a large number of epitaph rubbings. For example, one can compare epitaphs from Chang'an to those from Luzhou 潞州 in the collection *Xi'an beilin bowuguan xincang muzhi huibian*.

Perhaps a more striking distinction between capital and provincial elites involved their relative statuses in the political hierarchy. Examining transgenerational officeholding patterns reveals that capital elites and provincial elites were fundamentally different in two important ways. First, capital elites were much more likely to hold office generation after generation. Figure 2.4 categorizes excavated epitaphs according to family traditions of officeholding. Three-quarters of capital elites and over half of elites in the capital corridor demonstrated "strong" traditions—meaning that at least three of the five most recent generations had held office. Only 4 percent of epitaphs from Chang'an and from Luoyang were composed for members of families without any known officeholders. The opposite is true of elite families living in large swathes of provincial China, especially in southern Hebei and Hedong (Weibo and Zhaoyi Provinces), the Lower Yangzi, and Northern Zhejiang, large numbers of whom had no links to officialdom. Even when men in these outlying regions did hold office, they were not infrequently the only known members of their families to do so. The most striking exception to this pattern concerns the autonomous Hebei province of Youzhou, which was unusual in that it functioned in many ways like a miniature version of the highly centralized Tang state.[30]

The family of Wang Zhaocheng* 王照乘 (795–856) provides a good example of patterns of government service among capital elites. Her epitaph identifies eight generations of officeholding ancestors, going back three hundred years to a minister who had served the Northern Qi (550–577) dynasty. Although most Tang era epitaphs only name the father, grandfather, and great-grandfather, combining data from epitaphs with other genealogical sources (see chapter 3) suggests that Wang's case was in no way unusual. A large portion of the late Tang capital elite could trace a continuous line of officeholding ancestors back to well before the founding of the dynasty.

Second, among officeholders, those from the capital were far more likely to hold offices of national prominence, whereas provincial elites who did serve in office generally served near their homes (fig. 2.5). In other words, capital-based elites held central government positions at the capital, helping to make decisions that affected the entire empire.

---

30. See chapter 4 for more on the autonomous provinces of Hebei.

Region of burial	Strong tradition	Weak tradition	No officeholding
Luoyang	82% (772/936)	14% (130/936)	4% (34/936)
Chang'an	72% (395/546)	24% (130/546)	4% (21/546)
Corridor	57% (60/105)	22% (23/105)	21% (22/105)
Autonomous Hebei	46% (61/133)	26% (34/133)	29% (38/133)
Youzhou	72% (43/60)	27% (16/60)	2% (1/60)
Chengde	40% (10/25)	28% (7/25)	32% (8/25)
Weibo	17% (8/48)	23% (11/48)	60% (29/48)
Lower Yangzi	13% (19/142)	23% (32/142)	64% (91/142)
Zhaoyi	11% (14/129)	46% (59/129)	43% (56/129)
N. Zhejiang	10% (2/21)	24% (5/21)	67% (14/21)
Elsewhere	45% (88/195)	35% (69/195)	19% (38/195)

FIGURE 2.4. Family traditions of officeholding among elites (by region) (800–880 CE)

Considers all epitaphs except very short or illegible ones, as well as those for concubines and slaves and—in order to maintain a roughly random sample—those preserved only in transmitted texts (especially in writers' collected works). A "strong tradition" of officeholding means that three or more of the most recent generations (including great-grandfather, grandfather, father, self or husband, and son) held office; a "weak tradition" means that at least one officeholding relative is mentioned; "no officeholding" means that there are no known officeholders among close relatives (excluding great-grandfather and earlier ancestors).

Alternatively, they received temporary appointments—usually with tenures of two to three years—to provincial offices at sites scattered all across the empire, from modern-day Inner Mongolia in the north to modern-day Hanoi in the south. In some cases, they were appointed through the regular bureaucracy to county- or prefectural-level positions; in other cases, they were recruited by provincial governors into a parallel system of provincial bureaucracies (a system described in more detail in chapter 4). A limited number of elites from the capitals—6 percent from Chang'an and 15 percent from Luoyang—did serve in the much coveted county- or prefectural-level positions at the capital. However, in most cases, their provincial appointments involved assignments far from home. In almost all such cases, capital elites were agents of the central government, not representatives of the local elite.

A good example involves the family of Sun Gongyi* 孫公乂 (772–851). His grandfather had served in a civilian capacity in one of the imperial armies. His father had served as prefect in far-flung parts of

Region	Exclusively national		Exclusively local		Mixed		"National elite"	
Luoyang	85%	(720/850)	3%	(24/850)	15%	(130/850)	77%	(657/850)
Chang'an	94%	(453/481)	1%	(3/481)	6%	(28/481)	74%	(354/481)
Corridor	64%	(46/72)	14%	(10/72)	36%	(26/72)	53%	(38/72)
Lower Yangzi	50%	(18/36)	22%	(8/36)	50%	(18/36)	14%	(5/36)
Autonomous Hebei	11%	(10/88)	72%	(63/88)	89%	(78/88)	5%	(4/88)
Elsewhere	12%	(25/204)	55%	(113/204)	88%	(179/204)	3%	(7/204)

FIGURE 2.5. National versus local prominence of officeholding elite (by region) (800–880 CE)

Considers all epitaphs included in figure 2.4, but excludes individuals for whom it is unclear where the majority of officeholding family members served in office (generally because only nonsubstantive honorific offices are noted in the epitaph). "Exclusively national" means officeholders in the deceased's family served exclusively in central government offices or in provincial positions outside of their provinces of burial. In a few cases, local offices were ignored if they were clearly part of a pattern of nationwide officeholding. "Exclusively local" means officeholders in the deceased's family began at one point in time serving exclusively in local offices. "Mixed" means officeholders served in offices of local prominence or of both national and local prominence. "National elite" refers to families both with "strong" traditions of officeholding (see fig. 2.4) and who served in offices of "exclusively national" prominence.

Hunan, Zhejiang, Anhui, and Jiangsu. Although Sun, himself, served a term as metropolitan governor of Henan—a prefectural-level position in Luoyang, where his family was based—this prestigious office was part of a broad rotation that sent him to a wide variety of different posts. He held multiple central government positions, including censorate recorder, vice director of the Treasury Bureau, and director of the Bureau of Sacrifices; he also held offices in the provinces, including sheriff of Tianchang County, assistant magistrate of Jiangyang County, administrative supervisor of Wuzhou, and, late in his career, prefect of a string of southern prefectures. Sun was an officeholder of national prominence.

By contrast, provincial elites, when they did serve in office, usually served locally. In most regions outside of the capital—the Lower Yangzi being the notable exception—nearly nine in ten officeholding families served at least to some extent locally. These families probably fell into two groups. One group consisted of migrants from elsewhere who had taken advantage of a provincial appointment to relocate to that site. These individuals had nationally prominent ancestors and arrived, themselves, either with central government appointments to county- or prefectural-level positions, or with relatively high-level appointments in the separate provincial bureaucracy. More will be said below about this elite migratory pathway.

A second group consisted of men from native families—based at the localities perhaps for generations—who had managed to secure a position in the provincial militaries or in the lower echelons of the provincial bureaucracies.[31] Zhu Shan* 朱贍 (809–65) fell into this group. Based in Chenzhou, he was the first known member of his family to hold office. He began his career as a common soldier, indicating that his family was neither wealthy nor well connected. Yet he rose up in the ranks of the Zhongwu 忠武 Army (based in Chenzhou), and his three sons would serve there as well. In the case of Yuan Shengjin* 元昇進 (770–845), who was buried in the western prefecture of Longzhou, he had attained a mid-level officer rank in the local military, as had his father. Information on his grandfather and earlier generations was "lost," presumably because these men had not served in office. Such families—particularly common in the Hebei autonomous provinces as well as other regions with important provincial militaries, such as Luzhou 潞州 in southeastern Hedong and Qingzhou 青州 in Shandong—would have served exclusively in their home regions and, as will be discussed in more detail in chapter 4, would only rarely have managed to infiltrate the national bureaucracy.

In sum, the difference between capital and provincial elites was remarkable. Capital elites tended to serve generation after generation in offices of national prominence; their counterparts in the provinces tended to serve occasionally and only in local offices. In fact, combining the two trends produces striking results. No less than 98.5 percent (1,018/1,033) of extant epitaphs for "national elites"—those individuals both serving in offices of national prominence and also having "strong" family office-holding traditions—come from tombs in Luoyang, Chang'an, or the zone in between.

It is worth considering how this situation differed from that of the Late Imperial period. Although information on Tang provincial elites is limited, it seems that they probably resembled in many ways the "localist" elite of the Southern Song and later, a group described in considerable

---

31. See chapter 4 for more on how to distinguish upper-echelon from lower-echelon positions in the provincial bureaucracies.

detail by Robert Hymes. Some were landowners, some became merchants, some served in the clergy; only on occasion did they hold government positions.[32] The key difference between these Tang families and the localist elites of the later imperial period was that Tang provincial elites, when they did serve in office, nearly never served in positions of national prominence. Moreover, the reason they rarely served in prominent offices was not because of the expansion in size of the literate, educated population and the heightened competition of the civil service examinations—factors profoundly affecting later social development—but rather because late Tang capital elites were strikingly successful in monopolizing offices all across the realm. Chapter 3 will seek to account for the tremendous success of this dominant political elite.

National Elites in the Provinces

Although national elites were rarely buried away from the capital region, and these capital-based elites generally did not own private residences in the provinces, figures 2.2 and 2.5 reveal exceptions to this rule. Chapter 1 has provided a clue to account for the exceptional cases—ninth-century epitaphs for provincial elites frequently assert than an ancestor had initially settled down at the family's current home base after serving there in office. A careful analysis of data from epitaphs suggests that, indeed, one important elite migratory pathway consisted of officeholders—usually from the capital—who reestablished themselves at sites of provincial appointments.[33]

Although figures 2.2b and 2.2c demonstrate that the majority of private residences of Chang'an and Luoyang elites were situated in the immediate vicinities of one of the two capital cities, what accounts for the nearly one-fifth (102/565) of privately owned homes situated elsewhere? Figure 2.6a maps the sites of these residences. Not surprisingly, almost two-fifths (41 of 109) were situated in the Chang'an–Luoyang corridor, within a few days of travel from the capitals, confirming that prominent families in the capital corridor should in many cases be treated as capital elites. Also well represented were Jiangling (10 of 109)

---

32. Tackett, "Great Clansmen," p. 111; Robert Hymes, *Statesmen and Gentlemen*.

33. For evidence that this phenomenon was occurring during the Tang in Quanzhou, in China's southeast, see Clark, "Consolidation," pp. 110–11.

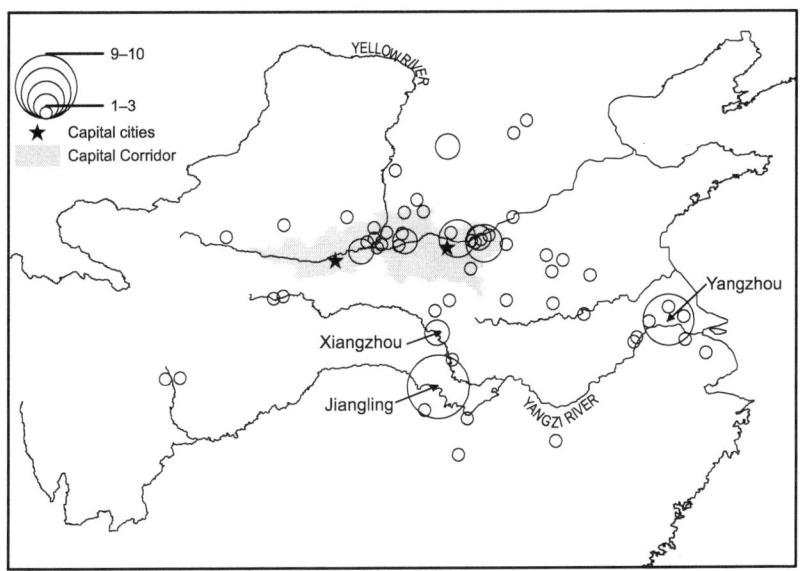

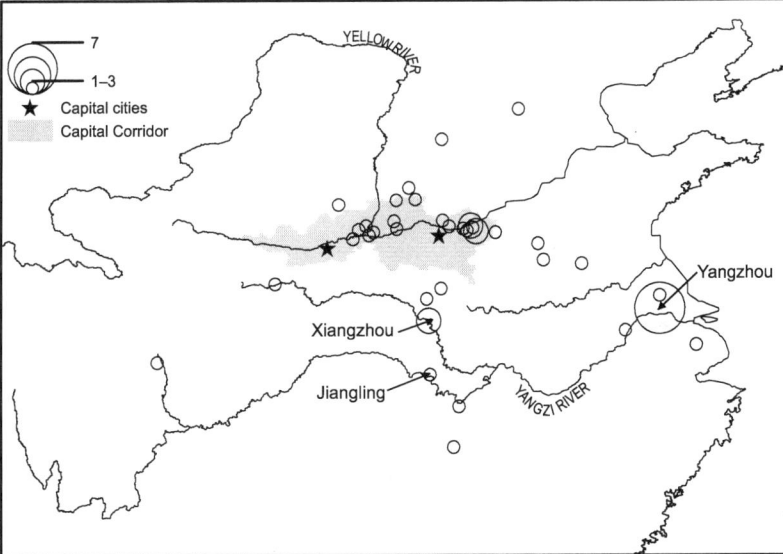

FIGURE 2.6. Private residences in the provinces belonging to Luoyang or Chang'an elites. (a) All provincial private residences of capital elites. (b) Provincial private residences of capital elites not known to have held office at locations in question.

Considers only private residences that were sites of death of epitaph subjects; see figure 2.2 for the definition of "private residence." "Provincial" includes all places outside of the two capital cities of Chang'an and Luoyang.

and Yangzhou (11 of 109).³⁴ Exploring with more care individual cases reveals an interesting pattern, exemplified by Pei Jian* 裴兼 (763–810). Pei's only bureaucratic appointment seems to have been that of adjutant of Songzhou 宋州參軍. According to his epitaph, "because of his office, his home was there" 因官而家焉. Indeed, he died at a "private residence" in Songzhou, though he would be reburied the following year at the ancestral cemetery in the Beimang hills. Ms. Yuan* 元氏 (770–804) constituted a similar example. She died in a "private residence" in Xiayang County in Tongzhou, where her husband was then serving as county magistrate. In other words, officials appointed to provincial posts did on occasion obtain permanent or semipermanent residences at the sites of their government service.

In some cases, they maintained these residences well after their term of appointment had come to an end. Cui Lifang* 崔立方 (787–855) died in a "private residence" in Xiayi County (also in Songzhou), where he had served as vice magistrate many years earlier. His wife, Ms. Li* 李氏 (804–33), had died in the same house two decades previously. Both, however, were brought back to Luoyang for burial. Similarly, Li Xun* 李愻 (d. 788) died in Gao'an 高安 County in Hongzhou 洪州 (modern-day Nanchang), where he was serving as county magistrate. Although he, himself, died in a state-owned building, his spouse would die in the same county twelve years later, having presumably established some roots there. Both husband and wife, along with their eldest son, were then buried "temporarily" at a site north of the Gao'an county seat. Although three decades later the younger son would rebury all three in Luoyang—their "hometown" 故鄉 according to the epitaph—it is clear that the family had lived in Hongzhou for some time. Their daughter, for example, had married the sheriff of Gao'an, who, as a central government appointee, represented a rare opportunity for the family to intermarry with a member of the national elite without having actually to return to the capital.

Among the relatively small number of provincial residences owned by capital-based elites, these examples do not seem to have been unusual. Over half (36/68) of private residences for capital elites situated beyond the capital and corridor regions were located at sites where

---

34. See "Fig 2_note34 provincial priv res" in database.

it is known that the deceased or a close relative (usually the father or spouse) was then serving or had once served in office.³⁵ Most of the remaining were situated either in Yangzhou or near Xiangzhou on the middle reaches of the Han River (fig. 2.6b). But it is not always easy to identify sites of past officeholding. Consider Zheng Guan* 鄭琯 (791–854) and her son Li Shu* 李述 (814–57), both of whom died in a private residence in Jiacheng County, Ruzhou. The epitaphs of Zheng and her son reveal only that Zheng's husband, Li Gongdu* 李公度 (784–852), served in Yingzhou at the end of his career. Fortunately, Li Gongdu's own epitaph also survives, and, from this inscription, one learns that he had served in Jiacheng earlier on and that, at one point while between two appointments, he had spent time at a villa he owned there. The epitaph of Pei Daosheng* 裴道生 (780–84), who died at a private residence south of the Yangzi, in Hongzhou, reveals only that her father, Pei Zha* 裴札 (728–84), had been prefect of Shaozhou 韶州. It turns out from Pei Zha's own epitaph, however, that he had served in office in Hongzhou before his final appointment further south. In both cases, had a second epitaph not fortuitously survived, it would not be possible to confirm that the family owned property at the site of a bureaucratic appointment.

Whereas the aforementioned cases involve families who were buried in the capital, some capital elites who obtained property in the provinces appear to have relocated there permanently. Figure 2.7a depicts the places of burial in the provinces of individuals with "national ancestries"—that is, whose *ancestors* were national elites, having held offices of national prominence for at least three generations.³⁶ The vast majority of individuals with national ancestries lived, died, and then were buried in Chang'an or Luoyang, and so do not appear on this map. Beyond the capital cities themselves, the Chang'an–Luoyang corridor is well represented (64 of 138 burials); there also seems to have been a small cluster of such families in Xiangzhou (5 of 138) on the middle reaches of the Han River and in Yangzhou (7 of 138).³⁷

---

35. See "Fig 2_note35 Prov res at site of office" in database.
36. Note that this group represents a slightly larger set of individuals than the provincially based "national elites" who appear in figure 2.5 because figure 2.5 only includes individuals who still were themselves of national prominence.
37. See "Fig 2_note37 National elites in provinces" in database.

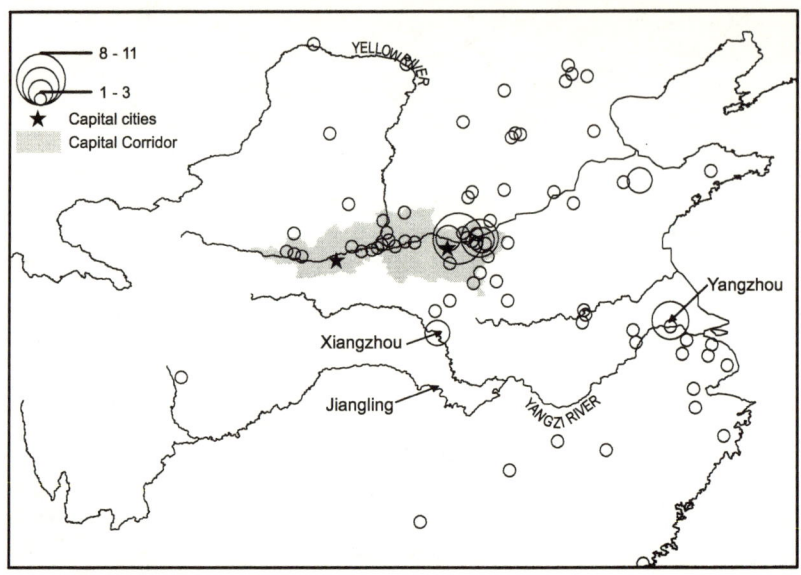
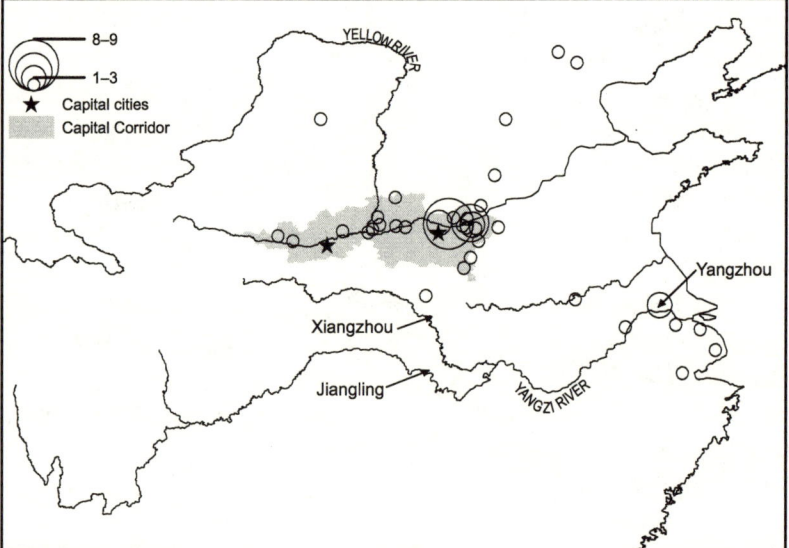

FIGURE 2.7. Places of provincial burial of individuals with national ancestries. (a) Places of provincial burial of all individuals with national ancestries. (b) Places of provincial burial of national elites not known to have served in office at their places of burial.

See figure 2.6 for the definition of "provincial." Figure 2.7b is the subset of data depicted in figure 2.7a that excludes individuals known to have served in office at their places of burial.

As in the case of provincial residences, most provincial burials of national elites followed a bureaucratic appointment to the place in question. Xue Zan* 薛贊 (762–840) provides a good example. His ancestors were nationally prominent, serving all over the empire. His great-grandfather had served as vice magistrate in a county adjoining Chang'an; his grandfather had served as prefect of Mingzhou in the southeast; and his father had been magistrate of Huazhou, east northeast of Luoyang. Xue, himself, had served in Jiangzhou in southern Hedong, as well as in Suzhou. In the end, he chose not to be buried with his ancestors, who were probably interred in one of the capitals: "Because the old place is far away, [the deceased] has not been returned home for burial, in accordance with his final wishes" 蓋舊里綿遠, 未遂歸葬, 從遺命也. Instead, Xue was buried in Xiacai County, on the Huai River, where he had once served as magistrate.

Such examples were typical in most parts of China. With the notable exceptions of the capital corridor and the Lower Yangzi region, three-quarters (43/60) of non-"temporary" provincial burials of individuals with national ancestries involved sites where the deceased or a close relative had once served in office.[38] As with provincial residences of capital elites, it is likely that these figures underestimate the extent of the phenomenon, as it is not always possible to identify all of the appointments of an individual's husband or father.[39] The exceptional number, in the Lower Yangzi region and in the Chang'an–Luoyang corridor, of burials of individuals who did not serve locally (fig. 7b) suggests that in these areas—and only in these areas—there may have existed in the late Tang small colonies of elites who maintained national prominence for several generations without a physical presence in the capital cities.

What explains the constant trickle of elite migrants relocating from the capital to sites of provincial appointments? The primary reason was probably economic, involving the expense of living at the capitals.

---

38. See "Fig 2_note38 Natl elites in prov served locally" in database.

39. For example, in the epitaph of Du Qiong 杜瓊 (767–831), who died and was buried in Xiangzhou, her unnamed husband is identified only as Mr. Li, administrator of Jiangzhou 絳州長史. An anecdote in the epitaph, however, reveals that Du initially came to Xiangzhou after her husband received an unidentified appointment to serve there. It is fortuitous that one learns this, as epitaphs for wives typically would not include such information.

In Chang'an and Luoyang, the wealthy scions of powerful families had driven up the costs of real estate, so that a single townhouse in a metropolitan ward might cost three million cash.[40] Simultaneously, the cost of importing grain to Chang'an—a severely grain deficient region—probably drove up the price of food there. Thus, when Wei Miao* 魏邈 (760–814) brought his family back to Chang'an after failing to find a position "within the four seas," he faced a relatively dire situation:

> With no place to rest his feet, he borrowed lodgings in the Shengye Ward of Wannian County [in metropolitan Chang'an]; because he clearly had nothing to rely upon [for a living], he went to his relatives and friends to eat. This lasted for five years. When he went out, there were no carriages [to transport him]; when he sat down, he lacked [even the basic] staple foods.
> 無投足之地, 賈居于萬年縣之勝業里, 顯然無託, 食於親知者, 首尾五祀. 出無車輿, 坐寡糧糗.

One solution was to purchase property in the capital corridor, where one could still be close enough to the capital to keep one's family politically relevant, yet real estate was likely more affordable. Thus, after retirement, Pan Kejian* 潘克儉 (782–842) "bought land and a cottage in western Huazhou [just east of Chang'an], where he lived his remaining years" 買田廬於華之西, 居歲餘. Men like Pan Kejian partly explain the relatively high presence of national elites in the broad zone between Chang'an and Luoyang.

A second solution was to acquire land—often through extralegal means—and resettle at a place where a family member held office.[41] One telling example involves Zheng Lu* 鄭魯 (c. 768–c. 824). After the death of his two elder brothers, Zheng felt it his duty to raise his nephews as

---

40. See record of conduct of Shen Chuanshi 沈傳師 (769–827).

41. There is little doubt that officials in the provinces took advantage of their positions to acquire resources. For a lengthy account of the "unlawful acquisition" of land by a provincial governor, see Peterson, "Corruption Unmasked"; Peterson, "Court and Province," pp. 521–22. For a discussion of how numerous scions of the great northern families agreed to serve as prefect of Quanzhou because of the potential for financial gain, see Clark, "Consolidation," pp. 89–97. Financial gain off of the South Sea trade may have been deemed a particular problem; in praising its subject for his honesty, the epitaph of Kong Kui 孔戣 (751–824) takes the trouble to note explicitly that he returned from office as governor of Lingnan (on the south coast) without any accrued wealth.

well as his own sons. However, he found these obligations to be unaffordable at the capital:

> It is said that, at the capital, it is difficult to feed oneself; one cannot in the end support widows and young ones. Formerly, the director of the Headquarters Bureau [Zheng's brother] had assisted the governor in Jingzhou and had once planted crops on several hundred *mu* of uncultivated land. These fields had lain fallow already for a dozen years. So, the Gentleman [Zheng] hurriedly headed south to recultivate the land there. He dug channels for irrigation, and erected embankments to demarcate the fields. It has now been three years, and the annual yield has reached a thousand bushels. This year, he sent out a request to invite his brothers' widows and orphans from the two capitals. In the third month in spring, Ms. Lu, wife of the prefect of Jiangzhou [Zheng's eldest brother], arrived from Chang'an with her four children; in the eighth month in Fall, Ms. Lu, wife of the director of the Headquarters Bureau, arrived from Luoyang. Alas! The Gentleman had fallen ill in the seventh month. The wife of the minister of works arrived just in time. When his sons announced [her arrival] to him, he arose to say: "The two widows have arrived; my family is now reunited! What shame is there now in shutting my eyes?" On the seventeenth day of that month, he died in his villa in the eastern suburbs of Jiangling County.
>
> 謂京師艱食, 終不能衣食嫠幼. 往歲工部佐戎於荆, 嘗植不毛之田數百畝, 蕪廢于茲亦一紀矣. 府君乃喟然南來, 復墾于是, 疏卑為溉, 陪高而畝, 及今三年, 而歲入千斛. 是歲分命迓二嫂氏泊諸孤于二京. 春三月, 絳州夫人盧氏從四子至自京師, 秋八月, 工部夫人盧氏至自洛陽. 噫! 府君遇疾於七月, 工部夫人之至蓋巫矣. 諸子以聞, 則軒然而作, 曰: 二嫂至矣, 吾家畢集矣, 吾於今而瞑, 庶無愧矣. 是月十七日, 終于江陵縣之東郊別業.

Although buried in the suburbs of Luoyang, in the general region where the family had buried its dead for at least a century, Zheng Lu was not the only family member to die in a private residence in Jiangling; several family members, including his children, Ms. Zheng* 鄭氏 (d. 808) and Zheng Gun* 鄭緄 (796–820), all died there over a two decade period.

Du Quan* 杜詮 (c. 791–c. 850), scion of a clan based in Chang'an for generations and grandson of the powerful late-eighth- and early-ninth-century chief minister Du You* 杜佑 (735–812), provides a similar example. After leaving his post as magistate of Jiangxia 江夏 County, near modern-day Wuhan, he built a house just across the Han River. Thereupon, according to the epitaph penned by his cousin Du Mu 杜牧:

[Under] the beating sun, he protected his head with a straw hat, personally supervising the farmhands. Within a year, food was ample; within two years, both food and other necessities were in excess. Within three years, he had renovated his home, the animals were fat and prolific, and he possessed all [necessary] implements and tools. In a period of fifteen years, beginning with the clearing of the land, he had become a wealthy man without relying one bit on the help of others. He would often tell people: "As for those who endure humiliation to become officials for no other reason than to support their families, how many have there been through the ages? They endure humiliation; I toil hard. Given that we both feed and clothe our families equally, what do you think when you see the likes of me?"

烈日笠首, 自督耕夫, 而一年食足, 二年衣食兩餘, 三年而室屋完新, 六畜肥繁, 器用皆具, 凡十五年, 起於墾荒, 不假人一毫之助, 至成富家翁, 常曰: "忍恥入仕, 不緣妻子衣食者, 舉世幾人, 彼忍恥, 我勞力, 等衣食爾, 顧我何如."

Du Mu, himself, answers this final rhetorical question in the rhymed *ming* that concludes the epitaph: "Given that they feed and support their families equally, he who has toiled hard is the man of virtue" 等衣食爾, 勞力者賢. The author's primary motive here is undoubtedly to convey a bucolic vision that Du Mu shared with a number of late Tang poets, a vision that went so far as to reject officeholding as a "humiliation." Nevertheless, hidden behind this idealism lies a strategy similar to that employed by the Zheng family. An official who obtained land not far from a place where he had served in office—quite possibly taking advantage of his bureaucratic ties in order to acquire this property—later finds life as a provincial landowner to be more stable and profitable than life amid the hypercompetitive environment of capital-based bureaucrats.

The examples of Zheng Lu and Du Quan provide a model for understanding why scions of capital-based families sometimes chose to relocate to the provinces. In both cases, however, although the individuals in question died in private residences in the provinces, they were later brought home to the ancestral cemetery for burial, to Luoyang in Zheng's case and Chang'an in Du's case. But it is not difficult to imagine that some of their descendants may have continued to operate the estates in subsequent years and that one or more descendants might eventually have considered the moves to be permanent, perhaps establishing a new clan cemetery nearby. In the short run, these branches of capital elite families gained the ability to profit off of a large estate; in the long run, they lost their connections at court, connections that—as will be discussed in more detail in the next chapter—were essential for maintaining status and prestige at the national level.

In other words, relocation to the provinces, constituted an act of downward social mobility. Downward mobility explains the backgrounds of provincial elites like Linghu Huaibin* 令狐懷斌 (834–58) and Yan Youming* 顏幼明 (785–866). Linghu, who was buried in Bozhou in the Weibo autonomous province of southern Hebei, claimed descent from a powerful capital-based clan that included two ninth-century chief ministers. His fourth-generation ancestor, the influential military man Linghu Zhang* 令狐彰 (d. 773), had served as governor of the region that would become Weibo during the campaign to pacify the An Lushan Rebellion; his great-grandfather had remained behind serving in a local office. Subsequently, neither Linghu nor his father and grandfather served in government.

Yan Youming, by contrast, was buried in the south, in Changshu County in the Yangzi Delta region. His fourth-generation ancestor Yan Moudao* 顏謀道 (642–721) had been a typical capital elite, whose ancestors had been government officials generation after generation for at least a century and a half and who, himself, had served all over the empire before his death and subsequent burial in Luoyang. Although it is not clear when or why some family members moved south, it is evident that the branch of the family that migrated to the south rapidly ceased to secure government positions. Neither Yan Youming nor his father or sons ever held office, though both the father and the sons prepared for the civil service exams, indicating that they probably had once hoped to serve. The downward social mobility associated with migration to the provinces also explains the abundant examples of elite families with weak or no officeholding traditions who claimed that an unnamed office-holding ancestor in the past had reestablished the family at its current location. Even if a certain number of these claims were fictive, the fact that the claims must have been deemed plausible if they were repeated so frequently suggests that they were modeled after an elite migratory pathway that was well recognized by contemporaries.

In sum, by the late Tang, most nationally prominent elites were based in the region surrounding the two capital cities of Chang'an and

Luoyang. Most who did not live in the cities lived in the capital corridor—that is, in the immediate vicinities of these cities and the zone linking them together. Small colonies of national elites may have aggregated at a limited number of locations beyond the capital region, notably in Yangzhou and the Lower Yangzi region—where some may have established permanent homes—and in Jiangling and Xiangzhou—where some capital elites maintained secondary residences. With the exception of these small colonies, most descendants of capital elites who relocated to the provinces—generally by taking advantage of property the family had accrued while serving in office in the same location—probably understood that it would be enormously difficult for their descendants to reenter national politics once they had lost touch with their relatives at court.

Other Elite Migratory Pathways

Besides the outward relocation of capital elites to places where they had served in office, there were a few other important elite migratory pathways. A large number of capital elites appear to have relocated to the south during the turmoil that followed the outbreak of the An Lushan Rebellion. Li Xie* 李頡 (710–62), for example, who was a distant relative of the reigning Tang emperors, abandoned his post in Henan in the wake of the rebel conquest of North China. Both he and his wife died and were later buried in the "Jiang-Huai" region—that is, the region between the Yangzi and the Huai Rivers, including Yangzhou and the Yangzi Delta. Even after the rebellion was quelled, the subsequent decade of unrest seems to have discouraged families from returning right away to the north. According to the early-ninth-century scholar Han Yu 韓愈 (768–824), into the late 760s, "the Central Plains having only recently quelled the revolt, a great number of elites remained in exile in the Jiang-Huai region" 中國新去亂, 士多避處江淮間.[42] In fact, as late as the 770s and early 780s, the family of Lu Yan* 盧沇 (712–74) was unable to return Lu's remains from Yangzhou to Luoyang because "at the time, the path of the country was still in difficulty, and obstructive armies [were stationed] in Heluo [i.e., the Luoyang area]" 頃以國步尚艱, 阻兵河洛.

---

42. Epitaph of Lu Dongmei 盧東美 (734–87).

These migrations, however, should not be thought of as part of the great southward demographic shift that spanned the eighth through thirteenth centuries; the Tang capitals remained a magnet for elites until the fall of the dynasty. Many of the officeholding families who fled south in the 750s and 760s began to return to the north at the end of the century. For example, Cui Qianli* 崔千里 (736–97) "wandered about in Jiang-Huai in order to avoid the chaos of the barbarian [rebels]" 因逆胡之亂, 流散江淮. Later, however, he returned to Luoyang, where he owned both a country villa and a private house, and where he died and was later buried. Liu Lun* 劉倫 (d. 782) also fled south to Yangzhou during the rebellion. Although he did not make it back north in his lifetime, he was eventually reburied in Luoyang, where his wife would later die, having reestablished residency there. And the grandfather of Liu Moran* 柳默然 (773–840) "went to Jiangnan to escape the Yan [i.e., An Lushan] bandits, thus cutting himself off from his official's salary" 避燕寇江南, 因自絕祿仕. But her grandfather was eventually buried near Luoyang, where Liu also died in a Daoist convent and where she and two of her sons would be buried.[43]

In numerous instances, especially in the cases of families who stayed in the south for years or even decades, the return north involved reburying a number of family members. The epitaph of Zheng Gao* 鄭高 (745–805) begins by recounting the mass elite migration to the south: "After the Tianbao era [which immediately preceded the An Lushan Rebellion], conflict was rife. People were buried temporarily in provisional tombs as they sojourned in the Jiang-Huai region. Seven or eight out of ten of them could not be brought home for burial" 自天寶已來, 四方多故, 權窆旅殯, 飄寓江淮, 未克歸葬, 十有七八. Later, however, Zheng sought to rebury his deceased family members back north, "exhausting his earnings to handle two generations [of kinsmen]" 磬祿俸之資, 舉兩代家事. Just after completing this task in 805, he died while already in residence back in Luoyang. There he was buried, not too far from where his great-grandfather Zheng Jinsi* 鄭進思 (626–75) had been interred a century earlier.[44] An even more dramatic example involves a branch of the Boling

---

43. The two sons, both with epitaphs, were Zhao Gui 趙珪 (806–47) and Zhao Huang 趙璜 (804–62).

44. Besides Zheng's epitaph, see also the epitaph of his spouse, Ms. Cui 崔氏 (770–806).

Cui family described by Patricia Ebrey. Over one hundred clansmen fled south together in the wake of the rebel onslaught, but many of the survivors returned to the capital region as early as 769. There, on the eighth day of the fourth month of the year 778—auspicious both as a *jiashen* day and as the day commemorating Buddha's birthday—several kinsmen who had died while the family was based in Jiang-Huai were reburied together at a new cemetery in the Beimang hills.⁴⁵

Returning to the capital in this fashion was so common that it seems to account for most relocation of bureaucratic families to Chang'an or Luoyang in the early ninth century. There are yet more examples. The father of Cui Bei* 崔備 (747–816), scion of one branch of the Qinghe Cui clan, had fled south during the rebellion, finding employment with the governor of Yangzhou, a very distant kinsman of his. When on his deathbed in a private residence in Chang'an a half century later, Cui Bei requested that his ancestors be brought back to the capital region. His son fulfilled his wishes by organizing a large reburial, performed on a single day in the year 816.⁴⁶

Then there was the family of Zhang Shiling* 張士陵 (763–816). For over fifty years, beginning shortly after An Lushan's rebellion, many of Zhang's clansmen were buried in the Yangzi Delta region. Zhang's spouse had died in Yangzhou, suggesting that the clan maintained an active presence in the south as late as the turn of the ninth century. However, on his deathbed, Zhang insisted to his son and younger brother that they relocate all clansmen buried in the south back to Luoyang in the north,

---

45. Ebrey, *Aristocratic Families*, pp. 97–98. This was a newly established cemetery; the older clan burial ground lay in Chang'an, at the other end of the capital corridor. Even after 778, a few stragglers still remained in the south. According to his epitaph, Cui Yi 崔倚 (d. c. 812) fled south while still quite young, "sojourning in Jiang-Huai while the caitiff dust rose up in the two capitals" 虜塵犯於兩京, 漂寓江淮. He obtained office in the retinue of a southern provincial governor. After he died, however, his body was "returned to the old country" 歸於舊國 in the capital region by his nephew.

46. Besides Cui Bei's epitaph, see also the epitaphs of Cui's grandmother Ms. Li 李氏 (d. c. 765) and Cui's brother Cui Huangzuo 崔黃左 (743–97). For confirmation that the clan had been buried in Luoyang prior to the rebellion, see the epitaphs of Cui Bei's grandfather Cui Taizhi 崔泰之 (667–723), and granduncles Cui Xiaochang 崔孝昌 (669–711) and Cui Ezhi 崔諤之 (671–719). The governor of Yangzhou in question, Cui Yuan 崔圓, was also from the Qinghe Cui clan, though their shared ancestor had lived and died well before the founding of the Tang. For Cui Yuan's tenure in Yangzhou, see Yu Xianhao, *Tang cishi kao* 3:1675.

a feat they accomplished. Numerous clan tombs dating back as far as the early eighth century have been discovered in the Beimang hills, suggesting that Zhang was indeed "returning home."[47]

The family of the well-known late Tang literary figure Quan Deyu* 權德輿 (759–818) offers yet another similar example. Quan's grandmother had fled the capital with her children after the outbreak of An Lushan's rebellion. After spending some time roaming aboard a "drifting boat" 扁舟, she eventually died in Hangzhou in 757, where she was buried. Quan's father and mother were also buried in the south, in Runzhou 潤州, where the father had died in 767. Decades later, in 817, Quan relocated the tombs of all three to a site south of Luoyang, not far from where family members are known to have been buried in the years preceding the great rebellion.[48] Thus, Quan's immediate ancestors had followed a now recognizable pattern. They had fled south in the 750s but then returned to the north sometime in the late eighth or early ninth centuries.

All of these relocations to the capital involved capital elites in exile. These families had undoubtedly maintained ties with the court and with court officials throughout the period of turmoil and presumably had deployed these connections when returning to the north late in the eighth century. There are only a few cases of migration to the capital in the ninth century involving bureaucratic elites with no apparent capital connections. The best example involves the Zhi 支 family. Zhi Song 支竦 was a member of a clan that had purportedly accompanied the Jin court to the south after the regime was forced out of North China in the

---

47. For other clansmen buried in Luoyang, see epitaphs of Zhang Qiqiu 張齊丘 (656–91), Zhang Shiyu 張時譽 (688–733), Zhang Hong 張翃 (709–78), Zhang Xiang 張翔 (724–79) and his spouse Ms. Yuan 源氏 (735–96), (Ms.) Zhang Chan 張嬋 (816–40), and (Ms.) Zhang Ying 張嬰 (834–55). It is possible that the court encouraged this recentralization of the bureaucratic elite. According to the epitaph of Chen Xuanlu 陳宣魯 (808–40), Chen's father had sought to reregister the family in Yangzhou after the death of Chen's grandparents. Emperor Dezong had refused. Eventually, although Chen's brothers were still living in the south, Chen, himself, was buried in Luoyang on new land that had apparently been purchased for this purpose.

48. See the epitaph of Quan's grandmother, Ms. Yang 楊氏 (d. 757), and the spirit marker 靈表 of Quan's father, Quan Gao 權皋 (723–68), both included in Quan Deyu's collected works. For evidence of a clan cemetery in Luoyang before the An Lushan Rebellion, see epitaph of Quan Jun 權均 (720–51), a descendant of Quan's fifth-generation ancestor.

fourth century. In the late eighth and early ninth centuries, the family was still burying its dead in the south. Before his death in Luoyang, however, Zhi Song announced to his sons, "I like it here; when I die, this is where you should bury me" 我樂於斯, 死當葬我. He also insisted on being laid to rest alongside his ancestors; thus, his descendants transported twenty-four bodies from six different generations to the Beimang hills north of the Tang Eastern Capital.[49] The epitaphs of one of his sons and of the wife of another son confirm that family members were still residing in Luoyang's Xingxiu 行修 Ward two decades later, in the 870s. Because six generations were involved, the Zhi family does not appear to have been an An Lushan era refugee clan. Nevertheless, the Zhi family was part of the national elite, having served for generations in offices of national prominence. A few similar examples exist.[50] Quite possibly, these families were members of the small colonies of nationally prominent elites based in the Lower Yangzi region.

Although civil bureaucratic families are most visible among extant epitaphs— presumably because they dominated the higher socioeconomic strata of society—it is possible to reconstruct the migratory routes of military and other types of elites. For example, there are rare cases of the migration of non-officeholders from the provinces to the capital. Li Hong* 李弘 (754–816) came down from Hedong in order to "serve the [Buddhist] sangha" 奉釋氏 at the Longmen temples south of Luoyang. Merchant elites, commonly encountered in Hebei and Yangzhou, occasionally migrated to the capitals as well.[51] One such merchant was Ma Qian* 馬倩 (743–812), whose family had moved first to Xuzhou 徐州— an important prefectural city situated at a key location on the Grand Canal riverine transport system—and then later to Chang'an. Among the merchants were undoubtedly a certain number of foreigners.[52] There were also eunuchs, whose recruitment is still poorly understood. Some

---

49. Tackett, "Great Clansmen," pp. 118–19.

50. See, for example, epitaphs of Luo Xian 駱遣 (737–85) and Xie Guan 謝觀 (793–865); both men had reestablished themselves and their families in Luoyang.

51. For a discussion of merchants in Hebei and Yangzhou, see Tackett, "Transformation," pp. 33–41.

52. The foreigners in Chang'an are well known. For a discussion of a Sogdian population residing permanently in Luoyang into the ninth century, see Mao Yangguang, "Xinjian si fang."

are believed to have been children or prisoners of war captured in the far south.⁵³ Their relocation to the capital might constitute an example of forced migration that nonetheless offered opportunities for upward advancement. Although most eunuchs never attained positions of prominence, a few eunuch clans became fabulously wealthy.⁵⁴

Perhaps more common than these groups were the military men from the provinces who were appointed to serve in one of the capital armies. An interesting example involves the descendants of Chen Chu 陳楚 (763–823) and Zhang Maozhao 張茂昭 (762–811), both of whom had governed Yiwu Province in northern Hebei. The two families had intermarried in Yiwu; later, kinsmen from both families relocated to the south together when Chen Chu was appointed to serve as military governor of Mengzhou, just north of Luoyang.⁵⁵ There are other examples of families relocating to Luoyang after serving in the Eastern Capital Command 東都留守.⁵⁶ Others, such as Fu Lin* 符璘 (734–98) and Zhang Liangfu* 張良輔 (754–814), transferred from the provinces to serve in the Chang'an-based Shence Army.⁵⁷

Finally, there were the military men who relocated from one province to another in the tow of a provincial governor or military commander who had been reappointed elsewhere. Although capital elites largely monopolized the upper echelons of the civilian positions in the governors' retinues, local men might secure military and other lower-level positions. From these positions, they might accompany their superiors

---

53. Dalby, "Court Politics," p. 571. Indeed, according to Ch'en Jo-shui, "Tangdai Chang'an," pp. 177–80, epitaphs for eunuchs (especially those dating to the first half of the Tang) often indicate that the eunuchs in question were from the south. For example, according to his epitaph, the eunuch Zhang Shuzun 張叔遵 (810–71) was from Jiaozhi 交趾, i.e., modern-day Hanoi. It is plausible that Zhang was captured in the far south. A few other eunuchs claimed as their immediate ancestors men who had served as "prefects" in the far south; these ancestors may have been tribal chieftains.

54. For a good overview of those eunuchs who did achieve positions of political prominence in the early ninth century, see Lu Yang, "Dynastic Revival," pp. 279–307.

55. Tackett, "Great Clansmen," pp. 126–27.

56. See the epitaphs of Ms. Zhou 周氏 (764–839), whose husband had served there and whose son subsequently reburied several people in Luoyang, as well as of Zhang Jirong 張季戎 (790–851), who also served in the Eastern Capital Command.

57. The court seems to have been quite eager to relocate some of these military commanders to the capital. Fu Lin, for example, was granted a townhouse in Chang'an's Jinggong 靖恭 Ward as well as over 10 *qing* of land in nearby Lantian County.

on their reassignments. Wang Nixiu* 王逆修 (c.773–c. 823), for example, began his career in Taiyuan, seat of the Hedong provincial government. When one of the military commanders there, a certain Li Jinglue 李景略 (732–86), was reappointed to a post on the fringes of the Gobi Desert in the far north, Wang accompanied him there. Thirty years later, he died there, where he was interred as well.[58] Similarly, according to the epitaph of Liu Zizheng* 劉自政 (782–851), his father accompanied a certain Zhu Zhongliang 朱忠亮 (d. 813) from Binzhou to Jingzhou farther west. Both father and son were later buried there.[59] So, too, Wei Guohua* 衛國華 (777–830), originally in the service of the provincial military in Chenzhou, accompanied a provincial governor to Luzhou, where he passed away.[60]

And there is the similar example of Yang Xiaozhi* 楊孝直 (751–835) and his son Yang Shan* 楊贍 (789–826). The elder Yang began his career in Chengde Province in Hebei. Given the political autonomy of this province, it is almost certain that the family resided there at the time. Indeed, Yang Xiaozhi's deceased wife was buried in Chengde, and at the time of his own death, one son was still based there and so could not attend his funeral. However, when Chengde's military governor Wang Chengyuan 王承元 submitted to the Tang court in 820, father and son accompanied Wang to his new office as governor of Yicheng Province, east of Luoyang. The elder Yang later encountered an old comrade-in-arms from Chengde, following this man to Xiangzhou farther south. The younger Yang remained in the retinue of Wang Chengyuan, accompanying him to his new post in Fengxiang Province, west of Chang'an. Both men died in private residences at their place of office and near where they were buried, Xiaozhi in Xiangzhou and Shan in Fengxiang.[61]

---

58. For a similar example, see epitaph of Qiu Zhicheng 仇志誠 (775–839).
59. Besides Liu's epitaph, see also Yu Xianhao, *Tang cishi kao* 1:283.
60. A somewhat similar example involves Cheng An 程安 (761–829). According to his epitaph, he began his career in the military in Songzhou, where his family had lived for several generations. After gaining the favor of a eunuch, he eventually ended up serving in the provincial army in Luzhou, where he died.
61. For an expanded account of the Yang family and its association with Wang Chengyuan, see Tackett, "Great Clansmen," pp. 136–37. A similar example involves the military officer Liu Yi 劉逸 (776–834), who, according to his epitaph, joined the retinue of Wang Chengyuan while Wang was governor of Yicheng Province. Liu then accompanied Wang to Fengxiang and, subsequently, to Pinglu (in modern-day Shandong),

Conclusion

According to the preeminent author and poet of the ninth century Bai Juyi 白居易 (772–846), "Since the Tianbao era [742–56], the great families East of the Mountains all relocated their tombs to the two capitals, as this was beneficial in terms of convenience and closeness" 自天寶以還, 山東士人皆改葬兩京, 利於便近.[62] According to Bai's contemporary Du Mu 杜牧 (803–52): "There is the Western Capital [of Chang'an] and the Eastern Capital [of Luoyang]. The Western Capital has the Son of Heaven; the lands and homes of the ministers and literati lie between the two capitals" 有西京、東京, 西京有天子, 公卿士人畦居兩京間.[63] This chapter has sought first and foremost to confirm these impressionistic accounts of ninth-century society—that the dominant political elite was overwhelmingly concentrated in the vicinities of the two capitals. In this way, it provides a new way of understanding the Tang elite. Scions of the great families of the pre-Tang period constituted far too large a status group to have all been part of the political elite. Instead, the dominant political elite consisted of a small subgroup, those based in the capital region of Chang'an, Luoyang, and the zone in between.

One implication of this geography of power is that social mobility was closely tied to migration. Thus, many migrants to the provinces were the sons of capital grandees who were unable to compete in the hypercompetitive environment of the capital and so took advantage of a provincial appointment to reestablish roots far from the center. There, they might have remained important in local society, but they quickly vanished from the historical record as they fell from national prominence. In later centuries, this option may not have existed, as entrenched "localist" elites acquired an ability to resist representatives of the central government.[64] But in the late Tang, the central government was apparently still able to dominate local society in such a way that its own representatives or their kinsmen could acquire land and status at the sites of provincial appointments.

---

where he died in 834, one year after Wang. He was buried in Qingzhou, the seat of Pinglu Province.

62. See Bai's epitaph for Cui Xuanliang 崔玄亮 (768–833).
63. *Du Mu ji xinian jiaozhu* 3:767.
64. Thus, after the Jurchen invasion, northern refugees, including individuals from politically prominent families, had great difficulty integrating into local society in the south. See Bol, *Neo-Confucianism*, p. 38.

In principle, the situation in the late Tang also meant that infiltrating capital society by physically relocating there may have been a way a family could improve its fortunes. However, this type of mobility probably was rare. Most individuals who relocated by choice or by force to the capital—eunuchs, soldiers, palace bondservants, and palace women—probably never succeeded in attaining prestigious positions in society; in any case, one learns little about them from extant sources. Epitaphs for burials in the capital occasionally do point to more recent inward migration of bureaucratic elites. But many of these cases did not involve "new" elites; rather, they were often the descendants of capital elites who had gone into exile in the south during the An Lushan Rebellion.

A second implication of the Tang geography of power is that it explains both how certain clans survived so long and, simultaneously, how they disappeared so suddenly at the turn of the tenth century. The following chapter will focus on the capital elite's long-term survival, arguing that their concentration in a relatively narrow geographic space helped reinforce the social networks that, more than anything else, ensured their survival until the end of the ninth century. This same geographic concentration, as chapter 5 will demonstrate, would contribute to their immediate demise once the capitals were sacked by the Huang Chao rebels in 880, leading both to the physical elimination of large numbers of capital-based elites and to the disintegration of the social networks that kept them in power.

3

The Capital Elite Marriage Network

Wei Feng* 韋渢 (735–810), who served both as magistrate of Luoyang and as vice prefect of Huazhou 華州司馬—two plum posts in the capital region—was clearly well connected. Several of his relatives were important provincial officials in their own lifetimes, including his father, two of his brothers, his father-in-law, and one of his sons, all of whom served as prefects at various locations around the empire. Another son was the father-in-law of Yang Hangong* 楊漢公 (785–861), who would later serve as governor of Tianping 天平 Province in eastern Henan and Jingnan 荊南 Province on the middle Yangzi. Wei also had connections to powerful central government officials. His grandfather, Wei Anshi 韋安石 (651–714), had been a chief minister during Empress Wu's regime. Both the husband of his niece, Li Xun* 李巽 (747–809), and his uncle, Wei Zhi 韋陟 (696–760), had served in the influential post of minister of personnel. Another uncle was father-in-law to a fourth-generation descendant of Wang Gui 王珪 (571–639), one of Taizong's chief ministers. His grandnephew was the father-in-law of Gao Ju 高璩 (d. 865), a late Tang chief minister. And his granddaughter would marry the mid-eighth-century chief minister Bai Minzhong* 白敏中 (792–861), making Wei a distant relative by marriage of the great late Tang poet Bai Juyi.[1]

By using information on place of burial contained in tomb epitaphs,

---

1. Besides the epitaph of Wei Feng, see the spirit-path inscription of his father, Wei Bin 韋斌 (d. c. 793); the epitaphs of Yang Hangong, Li Xun, Wang Tan 王譚 (813–64), Wei Chengsu 韋承素 (788–847), and Bai Minzhong; and relevant passages of the *XTS* genealogical table of chief ministers.

the previous chapter analyzed geographic data to reveal the degree to which capital-based elites were fundamentally different from provincial elites. This chapter elaborates on this observation by exploring what it was that allowed such capital-based families to monopolize nationally prominent bureaucratic positions generation after generation for centuries. Although the fame and prestige of some of the old aristocratic families undoubtedly helped them to hold on to power, the focus here will be on how social networks—reinforced by the geographic concentration of late Tang elites—played an even more important role. Wei Feng's case was in no way unusual. The most prominent bureaucrats as well as many of the most famous poets and other cultural figures were linked to each other in a dense marriage network implanted in the capital region, a network critical to this elite's long-term survival.

Reconstructing Patrilines

Chapter 1 focused on clans in the conventional sense of the term, referring to the very large group of individuals professing a particular pedigree identified by a specific choronym-surname combination. The problem with this approach, as discussed previously, is that claims to such aristocratic lineages were pervasive among elites at all levels of society. Such claims may well have reinforced individual status within local communities, but they can hardly be used by the historian to identify the political power elite of the late Tang. For analytical purposes, it is preferable to define kin groups on a more empirical basis. In the present chapter, the basic unit of analysis is the "patriline," which I define as the largest cluster of blood relatives that can be reconstructed on the basis of documented father-son (or father-daughter) relationships.[2] Claims of descent from a famous figure of the distant past are disregarded unless most of the intervening ancestors can be identified.

These reconstructions are possible by analyzing the thousands of extant late Tang tomb epitaphs and other funerary texts in conjunction with additional genealogical material. Epitaphs typically identify three generations of the deceased's ancestors as well as the deceased's sons and sons-in-law. Frequently, they also identify the father-in-law or

---

2. For the sake of convenience, in the context of the present chapter, the term "family" will be used interchangeably with the term "patriline."

other relatives by marriage, such as the maternal uncle.³ On the basis of such sources, it is sometimes possible to reconstruct patrilines that include several hundred individuals; in other cases, a patriline comprises only a few kinsmen named in a single epitaph.⁴ Most consist of small subbranches of the "great clans" described in chapter 1.

The information found in tomb inscriptions can be substantially expanded for the Tang political elite—the principal focus of this chapter—by means of the eleventh-century genealogical tables of the imperial clan, the chief ministers, and the most important provincial dynasts. These tables—preserved in chapters 70 to 75 of *Xin Tang shu* 新唐書 (New Tang History)—include the names of about 17,500 individuals, the vast majority of whom lived during the Tang period. Although the tables do contain discrepancies, overall they seem to have been grounded in highly reliable scholarship. The Northern Song scholar and statesman Ouyang Xiu 歐陽修 (1007–72), one of the two chief editors of *Xin Tang shu*, took genealogical studies particularly seriously. On one occasion, after encountering a Tang stele that listed centuries of clansmen, he was moved to criticize the people of his own era for knowing scarcely one or two generations of their own forebears: "What makes them different from the birds and the beasts is merely that they can name their father and grandfather" 其所以異於禽獸者僅能識其父祖爾.⁵ Ouyang's thorough scholarship into the great Tang lineages, the scholarship that culminated in the publication of the *Xin Tang shu* tables, was partly driven by his belief that accurate multigenerational awareness of one's ancestors was at the core of what it meant to be human; it was the possession of such knowledge that, in some sense, distinguished humans from animals.

In producing the *Xin Tang shu* tables, Ouyang also collaborated extensively with the historian Lü Xiaqing 呂夏卿 (*jinshi* 1042). Lü was known to have "mastered the study of clan genealogies" 通譜學, most of which would have consisted of Tang era compilations that had survived

---

3. Needless to say, by knowing the maternal uncle, one can conclude that that man's father is the father-in-law of the deceased's own father.

4. Because it is often difficult to demonstrate the parentage of a son-in-law, sons-in-law often appear as the sole members of their patrilines in the database.

5. *Ouyang Xiu quan ji* 136:2146.

by chance into the eleventh century.[6] The Southern Song scholar Hong Mai 洪邁 (1123–1202) observed that "the genealogical tables of chief ministers in *Xin Tang* [*shu*] all transmit [knowledge from] the clan genealogies of each family" 新唐宰相世系表皆承用逐家譜牒.[7] But the two editors consulted other source materials as well. In a note concerning the eighth-century stele of one of his own forebears—a certain Ouyang Wei* 歐陽琟 (697–761)—Ouyang Xiu revealed how he and Lü went about their work. Using the "old genealogy transmitted by the family" 家所傳舊譜 as a starting point, the two men collated this text with information culled from the dynastic history *Chen shu* 陳書, from the early-ninth-century national genealogy *Yuanhe xingzuan* 元和姓纂, from Ouyang Wei's stele, as well as from the excavated tomb epitaph of another ancestor, Ouyang Chen 歐陽諶.[8] Given both the rigor of their methods and Ouyang's own ideological commitment to genealogical research, there is ample reason to believe that the *Xin Tang shu* tables are generally reliable.

In a monumental work of scholarship, the contemporary archaeologist Zhao Chao 趙超 tested the accuracy of these tables by collating them against thousands of Tang era inscriptions.[9] Although Zhao identified a certain number of errors, overall his research strongly corroborates the accuracy of the tables. In compiling the biographical database for the present study, I have arrived at the same conclusion, finding it almost always possible to reconcile data from excavated epitaphs with the *Xin Tang shu* genealogies.[10] Discrepancies are usually minor, involv-

---

6. *SS* 331:10658.

7. Hong Mai, *Rongzhai suibi* 6:83. Although Hong Mai goes on to ridicule some of the errors in the *Xin Tang shu* tables, the errors he identifies concern the distant preimperial past. He does not seem to question the accuracy of the much more recent, Tang era genealogical information.

8. *Ouyang Xiu quan ji* 140:2250. Lü and Ouyang were not alone in employing epigraphic material in their genealogical research. In the eleventh century, the father of Han Qi 韓琦 (1008–75) is also said to have collected tomb epitaphs in an attempt to reconstruct the family's ancestry. See Ebrey, "Early Stages," p. 25.

9. Zhao Chao, *Xin Tang shu zaixiang*. In this work, the author brings together the collation notes to the genealogical tables composed by a number of scholars, to which he adds his own commentaries. Zhao Chao's use of inscriptional material is particularly worth paying attention to since he has coedited three volumes of epitaph transcriptions.

10. One of the few exceptions involves the family of the eighth-century chief minister Lü Yin 呂諲 (715–65). It is difficult to reconcile the epitaphs of his brother Lü Dejun

ing, for example, mistaking a posthumous office for an individual's last substantive office or a courtesy name for a personal name.¹¹ Given the pervasiveness with which men adopted the sons of their brothers—for example, when they did not have male heirs of their own—it also sometimes happened that an uncle was mistaken for a father.¹²

Additional genealogical data can be culled from a few other sources. Biographies in the two Tang standard histories occasionally identify fathers and grandfathers not mentioned in the genealogical tables. The most important chronicle surveying the Tang period, *Zizhi tongjian* 資治通鑑, as well as the annotations to this text by the Yuan scholar Hu Sanxing 胡三省 (1230–1302) also sometimes mention an individual's father or son.¹³ Song dynasty epigraphic collections, especially Chen Si's 陳思 (fl. 1225–64) *Baoke congbian* 寶刻叢編, can be useful as well, because they catalog inscriptions that have since been lost. Chen's cata-

---

呂德俊 (697–762) and father Lü Cangyuan 呂藏元 (669–736) with the genealogical table of chief ministers. Note, however, that either source of genealogical information implies he came from a capital-based family that had served in government since before the founding of the Tang.

11. In another commonly encountered problem involving names, the first of a two-character given name is sometimes left out or there is confusion over the multiple personal names a man might use in his lifetime. In the case of two-character given names, the generational component of the name appears to have been optional. For example, the epitaph of Zhi Zhijian 支志堅 (812–61) lists twelve of his brothers. Although several of these brothers are known in other inscriptions by names that adhered to the pattern 叔X, the character 叔 is dropped from all of their names in this inscription. The fluidity of people's given names is most apparent early in their lives. Even if one disregards infant nicknames 小名, the names of children often differ between the epitaph of a husband and that of his spouse. Compare, for example, the epitaphs of Dong Tangzhi 董唐之 (804–58) and of his wife, Ms. Wang 王氏 (824–70). It is not surprising, then, that the names of sons (as opposed to the names of ancestors) are more likely to diverge from the names of sons given in the *Xin Tang shu* tables.

12. For one of many examples of a man adopting his brother's son, see the epitaph of Wei Ting 韋挺 (770–825). Another particularly interesting example involves the epitaph of Miao Hongben (797–855), which explicitly states that his father had been adopted by his father's uncle. The epitaphs of two of Miao's brothers as well as the genealogical table of chief ministers simply state that the father is the son of the uncle, without mentioning the adoption. In addition to mistaking an uncle for a father, sometimes the *Xin Tang shu* tables skip a generation, listing a man's grandfather as his father.

13. Although it is very unusual for standard history biographies to identify the spouses of their subjects, the biographies of imperial princesses are exceptional in identifying their marriage partners. For the biographies of imperial princesses, see *XTS* j. 83.

log does not include the texts of transcriptions, but it does indicate where the inscriptions were found, which helps to localize the residences of certain patrilines. Finally, over the last few centuries, scholars have succeeded in reconstructing large portions of the imperially sponsored national genealogy *Yuanhe xingzuan*, which surveys a vast number of surnames, including those of non-Chinese families, such as the Tibetan Blon 論 clan. In his preface, the author, Lin Bao 林寶 (ninth c.), made clear the extent of his own research: "as for the various family genealogies, there are none that I have not consulted with care" 諸家圖牒, 無不參詳.[14] Although the extant edition remains incomplete, it nevertheless contains substantial genealogical information regarding pre-ninth-century individuals contained nowhere else.[15]

In the process of compiling all of this data into a single database, I took particular care to identify correctly the individuals mentioned multiple times in disparate sources. Needless to say, identical names do not necessarily indicate a single individual; additional corroborating evidence—such as the same courtesy name—is critical before making such an assumption.[16] Because sons-in-law are frequently known only by family and given names with no additional identifying information, it is usually impossible to equate them with other men of the same name.[17]

---

14. Preface to Lin Bao, *Yuanhe xingzuan fu si*, p. 1. For the Blon family, see ibid. 9:1280–82. The Blon family was originally surnamed mGar; at some point, clansmen apparently took on the Tibetan bureaucratic title *blon* as their surname. For a discussion of the Blon clan, see Tackett, "Transformation," pp. 60–61; Chen Kang, "Cong Lun Boyan muzhi."

15. Portions of this work were already lost by Southern Song times so that, by the eighteenth century, the *Siku quanshu* editors were forced to rely on a reorganized and fragmented version contained in *Yongle dadian*. Scholars of the nineteenth and twentieth centuries were able to reconstruct some missing portions of the text on the basis of additional scattered fragments.

16. Other corroborating evidence might include (a) if the two men with the same name also held the same last substantive office or offices, and this office was relatively uncommon; (b) if the two men also had fathers with the same name; and (c) if both the surname and the given name of the two men were unusual.

17. One of the problems is that sons-in-law were generally still at early stages in their careers when their names appeared in their father-in-law's epitaph. The office the son-in-law held at that time was unlikely to be his last substantive office—that is, the office by which the son-in-law would be identified in the *Xin Tang shu* tables or in epitaphs of later generations.

After duplicate names were reconciled, each group of individuals linked through the same patriline was assigned a unique clan number. In the end, the approximately thirty thousand Tang era individuals included in the database were aggregated into about four thousand patrilines. These include eighty with more than fifty known members and forty six with more than one hundred known members.[18] This database provides a means for defining large clusters of blood relatives in a far more concrete and precise way than by relying on claims to pedigree alone.

Localizing Patrilines

Once clusters of related kinsmen have been identified, it is possible to determine where each of these patrilines was based in the late Tang. Indeed, given a family's desire to bury its dead together in order to facilitate the performance of rituals at the family cemetery, it is highly likely that the epitaph of one single individual reveals the place of burial of the great majority of his kinsmen and that one might thus be able to localize the place of residence of entire clans on the basis of a relatively limited number of epitaphs. It is the premise of this study, based on the overwhelming evidence of the genealogical record, that members of each patriline resided and were buried in the same region and that, in the case of political elites, virtually all resided in a relatively restricted area composed of the twin Tang capitals and the adjoining capital corridor.

Indeed, a systematic examination of the largest elite lineages provides strong empirical evidence for such a hypothesis. Figures 3.1 and 3.2 depict the family trees of several of the largest reconstructed Tang patrilines among the political elite. These trees identify clansmen whose places of burial are known—or for whom the place of burial of a wife is known—on the basis of burial data contained in tomb epitaphs or funerary steles. As in chapter 2, temporary 權 burials are disregarded unless the epitaph in question explicitly indicates that the temporary burial was near the ancestral cemetery. Besides extant epitaphs, these figures also include data on the places of discovery of a number of spirit-path steles—funerary biographies placed outside of the tomb—as recorded in the Song

---

18. In addition, there were 226 patrilines with more than fifteen known members. See "Fig 3_note18 Top clans in number of known members" in database.

a. Patriline 6091: Longxi Li (Guzang branch)　隴西(姑臧房)李氏

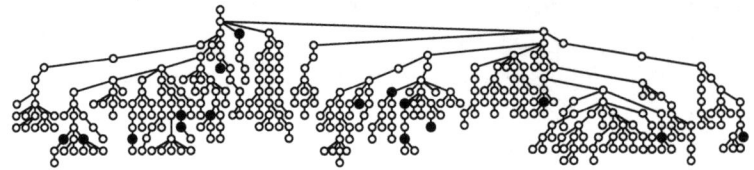

b. Patriline 5791: Le'an Sun　樂安孫氏

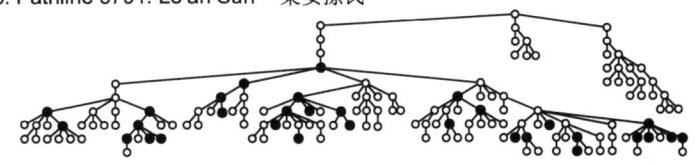

c. Patriline 5782: Jingzhao Wei (Yun Gong branch)　京兆(鄖公房)韋氏

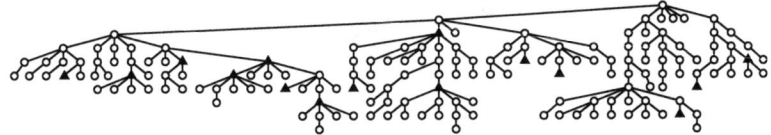

d. Patriline 6035: Qinghe Cui (lesser branch)
清河(小房)崔氏

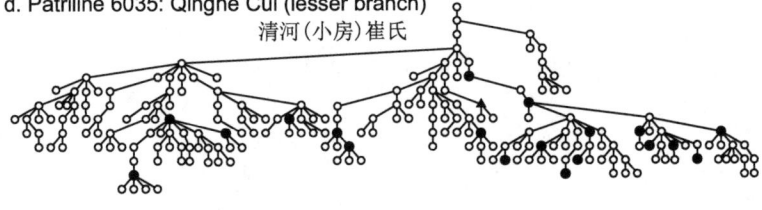

e. Patriline 8196: Henan Yu
河南于氏

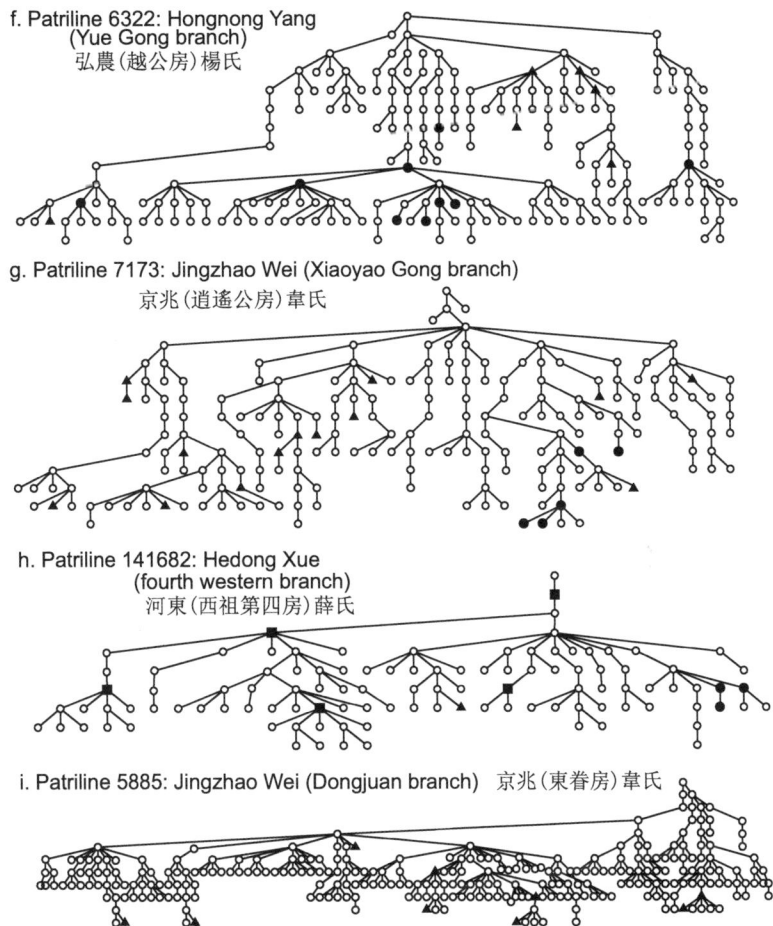

FIGURE 3.1. Places of burial of members of select patrilines

All family trees were drawn with NodeXL using the Sugiyama algorithm. Patrilines are identified by number (as recorded in the database) as well as by great clan (and subbranch) name. ● = individual (or wife) buried in Luoyang or neighboring prefectures of Mengzhou and Zhengzhou; ▲ = Chang'an or neighboring prefecture of Huazhou; ■ = elsewhere in the capital corridor; ○ = place of burial unknown. Temporary 權 burials are ignored unless it is unambiguous that the temporary burial was near the ancestral cemetery. A few individuals were eliminated from trees to reduce clutter.

dynasty epigraphic collection *Baoke congbian*.[19] The figures distinguish three regions: Luoyang and vicinity, Chang'an and vicinity, and the capital corridor. With only a single exception, no Tang era tomb epitaphs of any of these families have been discovered outside of the capital region.[20]

A survey of the family trees of most of the largest reconstructed patrilines reveals a limited number of patterns. In many cases, epitaphs provide nearly irrefutable evidence that the family was buried in its entirety in a single region (fig. 3.1a, b, c) or predominantly in a single region (fig. 3.1d, e). There are also examples of patrilines with subbranches in both capital cities or at more than one location in the capital corridor (fig. 3.1f, g, h). The particular branch of the Hedong Xue clan depicted in figure 3.1h is probably typical of clans in the eighth and ninth centuries that seem still to have been in the process of relocating from a base in the corridor to either Chang'an or Luoyang. Most known pre–An Lushan burials of both the Hedong Xue and the Hedong Pei clans took place at the sites of clan origin, in Hezhong 河中府 and Jiangzhou 絳州, respectively (both within the Hedong region).[21] In the late Tang, by contrast, most members of the two clans were buried in one of the two capitals. In these cases, even though the geographic scope of the family was not confined to a single capital city, the burials were all within the zone that includes the two capitals and the intervening corridor.

Figure 3.2 provides more precise details on the places of burial of two particular Luoyang-based patrilines, consisting, respectively, of the "greater northern" and "second northern" branches of the Fanyang Lu clan. In the first case, one can make out several important subbranches of the family, including one buried exclusively in the Beimang hills just north of Luoyang and one buried near Mount Wan'an south of the

---

19. Although the texts of these inscriptions—which would indicate if the burials were "temporary" and if they were at the site of the ancestral cemetery—do not survive, it is unlikely that an expensive stele of this type would have been erected at the site of a temporary burial. By contrast, epitaphs—as opposed to spirit-path steles—cited in *Baoke congbian* were excluded precisely because one cannot determine if the burial was "temporary" or not.

20. The sole exception involves an inscription for the wife of a Fanyang Lu clansman found near Fanyang (modern-day Beijing) that dates to the very first decade of Tang rule.

21. See "Fig 1_note54 Pei clan home base over time" and "Fig 3_note21 Xue clan home base over time" in database.

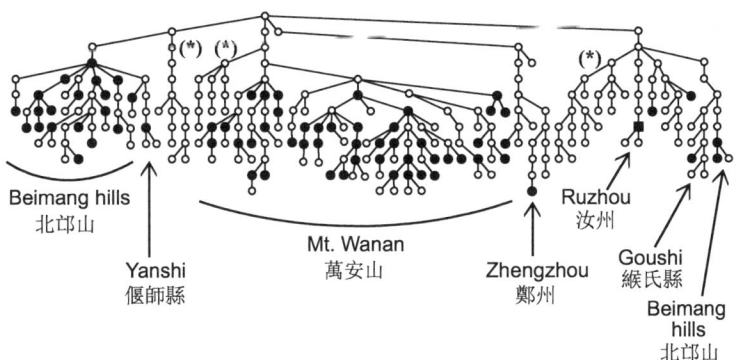

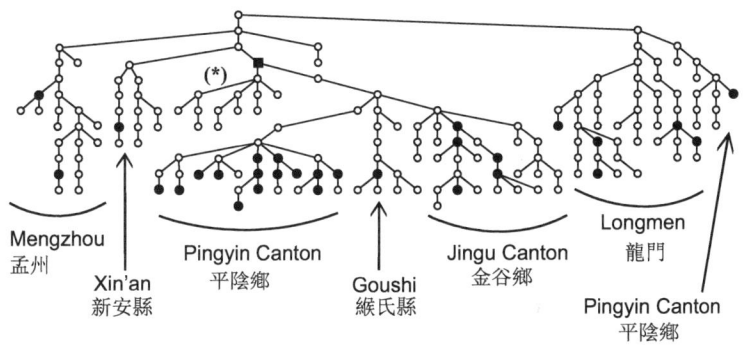

FIGURE 3.2. Suburbs of burial of branches of two Luoyang-based patrilines
Family trees drawn as described in figure 3.1. (*) = patriline subbranch with no burial data.

city. It appears that a few of these subbranches subdivided themselves further, establishing new cemeteries elsewhere—including in Yanshi and Goushi Counties, and Ruzhou and Zhengzhou Prefectures—but all were within a fifty-kilometer radius of the Eastern Capital. In the case of the "second northern" branch of the clan, one can also discern several subbranches: two with cemeteries in the Beimang hills, in Jingu and Pingyin Cantons, respectively; one in Mengzhou, a few kilometers north of Luoyang; a fourth at Longmen, just south of the city; and two more at nearby Xin'an and Goushi Counties. Clearly, subbranches of these two patrilines did establish cemeteries in new locations—perhaps when an older cemetery filled up—but the new sites were always within the same relatively small general region in which the family was based.[22]

Given the interment patterns depicted in figure 3.2, one can better understand why the place of burial of many subbranches of even the largest patrilines remains unknown. The identification of the various clan cemeteries in figure 3.2 has depended on the chance discovery of one tomb at each discrete location. After the discovery of a first tomb at a given site, archaeologists or tomb robbers would commonly excavate the neighboring tombs, leading to the discovery of a cluster of epitaphs for closely related kinsmen. But without the discovery of the initial tomb, the place of burial of that entire sub branch of the family would remain unknown. Indeed, in the case of the Fanyang Lus, no burial data exists for several sub branches—marked by asterisks in figure 3.2. These asterisks undoubtedly represent clusters of clansmen interred at yet undiscovered branch cemeteries that were, nevertheless, situated in all likelihood in the Luoyang area. Figure 3.11 depicts an additional patriline with incomplete burial data. Although epitaphs excavated to date for this family have been found exclusively in the Chang'an region, there is no burial data for most of the subbranches. Yet, as in the case of the Fanyang Lus, it is highly probable that all subbranches buried their dead in Chang'an as well, in branch cemeteries that have not yet been discovered.

Finally, one can consider the case of families for which burial data exists for only one or two members. Often, the data in question comes not from the discovery of tombs but from epitaphs included in literary collections or from records preserved in *Baoke congbian*. Unlike the fruits of archaeological excavations, these two sources would not normally include inscriptions for clusters of related kinsmen. Nevertheless, given the clan burial patterns revealed in figure 3.1, one can assume, I would argue, that even a single epitaph can be sufficient to identify the general region of interment of most members of a patriline.

---

22. Whereas one might imagine that a subbranch of a Luoyang family that had moved away from Luoyang might continue to bury family members there for a generation or two, it is difficult to believe that a family that had in any case decided to establish a new cemetery at some distance from the old cemetery would select a location far from where family members then resided.

Geographic Distribution and Size of the Late Tang Political Elite

The methodologies described above provide powerful tools for determining with some precision both the geographic distribution of the dominant political elite of the late Tang and its overall size. Figure 3.3 identifies the regions of burial of the seventy-five patrilines with the largest number of known officeholders. This group of families included the imperial clan as well as numerous subdivisions of the "marriage-ban clans," notably five branches of the Boling Cui clan and four branches each of the Qinghe Cui, Zhaojun Li, and Fanyang Lu clans. Several thousand men from these seventy-five families are known to have served in nationally prominent offices over the course of the ninth century.[23] Moreover, because of their large sizes, these patrilines constitute a particularly valuable sample for assessing geographic distribution.[24] Indeed, all but two of the seventy-five can be localized.

Figure 3.3 provides an alternative means of corroborating the conclusions of chapter 2—that the dominant political elite of the late Tang was concentrated at the political center of the empire. Of patrilines for which burial data exists, 97 percent (71 of 73) were based in the capital region. Of the two apparently based in the provinces, one—the family of the early-eighth-century chief minister Zhang Jiuling 張九齡 (678–740), who hailed from Shaozhou 韶州 in the far south—may well have been in the process of relocating to the capital by the ninth century; one of Zhang's descendants was, in fact, buried in Luoyang in 837.

But if Chang'an and Luoyang both possessed high concentrations of upper-class families serving in nationally prominent offices generation after generation, the two cities differed in important ways in the compositions of their elite populations. Overall, the evidence suggests

---

23. After estimating the dates of death of all clansmen (using techniques described below), one can date the deaths of approximately five thousand members of these clans to the ninth century. See "Fig 3_note23 Top 75 clans death dates by half century" in database. A quick survey of samples of these clansmen suggests that most held offices of national prominence.

24. Whereas it is not uncommon to encounter zero surviving epitaphs for small clans with few individuals, it is much more likely that burial data survives for at least one member of the larger clans.

Place of burial	Number of clans
Capital region (including capital corridor)	71
Luoyang predominantly	35
Chang'an predominantly	10
Elsewhere	2
No data	2

FIGURE 3.3. Places of burial of the top seventy-five officeholding patrilines

See the main text for methodological details. Patrilines are localized to the capital region if the number of known burials in Luoyang, Chang'an, or the capital corridor exceeds the number of known burials elsewhere by a factor of at least four. "Luoyang predominantly" and "Chang'an predominantly" mean burials in Luoyang or Chang'an, respectively, exceed burials elsewhere in the capital region by a factor of at least four. "No data" indicates that there is no burial data for any family member. All temporary 權 burials are excluded from calculations.

that the Eastern Capital of Luoyang was a more important home base for the largest officeholding families. Of the 71 capital-based patrilines described above, 48 percent (34/71) were predominantly based in Luoyang, 14 percent (10/71) predominantly in Chang'an, and the remainder had subbranches distributed in both Chang'an and Luoyang or in the corridor in between. As shown in figure 3.4, the vast majority of men buried in Luoyang were civil bureaucrats, whereas only a small minority had made their careers in the military, primarily through service in the Eastern Capital Command 東都留守 or the Henan prefectural army. By contrast, the Chang'an elite was more diverse. There was a much larger percentage of military men (24 percent), presumably reflecting the greater concentration of military troops in the Western Capital. One also finds a large number of epitaphs for eunuchs (20 percent), who, in imitation of their civilian bureaucrat counterparts, took on wives and adopted sons. Among the more influential multigenerational eunuch clans—whose patrilines were based on adoption rather than birth—one finds the descendants of Liu Honggui* 劉弘規 (775–826) and of Xuanzong's eunuch-advisor Gao Lishi 高力士 (690–762).

Luoyang and Chang'an also differed in the relative success of their elites in attaining the office of chief minister, the most powerful and prestigious position in the Chinese bureaucracy. As tabulated in figure 3.5, among Luoyang epitaphs, no fewer than 41 percent were composed for descendants of the patrilines of such ministers. By contrast, 20 percent in Chang'an, 21 percent in the capital corridor, and just 1 percent

Elite type	Luoyang		Chang'an	
Civil bureaucrats	405	(91%)	172	(56%)
Military men	42	(9%)	72	(24%)
Eunuchs	0	(0%)	61	(20%)
Total	447	(100%)	305	(100%)

FIGURE 3.4. Major types of capital elites (Chang'an versus Luoyang)

Includes only officeholding males with excavated epitaphs; excludes elite types seldom encountered among excavated epitaphs from the capitals (e.g., imperial princes, religious masters).

Region	Percentage of epitaphs for kinsmen of chief ministers	
Chang'an	20%	(110/539)
Luoyang	41%	(388/950)
Capital Corridor	21%	(7/33)
Elsewhere	1%	(6/586)

FIGURE 3.5. Percentage of burials for kinsmen or kinswomen of chief ministers (by region)

Individuals are identified as "kin" of a chief minister if they belonged to a patriline that produced a chief minister at any time during the Tang dynasty. Only excavated epitaphs are counted; temporary burials are excluded unless they are explicitly said to have occurred at or near the ancestral cemetery.

elsewhere claimed such an ancestry. Given that many of these patrilines produced only a single chief minister, one should think of them as representing a subset of a pool of influential political lineages. Thus, among the wealthier strata of residents in the capital region in general and in Luoyang in particular, a very large percentage descended from the most powerful Tang bureaucratic families. These same families were nearly entirely absent from the social landscape elsewhere in the empire.

Finally, the extraordinary richness of the genealogical record allows us to estimate the total population of the capital elite at the end of the Tang. The details of the calculation are a bit complex (see appendix B for a full account). Since we know, for the period 800 to 880, the total number of (1) chief ministers and their descendants, (2) inscriptions found for this group of individuals, and (3) inscriptions found for all capital elites, it is possible to extrapolate the total number of adult male capital elites (over the age of fifteen) during the eighty-year span, which comes to 37,510. Thus, from what we know of life expectancy, it seems likely that about 19,700 were alive at any given moment in this period.

It should be stressed that this can only be a very approximate figure. It is notable, nonetheless, that it is of the same order of magnitude as that of the total number of ranked officials in the regular bureaucracy during the Tang.[25] Unfortunately, there is insufficient data to assess the size of provincial elites using the same methods. It is clear, however, that the capital elite represented a relatively small group of people. Despite dominating bureaucratic positions, it constituted only a tiny fraction—less than one-tenth of one percent—of the total population of Tang China, generally estimated to have been over 50 million.[26]

The Social Landscape of the Capitals

The dominant political families of the late Tang were not only concentrated in the geographic zone around the two capital cities, they were also bound together by ties of kinship. Figure 3.6 depicts a large network of marriage ties involving Tang elite families. Each vertex represents a single patriline; the lines connecting the vertices denote marriage connections, with thicker lines indicating a greater number of known ties between the two given families. The shapes and the shading of each vertex indicates, respectively, the family's home base (Chang'an, Luoyang, the capital corridor, or elsewhere) and the length of the family's bureaucratic service. Included in the figure are all father-in-law–son-in-law relationships documented in ninth-century epitaphs as well as a number mentioned in late-eighth-century epitaphs and in other historical texts.[27] Most marriages were contracted in the period from 750 to

---

25. Specifically, as of the year 737, there were 18,805 officials belonging to the Nine Ranks. See Bol, *This Culture*, p. 41.

26. For a table listing the various population figures for the mid-eighth century, which hovered around 50 million, see Yang Zihui, *Zhongguo lidai renkou*, p. 537. As these were official census figures, they did not include unregistered individuals; thus, the true population was probably somewhat higher. After the An Lushan Rebellion, the central government's ability to take accurate censuses declined substantially, so ninth-century population figures are not reliable. Nevertheless, the population is unlikely to have declined substantially from mid-eighth-century levels.

27. In particular, I also included marriage ties mentioned in the dynastic history biographies of late Tang individuals, including imperial princesses, as well as marriage ties mentioned in relevant chapters of *ZZTJ*. Although I have not systematically entered data into the database from pre-800 epitaphs, I did include the data from a certain number of these earlier epitaphs in figure 3.6.

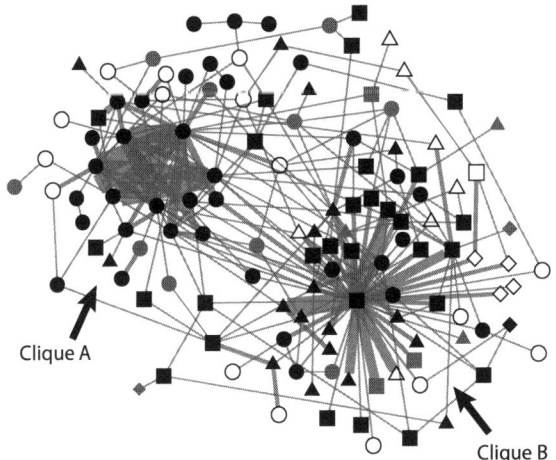

FIGURE 3.6. Marriage network of late Tang elite families

Each shape represents a single patriline, as the term has been defined in the text of this chapter. Thicker lines represent a larger number of known marriage ties. Shapes indicate home base: circles = patrilines based primarily in Luoyang; triangles = patrilines in Chang'an; squares = patrilines in the corridor between Luoyang and Chang'an, or in both Luoyang and Chang'an; large diamonds = patrilines outside of the capital region; small diamonds = patrilines whose home base cannot be identified. Colors indicate length of family officeholding tradition: black shapes = patrilines who served in office nearly every generation since before the founding of the Sui; grey shapes = patrilines who served since the Sui; white shapes = patrilines for which there is no documentary evidence that members served in office in the Sui or earlier.

850, although some may have dated to an earlier period. Unfortunately, it is not possible to identify unambiguously the natal patrilines of most spouses and sons-in-law mentioned by name in epitaphs; these marriage ties are excluded. In addition, in order to avoid cluttering the diagram, patrilines containing fewer than fifteen known members and those with no documented ties to any families in the network are also excluded.[28]

Although not comprehensive due to the limitations of surviving data, the marriage network depicted in figure 3.6 can be thought of as a visual representation of the dominant political elite of the late Tang. With only

---

28. Note that many of the very small "patrilines" are reconstructed from epitaphs for individuals with no confirmed genealogical link to the large clans but who—on the basis of their claims as well as their places of burial—were nevertheless almost certainly descendants of these larger clans. As more epitaphs come to light, some of the small clans in the dataset will merge with the larger clans.

six exceptions (the six large diamonds on the right side of the figure), its component patrilines were all based in the capital region. Most clans had held office generation after generation since either the Sui dynasty (grey vertices) or the pre-Sui period (black vertices); many of the other clans (white vertices) may also have had similarly lengthy officeholding traditions, but this cannot be demonstrated from extant data. The marriage network included 65 of the 75 patrilines with the largest numbers of known officeholders.[29] With a combined membership in the ninth century of 5,450 capital-based individuals, the network represented over three-fifths (5,450/8,746) of known capital elites.[30] It included the imperial house, a number of military families, and the clans of the eminent ninth-century writers and poets Du Mu, Bai Juyi, Liu Zongyuan, Han Yu, and Yuan Zhen. In addition, 72 of 104 chief ministers serving in the period 800 to 880 were from clans appearing on this diagram.[31] The only component of the political power elite not represented was the corps of eunuchs.

Given that only a fraction of all marriage connections have been identified, the density of the marriage network is all the more remarkable. Consider the example of a certain Ms. Li* 李氏 (d. 874). From her epitaph, we learn that her mother, grandmother, and great-grandmother all descended from the "second northern" branch of the Xingyang Zheng clan 滎陽北祖第二房鄭氏, yet only her mother's father is identified by name, so only this one tie is included in the diagram. Cases of this sort are common. Thus, as new inscriptions come to light, they will likely demonstrate that many of the marriage ties represented in figure 3.6 were much thicker than currently depicted. Anecdotal evidence of the impact of a high degree of inbreeding is sometimes evident, as in the epitaph of Lu Zhizong* 盧知宗 (816–74), who married in succession two women from a clan with which his family had several known ties. His four sons born of the principal wives were "extremely odd in appearance" 器貌特異, and all died young. Only Lu's two sons born of concubines 別子 were perfectly healthy. Indeed, the widespread practice of concubinage and the recognition of the sons of concubines as

---

29. See "Fig 3_note29 Top 75 in marriage network" in database.
30. See "Fig 3_note30 Marriage net total capital membership" in database.
31. See "Fig 3_note31 Chief ministers in marriage net" in database.

legitimate heirs probably ensured a fairly diverse gene pool despite the intensive endogamy.

A more careful examination of the marriage network reveals that it was organized around two prominent clusters (clique A and clique B). Figure 3.7 focuses on these two cliques, eliminating the clans from figure 3.6 that were not closely linked to the cliques' core families.[32] There were several crucial distinctions between these two groups of families. Clique A had no single dominant patriline, whereas clique B was organized around the imperial clan. Clique A had few ties to the military, whereas clique B included several military families, including the descendants of Guo Ziyi 郭子儀 (697–781), the great war hero who helped put down the An Lushan Rebellion, as well as the descendants of three Hebei military governors—the former northeastern tribesman Zhang Xiaozhong 張孝忠 (730–91), governor of Yiwu Province; Tian Chengsi 田承嗣 (704–78), governor of autonomous Weibo Province; and the Khitan Wang Wujun 王武俊 (735–801), governor of autonomous Chengde Province (fig. 3.7a). Perhaps even more striking is the fact that, although clique B included many important patrilines, most were branches of the "northwestern" aristocracy, as defined by the Tang genealogist Liu Fang (fig. 3.7b). Clique B contained virtually no members of the prestigious "marriage-ban" clans from "East of the Mountains." The core of clique A, by contrast, was composed almost entirely of subbranches of these most eminent clans (fig. 3.7c).

Differences in the geographic distribution of the two cliques are remarkable. Clique B exhibited a greater diversity, with a few Luoyang-based clans, several Chang'an-based clans, and a few other clans based in multiple locations in the Chang'an-Luoyang region. Clique A, in contrast, consisted almost entirely of families residing in Luoyang, with only two exceptions, both of which had, nevertheless, at least a few family members buried near the Eastern Capital. Given the existence of such a clique, it is not surprising that a late Tang elite male from Luoyang was over seven times more likely (177 vs. 24) to marry into a Luoyang-based elite family than into a Chang'an-based one.[33]

---

32. It is possible that, as more epitaphs are discovered, it will become more apparent in what ways the excluded families were themselves also tied to one or both of the cliques.

33. See "Fig 3_note33 Marriage ties of Luoyang males" in database.

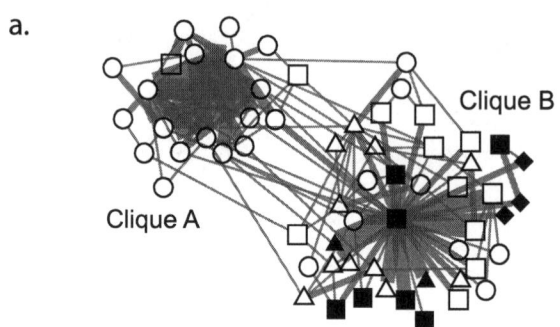

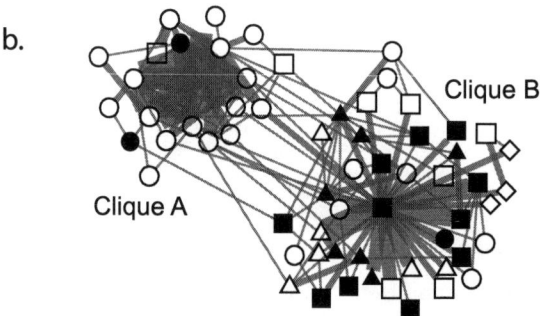

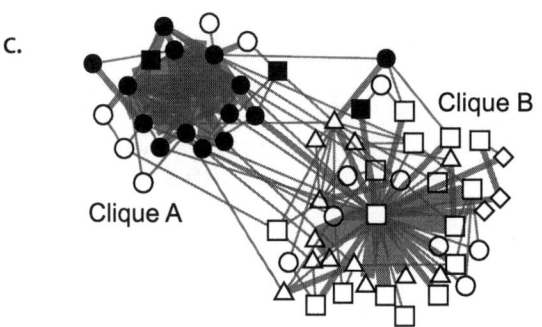

FIGURE 3.7. Composition of capital-based marriage cliques. (a) Military families: black shapes = patrilines with multiple generals among kinsmen. (b) Northwestern aristocracy: black shapes = Guanzhong and Daibei patrilines, as identified by Liu Fang. (c) Marriage-ban clans: black shapes = subbranches of seven marriage-ban clans.

Because the Western Capital of Chang'an was the site of the imperial court, Luoyang-based elites regularly spent time there as well, serving in central government offices, preparing for the examinations, or accompanying relatives. Since they would occasionally die while sojourning there, one can get a sense of where they lived in the city—be it at an inn or in a private residence—on the basis of their places of death as recorded in their epitaphs. The distribution of Luoyang elites within the wards of Chang'an suggests that residential proximity correlated with marriage ties. Figure 3.8 depicts the residency patterns of four groups: civil bureaucrats from Chang'an-based families, eunuchs, members of clique A, and members of clique B. Generally speaking, Chang'an-based civil bureaucrats lived in wards scattered all across the capital city. But some groups of families were confined to fairly circumscribed neighborhoods.[34] Eunuchs concentrated in the northern wards, on either side of the imperial palace. Both of the highly endogamous marriage cliques, by contrast, tended to reside together in the same small cluster of wards, in this case south of both the Administrative City and the Eastern Market.[35]

In sum, a fairly strong correlation existed between the geographic localization of clans and the scope of their marriage ties. Ch'en Jo-shui 陳弱水 came to a similar conclusion in his recent study of Tang period eunuchs. Ch'en discovered not only that eunuchs intermarried with certain military families, he also showed that members of this "community" 社群 of military and eunuch clans lived together in the same wards of Chang'an.[36] Similarly, the tightly knit marriage network composed of the powerful clans that dominated Tang political life was heavily concentrated in the single region surrounding the two Tang capital cities of Chang'an and Luoyang—a region that could be traversed in a matter of a few days. One of the two marriage cliques that constituted the foundation of the marriage network demonstrated an even sharper regional concentration. The bulk of clans in clique A, the cluster of families descending from the very most eminent aristocratic families, were

---

34. For an excellent and detailed description of Chang'an's social landscape, see Seo, *Chōan no toshi kekaku*, esp. pp. 175–226.

35. Extant literary sources confirm that the east-central part of the city was indeed home to many prominent Tang figures of the seventh and eighth centuries. See Xiong, *Sui-Tang Chang'an*, pp. 219–24.

36. Ch'en Jo-shui, "Tangdai Chang'an."

a. Chang'an-based civil bureaucrats

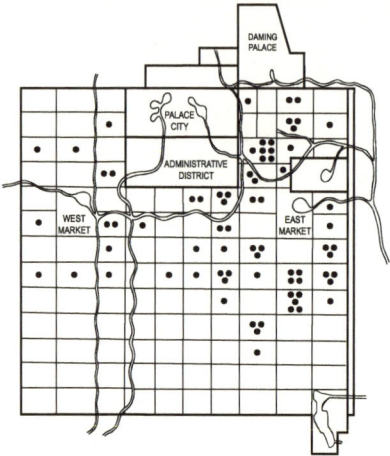

b. Eunuchs

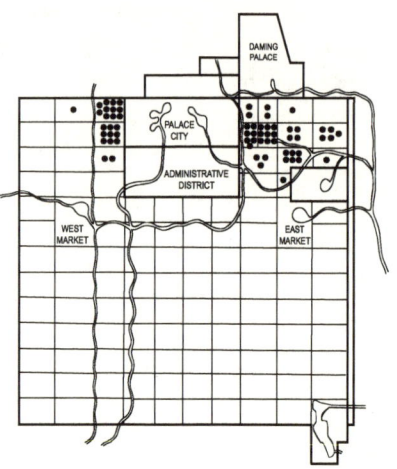

c. Members of clique A

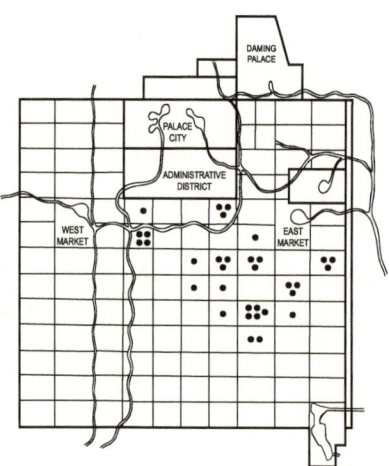

d. Members of clique B

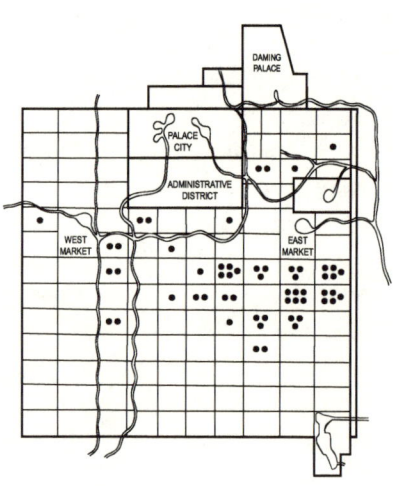

FIGURE 3.8. Elite residency patterns in Chang'an. (a) Chang'an-based civil bureaucrats. (b) Eunuchs. (c) Members of clique A. (d) Members of clique B.

Dots represent places of death of single individuals. Base maps adapted from Xu Song, *Zengding Tang liangjing chengfang kao*, p. 17; Victor Xiong, *Sui-Tang Chang'an*, fig. 8.1. Map formats inspired by Seo Tatsuhiko, *Chōan no toshi kekaku*, esp. pp. 196, 198; Rong Xinjiang, ed., *Tang yanjiu*, vol. 15.

based in Luoyang. When they did sojourn in Chang'an to serve in office, they resided together in a small cluster of wards at the center of the city.

Although there are no examples of Tang writers reflecting on the close link between geography and marriage, the link is not entirely unexpected. One would imagine that individuals would choose to live near their relatives; simultaneously, they would choose marriage partners for their children from among the people with whom they were most likely to interact. In either case, physical proximity played a role in reinforcing marriage ties. It was the very geographic concentration of the dominant political elite that helped ensure its strongly endogamous marriage patterns. As we shall now see, marriage endogamy also helps to explain the Tang political elite's remarkable longevity despite avenues of upward social mobility that might otherwise have threatened its monopoly on political power.

Marriage Networks and Social Capital

Family relationships—both by birth and by marriage—invariably played important roles in Tang China in a variety of contexts. Orphans from elite families were often brought up by their paternal uncles, who might also help to arrange their marriages.[37] Men without male heirs frequently adopted a nephew or another close kinsman.[38] After her husband's death, a widow might return to her natal clan to live with her parents or with a brother or uncle.[39] And when war or rebellion broke out, clansmen helped each other to survive, even pooling their resources to ransom a relative captured by enemy soldiers.[40] Finally, as frequently noted in epitaphs, men were generally responsible for arranging the burials of their kinsmen. Thus, after Li Duanyou* 李端友 (811–53) died in Yanzhou 延州, where he was serving in the prefectural government, a

---

37. Epitaphs of Dugu Yu 獨孤郁 (776–815), Han Fu 韓復 (783–851), Ms. Li 李氏 (830–55), and Ms. Pei 裴氏 (792–821).

38. The adoption of a kinsman was very common. For one example, see the epitaph of Cui Shao 崔紹 (834–77). In some cases, when a man died without a male heir to take care of the sacrificial rituals, he was granted post-mortem a son from among his nephews.

39. Epitaphs of Ms. Pei 裴氏 (792–821) and Ms. Lu 盧氏 (811–58).

40. Ebrey, *Aristocratic Families*, pp. 97–98; epitaph of Cui Yifu 崔夷甫 (704–56). For the ransomed clansman, see epitaph of Bi Jiong 畢坰 (751–811).

brother accompanied his body back to Luoyang, an uncle financed the burial, and the deceased's nephew was asked to officiate at the funeral. When Wei Jinghong* 衛景弘 (812–55) died, his eldest brother sent 200 strings of cash from Sichuan to finance the burial and commissioned a cousin to pen the text of the epitaph. Countless epitaphs were composed by brothers, sons, or cousins of the same surname.[41]

But it was not just the paternal side of the family to whom one could turn for assistance in times of need. Many children of elite families went to live with maternal grandparents or with one of their mothers' brothers or sisters after their fathers died (or, in one case, after he had run off).[42] In some cases, a man might formally adopt his sister's child.[43] There were also instances of a young man marrying the daughter of the maternal uncle who raised him.[44] One woman who brought up her younger sister's orphan articulated what must have been a common sentiment: "My son is like my nephew; my nephew is like my son" 子如甥焉, 甥如子矣.[45] A widow with no kinsmen to rely upon might find shelter with her relatives by marriage, with the family of her father's sister,[46] or—more frequently—with her daughter and son-in-law.[47] Usually, such widows had no adult sons, but, in some cases, the sons had simply

---

41. Epitaphs composed by agnates are far too common to list here. For examples of a brother, son, and cousin, respectively, see epitaphs of Lu Qu 盧衢 (815–57), Ms. Li 李氏 (788–843), and Lu Houde 盧厚德 (d. c. 844).

42. Epitaphs of Huangfu Ying 皇甫映 (793–864), Lu Quanjiao 路全交 (c. 797–c. 854), (Ms.) Ma Wan 馬琬 (835–58), (Ms.) Lu Qi 盧綺 (792–850), and Li Ju 李舉 (750–814). The father who "ran off" 游不歸 appears in the epitaph of Li Hong 李弘 (754–816), who consequently brought up his younger sister's son. Other relatives could play a similar role. According to their epitaphs, Ms. Lu 盧氏 (767–818) was brought up by her elder sister, and Li Jing 李荊 (749–821) was brought up by his mother's affine, probably his maternal great-aunt.

43. Epitaph of Yuan Weicheng 袁惟承 (753–814).

44. Epitaph of Wei Xingsu 韋行素 (793–827).

45. Epitaph of Tao Ying 陶英 (737–801). For a similar example, see epitaph of Ms. Zheng 鄭氏 (762–803). The author—Ms. Zheng's affinal cousin, quite possibly the son of her father's sister—explained: "I was born and brought up in my mother's family. In the end, although I had no brothers, my [maternal cousins] treated me as one of their own blood so that our intimacy exceeded ordinary feelings" 景亮生長外家, 終無昆弟, 姊妹視猶同氣, 睦異常情.

46. Epitaph of Ms. Wei 韋氏 (802–57).

47. Epitaphs of Zheng Fang 鄭魴 (777–834), (Ms.) Bai Tiao 栢苕 (d. c. 839), Ms. Li 李氏 (720–800), Ms. Li 李氏 (771–822), and Lu Guang 盧廣 (c. 738–c. 775).

shirked their duties. Such was the case for Ms. Li* 李氏 (740–815) from Chang'an, who lived with her daughter and son-in-law in Sichuan for many years, and whose funeral was later organized by her daughter's daughter. Her epitaph includes her own account of the indignation of her situation: "By misfortune, I have three sons, none of whom adhere to the teachings of the ancient kings. They have wandered off to other lands and have become distant from me like strangers" 吾不幸有子三人, 皆不由先王訓, 遊蕩異土, 邈如他人. A man too might spend time with his wife's relatives, while traveling, or, perhaps, when he was down and out and had nowhere else to go.[48]

Like blood relatives, relatives by marriage might also involve themselves in funerary matters. Hundreds of ninth-century epitaphs were composed and funerals organized by such relatives, often by the son-in-law. One interesting example involves Li Yuzhong 李虞仲 (772–836), whose only son had died at the age of three. When interviewing suitors seeking his daughter's hand in marriage, he insisted that they first promise to take charge of arranging his burial when his time came. After Li died in Chang'an, while serving there as vice minister of personnel, the son-in-law dutifully kept his word, returning Li's body along with that of Li's wife for burial in Luoyang. The son-in-law and his wife then brought up and educated an orphaned younger daughter, later arranging her marriage to a respectable official.[49] This case seems not to have been atypical.[50] In the case of Fan Yi* 范弈 (739–95), it was his second wife's maternal uncle who took charge of reburying him in Luoyang a decade after his death.[51] Relatives by marriage might also finance the ceremonies, as in the case of Ms. Zhang* 張氏 (761–817), whose funeral, organized by her daughter and brother, was partly paid for with a generous gift of 300 strings of cash from her son-in-law. In addition, several

---

48. According to their epitaphs, Lu Qu 盧衢 (815–57) died in his wife's family's Luoyang mansion; Lu Xian 盧況 (714–801) died, at the ripe age of eighty-eight, in a compound belonging to his wife's kinsmen; and Zheng Shaofang 鄭紹方 (768–809) died after having gone to live with his younger sister and her husband.

49. See the epitaph of Li Yuzhong's daughter Ms. Li 李氏 (814–62).

50. For other examples of young men taking the lead in organizing their father-in-laws' burials, see epitaphs of Zheng Juzhong 鄭居中 (784–837) and Ms. Zhang 張氏 (751–824).

51. For similar examples, see epitaphs of Ms. Wang 王氏 (c. 771–c. 804) and (Ms.) Zheng Xuan 鄭絢 (722–86).

children were interred in their mother's ancestral cemetery when it was inconvenient or inauspicious to relocate their bodies back to their own clan burial grounds.⁵² Similarly, Han Yu's sister-in-law Ms. Wei* 韋氏 (771–802) was buried with her son-in-law's clansmen; the defrocked monk Wang Yuanzhen* 王元貞 (c. 781–c. 860) was laid to rest alongside his mother's brother; and the military man Qing Zhixia* 青陟霞 (760–852) was buried on land belonging to the clan of his spouse's mother.

Given the importance of relatives in providing support in a wide variety of contexts, one would expect that they also played a role in helping young men advance in their government careers. Obtaining a ranked position in the regular bureaucracy was a two-step process. One first needed to be entered on the official rolls 出身, by means of which one acquired a lifetime eligibility to serve in office. An important means of gaining this status was through the hereditary *yin* 蔭 (protection) privilege, which gave high-ranking officials the right to select a specified number of sons and grandsons for government service. But there were other avenues of entry into officialdom, including an extensive period of service in a low-level clerical position or success on one of several examinations—notably the *jinshi* 進士 "civil service" examination described below.⁵³

Even after having been inscribed on the eligibility rolls, however, one was not guaranteed a salaried position. Actual appointments were controlled by a separate selection process. Promotions to ranks five and higher (among a total of nine ranks) were determined directly by the chief ministers, probably more or less as they saw fit and with no real oversight. By contrast, the formal procedures of "assessment and selection" 銓選 for posts below rank five—that is, for the bulk of the bureaucracy and for essentially all young men early in their careers—involved an examination administered by the Ministry of Personnel 吏部. This selection examination—which should not be confused with the *jinshi* examination—was held both in Luoyang and in Chang'an throughout

---

52. Epitaphs of (Ms.) Zheng Sanqing 鄭三清 (844–52), Fu Yin 傅鋆 (748–813), and (Ms.) Wang Jinpo 王金婆 (829–62).

53. Huang Ch'ing-lien, "Recruitment and Assessment," pp. 21–34; Herbert, *Examine the Honest*, pp. 20–26. In addition, there were a few less frequently exploited means of entering officialdom, including through one of the very few inherited titles of nobility; through a tie of kinship to an emperor, empress, or empress dowager; or through raising money for the government while managing public funds.

most of the dynasty. It assessed deportment, speech, calligraphy, and the ability to compose administrative documents, and was highly competitive. Mid-eighth-century sources report that only one in eight or nine men entitled to serve actually succeeded in securing employment as a ranked bureaucrat.[54]

Capital elites held a substantial advantage over their provincial peers in this system. Part of this advantage lay in cultural factors. Through their upbringing and social milieu, they invariably understood the subtle language of the aristocracy and the potential for social gaffes amid the snobbery at the capital. One hapless young man from the southeast greeted in public a eunuch he had once met, not realizing that this act would doom his chances of a successful career.[55] In addition, the language assessment portion of the selection examination probably favored men with proper metropolitan accents. Above all, however, capital elites benefited from their social connections. Figure 3.9 identifies the home base of the patrilines of ninth-century chief ministers and ministers of personnel, the men with the greatest influence over promotion decisions. Nearly all were from capital families, with Luoyang-based ones holding the lion's share of such positions. Perhaps the two most famous chief ministers of the ninth century—Niu Sengru 牛僧孺 (780–848) and Li Deyu 李德裕 (787–849)—were from families long entrenched in Chang'an and Luoyang, respectively. And the three patrilines producing the most ministers of personnel, subbranches of the Xingyang Zheng, Lanling Xiao, and Qinghe Cui clans, were all based in Luoyang.[56] Figure 3.9 also indicates that the majority of these ministers had demonstrable ties to the large capital-focused social network depicted in figure 3.6.[57] In the bureaucratic selection process, relatives

---

54. Herbert, *Examine the Honest*, esp. pp. 27–34, 67, 69. Most candidates were required to travel to one of the two capitals for the selection process. The exception was the "southern selection" 南選 system for residents of the southernmost provinces; see ibid., pp. 189–90.

55. *ZZTJ* 250:8093–94.

56. These three clans each produced three ministers of personnel over the course of the ninth century.

57. Many of the ministers without known ties to this marriage network served in the decades after 850, when genealogical data becomes increasingly sparse; a number of these men undoubtedly were linked to the marriage network, though there is no extant genealogical evidence.

	Chief ministers	Chief examiners	Ministers of personnel
Patriline home base			
Capital region	83	64	41
Luoyang primarily	39	38	26
Chang'an primarily	17	12	8
Elsewhere	0	0	0
No data	21	11	5
Total	104	75	46
Marriage network			
Ties to capital network	79	61	37
Clique A	23	24	14
Clique B	17	11	7
Clique B (excl. imperial clan)	11	7	5
No known ties	25	14	9
Total	104	75	46

FIGURE 3.9. Top ninth-century officials by patriline home base and marriage network

"Ties to capital network" refers to patrilines depicted in figure 3.6 as well as to patrilines with marriage ties to those families (but who are excluded from figure 3.6 because they had fewer than fifteen documented members). Chief ministers are identified on the basis of the *Xin Tang shu* genealogical table of chief ministers (jj. 71–75) and monograph on chief ministers (jj. 62–63). Chief examiners are identified using Xu Song, *Dengke jikao buzheng*, excluding two examiners Xu Song identified on the basis of much later local gazetteers. Ministers of personnel are identified using Yan Gengwang, *Tang pu shang cheng lang biao* 2:514–33, with one addition based on data from a recently excavated epitaph. Note the likelihood that many men for whom there is "no data" were, in fact, part of the capital-based marriage network. For example, if Watanabe Takashi is correct in equating the Liu Sanfu 劉三復 who served under Li Deyu with the Liu Sanfu who composed an epitaph for one of his Luoyang kinswomen (see discussion in chapter 4), then his son Liu Ye 劉鄴 (d. 880), who served as chief minister under two very late Tang emperors, would indeed have been a member of the marriage network, even though he is not counted as such in this figure.

of these powerful ministers were invariably in an advantageous position. There are countless examples of chief ministers intervening to promote a clansman, a son-in-law, or a sister's son. For example, immediately after Quan Deyu 權德輿 (759–818) became chief minister, he appointed his son-in-law Dugu Yu* 獨孤郁 (776–815) to the post of vice director of the Bureau of Evaluations 考功員外郎, a "pure and important" 清要 position that put Dugu on track for rapid promotion to even higher office.

In the case of lower-ranked offices, selection procedures were more routine, but political connections were no less important. Even in the case of appointments below rank five, it was necessary first to obtain the support of five metropolitan officials to serve as guarantors.[58] This requirement would have been far less daunting for members of the well-connected capital elite. Although there is no way to assess in a systematic fashion the impact of favoritism on selection, there is ample anecdotal evidence of the power of patronage.[59] Ministers of personnel had more say than any others on promotions and bureaucratic advancement, giving them enormous influence over the composition of the civil bureaucracy. It was undoubtedly for this reason that the "dictator" Li Linfu 李林甫 (683–752), chief minister late in Xuanzong's reign, arranged concurrently to hold the title of minister of personnel, a position he held from 739 until his death.[60] It was also for this reason that someone like Li Ju* 李璩 (814–71), nephew of the chief minister Li Jiang 李絳 (764–830), was able to make an impressive career. His excavated epitaph confirms that he attained a series of important positions in government, including coveted stints in the Chang'an and Luoyang metropolitan counties of Wannian and Henan. In fact, by all accounts, he seems to have been something of a dolt, unlikely to have been competitive in selection examinations. His contemporaries ridiculed him as a "profligate descendant" 紈褲 of a great family, with only poor grammar and writing skills.[61] Presumably, his successful career had initially depended on his uncle's intervention.

Besides the regularized formal appointment procedures, there were also informal selection processes involving direct recommendations. Anecdotal evidence suggests that family connections often played an important role here as well. Li Shao'an* 李少安 (759–808), for example, served as a county sheriff in Jizhou 冀州 "upon the recommendation of

---

58. Herbert, *Examine the Honest*, pp. 29–30.

59. Ibid., pp. 127–32.

60. Li Linfu was succeeded as minister of personnel by the next powerful chief minister, Yang Guozhong 楊國忠 (d. 756). See Yan Gengwang, *Tang pu shang cheng lang biao* 2:508.

61. Besides his epitaph, see Yang Jidong, "Making, Writing, and Testing," pp. 148–49; Li Fang, *Taiping guang ji* 261:2038. Although *Taiping guangji* has a variant form of Li's given name, the reference is unambiguously to the same man, as both this text and the epitaph assert that Li served as vice magistrate of Mianchi 澠池 County, Henan, early in his career.

kinsmen" 爲所親者薦. Similarly, Cui Maozao* 崔茂藻 (836–75) became sheriff of Jiaocheng 交城 County near Taiyuan on the recommendation of his second cousin 再從昆仲 Cui Yanzhao 崔彥昭 (d. 879). Even after Zhi Mo* 支謨 (829–79) had earned a *mingjing* degree, he was only able to obtain the position of administrative assistant to the Commission of Palace Construction 内作使判官 when his maternal great uncle 外叔祖 appealed to the throne on his behalf.

The patronage of relatives operating through informal channels was particularly critical in the case of scions of capital clans who, by misfortune, were trapped in provincial service. Mr. Li* 李公 (764–820) was from a Luoyang-based family; his grandfather was buried in the Beimang hills north of the Eastern Capital. His father, however, relocated to northern Hebei, probably at the time of the An Lushan Rebellion. Li grew up there and eventually served in a minor post under one of the autonomous Hebei governors. He was able to return to the capital to serve the Tang only because "his maternal uncles were all in pure and illustrious [offices]" 諸舅皆在清顯. Lu Shou* 盧綬 (751–810) began life in Binzhou 邠州, northwest of Chang'an, where his father had acquired a modest estate, probably while serving there in office. Lu lost his chance to use the *yin* privilege when his father died, so he first sought employment in the local provincial government. His last hope to serve in an office of national significance lay with his elder brother, a successful bureaucrat, who did eventually succeed in finding him a post in the regular civil service.

Because of political pressures discouraging open favoritism for one's kinsmen, it is not always easy to identify all such acts of patronage, which are often concealed from view in surviving source material. In some instances, such relationships can be reconstructed through multiple sources of genealogical data. From the funerary inscription of Lu Xiang* 盧湘 (d. 787), for example, one learns that a certain Pei Tian 裴腆 had used his influence to have Lu put in charge of taxes and transport in Sichuan. However, it is only by consulting the epitaph of Lu's kinsman Lu Chuyue* 盧處約 (780–834) in conjunction with the genealogical table of chief ministers that one discovers that Lu Xiang's second cousin Lu Shiying 盧士瑛 was married to the daughter of Pei Tian's cousin Pei Xu 裴諝. The case of Lu Pu* 盧溥 (786–850) is similar. His epitaph states only that he served in Huzhou 湖州 under the patronage of Zhang Wengui 張文規. But other sources reveal that Zhang was the son-in-law of Lu's father's cousin.⁶² It is quite possible that, in both of these cases, the men in question were bound together by additional ties of marriage not indicated in extant documentary sources. If more extensive records of this sort existed, similar webs of influence via family and marriage relationships would almost certainly be found pervasive throughout the upper reaches of Tang society.

Although the bureaucratic processes described above greatly favored the entrenched political oligarchy, it has been argued that certain institutional changes of the mid-Tang threatened the old clans' hold on power by providing new avenues of upward mobility. One such development involved the informal system used by provincial governors to bypass formal bureaucratic selection procedures, a system examined in chapter 4. But probably the change most commonly cited by historians is the expansion of the civil service examination. Empress Wu is believed to have played a particularly significant role in this development, perhaps as part of a deliberate strategy to weaken the power of the great families and promote a "newly risen class" 新興階級.⁶³ During the two centuries of Tang rule following Empress Wu's abdication, it was increasingly possible to use the examinations in lieu of the *yin* privilege to enter officialdom. Although at no time in the dynasty did the bulk of the bureaucracy hold examination degrees, an ever greater percentage of the very highest officials did. Even those officials who had acquired bureaucratic status through protection often took the examinations as well, as a way of bolstering their credentials and augmenting their chances of success.⁶⁴

Indeed, by the late Tang, the examinations had become a fixture of elite culture. Already in ninth-century texts, one begins to encounter a scattering of rags-to-riches stories not unlike those that would become so common in the Late Imperial period. In one epitaph, Han Yu describes just such an ascension: "The deceased, in the beginning, traveled all alone to Chang'an for the *jinshi* exams; he attained offices [that ranked] among the Nine Chamberlains; [his family] became a great household,

---

62. See the epitaph of the father's cousin Lu Shigong 盧士琫 (745–821) in conjunction with the appropriate section of the *XTS* genealogical table of chief ministers.
63. Chen Yinke, *Tangdai zhengzhi shi*, esp. pp. 20–24.
64. Wittfogel, "Public Office," pp. 25–30; Mao Hanguang, "Tangdai da shizu," p. 347.

his seven sons were all educated and principled, and his daughters all married famous men" 公始以進士孤身旅長安, 致官九卿, 爲大家, 七子皆有學守, 女嫁名人.[65] Also, as in later dynasties, there are sad tales of men failing the examinations on multiple attempts. The father of Lu Qu* 盧衢 (815–57) competed for the *jinshi* six times before giving up, eventually pinning his hopes on his sons. "Elevating [the status of] our clan rests on your generation" 興吾宗者, 當在汝輩, he would tell them. By the tenth century, the exams had become such an important element in elite culture that an era without them was difficult to conceive. One anachronistic anecdote evoked an imaginary parade of *jinshi* graduates before Emperor Taizong (r. 627–49), who had ruled Tang China several decades before such a ritual existed.[66]

But there are two problems with the theory that the examinations fueled upward social mobility. First, as we have seen, these tests merely granted official eligibility; the subsequent appointment procedure, including the separate selection examination, was far more important for determining the actual composition of the bureaucracy. Second, as Tonami Mamoru has argued, the civil service examinations were largely coopted by the old families and did not at all play the role that they would assume in later centuries.[67] There were a variety of reasons for this. Before the expansion of printing in the eleventh century, only wealthy and well-connected individuals had access to the manuscript editions of the books whose contents needed to be internalized if a candidate was to be successful. The Sui dynasty ancestors of the ninth-century chief minister Niu Sengru*, for example, had been granted several *qing* of land south of Chang'an and a thousand-volume library as an imperial favor. These resources were still in the family's hands three centuries later, and, according to his epitaph, were critical for Niu's studies in his youth.[68] In addition, under the influence of those in power, the examination system was modified to favor the capital-based elites. Thus, the top

---

65. Epitaph of Hu Xiang 胡珦 (740–818). As in the case of Late Imperial stories of this type, there is reason to doubt that Hu's background was really as disadvantaged as suggested in this piece.

66. Moore, *Rituals of Recruitment*, p. 174.

67. Tonami, "Chūsei kizokusei," pp. 250–54; Tonami, "Sōdai shitaifu," pp. 197–201.

68. For more on the libraries and study halls of the old elite, see Sun Guodong, "Tang Song zhi ji shehuimendi," pp. 221–24.

ten candidates from the Chang'an prefectural exams earned the status of "degree worthy" 等第, which often guaranteed them a place on the final pass list of the national exams. Another policy, called "freeing the dispatch" 拔解, allowed men living in Chang'an or Luoyang to register as candidates from elsewhere, thus bypassing entirely the prefectural level examinations.[69]

But advantages in the exams did not come only from residence in the capital. One's social network played an equally important role. Patron-client bonds were evident at all stages of the examination process. Before the tests, candidates circulated poems and prose pieces to potential patrons as well as to the chief examiner, hoping to gain the favor of a powerful ally. Later, successful graduates personally thanked their patrons in the important "ceremony of gratitude" 謝恩, demonstrating through the very performance of this ritual that their success had depended more on political connections than on an impartial exam score.[70] Rumors that the pass lists had been determined beforehand reflected persistent suspicions about the fairness of the examinations.[71] In particular, it was well understood that close relatives of the examiners held particular advantages. Thus, when the son of Gao Kai 高鍇, chief examiner from 836 to 838, repeatedly failed the exams despite these advantages, he was excoriated by his peers in a popular couplet: "one hundred twenty dung beetles cannot lift up this one piece of crap" 一百二十個蜣蜋, 推一個屎塊不上.[72]

Gao was not alone in having family connections to an examination official. Figure 3.9 reveals that all chief examiners whose clans can be localized were based in the capital region, with three times more residing in Luoyang than in Chang'an; moreover, 84 percent of them (61/75) are known to have come from patrilines belonging to the capital elite marriage network.[73] Indeed, among a sample of Chang'an and

---

69. Moore, *Rituals of Recruitment*, pp. 82–83.

70. Ibid., esp. pp. 141–52, 186–90, 204.

71. Ibid., p. 160.

72. Ibid., p. 353; Wang Dingbao, *Tang zhi yan*, p. 307. It is possible that the unusual vernacular grammar of this couplet contributed to the force of the insult.

73. The dozen examiners whose clan home base is unknown are largely men from the very late period, when it is increasingly difficult to find material to confirm their genealogies and clan home bases. Nevertheless, some of these men may indeed have

Luoyang epitaphs, one encounters the cousin and the second cousin of Yu Chengxuan 庾承宣, chief examiner in 818–819; both the father and the granddaughter of Cui Yan 崔郾, chief examiner in 827 and 828; the uncle as well as the niece of Li Jingrang 李景讓, chief examiner in 840; and the younger sister of Zheng Hao 鄭顥, chief examiner in 856 and 859.[74]

Thus, although candidates from all prefectures in the empire traveled to Chang'an to participate in the exams, success was largely monopolized by men living in the capital.[75] According to one late Tang observer, Sun Qi 孫棨 (fl. 889), who hailed from a Luoyang-based clan, even after the expansion of the examination system in the 850s, there was little room for new blood:

> Ever since the Dazhong Emperor [Xuanzong] began favoring Classical studies and paying special attention to the examinations, . . . *jinshi* recipients became especially numerous; earlier eras were incomparable [in total numbers]. But the majority were the scions of wealthy families; those from ordinary families were never more than three per year.
>
> 自大中皇帝好儒術, 特重科第 . . . 故進士自此尤盛, 曠古無儔, 然率多膏梁子弟, 平進歲不及三數人.[76]

In his well-known "Record of the Interior of a Pillow" 枕中記, Shen Jiji 沈既濟 (fl. 780s) described in striking terms the capital's monopoly over *jinshi* degrees. In the tale, a young, wealthy landowner from Handan in southern Hebei tells a master of the Dao of his great political ambitions, upon which the master presents him with a porcelain pillow. As the young man rests his head on it, he wakes up in an alternate life, in which he weds a woman of the distinguished Qinghe Cui clan. Presumably with the assistance of his wife's family, he earns a

---

been from outside of the capital region, notably Gao Ying 高郢, chief examiner in 800 and 801.

74. See, respectively, epitaphs of Yu Chenghuan 庾承歡 (767–820) and Yu Youfang 庾游方 (c. 818–c. 859); Cui Chui 崔陲 (727–91) and (Ms.) Li Daoyin 李道因 (d. 876); Li Ning 李寧 (774–856) and Ms. Li 李氏 (d. 874); and Ms. Zheng 鄭氏 (827–58). For identification of the chief examiners in question, see the relevant pages in Xu Song, *Dengke jikao buzheng*.

75. For the assertion that examination success was dominated by men from the capital, see Moore, *Rituals of Recruitment*, pp. 68–69, 80, 82, 89.

76. Sun Qi, *Beili zhi*, p. 22. Sun was, himself, a member of the Luoyang-based Le'an Sun clan (patriline 5791) depicted in figure 3.1b.

jinshi degree the very next year, has a long career in government, and marries off his own sons into a marriage network 姻媾 containing the "greatest families under Heaven" 天下望族. As he nears death, he wakes up from his dream. The *jinshi* degree, the long career, and the impressive marriage ties were but a fantasy for this son of a provincial elite family.[77]

In sum, capital elites were remarkably successful at maintaining their influence over the bureaucracy. They were the prime beneficiaries of both the *yin* privilege and the civil service examinations, allowing them to dominate membership on the official rolls. Once they gained official status, they also had advantages in the selection examinations, obtaining appointments to choice offices at the expense of those exceptional outsiders who had managed to secure eligibility for a ranked office. In some cases, the advantages enjoyed by capital elites were institutionalized, as in the case of the "degree worthy" status. Even more crucial, however, was their extensive network of kinship and marriage ties. Those linked by birth and marriage provided support for each other in a variety of contexts. In such an environment, it is no surprise that governors, ministers, and examiners served as critical political patrons to their younger relatives.

Conclusion

The previous chapter demonstrated the existence of a stark divide between elites based in the Chang'an-Luoyang region and elites based in the provinces, involving fundamental differences in terms of the geographic scope of their political influence, the length of their family traditions of officeholding, and their relationship to the bureaucratic power structure. This chapter has explored in more detail the composition of the capital elite and the reasons it managed to perpetuate itself in power for so long. In order to approach this problem, I have analyzed capital elites in terms of their membership in specific patrilines—defined not on the basis of claims to particular prestigious ancestries, but rather on the basis of kin networks reconstructed from demonstrable father-son ties. Using this approach, it has been possible to identify a fairly limited number of

---

77. *WYYH* 833:4395–97.

families of great political influence who constituted a small subgroup of the great clans described in chapter 1.

Not only were these families based overwhelmingly in Chang'an, Luoyang, or—to a lesser extent—the corridor between the two capitals, but they were also linked together by a dense network of marriage ties. Geographic proximity no doubt played a critical role in maintaining this intricate network. Indeed, one specific marriage clique was based almost entirely in Luoyang; when assigned to a posting in a central government ministry or bureau, its members sojourned in a small cluster of contiguous wards in the center of Chang'an. New epitaphs that come to light will undoubtedly allow future researchers to complicate the social network depicted in figure 3.6 and to explore further the bonds of marriage, and perhaps also friendship, that tied together the upper reaches of society. Nevertheless, figure 3.6 can be thought of as embodying, roughly speaking, the political power elite of the late Tang.

It has often been observed that two new institutions emerged in the Tang that provided avenues of upward mobility for those outside the capital clans—the civil service examinations and the provincial bureaucracies. These institutions, it has been argued, set in motion a series of developments that culminated in the demise of the old entrenched elite. This chapter has addressed the issue of the examinations; the next chapter will explore in more detail the provincial governments. As it turns out, the same subbranches of the great clans that had served in office generation after generation since even before the founding of the dynasty, the same group of elites concentrated in the capital region and reinforced by the marriage network readily adapted to the new institutional developments, coopting both of these channels for their own advancement and then perpetuation in power.

To be sure, not all descendants of the old aristocracy succeeded. As discussed in chapter 1, there were simply too many of them. Both entry into officialdom and appointments to bureaucratic posts involved intensely competitive processes, as large numbers of great clan scions fought for a limited number of prestigious *jinshi* degrees, and numerous cousins competed with each other for the patronage of a powerful uncle. In this environment, it was believed almost universally that talent, virtue, and merit should determine the success of one's political career.[78] Thus, in the case of both the *jinshi* and the selection examinations, there were frequent complaints about the lack of fairness. And in the case of informal appointment procedures, such as those used by chief ministers for high-ranking positions and by governors for positions in the provincial governments, it was assumed that wise men in charge had the ability to recognize true talent.[79]

But this exaltation of talent did not mean what it would come to mean in the Song dynasty.[80] The Tang elite maintained faith in an "aristocratic" ethos holding that descendants of the great bureaucratic clans were far more likely to possess talent, to have accumulated the merit of their forebears. Such an ideology legitimated a number of procedures built into the structure of the bureaucratic recruitment and appointment system, including the *yin* privilege and "degree worthiness." Although the hereditary *yin* privilege might well appear nepotistic by latter-day standards, as I argued in chapter 1, epitaphs of the ninth century praised their subjects for obtaining positions through protection, as this constituted evidence of the distinction and prestige of their officeholding forebears.[81] Thus, for the Tang elite, a discourse of talent in no way seemed discordant with their own continued domination through geographically concentrated social networks of power.

---

78. For a discussion of talent, virtue, and merit as the primary criteria in the selection examinations, see Herbert, *Examine the Honest*, pp. 91–97.

79. For example, it was common for epitaphs to assert that the deceased was appointed to a provincial government after the governor came to recognize the man's talent. One interesting articulation of this notion of the recognition of talent involved the recurring motif, particularly common in ninth-century writings, of the fabulous horse whose hidden talents could be recognized only by the most perspicacious minister. See Spring, "Fabulous Horses."

80. For the Song exams, see John Chaffee, *Thorny Gates of Learning*.

81. Defenses of the *yin* privilege also argued that sons of court officials grew up in an environment that provided them with a more solid foundation for their future responsibilities as bureaucrats. For example, the mid-ninth-century chief minister Li Deyu argued in 840: "The outstanding officials of the court ought to be the sons of the highest officials. Why? Because from childhood on they are accustomed to this kind of position; their eyes are familiar with court affairs; even if they have not been trained in the ceremonial of the palace, they automatically achieve perfection. Scholars of poor families, even if they have an extraordinary talent, are certainly unable to accustom themselves to [its routine]." See Wittfogel, "Public Office," p. 29.

Pierre Bourdieu's notion of social capital is useful for explaining these families' continued dominance.[82] The social connections of capital elites constituted a fungible resource that was itself valuable and could be exchanged for lucrative posts in government. It was this social capital, embedded in the Chang'an- and Luoyang-based elite marriage networks, that provided select subbranches of the old great clans such exceptional advantages in the competitions for talent. Such social capital would have functioned differently in different contexts. The capital marriage network seems to have been composed of two marriage cliques that reflected two very different ways in which elites related to the political regime and the power structures. Clique B was more diverse in its geographic distribution, with families based in both Chang'an and Luoyang; it was also more varied in its composition, containing both military families and civil bureaucratic clans. What the families in clique B shared was a high degree of intermarriage with the imperial clan. Thus, clique B represented families intimately tied to the Tang regime, including those of the great military heroes who had helped the regime survive the An Lushan Rebellion. From the perspective of the imperial family, a more diverse marriage network may have helped bolster its influence over a broader segment of the power structure. Simultaneously, it is possible that it was intermarriage with elements of clique B, rather than the civil service exams or the provincial bureaucracies, that offered rare opportunities for outsiders to enter the political elite.

Clique A was far more homogeneous, composed of subbranches of the most eminent old clans, nearly all of whom were based in Luoyang. These families were connected to each other by a particularly dense marriage network. They also seem to have played an especially influential role in the bureaucracy and its reproduction. Members of clique A were much more likely than members of clique B (excluding the imperial clan itself) to occupy the top positions in the civil bureaucracy, including those of chief minister, chief examiner, and minister of personnel (see fig. 3.9). If one compares elites in Luoyang—many of whom were linked by marriage to clique A—with those in Chang'an, the dispar-

---

82. A clear and succinct enunciation of the notion of social capital can be found in Bourdieu, "Capital social." Watanabe Takashi was one of the first Tang historians to note the applicability of Bourdieu to ninth-century China. See "Tōkō hanki," esp. pp. 59–60.

ity appears even greater. Although one should not exaggerate the differences between the two marriage cliques, clique A does seem to have been less dependent on the Li imperial clan and the Tang regime, and more connected to the Chinese political system itself. There is evidence that the families in clique A had intermarried with each other since well before the founding of the dynasty.[83] It is plausible that clique A would have survived even if An Lushan had succeeded in overthrowing the Tang in the mid-eighth century. But before discussing the final collapse of the dynasty, it is necessary to return to the question of the late Tang provincial governments, which have been credited—erroneously, I argue—with bringing down both the Tang regime and the great clans of medieval China.

---

83. Although a complete survey of the pre-Tang marriage ties of these families is well beyond the scope of this study, there is good evidence that the "eastern" branch of the Zhaojun Lis was already intermarrying with the "second" and the "great" branches of the Boling Cuis as early as the sixth century. See epitaphs of Li Xili 李希禮 (511–56), Li Xian 李憲 (c. 480–c. 537), and Cui Ang 崔昂 (508–65). Some of the old families may have relocated to Luoyang as a social network, providing them with the resources as a group to outcompete other early Tang elites.

4

The Late Tang Provinces

An abundance of scholarship on late Tang political, economic, and social history has demonstrated the far-reaching implications of the An Lushan Rebellion. An Lushan 安祿山 (c. 703–57) had risen through the ranks of the frontier military to become one of the most important Tang military commanders of the mid-eighth century.[1] By the late 740s, after spending time in Chang'an, he had become a particular favorite of the reigning emperor Xuanzong 玄宗 (r. 712–56), while maintaining good relations with the powerful chief minister Li Linfu. Largely as a result of his connections at court, An was put in charge of three adjoining frontier commands and was allowed to maintain these commands for several consecutive terms of office. After Li Linfu's death, however, his relations with the court soured. Finally, in late 755, amid his growing rivalry with Li's replacement, An rose up in rebellion, marching across Hebei with 150,000 troops and seizing the Eastern Capital less than a month later. As a man of the regime, An well understood Chinese political culture and realized that he had a legitimate claim to the Chinese throne.[2] Only a few weeks after revolting, he proclaimed himself emperor of a new Yan dynasty. A few months later, he seized Chang'an, forcing Xuanzong to flee southwest to Sichuan. Under An and his successors, the Yan regime survived for a full seven years before it was finally crushed by Tang loyalist armies.

---

1. For a good account of the rebellion, see Peterson, "Court and Province," pp. 468–84.

2. According to traditional Chinese political theory, a successful rebellion was in itself evidence of Heaven's support of the rebels.

Probably the most immediate effect of the rebellion involved substantial territorial losses. The Tang armies protecting the trade routes into Central Asia were recalled to the interior to fight the rebels, allowing vast swathes of the northwest to come under Tibetan and Uighur control.³ Meanwhile, Hebei in the northeast fell into the hands of autonomous provincial military oligarchies. But there were other effects equally dramatic in their long-term implications. The destruction of the tax registries during the upheaval dealt a profound blow to state finances in post-rebellion years, while simultaneously debilitating the land allocation system that had once constrained the sizes of individual landholdings.⁴ The simultaneous relaxation of stringent restrictions on commerce—notably the breakdown of government control over urban marketplaces—inadvertently fueled the expansion and diversification of commercial activity in the late Tang.⁵ Finally, the rebellion led to an institutional restructuring, with the establishment of new provincial administrations that existed in parallel with the regular bureaucracy.

Many scholars of Tang China have assumed that this set of developments played a critical role in the demise of the great families. These scholars note that the deregulation of commerce and property rights led to the emergence of new merchant and landed elites.⁶ Meanwhile, the informal bureaucratic recruitment methods employed by the provincial governments created, in principle at least, new channels of upward mobility. Thus, it has been argued, men with "backgrounds unheard of in civil servants before the rebellion" began to enter government service and threaten the old clans' monopoly on power, becoming "full-ranking members of the regular bureaucracy."⁷ The previous two chapters

---

3. Peterson, "Court and Province," p. 486; Beckwith, *Tibetan Empire*, esp. pp. 143–156.

4. Twitchett, "Introduction," pp. 24–28.

5. Twitchett, "Merchant, Trade, and Government"; Twitchett, "T'ang Market System."

6. For a detailed account of the property accrued by one North Chinese landowner, see Tackett, "Transformation," pp. 37–38, 51. These developments in land tenure and the economy were paralleled by what one might think of as a "deregulation" of intellectual life, as court sponsorship of scholarly projects declined over the course of the Tang, giving rise to scholarly and literary independence from the state. See McMullen, *State and Scholars*.

7. Twitchett, "Introduction," p. 21; Twitchett, "Composition," p. 79.

have demonstrated that a Chang'an- and Luoyang-based elite, largely by means of the social capital embedded in a tightly knit network of intermarrying clans, dominated the imperial bureaucracy of the late Tang. But what of these provincial bureaucracies? If the influence of the political oligarchy of capital-based aristocrats failed to extend to the provinces, then local bureaucracies might indeed have become the breeding ground for an increasingly powerful new elite.

The present chapter reevaluates the impact of developments in the provinces on late Tang politics and society. I begin by mobilizing new evidence in support of revisionist scholarship that downplays the extent of political decentralization in the ninth century. Whereas historians for a thousand years have tended to portray the post–An Lushan Tang as a long period of gradual dynastic decline, I suggest that the dynasty remained relatively stable until quite late in the ninth century.[8] Then, using methodologies described in the previous chapter, I show how capital elites adapted effectively to institutional restructuring. Much in the way that they succeeded in coopting the civil service examinations, they managed also to benefit directly from the late Tang provincial order. Though the An Lushan Rebellion may have constituted a critical turning point in China's economic history, its impact on China's great families was relatively minimal. As we shall see in chapter 5, it was the catastrophic rebellions of the last two decades of the ninth century, in fact, that destroyed, quite suddenly, both the medieval aristocracy and the Tang state itself.

---

8. According to the Song historian He Qufei 何去非 (fl. 1082–90), in the post–An Lushan period, "the power of the empire had been doled out to subordinates [i.e., to the provincial governors]" 天下之權已分於下; thus, "the demise [of the Tang dynasty] did not lie in the era of Xizong and Zhaozong [the last two emperors], but rather in the years of the Tianbao era [immediately preceding the An Lushan Rebellion]" 其亡不在乎僖昭之世而在乎天寶之載焉. A few centuries later, the great Qing historical critic Zhao Yi 趙翼 (1727–1814), who described the late Tang provincial system as a "disaster" 禍, marking a period when "arrogant soldiers" 驕兵 ruled the day, argued that provincial separatism plagued the Tang state continuously from the mid-eighth century until its ultimate demise at the turn of the tenth century. See He Qufei, *He boshi* 64a–65a; Zhao Yi, *Nian er shi* 20.7a–8a, 9a–10a. The theory of post–An Lushan decline is widely held by historians of Tang China today.

The Late Tang Provincial System and the Hebei Autonomous Provinces

The provincial system of the late Tang had roots in two institutional developments of the early eighth century.[9] First was the creation of a third tier of local administration in China's interior. In the initial century of Tang rule, the empire had been divided into only two levels of administrative units: prefectures and their subordinate counties. In 706, due to concerns about the declining quality of local government, the court began to appoint special commissioners, initially holding the title of inspection commissioner 按察使. They took charge of ten newly created provinces 道, to which the prefectures and counties were now subordinated. In subsequent decades, these men acquired increasing powers of oversight over the lower levels of administration within their jurisdiction. By 734, when the system was formalized, the inspectors—now known as investigative and supervisory commissioners 採訪處置使 (often abbreviated 採訪使)—oversaw a total of fifteen provinces.

The second development involved a fundamental reorganization of frontier defense. In the early years of the dynasty, the armed forces were organized into a militia system, with no large permanent armies. When it was necessary to organize major campaigns, temporary commanders were put in charge of expeditionary armies composed of mobilized militia troops and other conscripts.[10] In the second decade of the eighth century, an increase in border pressures compelled the court to establish a series of ten large, permanent garrisons on the northern and southwestern frontiers, each under the command of a military commissioner 節度使. Although these commissioners were initially civil bureaucrats, the court came increasingly to rely on professional military officers. Over time, the military commissioners were granted greater authority over local administration, finance, and food supply, giving them unrivaled power over the territories they controlled. Simultaneously, they acquired

---

9. The following account of the development of the provinces through the An Lushan Rebellion is based on Peterson, "Autonomy," pp. 2–8; Twitchett, "Hsüantsung," pp. 366–70, 402–4; Peterson, "Court and Province," pp. 465–67, 476, 486–89; and Zhang Guogang, *Tangdai fanzhen yanjiu*, pp. 9–20.

10. For more on the earlier militia system, see Wechsler, "T'ai-tsung," pp. 207–8.

substantially more troops so that, by the 730s, as much as 85 percent of active Tang military units were under their command.[11]

An Lushan was one of these military commissioners, who, after gaining the trust of the emperor, had been unwisely placed in charge of three contiguous frontier commands. When he rebelled in 755, there were initially no imperial armies that could match his forces in troop strength. During the years of rebellion, as an expedient to provide military support to loyal regions of the empire, the court allowed each of the fifteen interior provinces to establish a permanent army modeled along the lines of the frontier commands. The new military commissioners of the interior provinces were also given all the responsibilities formerly held by the investigative commissioners. Within two decades after the end of the rebellion, all prefectures in the empire were subordinate to provinces that now maintained their own permanent provincial armies.

Because the late Tang provincial system emerged in piecemeal fashion and was never fully rationalized, governors in the post–An Lushan period were known by a number of different titles. This variety of titles has sometimes led to confusion among historians, some of whom have assumed that a distinction existed between military and civil governors.[12] In fact, governors had both military and civilian responsibilities, usually holding the civilian title of surveillance commissioner 觀察使 conjointly with that of military commissioner or of chief military training commissioner 都團練使. There are no cases of power being divided in a province between separate military and civilian governors. To add to the confusion, the surveillance and military commissions of some provinces were known by two different names. For example, the surveillance commissioner of E'yue 鄂岳觀察使 also held the title of military commissioner of the Wuchang Army 武昌軍節度使, and the surveillance commissioner of Zhexi 浙西觀察使 simultaneously held the position of military commissioner of the Zhenhai Army 鎮海軍節度使. Finally, the governors of the Eastern Regional Command based in Luoyang usually held the title of regent 留守. But regardless of the variety of titles and

---

11. Twitchett, "Hsüan-tsung," pp. 415–16.
12. See, for example, Hucker, *Dictionary of Official Titles*, p. 33; Twitchett, "Varied Patterns," pp. 100–101.

names involved, it is appropriate to think of the late Tang empire as being divided into provinces, each headed by a single "governor."

In the decades immediately following the An Lushan Rebellion, the Tang central government had some initial difficulty reasserting its control over all of the provinces. Indeed, three provinces in Hebei—Youzhou, Chengde, and Weibo—were able to maintain their autonomy until the end of the dynasty.[13] All three were founded by former rebels. Li Huaixian 李懷仙 (d. 768), Li Baochen 李寶臣 (d. 781), and Tian Chengsi 田承嗣 (704–78), who served as governors there during the 760s and 770s, had all been military commanders under An Lushan. As part of the peace that brought the rebellion to a close, they were allowed to stay on as governors after surrendering their territories to nominal Tang rule.[14]

Over the course of the next century and a half, however, the three provinces maintained strong separatist traditions. Thus, throughout the ninth century, the Tang court had minimal influence over the selection of their governors. More often than not, governorships were transmitted according to the principle of hereditary succession, a principle that came to be known as the "Hebei custom" 河北舊事.[15] The kinsmen of Tian Chengsi, for example, ruled Weibo for nearly sixty years following the initial creation of the province in 763.[16] In Chengde, the descendants of Wang Tingcou 王庭湊 (d. 834)—the military commander who seized control of Chengde in 822 and who was, himself, the adopted son of an earlier governor—stayed in power for a full century.[17] In other cases, governors were overthrown by their subordinates. Ninth-century Youzhou was particularly unstable, with nine military coups organized by the provincial army in the period 821 to 876.[18] Given that even hereditary succession required the tacit approval of the army, it is no exaggeration to say that the Hebei governments were under "garrison rule."[19]

---

13. For the best survey history in English of autonomous Hebei in the late Tang, see Peterson, "Autonomy." Peterson did not have access to the abundant epigraphic material that now allows for a more in-depth understanding of this region.
14. Ibid., pp. 48–52.
15. Ibid., p. 104.
16. Yu Xianhao, *Tang cishi kao* 2:1381–84.
17. Ibid. 3:1485–88.
18. Ibid. 3:1609–14.
19. Peterson, "Court and Province," p. 548.

As a consequence, the Tang court had very little control over political decisions made at the provincial level in the autonomous provinces. Regulations restricting the sizes of armies and the distribution of soldiers between province and subordinate prefectures were unenforceable in Hebei.[20] Although the Tang regularly depended on contingents of provincial troops during major military campaigns, the autonomous Hebei regimes rarely contributed, except when allying with Tang against each other.[21] On numerous occasions, they engaged in open warfare with the Tang court. Youzhou, in particular, seems even to have conducted its own foreign policy with non-Chinese states. One career Youzhou bureaucrat, Zhang Jianzhang* 張建章 (806–66), was dispatched by the provincial authorities on a diplomatic mission to the Manchurian state of Parhae. Later, at the time of his death, he held the title of vice envoy to the Xi and Khitan nations.[22]

In addition, although it was generally the prerogative of the Tang court to appoint prefects and county magistrates, the provincial governors in the autonomous provinces usurped this authority.[23] Ninth-century

---

20. For example, in 779, the court failed miserably in its attempt to reduce the size of the Weibo army from 70,000 to 30,000 troops. See Peterson, "Autonomy," pp. 82–83. The armies of the autonomous provinces probably contained between 150,000 and 200,000 troops. See ibid., p. 57.

21. For example, Youzhou and Chengde joined forces with imperial troops in 775 to pressure Weibo into giving up territory it had seized in southwest Hebei. See Peterson, "Autonomy," p. 60. For a prominent exception to this rule, see the epitaph of Lun Boyan 論博言 (805–65), a man of Tibetan descent, who—while in the employ of the Youzhou provincial government—led a contingent of troops from Youzhou in an imperially sponsored counterattack against the southwestern kingdom of Nanzhao 南詔. For evidence that the Hebei provinces also occasionally provided troops to help defend the northwest from Tibetan incursions, see ibid., 174–76.

22. At the time, the Youzhou governor held the concurrent title of "envoy to the two border states" 兩蕃使, a title granted to the governor by the throne. It is likely that the Tang court was, in fact, delighted to delegate diplomacy with Manchuria to the Youzhou authorities, though the court probably had little control over the contents of these negotiations. Peterson cites the minister Niu Sengru's observations about the succession of a new Youzhou governor: "We shall have him guard the frontier against the northern barbarians; it is irrelevant, therefore, whether he is [by origin] an usurper or a loyal official" (ibid., p. 173).

23. Past scholarship has provided ample "negative proof" of this fact, based on the absence of evidence that the court successfully appointed magistrates or prefects to the autonomous provinces. See ibid., p. 58. Epitaphs from Hebei that have come to light in

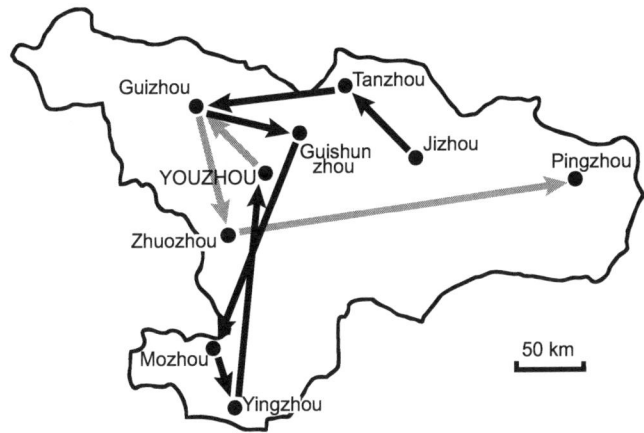

FIGURE 4.1. Office rotations of two ninth-century Youzhou officials
Black arrows = career of Yue Bangsui; grey arrows = career of Zhou Yu. Offices for which the place of office is ambiguous are excluded.

epitaphs excavated in recent decades in Hebei have demonstrated that provincial elites with close ties to provincial governments frequently served in prefecture- and county-level positions within their home provinces. Bureaucrats in the service of the Youzhou government, in particular, were often rotated in sequence to offices in several of the nine prefectures under the control of this northeastern regime. Figure 4.1 shows the prefectural offices held by two fairly high ranking Youzhou officials, Zhou Yu* 周璵 (787–856) and Yue Bangsui* 樂邦穗 (827–77), who together served in all nine prefectures under the province's control. Zhou and Yue were by no means unusual.[24] Youzhou emulated the imperial Tang regime in rotating officials residing at the capital—in this case, the provincial capital—throughout its subordinate territories.

Finally—and perhaps of greatest concern to the Tang regime—the autonomous provinces never submitted tax revenues to the court,

---

recent decades provide a rich picture of prefecture- and county-level appointments in Youzhou, Chengde, and Weibo.

24. For other examples, see the epitaphs of the military man Geng Zongyi 耿宗倚 (823–81), who held no less than nine different appointments in three different prefectures under the command of the Youzhou government; and of Wang Gongshu 王公淑 (780–848), Lun Boyan 論博言 (805–65), Yan Haowen 閻好問 (810–73), and Wen Lingshou 溫令綬 (806–74).

although they did occasionally offer gifts.²⁵ To be sure, because of the costs of maintaining defensive forces, there were also a number of loyalist provinces that paid no taxes, even sometimes receiving state subsidies.²⁶ Hebei, however, was one of China's breadbaskets; the loss of tax revenue from the autonomous provinces in the post–An Lushan period permanently decreased the grain resources available to the Tang court.²⁷ Moreover, before the rebellion, most of China's silk and virtually all of the highest-quality silk—one of the more famous types being the twilled silk 綾 of Fanyang (in northern Hebei)—was produced in Hebei and northern Henan.²⁸ One indicator of Youzhou's wealth is the impressive list of donors carved on the back of the Buddhist stone classics of Fangshan 房山. A large number of the fifteen thousand steles were produced in the late ninth century; on these stones are inscribed the names of tens of thousands of individual donors, including numerous officials of the Youzhou regime.²⁹ In addition, several great commercial centers emerged in Hebei in the late Tang, partly as a result of important international trade routes coming down from the northeast. The Youzhou provincial seat contained thirty trading streets 行 as well as a "barbarian market" 胡市, set up specifically for trade with foreigners, where goods from all over China were for sale.³⁰ Already in the seventh century, the large amount of trade that passed through Hebei, between the Yellow River in the south and Youzhou in the north, had necessitated the construction of an important canal, with major storage and transit

---

25. Peterson, "Autonomy," p. 81.

26. For a table that identifies four types of late Tang provinces partly on the basis of whether or not they contributed taxes to the state coffers, see Zhang Guogang, *Tangdai fanzhen yanjiu*, p. 59.

27. Twitchett calculates that, as of the 740s, as much as a quarter of China's registered population (i.e., the population that paid taxes) and an even greater percentage of grain reserves were situated in regions that became autonomous after An Lushan. See Twitchett, "Provincial Autonomy," pp. 214–16. However, Twitchett includes in his calculations portions of Hebei and Shandong that were brought back under court control in the early ninth century, so the actual loss to the court was ultimately not this large.

28. Twitchett, "Merchant, Trade, and Government," p. 76; Twitchett, "Provincial Autonomy," pp. 224–30.

29. *Fangshan shijing tiji huibian*.

30. Lu Xiaofan, "Tang Youzhou zhufang," p. 79.

depots at Weizhou 魏州 and Beizhou 貝州.³¹ This canal seems still to have been svery much in use in the ninth century.³²

With their own finances, foreign policy, and bureaucratic recruitment and selection procedures, the autonomous provinces operated in many ways like miniature replicas of the Tang state. Youzhou, Chengde, and Weibo were not, however, completely free of attachments to the Tang court. In what was probably a fiercely competitive political environment, their governors often depended on the legitimacy afforded by court sponsorship. As the ninth-century chief minister Li Deyu observed, "Although the armies in Hebei are powerful, [their leaders] cannot stand on their own; they depend on the orders of appointment from court to assuage their troops" 河朔兵力雖強, 不能自立, 須借朝廷官爵威命以安軍情.³³ In this sense, in their relationship with the central government, the Hebei leaders saw themselves much like the great lords of the preimperial Warring States Period.³⁴ Even during a period of open revolt against the throne, in late 782, the governors never denied a role for the emperor; instead, they proclaimed themselves "kings" 王—a title unambiguously subordinate to that of "emperor" in Chinese political theory—and temporarily converted their own provincial bureaucracies into "feudal" courts and hierarchies, self-consciously employing terminologies harking back to the Warring States.³⁵

Recentralization after the Xianzong Restoration

Much twentieth-century scholarship on the provincial system of the late Tang, inspired by seminal works in the 1940s and 1950s by Hino Kaisaburō 日野開三郎 and Hori Toshikazu 堀敏一, has focused primarily on the autonomous provinces, treating them as representative of all

---

31. Twitchett, *Financial Administration*, pp. 188–89. The canal in question was the Yongji Canal 永濟渠.

32. For reference to tax grain in Youzhou apparently being transported by boat, see the epitaph of Dong Tangzhi 董唐之 (804–58).

33. Zhang Guogang, *Tangdai fanzhen yanjiu*, p. 49.

34. In the ninth century, provincial governors were not infrequently compared to feudal lords 諸侯. See Wang Shounan, *Tangdai fanzhen*, p. 1. It should be noted that the term "feudal lords" is misleading; the governors and their underlings were, for the most part, all salaried bureaucrats.

35. Peterson, "Autonomy," pp. 91–92; *ZZTJ* 227:7335–36.

parts of China.³⁶ According to this model, the An Lushan Rebellion resulted in a "powerful decentralized provincial order," in which the state—which "deteriorated by degrees" after the rebellion—was "repeatedly on the brink of becoming a loose patchwork of virtually autonomous satrapies."³⁷ This was said to be an era of "chronic militarism," where "professional armies . . . usurped many of the normal functions of government and, while nominally owing allegiance to the T'ang, were constantly unruly, sometimes virtually independent."³⁸ The division of the whole country into independent kingdoms during the Five Dynasties period was, it has been argued, "the culmination of this process."³⁹

In fact, these portrayals of near total disintegration of central authority in the post–An Lushan period are greatly exaggerated. Ōsawa Masaaki 大沢正昭 was one of the first modern scholars to distinguish between the provinces in a systematic manner. In two studies focusing on the reigns of Dezong 德宗 (r. 780–805) and Xianzong 憲宗 (r. 806–20), he identified three types: those that were essentially autonomous, in Hebei; those that were autonomously minded, especially in Henan; and loyal provinces, mostly situated in the south.⁴⁰ Subsequently, Denis Twitchett proposed a similar model, arguing, in addition, that the north remained much more militarized than the south in the late Tang.⁴¹ A decade later, Zhang Guogang 張國剛 put forward a more complex typology, which took as its starting point an analysis of the provinces by the ninth-century statesman and poet Du Mu. For Zhang, there were four types of provinces, which differed both in degree of loyalty to the Tang court and in their dependence on the Tang regime for financial and logisti-

---

36. Hino Kaisaburō, *Shina chūsei*; Hori, "Tōmatsu shohanran"; Hori, "Hanchin shineigun." Both Hino and Hori were undoubtedly themselves influenced by earlier scholarship, including that of the Song and Qing era scholars He Qufei and Zhao Yi. See note 8.
37. Peterson, "Court and Province," p. 464; Twitchett, "Government of T'ang," p. 322; Hucker, *Dictionary of Official Titles*, p. 28.
38. Pulleyblank, "An Lu-shan Rebellion," p. 35.
39. Ibid., p. 59.
40. Ōsawa, "Tōmatsu no hanchin."
41. Twitchett, "Varied Patterns." Note that Twitchett, nevertheless, asserts elsewhere that "everywhere the forces of local autonomy and of particularism had grown markedly." See Twitchett, "Introduction," p. 17.

cal support.⁴² Although these typologies have proven useful for better understanding the power structure of the late Tang, one should bear in mind that the sharpest distinction of all was between the autonomous provinces of Hebei and the rest of the Tang empire.

In particular, outside of Hebei, the court embarked on largely successful recentralization efforts under the emperors Dezong and Xianzong.⁴³ One aspect of this recentralization involved military campaigns. Upon the death of Emperor Daizong in 779, seven provinces—Youzhou, Chengde, and Weibo, as well as Pinglu in Shandong, Xiangyang in northern Hubei, Jiannan Xi in Sichuan, and Huaixi in the Huai River valley—remained largely outside the control of the court, with their governors selected by the provincial armies rather than by the central government. Two of these recalcitrant provinces were brought back under central control after several military campaigns instigated in the early years of Dezong's reign. Simultaneously, two small splinter provinces were created from territory forcibly taken from the largest Hebei autonomous provinces. Thereafter, Dezong's successor, Xianzong, embarked on successful campaigns to subjugate the remaining breakaway regimes, campaigns that culminated in the early 820s, when the court was even able to appoint governors to the autonomous Hebei provinces.⁴⁴ Although the military oligarchies in these three provinces soon overthrew the court-appointed governors, the Tang state had, by the 820s, succeeded in reestablishing authority in all other parts of the empire.

These military campaigns, however, constituted only one component of the recentralization efforts. The court simultaneously restructured provincial institutions in a number of important ways. In the late 770s, governors were forbidden from becoming involved in the appointment or firing of their subordinate prefects, who were thereafter chosen through central government selection procedures. Later, Dezong succeeded both in augmenting

---

42. Zhang Guogang, "Tangdai fanzhen leixing"; Zhang Guogang, *Tangdai fanzhen yanjiu*, pp. 42–59.

43. The best accounts of the recentralization efforts of the emperors Dezong and Xianzong, on which the following discussion is based, are by Charles Peterson. See "Restoration Completed" and "Court and Province," pp. 497–552. See also Ōsawa, "Tōmatsu no hanchin"; Tsuji, "Tōchō no tai hanchin."

44. For interesting recent accounts of Xianzong's military efforts in the southwest and southeast, see Lu Yang, "Cong Xichuan he Zhexi shijian" and "Cong xinchu muzhi zai lun."

the size of the Palace Armies, to serve as a counterweight to provincial forces, and in establishing a system of army supervisors 監軍.⁴⁵ Staffed by eunuchs from the Inner Palace, these supervisors were dispatched to the provinces in order to keep tabs on the governors. Additional reforms were implemented under Xianzong. An important new tax policy put into practice in 809 by the chief minister Pei Ji 裴垍 (d. 811) deprived the provincial governments of part of their revenue base. Henceforth, they derived their incomes from only one subordinate prefecture; the remaining prefectures sent excess revenue directly to court. Finally, in 819, some troops in the provincial armies were put under the command of the prefects—who had previously held no military responsibilities—thus reducing the military power of the governors. Although additional reforms were implemented in subsequent decades—notably reforms involving the regularization of the appointment procedures for provincial authorities—the bulk of the recentralization process was complete by the year 820.

Scholars have only gradually come to appreciate the full implications of the Xianzong Restoration on the late Tang provincial order. Until quite recently, the tendency has remained to envision the provincial governors and their staffs as fundamentally antagonistic to centralized control, as constituting a centrifugal force that culminated in the breakup of China into separate states at the turn of the tenth century. In the case of the typology of provinces posited by Ōsawa Masaaki, the provinces differed from each other only in terms of how loyal or disloyal they were to the throne. For Denis Twitchett, the provinces existed in a "broad spectrum of 'autonomy.'"⁴⁶ At issue in both cases is the degree to which provincial governments obstructed central government authority.

In the 1980s and 1990s, scholars in East Asia pioneered a new way of understanding the Tang provinces, viewing them as essentially no more antagonistic to central rule than were the provinces of later dynasties. Zhang Guogang, for example, demonstrated that mutinies—sometimes envisioned by historians as manifestations of anticourt sentiment—dealt more often than not with issues that were entirely local in nature.⁴⁷ Other scholars reexamined institutional developments of the ninth

---

45. On the importance of army supervisors under Emperor Xianzong, see Lu Yang, "Dynastic Revival," pp. 283–88.

46. Twitchett, "Varied Patterns," p. 105.

47. Zhang Guogang, *Tangdai fanzhen yanjiu*, pp. 60–71.

century in order to demonstrate how the court maintained direct channels of communication with prefectural authorities without interference from the provinces or how bureaucratic service in the provincial governments often culminated in promotion to central government positions.[48]

An even bolder theory was put forward by Nakasuna Akinori 中砂明徳, who showed that the central government at times actively exploited provincial governments in order to assert greater control at the local level. In a study of an early-ninth-century drought affecting the Jiang-Huai region, China's southern breadbasket, he argued that provincial authorities worked closely with the central government to organize hydraulic infrastructure development projects and to provision urban centers with food.[49] Inspired by Nakasuna, Cheong Byungjun 鄭炳俊 demonstrated—largely on the basis of mid-ninth-century court directives—that the central government sought to delegate a number of duties to provincial administrators, with the goal of enhancing bureaucratic efficiency. Thus, provincial governments were put in charge of keeping track of population counts and the total cultivated acreage of their subordinate administrative units, of overseeing criminal cases handled by subordinate prefectures and counties, and even of supervising the selection of prefectural candidates for the civil service examinations.[50] The text of the emperor's great amnesty 大赦 of 866 is illuminating in this context in terms of the responsibilities given to the governors, here referred to as "surveillance commissioners":

> Prefectural and county officials everywhere rarely study with care the codes and statutes; they do not know about aggravating and mitigating factors. By merely leaving [these matters] to low-level officials, they have brought about [judicial] excesses. We entrust the surveillance commissioners to investigate and report back to Us. Moreover, the prefects and the county magistrates often occupy themselves with amusements and banquets without minding their official duties. Since the administration of justice is obstructed, the prisons naturally fill up. As for constant talk of brimming resentment, how can it not stem from this? We entrust the surveillance commissioners to supervise the classification [of criminals] in order to punish [only] the most profoundly heinous.

---

48. Cheong, "Tōkō hanki"; Watanabe, "Chūban Tōki ni okeru kanjin."
49. Nakasuna, "Kōki Tōchō no Kōwai shihai."
50. Cheong, "Tōdai no kansasshochishi."

> 其天下州縣官等, 皆罕悉律令, 莫知重輕, 唯任胥徒, 因多枉濫, 委本
> 道觀察使覺察聞奏. 又刺史縣令, 多務遊宴, 不思官常, 決遣既妨, 囹圄自
> 滿, 永言冤滯, 豈不由斯? 委觀察使表率條流, 以懲深弊.[51]

In this directive entrusting provincial authorities with the oversight of amnesty procedures in their subordinate prefectures and counties, the governors played a key role in controlling malfeasance and incompetence at the local level. Far from constituting a centrifugal force, they were, in all appearance, agents of the court.

The Tang Political Oligarchy and the Provinces

Most of the scholarship on the Xianzong Restoration described above has focused on analyzing the provinces from the perspective of institutional structures and practices. The last component of recentralization in the early ninth century involved a gradual transformation in the composition of the governors and their staffs. Part of this transformation had already begun under Dezong and involved the replacement of military men with civilian bureaucrats. Thus, whereas 75 percent of governors at the end of the rebellion had military backgrounds, only about 60 percent did by the year 779.[52] The most important moment of transformation, however, seems to have occurred at the very end of Xianzong's reign. In 817, the aristocrat and then chief minister Pei Du 裴度 (765–839) asked to be appointed governor of Huaixi in order to lead the court's assault on the rebellious provincial military based there. He also requested the appointment of several court officials, notably the aristocrats Han Yu and Ma Zong 馬總 (d. 823), to assist him.[53] Pei was so successful in his endeavor that his approach was used as a model—the "Pei Du precedent" 裴度故事—leading to a more concerted effort to dispatch prominent bureaucrats to occupy key positions in provincial governments elsewhere.[54]

One can assess the changing composition of the corps of governors in a systematic way by means of a comprehensive analysis of extant biographical data. This empirical approach largely confirms the revisionist view

---

51. *QTW* 85:899; cited in ibid., p. 60.
52. Peterson, "Court and Province," p. 492.
53. *ZZTJ* 240:7737.
54. *ZZTJ* 249:8045.

positing that the end of Xianzong's reign, around the year 820, constituted an important horizon in the relationship between the court and the provinces. Figures 4.2 through 4.5 graphically depict year-by-year changes in the types of men serving as governors in thirty-one select provinces. The period covered begins with the year 770, shortly after the end of the An Lushan Rebellion, and concludes in 900, at which point the Tang regime had lost nearly all authority over the empire. The analysis depends largely on previously compiled lists of Tang governors, supplemented with data from excavated epitaphs and other biographical sources.[55]

Figures 4.2 and 4.3 identify methods of accession to office (appointed by court versus seized or inherited power) and career backgrounds (civilian versus military) of the governors. Both figures reveal conspicuous regional and temporal patterns. In terms of regional variations, the southern provinces were unique in having been consistently governed by court appointees with civilian backgrounds. By contrast, governors of the northwestern provinces tended to be court appointees with military backgrounds. But the most striking distinction involved the autonomous provinces of Hebei. Only the three Hebei provinces continued to appoint their own governors throughout the late Tang (fig. 4.2). Only Hebei remained entirely militarized, as attested by the military backgrounds of all but one of its governors (fig. 4.3).[56]

In terms of temporal variations, figures 4.2 and 4.3 both reveal important horizons around the years 820 and 880. As predicted by the institutionalization of the "Pei Du precedent," the number of provinces with court-appointed governors increased after 820 (fig. 4.2). A large percentage of these governors were professional bureaucrats, many of whom had served or would serve as governor in another province or as minister at the capital.[57] Simultaneously, North China became increasingly demilitarized after 820 (fig. 4.3). Figure 4.3, in particular, also reveals—with the more frequent changes in shading within a single column—the briefer tenures of office after 820, apparently an indication of the central government's determination to prevent governors from building independent bases of

---

55. For lists of Tang governors, see Wu Tingxie, *Tang fangzhen nianbiao*; Yu Xianhao, *Tang cishi kao* ; Wang Shounan, *Tangdai fanzhen*.

56. The exception was Liu Ji 劉濟 (757–810).

57. A perusal of the tables in Wang Shounan, *Tangdai fanzhen*, pp. 451–926, leads to this conclusion.

Key to Province Numbers

1	Youzhou 幽州	17	Binning 邠寧
2	Chengde 成德	18	Fengxiang 鳳翔
3	Weibo 魏博	19	Jingyuan 涇原
4	Pinglu 平盧	20	Fufang 鄜坊
5	Tianping 天平	21	Shannan Dong 山南東
6	Yanhai 兗海	22	Shannan Xi 山南西
7	Xuanwu 宣武	23	Jiannan Xichuan 劍南西川
8	Wuning 武寧	24	Xuanshe 宣歙
9	Zhongwu 忠武	25	Huainan 淮南
10	Heyang 河陽	26	Zhexi 浙西
11	Yiwu 義武	27	Jingnan 荊南
12	Zhaoyi 昭義	28	Fujian 福建
13	Shanguo 陝虢	29	Lingnan 嶺南
14	Yicheng 義成	30	Jiangxi 江西
15	Hedong 河東	31	Eyue 鄂岳
16	Hezhong 河中		

Governors are identified on the basis of Wu Tingxie, *Tang fangzhen nianbiao*; Yu Xianhao, *Tang cishi kao quanbian*; and Wang Shounan, *Tangdai fanzhen yu zhongyang guanxi zhi yanjiu*. Method of entry into office (fig. 4.2) and civilian or military backgrounds of governors (fig. 4.3) follow Wang Shounan, with minor adjustments; family background (fig. 4.4), residency at capital, and ties to the capital network (fig. 4.5) are based on patriline reconstructions, as described in chapter 3. Governors "with ties to capital marriage network" (fig. 4.5) include all governors from patrilines that intermarried with the marriage network depicted in figure 3.6 except governors not appointed by the court. For example, the descendants of Tian Chengsi 田承嗣 (704–78)—who controlled Weibo for several decades—are not deemed members of this network while still serving in Weibo, even though they intermarried with the imperial clan. After the family relocated to the capital around 820 and began accepting appointments in other provinces, they appear in figure 4.5 as members of the capital network.

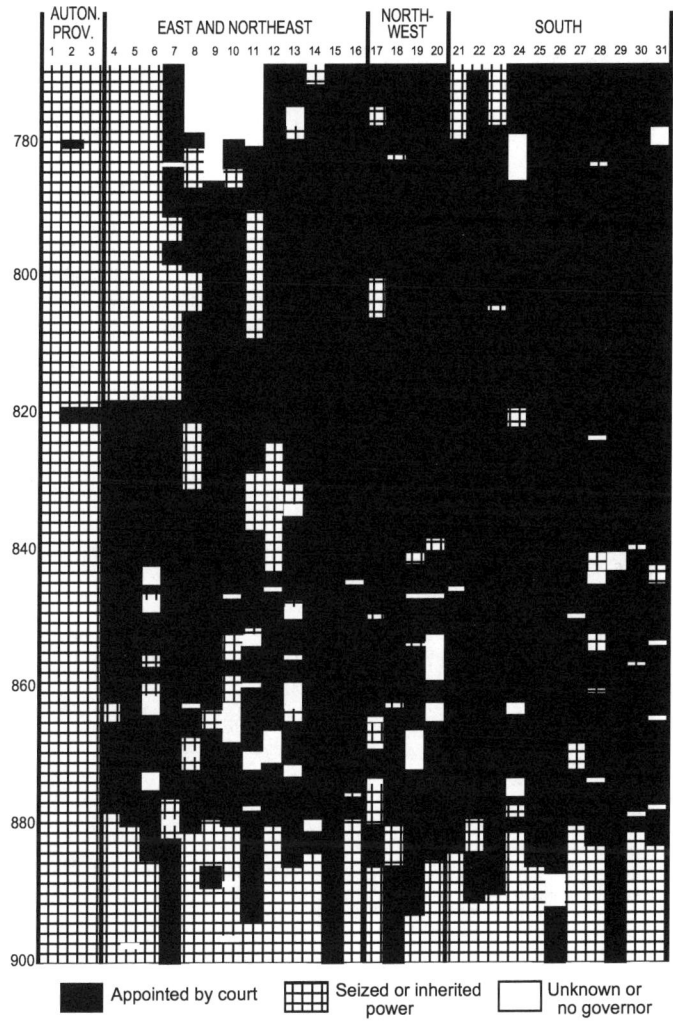

FIGURE 4.2. Methods by which governors of select provinces acceded to office (by year and province)

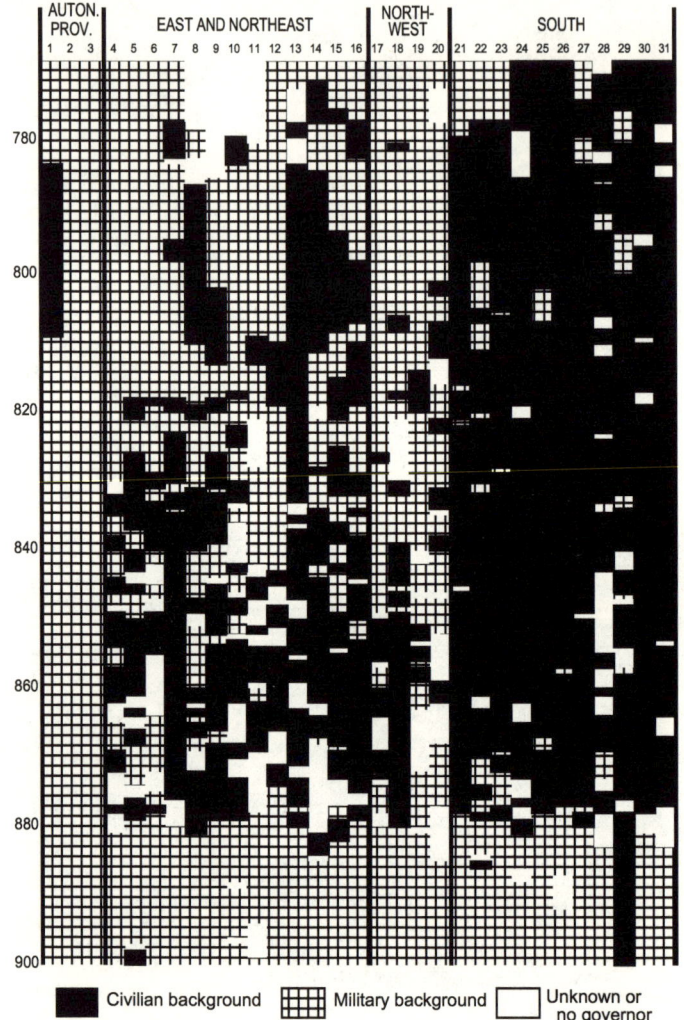

FIGURE 4.3. Backgrounds (civilian or military) of governors of select provinces (by year and province)

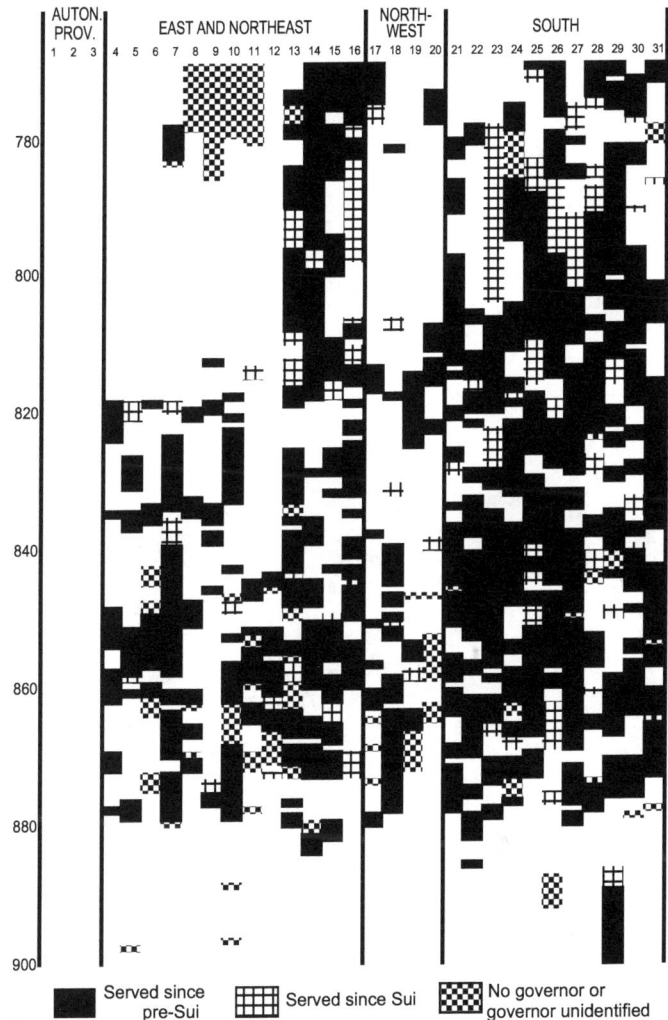

FIGURE 4.4. Governors with family history of bureaucratic service (by year and province)

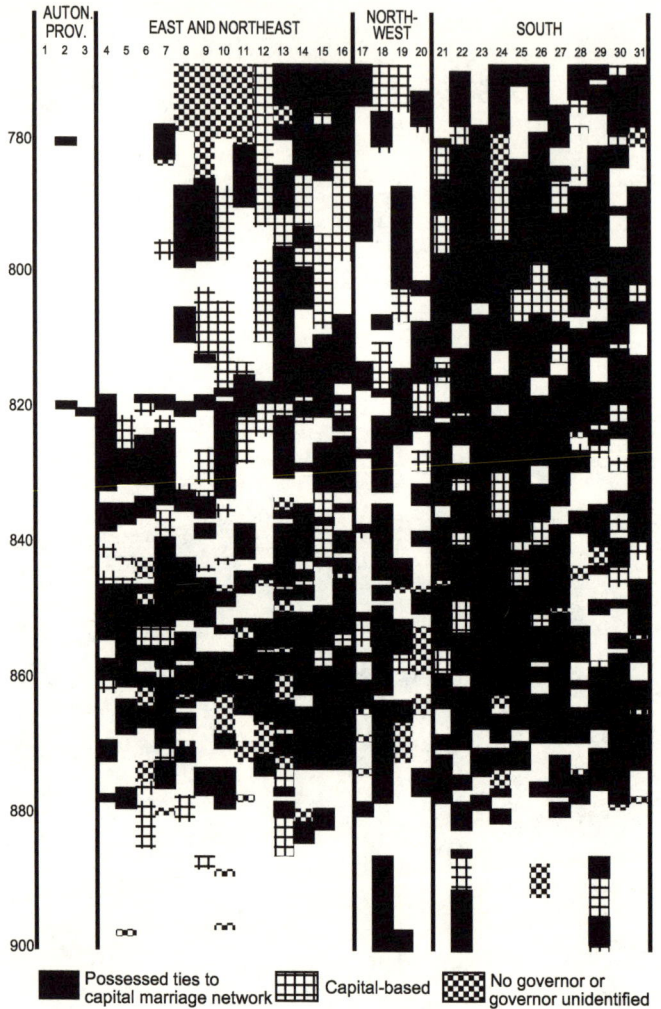

FIGURE 4.5. Governors based in the capital or with ties to the capital marriage network (by year and province)

power at their places of office. Indeed, whereas earlier governors often had served for a decade or more in the same place, after the Xianzong Restoration, their tenures in office tended not to exceed six years.[58]

The trends apparent in figures 4.2 and 4.3 are further confirmed by patterns of provincial mutinies, as recorded in data compiled by Wang Shounan. Most provinces in China seem to have been relatively stable in the period between the 820s and the 870s. Excluding autonomous Hebei, there were 1.28 recorded mutinies per year for the period 770 to 822 and only 0.65 per year in the subsequent five decades.[59] Only in Hebei did rebellions erupt with particular frequency throughout the ninth century. Indeed, if one takes into account the multiple mutinies that sometimes broke out in Youzhou and Weibo in a single year, one finds that the three Hebei provinces accounted for over two-fifths (19/45) of recorded rebellions in all of China during the period 821 to 873. Power struggles amid the military oligarchies of the autonomous provinces seem to have created a zone of political instability. But these Hebei provinces were unusual. In general, after the recentralization efforts during the reign of Xianzong, the mid-ninth century was a period of general stability and of relatively strong central government authority over most parts of the empire.

The situation changed dramatically and suddenly, however, after the year 880. Almost immediately, court appointees among the governors declined substantially in numbers, as many were overthrown or killed by local strongmen (men who did not necessarily have any ties to the provincial armies). Most of those who remained in office probably ceased quite rapidly to heed court directives. For example, Wang Chucun 王處存 (831–95), who was appointed to Yiwu Province in Hebei in 879 (column 11 of the figures), began as a loyal agent of the throne. He apparently wept for days when he heard that the rebel Huang Chao had captured the capital. But in 885, with dynastic authority swiftly crumbling, he refused to comply with a court order to transfer to Hedong Province. Ten years later, he was succeeded by his son as governor of Yiwu and a few years after that by his younger brother Chuzhi.[60] Along with the decline in court appointees after the year 880 came the near

---

58. Wang Shounan, *Tangdai fanzhen*, pp. 56–72.
59. Ibid., pp. 202–27.
60. *JTS* 182:4699–4701.

complete disappearance of governors with civilian backgrounds. The single exception was the province of Lingnan in China's far south, where the court somehow managed to maintain influence until Liu Yin 劉隱 (873–911), founder of the Southern Han Kingdom, seized power in 901. These developments were accompanied by a drastic increase in provincial mutinies—an impressive 2.09 per year in the final decades of the Tang, according to Wang Shounan's data.[61]

Exploiting techniques described in chapter 3 offers even more compelling evidence of the persistence of central control over the provinces throughout the ninth century. In particular, by classifying governors according to their patrilines, it becomes clear that metropolitan elites dominated multiple levels of the provincial bureaucratic hierarchy in most regions of China. Figure 4.4 identifies governors whose ancestors are known to have served in office nearly every generation since before the founding of the Tang dynasty. These men were part of a national elite tied to the Tang regime since its very inception. Figure 4.5 identifies governors whose families were based in the capital or whose families belonged to the capital-based marriage network described in chapter 3. These men were likely to return to the capital upon completing a term of office and, therefore, had little incentive to promote regional autonomy. In the case of both figures, one should bear in mind that the decline in scope of extant documentary sources, especially for the decades between 840 and 880, often makes it impossible to determine the ancestry of a particular governor. In the post-840 period, it is often simply not known who served as governor. Even when a governor is identified by name, there is sometimes nothing else known about the man.[62] Lacunae in source materials account for many of the blank spaces in the diagrams.

Again, these figures point to two significant turning points, one around 820 and the other about 880. From the culmination of Xianzong's recen-

---

61. Wang Shounan, *Tangdai fanzhen*, pp. 218-25. The total 2.09 is particularly striking given the decline in quality of historical source material covering the final three decades of the Tang.

62. One example involves Liu Ye 劉鄴 (d. 880), who served as Huainan governor from 874 to 879; he appears as a blank space in both figures. However, if Watanabe Takashi is correct in equating the Liu Sanfu 劉三復 who served Li Deyu with the Liu Sanfu who composed an epitaph for a Luoyang kinswoman (see discussion below), then his son, none other than Liu Ye, would indeed have been a member of an old capital-based patriline (patriline 5973).

tralization efforts in the second decade of the ninth century through the outbreak of the Huang Chao Rebellion, large numbers of governors were in fact members of the families who had largely monopolized top offices for centuries, who frequently intermarried with one another, and who resided in the capital region when not serving elsewhere in office. Even when governors had no known ties to the capital-based social network described in chapter 3, many were nevertheless from families buried in either Chang'an or Luoyang. For example, certain generals of the Chang'an-based Shence Army were dispatched to serve as governors, most frequently to one of the northwestern provinces.[63] Undoubtedly some of these capital-based generals were tied to the capital elite social network through as of yet unidentified marriage ties. To be sure, there were exceptions. Although many of the blanks spaces in figures 4.4 and 4.5 result from gaps in the historical record, there were also a handful of governors who seem to have been genuine outsiders. For example, the brothers Li Guangjin* 李光進 (759–815) and Li Guangyan* 李光顏 (762–826), who served tenures as provincial governors all over the empire, were buried along with their father, Li Liangchen* 李良臣 (728–63), in Taiyuan in central Shanxi.

Individuals such as the Li brothers were clearly exceptional in the context of the provinces in which they served. Yet one region of China stood out as fundamentally different from the others: autonomous Hebei. As shown in figures 4.4 and 4.5, no scions of the old pre-Tang great families ever served in Hebei as governor, nor, with very few exceptions, did representatives of the capital-based power structure.[64] The families of some Hebei provincial dynasts did intermarry with the imperial clan, as part of the court's attempt to placate these autonomously minded power holders through strategic marriage alliances. And the descendants of some of these family dynasties later sought refuge in Chang'an after being overthrown and chased away by their own subordinates. Nevertheless, while in power in Hebei, these governors were never members of the capital-centered Tang political elite.

In sum, examining the backgrounds of men serving as provincial governors during the late Tang provides particularly strong evidence

---

63. For example, in the 820s and 830s, four different Shence generals were sent out to govern Fufang 鄜坊 Province. See Wang Shounan, *Tangdai fanzhen*, pp. 561–62.

64. The exceptions in fig. 4.5 represent the very brief moments when the court was able to appoint governors to these provinces.

of the enduring influence of the center on provincial China before the outbreak of the Huang Chao Rebellion as well as the exceptional nature of the Hebei provinces. To be sure, a governor's behavior in office might belie his family background, as in the case of the imperial clansman Li Qi 李錡 (d. 807), who famously rebelled while serving in southeastern Zhexi Province during the first decade of the ninth century.[65] But in the vast majority of cases, governors, prefects, and magistrates serving all over the empire came from families living in the capital region, and, for the most part, they would return there upon their retirement. These men had little incentive to promote provincial autonomy while serving as governor. It was this reality above all else that explains the longevity and relative stability of the Tang empire in the post–An Lushan period.

Social Mobility in Provincial Governments

The recentralization of the provincial system was as beneficial to the aristocracy as it was to the Tang regime. Pei Du's victory against the separatist Huaixi governor provided the old families with renewed relevance. Thus, when the chief minister Bai Minzhong asked the emperor in 851 to make use of the "Pei Du precedent" in the northwest by appointing "court officials" to assist the governor there, the practical result was to staff the provincial government in question with scions of the old families. It is now possible to return to the question of social mobility in the late Tang in order to see how service in provincial governments helped to reinforce the power and influence of the capital-based political oligarchy.

As discussed in chapter 3, the newly instituted Tang civil service examination was not yet a significant means of social advancement. But the civil service examination was not the only major institutional development within the mid-Tang bureaucracy. A second significant development involved the expanded use of special commissioners to deal with administrative matters that existing officials were ill equipped to handle. These offices included the Salt Monopoly Commission 鹽鐵使, Transport Commission 轉運使, and Special Supply Commission

---

65. Peterson, "Court and Province," p. 525.

租庸使, all developed as ad hoc means for the state to profit from the burgeoning commercialization of the eighth and ninth centuries.[66] Provincial governors—who held the joint titles of military and surveillance commissioners—might also be included in this category. Although the commissioners were appointed by the throne, they generally could select their own staff members, needing merely to notify the court to obtain formal recognition of their most important subordinates. This "informal recruitment system" 辟召制 entirely bypassed the complex selection procedures that structured recruitment into the regular civil service.[67] Tonami Mamoru theorized that, through this informal recruitment system, the provincial governments provided employment for a strata of upwardly mobile local elites who were not otherwise eligible for regular bureaucratic service. As a consequence, "newly risen" 新興 elites gained access to a channel by which they could compete directly with the old aristocracy.[68] Numerous scholars have concurred with this thesis.[69] Some evidence in support of Tonami's theory can be found in the observations of the earliest historians of the Tang. According to Ouyang Xiu:

> By means of the informal recruitment of scholars, the regional commands [i.e., provinces] of the Tang competed with each other for greatness. Consequently, at that time, among [poor] scholars wearing plain clothes and ordinary belts, those who were either renowned in the village lanes or celebrated in the plazas would be hired by the regional commands. The great men of those days who went to court to serve as general or minister had all emerged from the staffs of the feudal lords [i.e., provincial governors].

---

66. For more on these three commissions, see Twitchett, *Financial Administration*, pp. 92–94, 109–11.

67. Narratives of official careers often explicitly assert that provincial-level posts were obtained through informal arrangements whereby the governor directly contacted the court by letter or memorial (usually 署, 表, 奏, or 辟). By contrast, prefectural- and county-level offices are rarely said to have involved irregular interventions of this sort, with the notable exception of county sheriffs.

68. Tonami, "Chūsei kizokusei," esp. pp. 254–64; Tonami, "Sōdai shitaifu," pp. 201–3.

69. For example: Peterson, "Court and Province," p. 517; Twitchett, "Introduction," p. 21; Zhang Guogang, *Tangdai fanzhen yanjiu*, pp. 141–44; Ning Xin, *Tangdai xuanguan yanjiu*, p. 121.

唐方鎮以辟士相高. 故當時布衣韋帶之士, 或行著鄉閭, 或名聞場屋者, 莫不爲方鎮所取. 至登朝廷, 位將相, 爲時偉人者, 亦皆出諸侯之幕.[70]

Similarly, according to Liu Chang 劉敞 (1019–68):

> Formerly, when the Tang controlled the world, the feudal lords [i.e., provincial governors] themselves recruited the scholars [who served] in their provincial governments. Only talent [was considered]; they did not ask about their origins. The court, then, recruited these men of talent to fill vacancies in the imperial bureaucracy.
>
> 昔唐有天下, 諸侯自辟幕府之士, 唯其才能, 不問所從來. 而朝廷常收其俊偉, 以補王官之缺.[71]

Both men attributed to the Tang provinces the birth of a meritocratic principle that they, like many men of the eleventh century, would have held dear. Recruitment into the provincial governments, according to Ouyang and Liu, provided talented scholars without prestigious pedigrees an opportunity to serve first in local government and later in the highest offices of the land. But whereas Ouyang and Liu were correct, as we shall see, in believing that many of the powerful men of the Tang had once served the provincial governments, they exaggerated their importance as a source of upward mobility.

In a series of recent studies, Watanabe Takashi 渡邊孝 has demonstrated that, although a lower echelon of petty clerks was staffed by local elites, the key civilian offices in the provincial governments were dominated by men with close ties to the central government. Despite an abundance of "exilic" literature from the late Tang bemoaning the misery of serving in posts away from the capital, there can be no doubt that these posts proved invaluable to the capital elite. Provincial governments constituted outlets for the sons of great families who could not initially find employment in the capital. Moreover, by serving in provincial governments, an ambitious young man might well find a pathway toward rapid promotion. In particular, by attaching himself to a provincial governor, he could hope to follow the latter in his entourage after the

---

70. *Ouyang Xiu quan ji* 142:2291. This comes from a colophon Ouyang composed for a Tang era stele commemorating a provincial governor.

71. *Quan Song wen* 30:37 (59:37 in the 2006 ed. of *Quan Song wen*). This comes from an appointment edict Liu composed on behalf of the court.

governor's reappointment to a ministerial position in Chang'an.⁷² As Bai Juyi observed in an appointment order drafted on behalf of the court in the early 820s:

> The men of outstanding talent of the present day are first recruited by the regional commands [i.e., provincial governments] before being elevated to court. Thus, those chosen by the provincial bureaucracies are only one grade in rank beneath [officials of] the central government. Eight or nine out of ten of them will some day become court officers or great ministers. 今之俊乂, 先辟于征鎮, 次升于朝廷. 故幕府之選, 下臺閣一等. 異日入爲大夫公卿者, 十八九焉.⁷³

Indeed, according to Watanabe's calculations, three-quarters of ninth-century chief ministers had served earlier in their careers on the staffs of provincial governors.⁷⁴

But upward mobility through service in the provincial bureaucracy was by no means open to locally born individuals without ties to the great families in the capital. Ouyang Xiu, living two centuries after Bai Juyi, may have imagined that "poor scholars wearing plain clothes" could take advantage of this system. But Ouyang was reinterpreting the past through his own experience in the Song. In fact, entrenched elites made full use of their social connections first to secure such provincial positions and then to move back to the capital. Indeed, there is good evidence that governors selected many of their subordinates at the capital before setting off to their appointments.⁷⁵ Watanabe has identified numerous examples of governors bringing out relatives or friends to serve under them.⁷⁶ My own survey of ninth-century tomb epitaphs

---

72. Watanabe, "Chūban Tōki ni okeru kanjin"; Watanabe, "Tōkō hanki"; Watanabe, "Re-Examination."
73. *Bai Juyi ji jianjiao* 5:2924, cited in Watanabe, "Tōkō hanki," p. 34.
74. Watanabe, "Chūban Tōki ni okeru kanjin," p. 359.
75. Although it is clear that governors sent "memorials" 奏 to the throne with their choice of staff members, the question is whether or not they did so before setting off from the capital to their assignments. In the aforementioned case of Pei Du, it is clear he did just this. Another famous example involves Zheng Congdang 鄭從讜 (d. 887), who was appointed governor of Hedong in 881. Before setting off, he requested as his subordinates a distinguished group of colleagues then serving in Chang'an—a group of men who, together, would be known by contemporaries as the "mini imperial court" 小朝廷. See *ZZTJ* 253:8222.
76. Watanabe, "Tōkō hanki," p. 52.

provides substantial additional evidence that patronage in the provinces adhered to patterns essentially identical to those described in chapter 3. Although governors seem rarely to have appointed their own sons to their staffs, they regularly selected relatives by marriage.77 Sons-in-law were particularly common choices. Xiao Fang's* 蕭放 (742–83) first offices involved posts in a provincial government in the court-controlled portion of southern Hebei, where his father-in-law, Xue Song 薛嵩 (d. 772), was then serving as governor. Yang Qianguang* 楊乾光 (794–853) served as a legal administrator 推官 to his father-in-law, Wu Chongyin 烏重胤 (761–827), then governor of Tianping 天平 Province in eastern Henan. And Han Shou* 韓綬 (821–78) was offered a position in Tiande 天德 Province working for his father-in-law, Li Dang 李瑭, though Han would ultimately turn down the job offer in order to pursue a life of carefree leisure.78

Men who could not turn to their fathers-in-law for assistance might count on other affines to recruit them into provincial service. In the case of Pei Zha* 裴札 (728–84), it was his wife's uncle rather than her father who asked the throne to secure him a position in the Jiangxi provincial government in Hongzhou. Maternal uncles might also serve as a man's patron. Linghu Mei's* 令狐梅 (793–854) first significant office seems to have been that of chief of staff 節度押衙 for his mother's brother Xue Ping* 薛平 (757–836), who was then serving as governor of Yicheng Province, situated just east of Linghu's home base of Luoyang. When Xue was reassigned to Pinglu Province farther east two years later, Linghu followed him there, maintaining his title of chief of staff. Lu Jiu* 盧就 (794–851) similarly began his career in the service of a maternal uncle. Even before earning his *jinshi* degree, he was recruited by Li Jue 李珏 (785–853) to a provincial-level post. In 838, when his uncle became chief minister, Lu was promoted to two central government positions in the

---

77. Huang Ch'ing-lien, "Recruitment and Assessment," pp. 79–82, suggests that rules forbidding men to serve as subordinates under their close relatives only applied to relatives within the third degree of mourning—that is, patrilineal relatives and their wives.

78. There were also cases of governors choosing staff members to marry their relatives (rather than choosing staff members who were already their relatives). Pei Gao 裴誥 (801–50) had a subordinate marry his elder sister; the affinal ties were strengthened when this same subordinate composed Pei's epitaph.

capital. Later, the governor of a province in Sichuan, Lu Hongxuan 盧弘宣 (c. 774–c. 850), whom the epitaph describes as Lu's third cousin 從高祖兄, made a request to the court to have Lu serve on his staff. When this cousin was subsequently reassigned to Yiwu Province in northern Hebei, Lu accompanied him there as well. In other cases, patrons might include a man's wife's maternal uncle or his second cousin on his mother's side.[79]

Watanabe did not consider place of residence in his analysis, focusing instead on social class as defined by claims to prestigious pedigrees. In particular, he based his critique of Tonami's theory of social mobility in the provinces on an analysis of the three-tiered hierarchy of national clans 門閥, provincial clans 郡姓, and commoner clans 庶姓 proposed by Yoshioka Makoto.[80] But, as suggested in chapter 1, this hierarchy was increasingly irrelevant by the late Tang. In fact, classifying men instead on the basis of place of residence strengthens Watanabe's critique of Tonami. Several of the individuals identified as having "commoner" backgrounds in his tables of provincial staff members were, in fact, scions of the capital elite. For example, the families of Wang E 王鍔 (740–815), Dong Jin* 董晉 (724–99), and Liu Bochu* 劉伯芻 (755–815) seem to have had their home bases in, respectively, Shanzhou (in the capital corridor), Luoyang, and Chang'an.[81] In the case of Liu Sanfu 劉三復, an apparent native of Runzhou who rose to prominence after serving Li Deyu, Watanabe goes to some length to justify classifying him as a member of the provincial aristocracy. He notes that an epitaph of one of Liu's kinswomen provides evidence that Liu was already serving in the bureaucracy before Li Deyu's arrival in Runzhou.[82] But what is more important, it seems to me, is that Liu's kinswoman was buried in Luoyang. From another epitaph, we also learn that her fourth-generation ancestor and his wife were buried in the

---

79. According to their epitaphs, Huangfu Pi 皇甫鉟 (799–862) accompanied his wife's maternal uncle to Xiangyang 襄陽 to serve in the Shannan Dong provincial government, and Lu Fan 盧璠 (750–819) served in two provinces under Pei Ji 裴佶 (d. 813) and then in another province under Pei Ji's brother Pei Wu 裴武 (d. 826). In Lu's epitaph, the two Pei brothers are identified as second cousins on his mother's side 重表兄.

80. Yoshioka, "Hasseiki zenhan ni okeru Tōchō kanryō kikō"; Yoshioka, "Zui Tō zenki ni okeru shihai kaisō."

81. These three men appear as numbers 52, 11, and 42 in Watanabe, "Tōkō hanki," p. 41. In my database, they are members of clans 7106, 145661, and 5973, respectively.

82. Watanabe, "Tōkō hanki," p. 48.

vicinity of Chang'an, as was a distant cousin of hers. There can be little doubt that his descent from an entrenched capital-based family greatly aided him in his government career.[83]

Indeed, a careful analysis of data culled from extant epitaphs provides unambiguous evidence of the capital elite's monopolization of the top civilian positions in the provincial bureaucracies. Figure 4.6 breaks down appointments in provincial bureaucracies according to place of origin (capital, autonomous Hebei provinces, or elsewhere) and class of office. Included are tenures in office held by capital elites serving anywhere in the empire (with the exception of those serving in the Eastern Capital Command) and by provincial elites serving in their home provinces. In classifying types of offices, figure 4.6—with only one exception—follows Watanabe when distinguishing between upper-echelon and lower-echelon civilian offices.[84] In other words, upper-echelon offices consisted of those subject to fast-track promotion according to two early-ninth-century court directives, whereas lower-echelon offices included all other civilian positions listed in standard descriptions of provincial bureaucracies.[85] The most frequently encountered upper-echelon positions were those of executive administrator 判官, legal administrator 推官, provincial inspector 巡官, and deputy governor 節度副使 (or 觀察副使). Lower-echelon civilian positions consisted of offices that probably required less polished skills at composition and calligraphy—including record keeper 要籍, attendant officer 隨軍, clerk 孔目官, and express courier 驅使官.[86] Besides civilian offices, figure 4.6 also tabulates upper- and lower-echelon military positions.[87]

---

83. See the epitaphs of the kinswoman, Ms. Liu Yuan 劉媛 (794–818); of Liu Congyi 劉從乂 (719–805), a man descended from Liu Yuan's fifth-generation ancestor; of Liu Yuan's fourth-generation ancestor Liu Yingdao 劉應道 (613–80); and of Liu Yingdao's wife, the imperial clanswoman Ms. Li Wanshun 李婉順 (622–61). Note that Watanabe's analysis depends on the fact that the man named Liu Sanfu in standard historical sources is the same as the man named Liu Sanfu who authored Liu Yuan's epitaph; as a general rule, one probably should not draw this conclusion based only on the fact that the two men had the same name.

84. The one exception is the office of retainer 從事, an office not included in Watanabe's list yet frequently held by capital elites serving in provincial bureaucracies.

85. Watanabe, "Tōdai hanshin ni okeru kakyū bakushokukan," pp. 83–86.

86. Watanabe lists two additional lower-echelon civilian positions that I exclude because I did not encounter men holding these offices in my sample of provincial offices.

87. Upper-echelon positions are defined empirically on the basis of the two types

	Place of burial of official		
Class of office	Chang'an and Luoyang (serving empirewide)	Autonomous Hebei (serving in home province)	Elsewhere (serving in home province)
Civilian (upper echelon)	150 (84%)	16 (15%)	0
Civilian (lower echelon)	3 (2%)	18 (16%)	15 (10%)
Military (upper echelon)	18 (10%)	33 (30%)	60 (42%)
Military (lower echelon)	8 (4%)	43 (39%)	68 (48%)
Total	179 (100%)	110 (100%)	143 (100%)

FIGURE 4.6. Types of service in provincial bureaucracies (by home region and class of officials)

For source of data, see figures 4.7 and 4.8. Included are tenures in office held by capital officials serving empirewide, excluding those serving in the Eastern Capital Command (as it is unclear if the men in question resided in Luoyang as capital elites or as local elites tied to the local provincial government), as well as tenures in office held by provincial elites serving in their home provinces. The distinction between upper-echelon and lower-echelon civilian positions follows, with minor modifications, Watanabe Takashi, "Tōdai hanshin ni okeru kakyū bakushokukan ni tsuite," 83–86. Thus, civilian (upper echelon) refers to the following offices, all subordinate to either a military commission 節度使, a surveillance commission 觀察使, or a regency 留守: deputy governor 節度副使 (or 觀察副使, excluding associate deputy governor 同節度副使, which is treated as a separate office in *XTS* 49下:1309), military deputy 行軍司馬, executive administrator 判官, governor's agent 支使, counselor 參謀, chief secretary 掌書記, legal administrator 推官, provincial inspector 巡官, and retainer 從事. Civilian (lower echelon) refers to the following offices: record keeper 要籍, attendant officer 隨軍, clerk 孔目官, and express courier 驅使官. Military (upper echelon) refers to the various types of troop commanders 兵馬使 and military chiefs of staff 押衙 (or 押牙). Military (lower echelon) refers to all other military offices.

It is immediately evident from this analysis that, throughout the provinces under the court's control, upper-echelon civilian posts were held almost exclusively by capital elites, whereas lower-echelon positions were held almost entirely by local elites. Only in the autonomous Hebei provinces did locally based elites serve in both lower- and upper-echelon positions. To be sure, local elites held the bulk of military positions at all levels. But that is not to say that the dominant political elite in the capital had no ties to provincial armies. A limited number of men from the

---

of offices most commonly held by capital elites, those of troop commander 兵馬使 and military chief of staff 押衙 (or 押牙). Lower-echelon offices include all other military-type positions.

capital did serve in the provincial militaries, most frequently as military chief of staff 押衙. In any case, military offices would not have constituted stepping stones into the civilian bureaucracy at the capital.

Among provincial elites, Zhu Shan* 朱贍 (809–65) constitutes a good example. Although his epitaph identifies him as a scion of the Zhu clan from Wujun 吳郡—a "national clan" according to Yoshioka Makoto's tripartite hierarchy of clans—Zhu began his career as a common soldier, before gaining an office in the Zhongwu 忠武 provincial army. All three of his sons served in the Zhongwu army as well. The family was buried locally, in Chenzhou. In this case, one might argue that upward mobility allowed the Zhu family to secure low-level military posts in a provincial government. But these were posts that scions of the capital elite would probably never have deigned to occupy. Thus, although Zhu was purportedly a member of a "national clan," his claim of descent provided him with no particular advantages in securing a bureaucratic office. Without ties to the network of great families entrenched in the capital, his own family was unlikely ever to attain an upper-level civilian position in the provincial government, let alone rise into the ranks of the regular bureaucracy.

Provincial Cultures

Thus far, we have seen how both provincial governors and the upper echelons of the provincial bureaucracy were staffed predominantly with men from the capitals, except in the case of the autonomous Hebei provinces. Not surprisingly, a similar pattern is evident in the case of prefectural- and county-level appointments. As shown in figure 4.7, capital elites held such positions throughout the empire, with particular concentrations serving in the capital corridor, the Lower Yangzi, and Northern Zhejiang, regions of high population density.[88] Given such tendencies, the near absence of capital elite officeholders in the autonomous provinces appears all the more aberrant. Indeed, fewer than 2 percent of appointments to offices at all three levels of the provincial

---

88. Cf. Clark, "Consolidation," pp. 70–77, 80–83, which shows that the overwhelming majority of prefects of Quanzhou and of Hangzhou throughout the Tang were "northerners" or "northwesterners" (defined according to place of clan origin, rather than according to place of burial).

The Late Tang Provinces 179

hierarchy (province, prefecture, and county) involved appointments to the autonomous provinces.[89]

An analysis of where provincial (as opposed to capital) elites served in prefectural- or county-level offices within their home provinces produces nearly the opposite results (fig. 4.8). Because of the varying rates at which epitaphs are discovered today in different parts of China, it is not possible to compare the overall numbers of individuals in figure 4.8 to those in figure 4.7. Nevertheless, it is clear that the two maps complement each other. It was precisely in the region of China where capital elites were least likely to go that provincial elites were most likely to dominate local government.[90] The northernmost autonomous province of Youzhou seems to have been the most isolated from the center. In Youzhou, civilian bureaucrats in the provincial administration as well as county- and prefectural-level officials were all locally based. These included men, such as Yue Bangsui and Zhou Yu referred to in figure 4.1, who were rotated to various posts around Youzhou. Not only did the Tang court have minimal influence over the provincial power structure, but individual members of the Chang'an- and Luoyang-based political elite seem only rarely to have found employment in this northernmost province of Hebei.

Weibo and to a lesser extent Chengde were somewhat different. Although it is clear that the Tang court had little influence over political decisions made by these two provincial governments, a small number of scions of capital-based families seem to have found employment there. It is instructive, however, to examine in more detail these exceptional cases, involving a total of nine individuals.[91] One of the nine was Cui Hongli*

---

89. The actual percentage, based on the relatively large sample of offices held by capital elites described in the notes to fig. 4.7, is 1.9 percent (25/1,340). As this data was collected and counted manually, it is not available in the database.

90. The exceptions—that is, the places outside of the three autonomous provinces where provincial elites served locally—were also concentrated in Hebei. The circles in figure 4.7 located east of the autonomous provinces are actually part of Cangzhou; most of these circles represent government service dating to before Xianzong's reign, when this province was, itself, still autonomous.

91. The nine individuals, based on the sample of epitaphs of capital elites described in the notes to figure 4.7, were Zheng Cong 鄭潨 (747–93), Li Zhongchang 李仲昌 (d. 812), Lu Lü 盧侶 (c. 758–c. 814), Li Fan 李範 (786–855), Mr. Li 李公 (764–820), Cui Hongli 崔弘禮 (766–830), Xie Guan 謝觀 (793–865), Li Ji 李濟 (776–825), and Kang

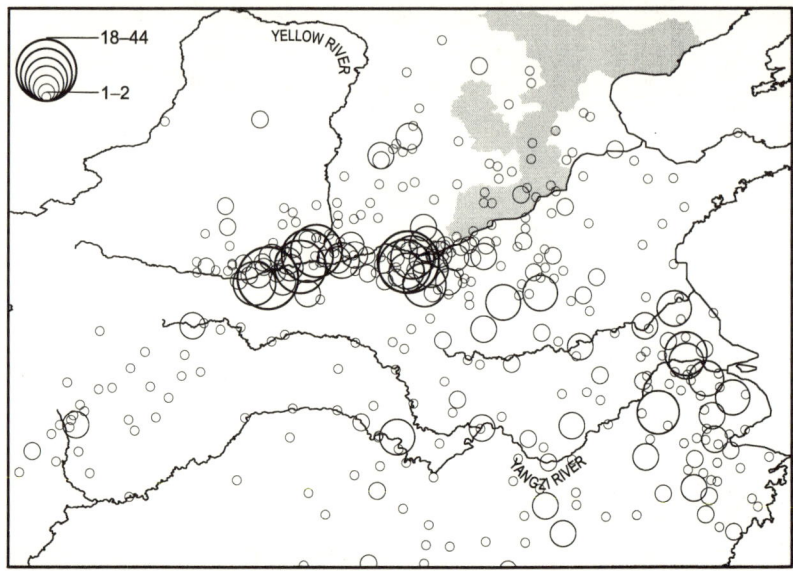

Figure 4.7. Places of county and prefectural service of capital-based officials

Includes data collected from about one thousand epitaphs for males buried in the immediate vicinities of Chang'an and Luoyang and dating to the period 800 to 880; each individual's last office was considered, as were the entire careers of a sample of about four hundred individuals. Included are appointments to ranked county-level offices, that is, magistrate 令, assistant magistrate 丞, registrar 主簿, or sheriff 尉; to ranked prefectural-level offices, that is, prefect 刺史 / 尹, vice prefect 司馬 / 少尹, chief administrator 長史, and a variety of other administrative positions, such as 錄事 and 參軍事; and to positions in the prefectural military. For a list of ranked county-level and prefectural-level offices, see P. A. Herbert, "Perceptions of Provincial Officialdom in Early T'ang China," 28–29. The autonomous provinces are shaded in grey.

崔弘禮 (766–830), who served in Weibo twice as prefect and once as vice governor, all in the years 818 to 820, an exceptional period when the governor Tian Hongzheng 田弘正 (764–821) had recently embarked on a rapprochement with the throne. Half of the remaining eight men served lengthy contiguous periods of time in office within a single province.

Zhida 康志達 (768–821). One man included in the sample of capital elites, Li Zaiyi 李載義 (788–837), is excluded from this list of nine. Though buried in the capital, he emerged from the Youzhou provincial army, eventually attaining the office of provincial governor. At this point, however, he was not yet a representative of the capital elite. As governor, he assisted the throne in military operations. So, when he was overthrown in a coup in 831, he was welcomed by the emperor and sent out to serve as governor in provinces under the court's control. It was only at this point that he settled his family in Chang'an.

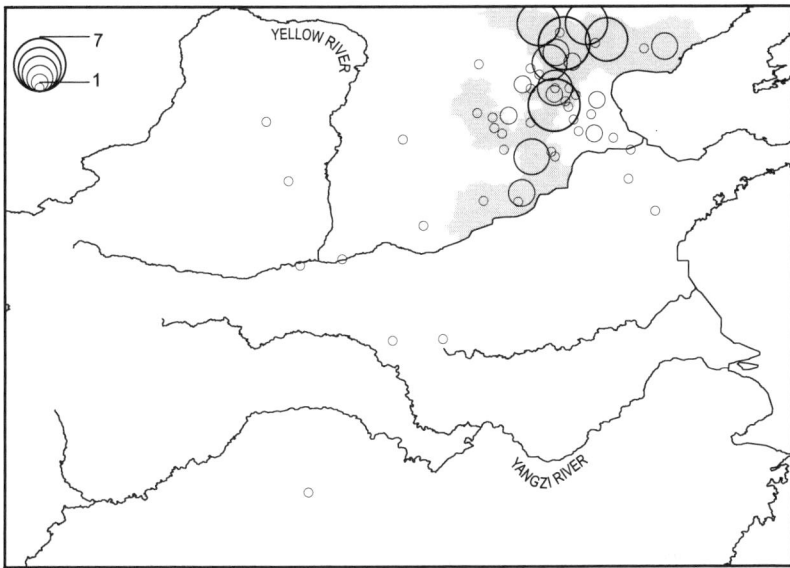

FIGURE 4.8. Places of county and prefectural service of provincial officials serving in their home provinces

Includes data collected from about 250 epitaphs dating to the period 800 to 880 for males buried anywhere other than the immediate vicinities of Chang'an and Luoyang; each individual's last office was considered, as were the entire careers of a sample of individuals. Unlike in figure 4.7, in order to increase sample size, offices of husbands and sons were included when known. Includes only appointments to county- and prefectural-level offices in individual's home province. County offices are as in figure 4.7; unlike in figure 4.7, however, only top-tier civilian prefectural officials are included. The autonomous provinces are shaded in grey.

There is the notable example of Mr. Li* 李公 (764–820)—mentioned in chapter 3—who became stuck for many years in Chengde after his father settled there during the turmoil of the An Lushan Rebellion. And there is the case of another man, Li Ji* 李濟 (776–825): although a member of the imperial clan—he was a sixth-generation descendant of the founding emperor Gaozu—he, nevertheless, served much of his career in Chengde. The fact that his wife was buried in Chengde and that a close kinswoman married the Chengde military governor together suggest that the family may well have considered relocating permanently to Hebei. In sum, even in the rare cases of capital elites serving in Weibo and Chengde, many remained in these provinces semipermanently. In the vast majority of cases, autonomous Hebei was never the destination for capital-based bureaucrats.

The particular geographic dispersal of power described here has two important implications. First, the fact that capital elites moved throughout the empire to serve in all of the top provincial-, prefectural-, and county-level positions implies a particular relationship between state and local society, a relationship very different from that pertaining in the Late Imperial period. In chapter 2, we saw the striking difference between national and local elites in terms of their officeholding patterns. The data presented in the current chapter provides an explanation for this discrepancy. For all practical purposes, during the Tang, the political center maintained a colonial-like relationship with other parts of the empire. Capital-based bureaucrats were sent out to all corners of the empire, monopolizing all of the top civilian posts and returning to the capital three or four years later at the end of their tenures of office. In later times, especially after the Southern Song, when top elites were not concentrated in the capital, these agents of the central government would have encountered blood relatives of influential ministers (or retired ministers themselves) based locally, individuals who possessed the prestige and connections to deal with these agents essentially as equals. Such was not the case in the late Tang; local elites could never rival representatives of the center in terms of status and power. How the state succeeded in maintaining control over military men in the provincial armies—men who seem to have been almost exclusively locals—is beyond the scope of this study.[92] But the low rate of mutinies before the Huang Chao Rebellion provides empirical evidence that the ninth-century state had succeeded in maintaining control of these armies by means of the provincial bureaucracies. Moreover, there is no indication that the Huang Chao rebels, who ultimately brought down the dynasty, had emerged from a provincial military power structure. Outside of Hebei, provincial militaries only began to assert their independence after the complete breakdown of imperial control.

Second, it is likely that the colonial relationship between the center and local society had implications for the development of regional

---

92. Certainly it was understood that military officers should be encouraged with promises of rewards. It was also understood that governors needed to be charismatic. *ZZTJ* 250:8099 preserves the record of a governor who maintained good rapport with the army partly by drinking and making merry with them; the subsequent governor did not establish such a rapport, provoking a mutiny.

cultures. Given the heavy concentration in the capital of the dominant elite, much of late Tang culture as we know it from extant documentary and literary sources was, in fact, a metropolitan culture. This metropolitan culture presumably evolved over time amid the tightly knit network of capital-based elites described in chapter 3. As was true in colonial situations at other times and places in history, it is likely that metropolitan culture influenced provincial culture as local elites sought to emulate some of the behaviors and practices of the politically powerful agents of the central government who lorded over them.

But the situation would have been substantially different in the one region where capital elites generally did not go—the autonomous provinces of Hebei. Not only did they rarely serve in office there, but—as shown in chapter 2 (see figure 2.7)—there is no evidence that they owned property there. In essence, local elite society in the autonomous provinces was largely isolated from metropolitan culture, thus potentially providing a fertile environment for the development over time of a unique regional elite culture. The notion of the uniqueness of Hebei culture is not new, having been popularized by the great mid-twentieth-century Tang historian Chen Yinke. But, by focusing on the presence in Hebei of large populations of peoples he classified as non-Han, Chen saw the region's unique culture as the product of a process of "barbarization" 胡化.[93] Figures 4.7 and 4.8 suggest a second important cause for this phenomenon—cultural isolation.[94]

Elsewhere, I have proposed that northeastern culture consequently came to diverge in significant ways from the center in terms of its mortuary traditions and spoken dialect.[95] More important to the present

---

93. Chen Yinke, *Tangdai zhengzhi shi*, esp. pp. 25–27. For a summary of Chen's thesis, see Peterson, "Court and Province," p. 471. For a more recent description of the Khitan influence on Hebei in the late Tang, see Li Hongbin, "Tangchao dui Hebei diqu."

94. Interestingly, Watanabe Takashi comes to a different conclusion in a study of the great clansmen and famous literati who served in independent Hebei. See his article "Gihaku to Seitoku." In this article, he argues that the service of these men ensured the maintenance of court influence over the Hebei provinces and that the governors themselves were still under the influence of Confucian hegemonic values. But it seems to me that, as long as these men remained a minority among the officeholders of the regional governments, there were clear limits to their abilities to exert cultural influence.

95. For an overview of these points, see Tackett, "Transformation," pp. 99–100, 135–36.

discussion, the northeast may have been less influenced by metropolitan society's particular means of defining prestige and status, and thus less susceptible to the capital elite's assertion of prestige based on particular pedigrees, an assertion ultimately critical to this elite's legitimacy. On this last point, the experience of the small number of capital officials who were invited to serve in autonomous Hebei may prove revelatory. The epitaph of Li Fan* 李範 (786–855), whose first office was that of prefectural instructor of Beizhou 貝州文學, in Weibo, remarks euphemistically that, "upon reaching his post, he came to realize that the Wei[bo] governor was without talent and so abandoned his post to return south" 到官, 遇魏帥非才, 棄官南歸. And Cui Hongli* 崔弘禮 (766–830) left one provincial post in Hebei after concluding that "because of the Hebei custom, he could not domesticate and thereby transform [the locals]" 以河朔舊事, 未可以馴致而變也.[96] Li Shao'an* 李少安 (759–808) was invited to serve as a county sheriff in Chengde Province, but, according to his epitaph, he was unhappy with this offer and, "in the end, did not deign to go there" 終不屑就.[97] Although the complaints of these men invariably reflected negative stereotypes of the northeast held by court officials, one suspects that central government officials may also have been unhappy that they were not treated locally with the respect they felt was warranted by their prestigious pedigrees. In any case, it is significant that Hebei elite culture was distinct from metropolitan elite culture. Many of the new elites of the post-Tang regimes, including the Song imperial clan itself, originated in China's northeast. Thus, understanding northeastern regional culture and its value system and notions of prestige becomes critical when seeking to explain cultural change after the fall of the Tang.[98]

---

96. In this instance, Cui was serving in Yiwu Province, which was not technically speaking one of the autonomous provinces. Nevertheless, figure 4.8 reveals an important contingent of locals within the regional bureaucratic hierarchy in this province as well.

97. Similarly, according to his epitaph, Lu Chong 盧重 (792–847) did not end up going to Youzhou, where he had been invited to serve in the provincial bureaucracy, although his reasons for not going are not explicitly articulated.

98. A subsequent study will describe the northeastern provincial mindset in more detail and account for how it came to replace the medieval aristocratic mentality. For an overview of the thesis, see Tackett, "Transformation."

Conclusion

A careful analysis of ninth-century provincial bureaucracies, based on newly available epigraphic and digital resources, permits a substantial revision of our understanding of late Tang political and social history. It is now clear that the second half of the dynasty was not as decentralized as has often been argued. By the 820s, the Xianzong Restoration had been largely successful in redressing the disorganization that followed in the wake of the An Lushan Rebellion. For most of the ninth century, outside of Hebei, provincial governments were not at all the unruly and semi-independent entities described in much of the historiography. Quite to the contrary, by the 820s if not earlier, they were once again under the solid control of the emperor and his court, with men from families based in the capital in charge of the provincial bureaucracies. Until the Huang Chao Rebellion, the Tang remained a strongly centralized empire; the late Tang provincial system did not preordain the collapse of the dynasty in the year 880.[99]

To be sure, it is not yet clear precisely how these bureaucrats from the capital kept in check the local elites who staffed the provincial armies. The threat of force, the promise of rewards, and the power of imperial ideology undoubtedly all played roles. Indeed, the fact that the rebels who ultimately brought down the dynasty seem not to have originated in these provincial armies suggests that a consensus may have been reached between the court, the capital-based aristocrats, and local power holders, possibly at the expense of the remnants of the local populations. In any case, the post–An Lushan Tang was anything but a long period of dynastic decline and increasing regional separatism. It was only after the Tang dynasty collapsed, quite suddenly at the end of the ninth century, that local elites and provincial structures of power acquired a new relevance as the core elements of the independent kingdoms that controlled China during most of the tenth century.

The endurance of centralized authority provides a context for understanding the continued dominance of the capital clans. David Johnson has already demonstrated the survival of an old political elite in the highest ministerships at the capital. As it turns out, this old political elite

---

99. Note that the Tibetans and the Uighurs, who had threatened the Tang frontier for decades, had also been neutralized by the mid-ninth century.

maintained a presence at all levels of government. Scholars who argue that the beginning of the downfall of the old families began in the eighth century tend to point to two new institutions: the civil service examinations and the informal recruitment procedures of the provincial governments. The previous chapter has shown how the old elite succeeded in dominating the examinations; the present chapter has explained how the same great families coopted provincial recruitment. The key to understanding elite survival is to be found in their geographic concentration in the capital, permitting the development of a tightly knit social network that, as I have suggested, played a critical role in provincial recruitment as well as in examination success. Of course, those descendants of the great clans who did remain in or relocate to the provinces would have rapidly lost touch with this network, thereby losing access to the principal avenues of entry into the bureaucracy. But the clansmen based in the capitals had little difficulty surviving in the late Tang political environment. Like the central government itself, the great families adapted very well to changing political and administrative conditions.

But one central question remains unanswered. I argue here—in the face of commonly held assumptions—that the An Lushan Rebellion was not nearly as important as the Huang Chao uprising for our understanding of the great changes affecting the medieval Chinese upper class. If the Huang Chao Rebellion was indeed so much more destructive and transformative, it is now necessary to explain why that might have been.

5

Huang Chao and the Destruction of the Medieval Aristocracy

Although the Tang state remained strong up until the 870s, the politics and events of that decade did not bode well for its long-term survival. In his monumental 294-chapter comprehensive chronicle of two millennia of Chinese history, the Northern Song scholar and statesman Sima Guang 司馬光 (1019–86)—whose own interests lay in using history as a "mirror to aid in governance"—identified a panoply of problems rooted in institutional failures.[1] First and foremost were the weaknesses at the highest levels of the state. The most powerful man at court was a eunuch who so dominated the young monarch Xizong 僖宗 (r. 873–88) that Xizong addressed him as "daddy" 阿父.[2] The most powerful military commander of the era "feared sharing his military glory with others" 恐分其功.[3] And the emperor, himself, was a frivolous young man whose passion for polo trumped any interest he might otherwise have had in governance. According to Sima, he once proudly asserted to an advisor, "Were I to take a *jinshi* examination in polo, I would certainly earn first place!" 朕若應擊毬進士舉, 須爲狀元. When rebuked by the advisor for his glib boast, he merely laughed.[4]

---

1. The mirror metaphor appears in the title of Sima Guang's chronicle.
2. *ZZTJ* 252:8176.
3. *ZZTJ* 253:8225.
4. *ZZTJ* 253:8221.

There were other problems. Because of the colonial-like relationship between the center and the provinces—described in chapter 4—capital-based bureaucrats seem not always to have found it worth their while to deal effectively with the economic problems and other issues affecting the far-flung counties and prefectures to which they were sent. Indeed, in the conclusion to his account of the year 873, Sima provided a broad litany of the troubles facing the provinces at this time:

> Beginning with [the time of] Emperor Yizong [r. 859–73], waste and extravagance [at court] became more extreme by the day, and troops were deployed without respite [so that] the need for tax receipts became more urgent. East of the Passes [in Henan], successive years of drought were not reported truthfully by the prefects and magistrates; those above and those below [in the bureaucratic hierarchy] were dishonest with each other. The common people wandered about in search of food with nobody [in government] they could appeal to for help; thus, they gathered into bandit gangs, moving about like swarms of bees. The prefects and magistrates had few soldiers at their disposal; moreover, because peace had reigned for so long, men were unaccustomed to fighting, and so, whenever they encountered the bandits, the government armies frequently suffered defeat. It was in this year [873] that the Puzhou man Wang Xianzhi first gathered together a band of several thousand men and rose up in Changyuan [in north central Henan].
>
> 自懿宗以來, 奢侈日甚, 用兵不息, 賦斂愈急. 關東連年水旱, 州縣不以實聞, 上下相蒙. 百姓流殍, 無所控訴, 相聚爲盜, 所在蜂起. 州縣兵少, 加以承平日久, 人不習戰, 每與盜遇, 官軍多敗. 是歲, 濮州人王仙芝始聚眾數千, 起於長垣.⁵

Sima's laconic reference to Wang Xianzhi belies the role this "bandit" played in the Tang empire's demise. Beginning in 873, Wang's armies pillaged the countryside of Henan and the middle reaches of the Yangzi River, as helpless prefects, "fearing the bandits, closed their city defenses" 畏賊嬰城守.⁶ Gradually, government armies did gain the upper hand. Wang was killed in early 878, and his chief accomplice, Huang Chao 黃巢 (d. 884), was forced to flee southward with his men.

Unfortunately for the Tang regime, however, Wang's death by no means marked the end of the rebellion. In the south, under Huang

---

5. *ZZTJ* 252:8174.
6. *XTS* 225下:6452.

Chao's leadership, the rebels sacked the chief southern port cities. Then, in the tenth month of 879, after droves of his followers had succumbed to tropical diseases, Huang gave in to their demands that he lead his troops back north.[7] Despite a series of government victories south of the Yangzi River, the Tang was unable to extinguish the rebels, who rebuilt their armies time and time again with what appears to have been an inexhaustible supply of willing recruits—men who, in the eyes of Sima Guang, were driven to banditry by their miserable conditions. In the seventh month of the year 880, after two of the Tang's most powerful military commanders, Liu Jurong 劉巨容 (826–89) and Gao Pian 高駢 (d. 887), chose not to engage the rebels in battle, Huang was able to slip across the Yangzi River.[8] North of the river, with the bulk of Tang forces now behind them, the rebels made their way over the North China Plain with relatively little opposition. In the ninth month, they crossed the Huai River, and, by the beginning of the eleventh month, they reached Ruzhou, just south of Luoyang.[9] Shortly thereafter, on the seventeenth day of the month, the Eastern Capital surrendered without a fight.[10] Although government armies attempted a defense at Tongguan pass, midway between the two capitals, the imperial defenses only briefly stalled the rebel army, which reportedly numbered 600,000 men.[11] Three days later, in the early evening of the fifth day of the twelfth month of the year 880 (equivalent to 8 January 881 in the Gregorian calendar), Huang's advanced troops entered Chang'an. The emperor had escaped westward earlier that day with a small contingent of soldiers.[12]

Given the key role Huang Chao's seizure of Chang'an played in the demise of the once great Tang dynasty—which survived in name only for another quarter century—enormous scholarly energy has been expended exploring the root causes of the rebellion, although few historians have

---

7. *ZZTJ* 253:8217.

8. According to Sima Guang, Liu refused to extinguish the rebels when he had the chance, in protest of what he saw as the court's disparaging treatment of military men. See *ZZTJ* 253:8219. By contrast, at the critical moment, Gao did not wish to sacrifice the strength of his own army by engaging the rebels. See *ZZTJ* 253:8229.

9. *ZZTJ* 253:8233.
10. *ZZTJ* 254:8235–36.
11. *ZZTJ* 254:8238–39.
12. *ZZTJ* 254:8239–40; *JTS* 19下:708–9.

strayed from the institutional focus of Sima Guang's eleventh-century analysis.[13] The present study does not seek to explain the rebellion but rather looks to demonstrate its impact on the demise of the medieval aristocracy. Previous chapters have shown how a circumscribed number of families had managed to serve in government generation after generation, monopolizing top offices in both the central government and the provinces into the late ninth century. Partly through their remarkable ability to adapt to new social and political developments, these families had survived the dynastic transitions that ushered in the Tang regime in the early seventh century, and they had maintained their political preeminence well after the An Lushan Rebellion of the mid-eighth century.

But despite having previously proven so adaptable to changing circumstances, they rapidly disappeared from the scene in the aftermath of the Huang Chao Rebellion. Their downfall was so precipitous after the year 880 that they ceased almost immediately to produce epitaphs for their deceased, as discussed in more detail below. Although a few descendants of the old capital elite reappeared in Luoyang epitaphs of the first half of the tenth century, they were now a small minority of the new governing elite.[14] By the time of the founding of the Song in 960, great clan scions were nearly nowhere to be found.[15] Why did these families, which had survived political upheaval in the past, disappear so completely with the fall of the Tang?

The present chapter will explore this question by focusing on the overwhelming violence and upheaval of the last twenty-five years of Tang rule, violence that far exceeded what had been witnessed in previous rebellions. Beginning in the 880s, large numbers of capital-based

---

13. The approach to Huang Chao that strays most from Sima's analysis is that of Chinese Maoist historians of the mid- to late twentieth century, who have seen Huang Chao as a "revolutionary hero" 革命英雄 and his "peasant uprising" 農民的起義 as proof of the Chinese peasantry's potential as a "true driving force of historical development" 歷史發展的真正動力. See Lin Yeqing, *Huang Chao*, pp. 1, 83.

14. A cursory survey of tenth-century Luoyang epitaphs makes this evident. More precisely, it was provincial elites from the northeast, many of whose ancestors had served the autonomous provinces, who came to dominate the new governments of the tenth century. See Tackett, "Transformation," pp. 163–64. A more systematic study of the tenth-century capital elite will be the subject of a future study.

15. Johnson, *Medieval Chinese Oligarchy*, pp. 141–48; Johnson, "Last Years," pp. 75–97.

elites lost their lives and their property; simultaneously, there was a near complete breakdown in the social networks that had played such an important role in their adaptation to political and social change in the past. Although, as we shall see, the epitaph record on which much of this study has been based declined substantially after the Huang Chao Rebellion, it is possible to supplement the analysis with traditional historical sources and, above all, with a large number of eye-witness accounts of the devastation of the 880s and 890s. One such testimony—Wei Zhuang's 韋莊 (847–910) "Lament of the Lady of Qin"—has already received substantial scholarly attention, but there are many others that are less well known. Writers like Wei Zhuang and his contemporary Sikong Tu 司空圖 (837–908) were both present in Chang'an when Huang Chao's armies arrived. Other members of this generation reported on the turmoil affecting other parts of the empire in subsequent decades. Many of these accounts take the form of poetic verse. Although one must always use poetry with care, the long-standing Chinese literary tradition of "singing of what is on one's mind," of composing verse with the explicit goal of conveying the poet's personal response to a given occasion or experience, can provide the historian with valuable insight into the psychological effects of the events of the day.[16] The corpus of such accounts and literary texts allows one to reconstruct in rich detail the final years of the Tang dynasty. Although English-language histories of the Huang Chao Rebellion already exist, I present a new narrative of the rebellion in order to analyze the death and destruction in more detail. Understanding the mayhem that affected the masses and elites alike, I argue, is critical for explaining the dissolution of the great clans. I will then focus more specifically on how precisely the turmoil that swept through the capital region in the late ninth century decapitated the old elite at its base of power, leading to its sudden and near complete demise.

Chang'an under Huang Chao

The occupation of Chang'an began relatively quietly. Huang Chao had first indicated imperial ambitions a few months before seizing the Tang empire's Western Capital. After crossing the Huai River in the ninth

---

16. Owen, *Anthology*, p. 378. The nature of the occasion in question is usually identified in the title of the piece.

month of the year 880, he had disciplined his men, ordering them to cease pillaging the countryside. Henceforth, during the rest of his northward push, in lieu of looting, he merely recruited new troops for his armies.[17] Undoubtedly, he sought to transform his image from that of an untamed bandit to that of a legitimate Chinese ruler. After seizing Luoyang, he initially emulated the persona of a paternalistic Chinese emperor, inquiring about the welfare of the populace, thereby putting the local residents at ease.[18]

The situation in Chang'an at the time, however, remained tense. Few residents had certain information, depending instead on circulating rumors. Even the top court officials were not immediately aware that the emperor had escaped the capital. Once the residents became cognizant of the situation, they and the remaining troops in the capital armies began to loot the palace.[19] The Daoist scholar Du Guangting, who had escaped Chang'an just before Huang Chao's arrival, described the ensuing panic in some detail in his account of a certain Luo Quansi 駱全嗣:[20]

> When Huang Chao attacked the court and the imperial city was lost, there was chaos and panic everywhere. On that day, [Luo] Quansi was by chance in his private residence. Suddenly, an official arrived to announce that all officials and commissioners had been ordered to the palace. He rushed on horseback straight to the Xing'an Gate, but the gate was already shut. He then galloped to the Wangxian Gate farther east, where people were crawling on top of each other so that no horses could enter. People there were saying that the imperial carriage had already fled westward. He then returned home, only to discover that the hundred or so members of his household had all scattered.... [Determined to leave the city,] he gripped his horse and galloped out to the Kaiyuan Gate. The gate was already packed with people, with some stealing horses. Many were killed or injured. [Luo] then headed to the Jinguang Gate [farther south], where people were fewer in number. He leapt through on horseback, exiting the city.
>
> 黃巢犯闕, 宮城失守, 南北紛擾, 中外倉惶. 全嗣其日偶在私第, 忽有官司報云諸司使並宣令入內. 單騎俓往至興安門, 門已閉矣, 東馳望仙

---

17. *ZZTJ* 253:8233; *XTS* 225下:6456.
18. *ZZTJ* 254:8236; *XTS* 225下:6457.
19. *ZZTJ* 254:8240.
20. For a description of Du's own escape from Chang'an, see Verellen, *Du Guangting*, pp. 65–66.

門, 人相踐踏, 馬不可進, 或聞人言駕已西去矣. 復還其家, 骨肉百餘口亦已奔散.... 遂秉馬馳出開遠門, 門亦壅咽, 奪馬殺傷甚多. 乃投金光門, 人稍少, 躍馬而出.[21]

In this condition of near anarchy, great bottlenecks at the city gates made it physically difficult to pass through; the mobs trampled each other and robbed each other's horses, undoubtedly stealing other possessions of value as well. Because large portions of the population were consequently unable to escape before Huang's arrival later that day, they must have felt a certain sense of relief when the rebels entered the city in a relatively orderly manner. One of Huang Chao's top generals, Shang Rang 尚讓, assuaged the city's residents, announcing to them, according to one account: "Prince Huang originally rose up for the sake of the common people. He is not like the [Tang imperial] Li family, which does not love you. You can live at ease without fear" 黃王起兵, 本為百姓, 非如李氏不愛汝曹, 汝曹但安居無恐.[22]

A relative degree of order was indeed maintained for a few days. Eight days after his armies first entered Chang'an, Huang Chao officially assumed the throne in a ceremony that involved the beating of several hundred war drums. He proclaimed a new dynasty, the Qi 齊; announced a new reign period, the Jintong 金統 era; and elevated his wife to the position of empress. Although officials of rank three or higher were all dismissed, those of lower ranks were asked to remain in office. Huang then appointed many of his closest followers to the top posts in the bureaucracy.[23] His generals Shang Rang and Zhao Zhang 趙璋 were promoted to the position of chief minister, and Ge Hong 蓋洪 was made vice director of the Department of State Affairs. But Huang also maintained many former officials of the Tang state in important positions within the new government. His two other chief ministers, Cui Qiu 崔璆 (d. 883) and Yang Xigu 楊希古, were both scions of old pre-Tang clans, as probably was Pei Wu 裴渥, whom Huang appointed

---

21. Du Guangting, *Daojiao lingyan ji* 6.7a–b. For an alternative French translation of this passage, see Verellen, *Du Guangting*, p. 69. For additional accounts of the panic on the eve of Huang Chao's arrival, see Yates, *Washing Silk*, pp. 109–10; Feng, "Youthful Displacement," pp. 76–77.

22. *ZZTJ* 254:8240. For a comparison of different versions of this speech, see Levy, *Biography of Huang Ch'ao*, pp. 28, 73–74.

23. *ZZTJ* 254:8241; *XTS* 225 下:6458–59.

to the Hanlin Academy.²⁴ Zhang Zhifang 張直方—the general who had led the procession of Tang military officers that surrendered the city to Huang—was rewarded with a high-ranking official title as well. Even one of the Tang imperial in-laws may have attained office in the new regime.²⁵

But despite the semblance of a smooth dynastic transition, Huang Chao ultimately failed at his ambitious enterprise. To begin with, he never convinced enough people to accept his new regime. The problem of legitimacy was probably especially pronounced outside of Chang'an, in places where he had overthrown Tang authority without reconstituting new structures of government. The few epitaphs that allude to his rule are unanimous in their condemnations. An inscription for a man buried in Binzhou, north of Chang'an, a few years after Huang's demise describes the passions with which some sought to defend the Tang state:

> Ever since disaster emerged south of the Yangzi and misfortune reached the critical passes [around Chang'an], soldiers charged forward, the beacon fires all lit up, calamity spread to the imperial capital, and turmoil accrued around the great ministers. The palace was occupied by a bandit, who surreptitiously usurped the throne. . . . When the imperial chariot left, both humans and spirits wept in bitterness.
> 洎災生江表, 禍及關防, 戈甲長驅, 烽煙競起, 害延京國, 釁積公卿. 官殿爲寇所居, 竊稱僞主.... 致鑾輅播遷, 人神怨哭.²⁶

The message in epitaphs from the time of Huang's occupation could be even more direct, sometimes equating the rebels with wild animals. According to a Luoyang inscription of 882: "Alas, that great bandit Huang Chao coveted the imperial treasures, and the great chariot [of

---

24. Although incontrovertible evidence is unfortunately lacking, the Pei Wu who served Huang Chao was probably the same as the Pei Wu who appears in the genealogical table of chief ministers as the brother of Xizong's chief minister Pei Che 裴澈 (d. 887). In any case, the Pei Wu who served Huang Chao was unambiguously well connected within the Tang regime. He served in important central government positions as well as in the position of prefect. See *JTS* 19下:691; *JTS* 19下:698. He was also the recipient of three poems included in the corpus of extant Tang poetry. See Yu Xianhao, *Tang cishi kao*, 3:1797–98.

25. A man named Zheng Hanzhang 鄭漢璋 was made vice censor-in-chief in Huang Chao's government. A man by this same name active in the 860s was the son of Emperor Xianzong's brother-in-law Zheng Guang 鄭光. See *JTS* 18下:644.

26. Epitaph of Guo Shun 郭順 (840–88).

the emperor] went westward. Neither ranked nor unranked officials have yet received any imperial commands, as we have already fallen into the lair of the beasts" 無何, 巨寇黃巢竊窺神器, 大駕西幸. 百執事已下, 未及聞詔, 已陷豺狼之穴.[27] Even in autonomous Weibo, where support for the Tang throne was undoubtedly less strong, Tang imperial legitimacy seems to have been recognized. Carved onto the side of an epitaph dated 882 is a note that, "In this year, Huang Chao occupies Chang'an; the Li emperor has fled to Sichuan" 其年黃巢坐長安. 李帝奔屬[sic].[28] Although the inscription does not use the typical honorifics to refer to the emperor, he—unlike Huang Chao—is clearly still identified as "emperor."

Moreover, if numerous Tang officials in Chang'an do seem to have joined the new regime, many others refused. Some of the most eminent Tang statesmen, including four current or former chief ministers, declined to attend Huang's court, hiding out instead in commoner residences.[29] Furious at his inability to acquire their support, Huang had them all tracked down and killed. Other officials committed suicide alongside their families. It was at this point that the body of chief minister Lu Xie 盧攜, who had killed himself on the eve of Huang's arrival in the capital, was put on display in the marketplace.[30] In a particularly notorious incident, one large group of Tang bureaucrats sought refuge in the home of Zhang Zhifang, in the Yongning Ward of the city, just southwest of Chang'an's Eastern Market. When they were discovered plotting to join the emperor in exile, they were all killed, along with Zhang and his entire family. Several hundred members of the great bureaucratic lineages may well have died in this massacre.[31]

As Huang Chao was responding violently to those rejecting the legitimacy of his new court, he also began to lose control of his own troops. Though he had forbidden his followers from "wantonly killing people"

---

27. Epitaph of Ms. Lu 盧氏 (818–81). This is the Ms. Lu discussed in the introduction.
28. Epitaph of Wang Zhi 王旺 (c. 802–c. 882).
29. The four in question were Doulu Zhuan 豆盧瑑, Cui Hang 崔沆, Yu Cong 于琮, and Liu Ye 劉鄴.
30. *ZZTJ* 254:8243.
31. *JTS* 200下:5394 says "several hundred" died; *XTS* 225下:6458 says "over a hundred." Both of these sources say that the four aforementioned chief ministers died in this massacre; *ZZTJ* 254:8243 treats the deaths of the four as a separate event.

妄殺人, his order seems largely to have been ignored. The traditional explanation for the breakdown of civil authority contends that "his underlings were bandits at heart" 其下本盜賊, but one must also imagine the great difficulties of controlling such a large army when no system of food provisioning had yet been put into place.[32] According to Sima Guang:

> After inhabiting [Chang'an] for a few days, all [of Huang's soldiers] went out for large-scale looting, burning down the marketplaces and killing people, filling the streets [with corpses]. [Huang] Chao was unable to prevent this. They especially detested bureaucrats, killing all those they got their hands on.
> 居數日, 各出大掠, 焚市肆, 殺人滿街, 巢不能禁; 尤憎官吏, 得者皆殺之.[33]

What ensued was one of the great urban massacres of premodern world history, described in great detail by the eye-witness Wei Zhuang in his oft-cited poem "Lament of the Lady of Qin": "In house after house blood flows like boiling fountains; / everywhere victims scream in bitterness, with screams that shake the earth" 家家流血如泉沸, 處處冤聲聲動地. Wei dwelt in particular on the rape and killing of young women, including the stabbing death of a girl of one wealthy family who refused to submit and the immolation of another who was unable to escape her burning house: "In the smoke, she loudly shrieks, still looking to be rescued; / Over a beam, her corpse hangs, already turned to ash" 煙中大叫猶求救, 梁上懸屍以作灰.[34] As word of the massacres spread across the empire, the poet Luo Yin 羅隱 (833–910), writing from the relative safety of the southeast, noted that "in the San Qin region [around Chang'an], rivulets of blood have converged into rivers" 三秦流血已成川.[35]

To make matters worse, it became increasingly difficult to exit the city. According to Du Guangting, after the massacre at the home of Zhang Zhifang, "the blockade became more stringent, with the interior

---

32. *XTS* 225下:6459.
33. *ZZTJ* 254:8240.
34. *Wei Zhuang ji jianzhu*, p. 316. For a full English translation of this poem, see Yates, *Washing Silk*, pp. 108–22. In *Washing Silk*, Yates has excellent translations of a large selection of Wei Zhuang's other poems.
35. *Luo Yin ji*, p. 103. Although the precise date of this poem is not known, another line in the poem implies the emperor has not yet returned to the capital from Sichuan.

and the exterior [of the city] cut off from each other."[36] Some sense of the difficulty of fleeing the slaughter is evident in Sikong Tu's account of his own harrowing escape from Chang'an, possible only after a fortuitous encounter with a former driver named Duan Zhang 段章:

> In the twelfth month of the Gengzi year of the Guangming era [the year 880], the bandits sacked the capital. I was then in temporary lodgings in the Chongyi Ward. On the ninth day [i.e., approximately when the great massacres began], I sought to change hiding places from the home of the ward head, Yang Qiong, to a spot underneath the public granary. As I was about to leave [for the granary], a group of bandits arrived one after the other. There was one who guarded the door with a halberd in hand. He examined me for some time. Then he came over, grasped my hand, and said: "I'm Duan Zhang. . . . I think back to your benevolent treatment of me, and today we meet again. It is Heaven's [will]! My commander General Zhang is seeking low-ranking officials. I'll take you to meet him; otherwise, you'll end up dead in a ditch." I swore I would never humiliate myself [by joining the rebels]. Zhang wept with disappointment. He then led me to the main road, and we parted ways. Thereupon, I was able to escape through the Kaiyuan Gate. I reached the Xianyang Bridge . . . and [from there] Hu County.
> 廣明庚子歲冬十二月, 寇犯京, 愚寓居崇義里. 九日, 自里豪楊瓊所轉匿常平廩下. 將出, 群盜繼至. 有擁戈拒門者, 熟視良久, 乃就持吾手曰, "某段章也....顧懷優養之仁, 今乃相遇, 天也! 某所主張將軍喜下士, 且幸偕往通他, 不且仆藉於济賑中矣." 愚誓不以辱, 章憫然泣下, 導至通衢, 即別去. 愚因此得自開遠門宵遁, 至咸陽橋,...乃抵鄠縣.[37]

Sikong later made it to a family estate in the hills of southern Hedong.

As Franciscus Verellen has pointed out, Du Guangting's miracle tales also include accounts of several Daoist practitioners who escaped Chang'an with celestial assistance.[38] A dramatic example involves a certain Cao Kui 曹戣, who was captured by the rebels in Chang'an and pressed into forced labor service. One night, a mysterious man approached him to help him flee: "this man grasped his hand and seemed to leap into the sky with him, returning to earth only after some time" 此人引其手若騰躍於空中良久履地.[39] In most cases, the benefi-

---

36. Verellen, *Du Guangting*, p. 81.
37. Sikong Tu, *Sikong Biaosheng shiwen ji jianjiao*, p. 227.
38. Verellen, *Du Guangting*, pp. 75–79.
39. Du Guangting, *Daojiao lingyan ji* 12.7a.

ciaries of divine aid remained on firm ground. Liu Cunxi 劉存希 left Chang'an holding before him the rolled up image of a heavenly master. Protected by this image, he alone in a party of some thirty refugees was able to escape death or serious injury.[40] Perhaps most fortunate of all was a certain Jia Xiang 賈湘. Jia never traveled anywhere without a scroll painting of the deified Laozi; with it in his possession, he managed to escape Chang'an with his large family and a load of gold and silk, despite traveling along roadways plagued with "marauders who knew no limits" 剝掠之人不知紀極.[41] In all these cases, however, Du is unambiguous that these men could not have escaped without exceptional assistance. Most individuals who sought to flee Chang'an in these times were killed or badly wounded; those, in particular, who tried to flee with cartloads of valuables could not have made it far without encountering marauding bandits or rebel patrols. In such a state of affairs, those who did manage to survive might easily have believed that they had benefited from divine assistance.

After the initial massacres, the violence may have subsided for a time. However, a new round of bloodshed erupted after someone posted a poem at the entryway to the Department of State Affairs that mocked the rebels. Though it is not possible to know the precise content of this poem, one might imagine it assumed the mocking tone Wei Zhuang employed in his own description of the rebel court:

> They wear lavish pins in their short hair;
> At night, they drape themselves with embroidered blankets
>   without removing their court robes.
> Their chief ministers hold their ivory tablets upside down;
> Their imperial diarists hang their golden fish insignia the
>   wrong way.
> In the morning, I hear them deliberating on their way to
>   court;
> In the evening, I see them howling their way to the tavern.
>
> 還將短髮戴華簪, 不脫朝衣纏繡被.
> 翻持象笏作三公, 倒佩金魚爲兩史.
> 朝聞奏對入朝堂, 暮見喧呼來酒市.[42]

---

40. Ibid. 8.2a.
41. Ibid. 7.1a–b.
42. *Wei Zhuang ji jianzhu*, p. 317.

Huang Chao's chief associate, Shang Rang, was enraged by the offensive portrayal of the regime. In his fury, he ordered the slaughter of over three thousand literati whom he deemed capable of having composed such verse. At this point, those government personnel still alive ceased showing up to work.[43] Huang Chao's troops perpetrated one last substantial massacre in early 881. Pro-Tang armies succeeded in briefly ejecting the rebels from the capital. Unfortunately for the populace, however, the loyalist troops themselves fell into disarray in a looting frenzy. Huang Chao seized the opportunity to march back into town. Angry that the population had, in his view, supported the government armies, he unleashed his soldiers, butchering, according to one account, tens of thousands of townspeople. He famously referred to the ensuing bloodbath as "cleansing the city" 洗城.[44]

As in all periods of warfare, not all deaths occurred by the sword. There is good evidence of at least one epidemic disease spreading through the population of Chang'an at this time. Wei Zhuang composed a poem in Chang'an while living "among the bandits" 賊中, probably in the year 881, bemoaning falling deathly ill with two friends. The first two lines of verse shed some light on his state of mind at the time: "Bedridden together with the gentlemen, only I continue to waste away./ I have no idea where my siblings are, as this warfare continues unabated" 與君同臥疾，獨我漸彌留。/ 弟妹不知處，兵戈殊未休。[45] Probably far more severe than the epidemics was the devastating impact of the warfare on agricultural production. Survivors in Chang'an's hinterland barricaded themselves in the mountain valleys south of town. For successive years, nobody farmed the fertile land of the Wei River valley. Because Huang's regime had no allies in the provinces willing to transfer grain taxes, food prices skyrocketed. People resorted to eating bark and, according to some rumors, even cannibalism.[46] Undoubtedly, many starved to death. According to Wei Zhuang:

---

43. *ZZTJ* 254:8247; *XTS* 225下:6460. *ZZTJ* dates this incident to the second month of 881; *XTS* implies that it occurred in 882.
44. *ZZTJ* 254:8250; *JTS* 200下:5402; *XTS* 225下:6459–60. Both *JTS* and *XTS* date this massacre to early 882, but *ZZTJ* dates it to the fourth month of 881, a date that is more plausible given the course of events.
45. *Wei Zhuang ji jianzhu*, p. 73.
46. *JTS* 200下:5394; *XTS* 225下:6460.

> The southeast is cut-off; there is no way to bring in grain.
> Ditches fill [with bodies] as the population gradually declines.
> Stiff corpses lie outside the gates of the Six [Capital] Armies;
> Victims of starvation fill the Seven Encampments [of the imperial army].
>
> 東南段絕無糧道, 溝壑漸平人漸少. 六軍門外以殭尸, 七架營中填餓殍.⁴⁷

When Huang Chao was finally expelled from the city for good in early 883, there were probably not many people left to kill. Nevertheless, Huang had one final opportunity to wreak devastation on the great metropolis: as he left town, he reportedly "burned down the palaces, government bureaus, and residential houses nearly completely" 焚宮闕、省寺、居第略盡.⁴⁸

After the Tang court returned to Chang'an, those officials who had escaped the turmoil discovered a scene of utter devastation, where "thistles and brambles filled the city, and foxes and hares darted in all directions" 荊棘滿城, 狐兔縱橫.⁴⁹ The fortunate Daoist Jia Xiang—who had escaped the city with his gold and silk—"came back to Chang'an's Chengxing Ward, and found that his old residence had been destroyed" 歸京承興里, 尋其舊第已隳折.⁵⁰ Most upper-class residents of the city would, like Jia, have found nothing left of their mansions; fewer yet would have recovered any of the valuables they left behind. Unfortunately for those families who did manage to rebuild, Chang'an was sacked several more times in the final two decades of the Tang. Government troops were no longer a match for the warlords that now encircled the capital city. The emperor became their pawn, spending as much time under their "protection" at their provincial capitals—twice in Fengxiang to the west and once in Huazhou to the east—as in Chang'an itself. Thus, in the last month of 885, when the Turk Li Keyong 李克用 (856–908) marched unopposed into Chang'an to punish the court for attacking him, his troops pillaged the city. Of the 10 to 20 percent of government buildings and residential houses rebuilt after Huang Chao's expulsion,

---

47. *Wei Zhuang ji jianzhu*, p. 317.
48. *ZZTJ* 255:8294.
49. *ZZTJ* 256:8320.
50. Du Guangting, *Daojiao lingyan ji* 7.2a.

none was left standing.⁵¹ The following year, after a loyalist army entered Chang'an to remove a usurper who had briefly seized the throne, the army pillaged the town once again, to the point that "the populace had no clothing left, and the ground was covered with those who froze to death" 士民無衣, 凍死者蔽地.⁵² A decade later, in 895, the emperor was forced to flee into the hills south of the capital, provoking yet another mass panic. Tens of thousands of residents abandoned the city. During the day, many died of exposure in the hot summer heat. At night they were attacked by the bandits flourishing in this era of weakening political authority: "the screeches [of the people] shook the mountain valleys."⁵³ The following year, it was the governor of Fengxiang who sacked the capital, the emperor this time fleeing eastward. Once more, anything that had been rebuilt since the 880s was burned to the ground.⁵⁴

Surviving poems from the 880s and 890s provide moving portraits of the destruction. In one poem titled "My Old Ward in Chang'an" 長安舊里, Wei Zhuang describes the ruins around his former home:

> On the ruined walls, thick spring grass fills my gaze,
> Amid the painful events of these painful times, [this sight]
>   pains my heart yet more.
> Today, where are the carriage wheels and the hoof prints?
> The twelve jade towers are nowhere to be seen.
>
> 滿目牆匡春草深, 傷時傷事更傷心. 車輪馬跡今何在, 十二玉樓無處尋.⁵⁵

All that remained by the 890s were the memories of the city's most magnificent buildings, edifices Wei compares to the "twelve jade towers" on the mythical Mount Kunlun. Zheng Gu 鄭谷 (c. 851–c. 910) presents a remarkably similar scene in part of a poem titled "At Chang'an, My Feelings Stirred" 長安感興:

> At sunset, foxes and hares cross
> Where the grandees of state resided but recently.
> How doleful to hear jade flutes,

---

51. *ZZTJ* 256:8328.
52. *ZZTJ* 256:8341.
53. *ZZTJ* 260:8472.
54. *ZZTJ* 260:8491.
55. *Wei Zhuang ji jianzhu*, p. 310.

> But not see the fragrant carriages go by.
> Lonesome amid the ruined walls,
> An apricot blossom is smothered by the spring gloom.
>
> 落日狐兔徑, 近年公相家. 可悲聞玉笛, 不見走香車.
> 寂寞牆匡裏, 春陰挫杏花.⁵⁶

Zheng, too, was struck by the complete disappearance of the powerful men who had dominated the city with their extravagant wealth up until the year 880. His overwhelming feeling of gloom at the magnitude of the loss effectively conveys the extent of the impact of the post–Huang Chao turmoil on the great city. In another poem that he apparently inscribed onto the wall of a former government office, Zheng paints a veritable postapocalyptic scene:

> Under the autumn sunlight, I cannot see the old pavilions and
>   terraces;
> In all directions, the scene is cold and bleak, with heaps of
>   tiles and rubble.
> But the power of fire cannot destroy the power of the soil:
> The yellow chrysanthemums I once saw before the upheaval
>   now flower before me.
>
> 秋光不見舊亭臺, 四顧荒涼瓦礫堆.
> 火力不能消地力, 亂前黃菊眼前開.⁵⁷

In this depiction of the total destruction of the city, Zheng's use of the temporal marker "before the upheaval" is worth noting. As we shall see, the literati elites of the final decades of the Tang well understood the catastrophic implications of the events they were witnessing, frequently marking time in relation to the outbreak of the post–Huang Chao turmoil.

The old family estates of the upper class in the outskirts of the great capital suffered similar devastation. In the early 880s, Wei Zhuang described the desolation of the hinterlands in his "Lament of the Lady of Qin": "Of a million households, not one survives;/In the abandoned fields, nothing remains but weeds;/The devastated orchards and bamboo groves have now no proprietor" 百萬人家無一戶, 被落田園

---

56. *Zheng Gu shi ji biannian jiaozhu*, p. 104.
57. *Zheng Gu shi ji jianzhu*, p. 251; *Zheng Gu shi ji biannian jiaozhu*, p. 169.

但有蒿，摧殘竹樹皆無主.[58] As the scion of one of the greatest of the Chang'an-based families, Wei, himself, possessed an estate southeast of the city, near the Han imperial mausoleum Duling. When visiting the region in the late 890s, he describes the desolate landscape: "I retreat to Fanchuan to visit my old haunts: / Evening light [shines on] withered grass at Duling in autumn" 却到樊川訪舊遊，夕陽衰草杜陵秋. Later on in the same poem, he provides further evidence of the collapse in agricultural productivity: "On a sea of a thousand mulberry trees, there is nobody in sight. / Hearing a lone note played from a flute, I shed a tear in the emptiness" 千桑萬海無人見，橫笛一聲空淚流.[59] Mulberry trees epitomized the productive wealth of the countryside. In normal times, peasants would have been hard at work cutting the leaves to feed the silk worms; instead, no one was in sight. In a similar poem composed upon visiting a country estate just east of Chang'an belonging to his cousin Wang Bin 王斌—undoubtedly also a descendant of a powerful late Tang family—Zheng Gu also described the death and destruction that had ravaged the region:

> Desolate and foresaken were the old fields
> In the river hamlet at Kusang.
> I had known this place as a child,
> So I was left speechless in my despondency.
> Inquiring in turn about each of the neighbors, [my cousin]
>   pointed over and over again toward the tombs.
> When I asked about the village paths, half had been rerouted.
> After prolonged shortages, the servants had all dispersed.
> With the return of better times, it was wild thistles that
>   flourished.

枯桑河上村，寥落舊田園. 少小曾來此，悲涼不可言.
訪鄰多指塚，問路半移原. 久歎家僮散，初晴野薺繁.[60]

These accounts demonstrate the degree to which the old Chang'an-based capital elite was devastated by the violence. Thousands of aristocrats probably died at the hands of rebels and bandits. Those who

---

58. *Wei Zhuang ji jianzhu*, p. 317.
59. Ibid., p. 309. This is the poem titled "Passing by My Old Home at Fanchuan" 過樊川舊居.
60. *Zheng Gu shi ji jianzhu*, p. 50. For a similar poem discussing the scene at his cousin's house "after the upheaval" 離亂後, see p. 383.

survived lost their houses in town; simultaneously, their provincial estates were no longer economically productive. But to make matters worse, it was now increasingly difficult to fall back on government employment, as the bureaucracy was rocked by waves of devastating political purges. The first began in late 886 after a failed attempt to replace the ineffective emperor Xizong with his distant cousin Li Yun 李煴 (d. 886), Prince of Xiang 襄王. From 20 to 30 percent of the hundreds of officials who participated in Li Yun's short-lived regime were executed.[61] Over the course of the next decade and a half, the political environment became increasingly violent. Thus, when an alliance of governors based around Chang'an decided to enter the capital in the middle of 895 to eliminate their political rivals, two chief ministers—Wei Zhaodu 韋昭度 and Li Xi 李谿—were executed.[62] In the first years of the tenth century, Zhu Quanzhong's 朱全忠 (852–912) chief ally at court, the chief minister Cui Yin 崔胤, likewise arranged for the deaths of a number of his political rivals.[63] Soon thereafter, in early 904, Cui and his closest associates were themselves killed when their erstwhile patron no longer needed their support.[64] Subsequently, Zhu saw to the deaths of a number of other prominent officials. Most famously, in the sixth month of the year 905, at the Baima post station, he ordered the execution of seven of the most influential ministers still alive. Their bodies were unceremoniously tossed into the Yellow River, in a sign that some of the new men who had risen in the ranks of Zhu's provincial government were no longer awed by the prestige of these ministers' ancestries.[65] At about the same time, several hundred officials still loyal to the Tang were condemned to death on trumped up charges of factionalism.[66]

Finally, in late 900, when the corps of eunuchs uncovered a plot within the palace to eradicate them, they killed almost everyone close

---

61. *ZZTJ* 256:8341; *ZZTJ* 256:8345. Many more would have been killed had it not been for the vigorous intervention of the minister Du Rangneng 杜讓能 (841–893).

62. *ZZTJ* 260:8470.

63. *ZZTJ* 262:8530; *ZZTJ* 264:8602.

64. *ZZTJ* 264:8624–25.

65. *JTS* 20下: 796; Xue Juzheng, *Jiu Wudai shi* 18:253. According to *ZZTJ* 265:8643, over thirty officials were executed at Baima. Zhu had also arranged for the murder of at least one other prominent official a few months earlier. See *ZZTJ* 264:8622. For a more detailed discussion of the massacre at Baima, see Wong, "White Horse Massacre."

66. Ouyang Xiu, *Xin Wudai shi* 35:375.

to the emperor, including at least one imperial prince. They then sought unsuccessfully to replace the emperor with their own chosen successor.[67] In retaliation, they and their allies were killed in large numbers in the first month of the following year.[68] The rest of the corps of eunuchs was eliminated two years later, under the instigation of Zhu Quanzhong. Zhu then had most of the remaining palace staff killed off in 904.[69] Finally, early the following year, nine of the most prominent imperial princes still alive at this point were slaughtered.[70] Although there had been bloody purges earlier in the dynasty, the late-ninth- and early-tenth-century political violence was particularly devastating because it came in multiple waves and was accompanied by decades of warfare and mayhem affecting the entire empire. Even if politically powerful individuals did manage to survive one or more massacres or purges, it was unlikely that they could maintain their political influence through the entire post–Huang Chao period of instability.

The final and permanent act of destruction to the city of Chang'an came in 904, after Zhu Quanzhong—who would formally overthrow the Tang and found the Later Liang 後梁 dynasty (907–923) three years later—forcibly relocated the emperor to Luoyang, at the center of his own base of power. To prevent the reestablishment of a legitimate capital city where his own armies were not in control, he ordered one of his subordinates to demolish everything. At this time, all remaining palaces, government buildings, and residences of the populace of Chang'an were destroyed. Everything of value was seized and sent downriver to Luoyang: "Chang'an, after this, was no more than mounds of dirt and empty wasteland" 長安自此遂丘墟矣. The great metropolis that had served as a dynastic capital for well over a millennium would be "almost a forgotten town" in subsequent centuries.[71] Its crumbling ruins scattered across the vast agricultural landscape became little more than a curiosity to later antiquarians.[72]

---

67. *ZZTJ* 262:8538–43.
68. *ZZTJ* 262:8544–45.
69. Somers, "End of the T'ang," pp. 780–81.
70. *ZZTJ* 265:8640.
71. Schafer, "Last Years of Chang'an."
72. For an account of an eleventh-century antiquarian exploring the ruins of Chang'an, see Rudolph, "Power of Places."

Devastation in Luoyang and the Provinces

During Huang Chao's occupation of Chang'an, Luoyang seems initially to have fared somewhat better. Wei Zhuang probably passed through in late 882 or early 883. In a poem composed in Luoyang at a time when "that [Huang] Chao bandit had not yet been pacified" 巢寇未平, Wei recognizes that times were tough—"nowadays the elders can only shed tears" 如今父老偏垂涕—but he hardly paints the portrait of a devastated city.[74] To be sure, heavy militarization of the surrounding region had dealt a blow to agriculture and commerce. According to the "Lament," as of spring 883, "east, west, north, and south, travel has been cut off" 東西南北路人絕.[75] Later in the poem, an old man describes the situation in a village west of town, after troops stationed near Luoyang sent foragers into the nearby villages:

> They enter our gateways and dismount like whirlwinds;
> They empty our houses and storage bags of every last item.
> Our valuables are all gone; our families have been separated:
> Today, I suffer alone in my old age.
> I suffer alone, yet is this anything to groan over?
> There are tens of thousands of families in the hills who,
> In the morning, starving, forage for buds and seeds atop the mountains and,
> At night, sleep in the frost among the reeds and flowers.

自從洛下屯師旅, 日夜巡兵入村塢; 匣中秋水拔青蛇, 旗上高風吹白虎.

---

73. The Ming era city walls that are seen in Xi'an today are much smaller in circumference than the Tang era walls; the Ming walls were built roughly on the site of the walls that surrounded the Tang era palace and government offices in the north center of the Tang city. For photographs dating to between 1906 and 1909 that show farmland abutting on the Ming era walls, see Adachi, *Chōan shiseki*, vol. 2, pls. 15, 17, 19. For evidence that the Big Goose and Little Goose pagodas—once well within the Tang city walls—were out amidst farmland as late as the turn of the twentieth century, see vol. 1, frontispiece; vol. 2, pls. 78, 86.

74. *Wei Zhuang ji jianzhu*, p. 109.

75. Ibid., p. 315.

入門下馬若旋風, 罄室傾囊如捲土. 家財既盡骨肉離, 今日垂
年一身苦.
一身苦兮何足嗟? 山中更有千萬家, 朝飢山上尋蓬子, 夜宿霜中
臥荻花.[76]

It was about this time that an addendum was scrawled onto the epitaph of a Luoyang-based great clansman bemoaning that "with the ravages of war overtaking Luoyang and Gong County, the people have no means by which to survive" 鞏、洛兵荒, 人無生理.[77] But although the population faced severe shortages, there are no reports from the first years of the decade of the type of total destruction that culminated in the obliteration of Chang'an.

The relative stability of Henan changed drastically for the worse, however, when Huang Chao was expelled from Chang'an in 883. After fleeing east, he joined forces with Qin Zongquan 秦宗權 (d. 889), the warlord based in Caizhou, in southern Henan, and the combined armies remained the preeminent military force in the North China Plain, bringing havoc to a region that had already suffered greatly at the hands of Wang Xianzhi in the late 870s. The epitaph of a certain Li Gongfu* 李公馥 (c. 830–c. 882) from Xuzhou 許州, just southeast of Luoyang, described the scene:

> In the Guangming era [880], alas, the [rebel] ants converged on the Qin passes [around Chang'an], while the dragon [i.e., the emperor] traveled to Sichuan. The Heavenly [i.e., imperial] soldiers defeated the bandits, who went east to Yancheng [in Xuzhou]. [Li Gongfu] evacuated the area along with other residents, ending up in a subsidiary building of the Chan hall west of the Longxing Temple in Xuzhou. With the door sealed, he silently meditated, breaking off contact with the world.
> 廣明中, 無何, 蟻結秦關, 龍遊蜀國. 會天兵敗寇, 東下郾城. 隨邑居人避地於許州龍興寺西禪院之別宇, 閉關默守, 不與時交.

Huang Chao, himself, was murdered by his own men in 884. But his death seems only to have worsened the situation. Qin Zongquan proclaimed himself Huang's successor as emperor, and, during a subsequent campaign to unite Huainan, Henan, and Hubei under his command, he left behind a trail of devastation throughout the region. Qin soon

---

76. Ibid., p. 318.
77. Epitaph of Li Shu 李杼 (802–50). This man was the husband of the Ms. Lu discussed in the introduction. The addendum was added in the year 882.

acquired a reputation for greater ruthlessness than Huang himself, ordering his armies—according to one rumor—to cart along salted human corpses for consumption while on the march.[78] Agricultural productivity continued to decline with the incessant warfare, with no farming activity at all for several successive years in parts of eastern Henan. An estimated three- to four-fifths of the population living between the Huai and Yellow Rivers may well have died in the late 880s and early 890s.[79]

Luoyang was ultimately sacked in the sixth month of 885. When Sun Ru 孫儒 (d. 892)—one of Qin's generals—occupied the city, he burned it to the ground, "departing only after looting [so systematically that it was] like rolling up [the city] like a mat; within the walls, all was dead quiet, with not a chicken or a dog in sight" 大掠席卷而去，城中寂無雞犬. So thorough was the destruction that the next general to march into town was obliged to set up temporary barracks in the marketplace on the west side of town.[80] Luoyang remained the site of fierce fighting the following year, with warfare also spreading to Heyang, north of the Yellow River, as well as to Zhengzhou just to the east.[81] It was not until 887 that Qin's armies were finally flushed out of the region. Unfortunately for the people of Zhengzhou and Heyang, as Qin and Sun Ru evacuated these two cities, they "butchered their entire populations, burning down their houses" 屠滅其人，焚其廬舍.[82] When the benevolent warlord Zhang Quanyi 張全義 (852–926) entered in mid-887, Luoyang was a scene of total devastation: "White bones littered the ground; thistles and brambles filled one's gaze; residents numbered fewer than a hundred households" 白骨蔽地，荊棘彌望，居民不滿百戶.[83] It was probably about at this time that the poet Luo Yin referred to the second largest metropolis of the Tang empire as an "empty city" 空城 and that Xu Yin 徐寅 (*jinshi* 892) wrote two lines of verse about the destruction he, himself, witnessed on the road heading west out of

---

78. *ZZTJ* 256:8318.
79. *ZZTJ* 256:8333; *ZZTJ* 259:8427. Many of the people who did survive depended on grain shipments from Li Keyong, who was then seeking allies in his emerging rivalry with Zhu Quanzhong.
80. *ZZTJ* 256:8324.
81. *ZZTJ* 256:8342.
82. *ZZTJ* 257:8357.
83. *ZZTJ* 257:8359.

town: "Bandits and soldiers have come and gone for many long years and months; wild mugwort fills the voids along ruined walls" 賊去兵來歲月長, 野蒿空滿壞牆匡.[84]

Fortunately, unlike Chang'an, Luoyang recovered. Zhang Quanyi proved an able administrator with a reputation for leniency and justice, and organized the reconstruction of the once great capital. The city became a refuge of safety for people in the nearby region.[85] Moreover, once Zhang agreed in 888 to join the new regime that Zhu Quanzhong was piecing together in the North China Plain, Luoyang no longer served as the battleground for rival warlords. As early as 896, Zhu began to see the potential to use Luoyang as the primary seat of the Tang government, a move that would greatly enhance his personal influence over the emperor. He ordered Zhang to rebuild the imperial palaces of the Eastern Capital.[86] Simultaneously, he invited the emperor to relocate there, an offer he would repeat on multiple occasions, before finally capturing him and bringing him back to Luoyang by force in 904.[87] Throughout the tenth century, even after the Tang was extinguished, Luoyang would remain either the primary or the secondary capital of successive North China–based imperial dynasties. Nevertheless, the toll of the bloody and destructive period from 885 to 887 on the great Luoyang-based families was immeasurable.

Besides Chang'an, Luoyang, and their surrounding areas, regions farther south were also devastated by the violence of the late ninth century. While Wang Xianzhi was still ravaging the north, smaller rebellions had broken out in both eastern Zhejiang and the Gan River valley of Jiangxi.[88] No sooner had these rebellions been quelled that Huang Chao crossed the Yangzi, sacking the southeast. The Buddhist monk Guanxiu 貫休 (832–912), who was possibly then living in Muzhou 睦州, near Hangzhou, described the devastation of one of the southeastern prefectural cities: "Household after household has been emptied

---

84. *Luo Yin ji*, p. 22; *Quan Tang shi* 709:8157.
85. *ZZTJ* 257:8359.
86. *ZZTJ* 260:8493; *ZZTJ* 262:8559; *ZZTJ* 264:8626.
87. *ZZTJ* 264:8630; *ZZTJ* 265:8636. Zhu had the emperor killed a few months later in order to place a young boy on the throne.
88. These were the rebellions of Wang Ying 王郢 and Liu Yanzhang 柳彥璋. See *ZZTJ* 252:8178–79, 8189, 8190; *ZZTJ* 253:8191–92, 8194.

of valuables; / Everywhere, refined mansions with elaborate eaves have burned to the ground" 黃金白玉家家盡，繡闥雕甍處處燒.[89] At this point, Huang's troops seemed unstoppable, sweeping through the region from one river valley to the next: "The mountains cannot hold back the massive bandit army: / A multitude of isolated towns burn in unison" 大寇山難隔，孤城數合燒.[90] Guanxiu, himself, seems to have fled into the mountains east of modern-day Shaoxing, where he describes a scene of complete chaos in a poem titled "Composed While in the Mountains Evading Bandits" 避寇上山作:

> Amid the towering jade mountains,
> Many refugees clamber with their possessions in tow,
> Occupying some land, whether near or remote,
> Not knowing if the soil there is good or bad.
> On any given patch of grass, one finds a household;
> Nobody is without a weapon for protection.
> When people meet, they gaze at each other with empty,
>   melancholy stares:
> Will we ever experience good times again?

山翠碧嵯峨, 攀牽去者多. 淺深俱得地, 好惡未知他.
有草皆爲戶, 無人不荷戈. 相逢空悵望, 更有好時麼?[91]

After capturing the governor of Zhedong, Huang Chao continued southward, attacking Fuzhou, where his troops "set fire to the houses and mowed people down like grass" 焚室廬殺人如薐.[92] He is said to have killed a hundred thousand people when he seized Guangzhou in the far south, and, on his march back north up the Xiang River valley in Hunan, he sacked Tanzhou (modern-day Changsha)—where "corpses covered the river as they floated downstream" 流尸蔽江而下—and he wreaked further havoc on the principal cities of the Middle Yangzi in early 880.[93] As of the eleventh month of that year, an epitaph for a young man from a local elite family in Hezhou killed by "that coarse bandit

---

89. Guanxiu, *Chan yue ji jiaozhu*, p. 442.
90. Ibid., p. 306.
91. Ibid., p. 198. For a poem describing a similar scene, see also p. 260.
92. *XTS* 225下: 6454.
93. The massacre in Guangzhou is reported in Abu Zaid's ninth-century account in Arabic. See Levy, *Biography of Huang Ch'ao*, p. 117. For the sack of Tanzhou, see *ZZTJ* 253:8217.

Huang Chao" 草賊黃巢 explained that "because everything was burned to the ground this year, people are not yet able to return home" 以其年焚燒赤盡, 人未歸焉.[94]

It was precisely during this period, between the mid-870s and the mid-880s, that two of the three sizable provincial colonies of national elites (described in chapter 2), Jiangling and Xiangzhou, were laid to waste. Shortly before his own demise, Wang Xianzhi plundered the outskirts of Jiangling, killing large numbers of people in the first month of 878.[95] Later the following year, as Huang Chao began his northward march from Guangzhou, reportedly with a half million troops, the military commander in charge of Jiangling's defenses fled in fright. The subordinate he left in charge exploited the breakdown in authority to loot the town, burning it to the ground and forcing the population to flee into the hills. With the arrival just at this time of an unseasonable snowstorm, many died, "their corpses filling the fields" 僵尸滿野.[96] Rumors of the devastation got round to the poet Zheng Gu, who had grown up in Baishe near Jiangling. In the first quatrain of a poem titled "Composed after the Upheaval at Dugong [i.e., Jiangling]" 渚宮亂後作, he wrote:

> Refugees arrived from my hometown with tales of the chaos;
> Shedding tears under broken sunlight, I inquired about the Jiangling region:
> At Baishe, there were likely already no elderly left,
> Yet the clear Yangzi meanders as before around the now empty city.
>
> 鄉人來話亂離情, 淚滴殘陽問楚荊. 白社已應無故老, 清江依舊繞空城.[97]

Xiangzhou initially fared somewhat better than Jiangling. In the tenth month of 879, pro-Tang armies stopped Huang Chao at Jingmen, well south of town.[98] In the years 883 and 884, however, Xiangzhou was attacked along with other cities in northern Hubei by successive generals

---

94. Epitaph of Cui Yisun 崔貽孫 (859–80). Consequently, the young man was buried in a temporary tomb "in the wilds" 荒野.
95. *ZZTJ* 253:8195.
96. *ZZTJ* 253:8217.
97. *Zheng Gu shi ji jianzhu*, p. 264.
98. *ZZTJ* 253:8219.

allied with Qin Zongquan.⁹⁹ To make matters worse, both Xiangzhou and Jiangling were already suffering from successive years of drought and locust plagues; in 886, there were reports from both cities of cannibalism.¹⁰⁰ Xiangzhou probably did not enjoy a sense of peace and stability until one of Qin's generals surrendered the city to Zhu Quanzhong in 888.¹⁰¹ As for the broader Jiangling region, political authority there declined so thoroughly that the region may have briefly reverted to tribal control.¹⁰²

To be sure, as late as the mid-880s, there were still a few pockets of safety among China's major population centers. The Lower Yangzi was still untouched by the chaos, protected by the powerful generals Gao Pian in Yangzhou and Zhou Bao 周寶 (d. 887) across the Yangzi in Runzhou. Both men had been central government appointees who remained in place well after Huang Chao seized Chang'an. Following his break with the Tang court in 882, Gao Pian acquired full control of one of the Tang's great commercial and agricultural centers, allowing him to support a large army with the lucrative local tax revenues.¹⁰³ Partly with the aid of a Korean administrator, Gao ran an efficient government, personally taking charge of the appointment of regional prefects and county officials, appointments that had been the prerogative of the court before the Huang Chao Rebellion.¹⁰⁴ Shanguo and Hezhong Provinces in the capital corridor also remained relatively safe, under the control of the brothers Wang Chongrong 王重榮 (d. 887) and Wang Chongying 王重盈 (d. 895) and their sons, who had managed to hold off Huang Chao by means of a series of clever alliances.¹⁰⁵ It was to this

---

99. *ZZTJ* 255:8300; *ZZTJ* 256:8315, 8318.

100. *JTS* 19下:724.

101. *ZZTJ* 257:8379.

102. *ZZTJ* 254:8261. Several tribesmen seized control of prefectures just south of Jiangling. To emphasize what Sima saw as their lack of civilization, the Song period historian explained that a feud had developed between two of them after they had once, like wild animals, fought over a piece of meat during a hunt.

103. *ZZTJ* 255:8270–71 preserves the letters Gao Pian exchanged with the emperor in 882, when he broke with the throne.

104. The Korean in question was Cui Zhiyuan 崔致遠 (b. 857). His extant works include many of the appointment documents Cui wrote on Gao's behalf. See especially Cui Zhiyuan, *Guiyuan bigeng ji jiaozhu*, jj. 13–14.

105. *ZZTJ* 254:8239; *XTS* 187:5435–41. The sons in question were Wang Gong 王珙 and Wang Ke 王珂.

region that Sikong Tu fled after his harrowing escape from Chang'an; it was also to Hezhong that the widow Wei Yuan* 韋媛 (810–81) escaped with her son in mid-881;[106] and it was this region that the Lady of Qin referred to as the "land of the living" in Wei Zhuang's "Lament."[107] Autonomous Hebei was also largely unaffected by the violence of the 880s, although neighboring Hedong had already begun to decline, as the Turk Li Keyong and his allies sacked numerous cities in the region while consolidating the regime that would eventually, in 923, reunify all of North China.[108] Finally, Sichuan—where the court had sought refuge during Huang Chao's occupation—was also in the mid-880s still relatively stable, as was Fengxiang at the western extremity of the capital corridor, a region Huang Chao had failed to capture.

But even these pockets of safety dissolved into turmoil in the late 880s and 890s. Zhou Bao and Gao Pian were overthrown and then killed in 886 and 887, respectively, plunging the Lower Yangzi into instability. The great metropolis of Yangzhou—the largest of the three provincial colonies of national elites—was particularly hard hit. The city had already suffered during the civil war that had brought down Gao Pian. After Gao's death, in the tenth month of 887, Yang Xingmi 楊行密 (852–905)—future founder of the Wu 吳 Kingdom (902–37)—lay siege to the city, during which over half of the urban population is thought to have died of starvation. Immediately after Yang entered the city, Sun Ru—who had just been chased out of the north after laying waste to Luoyang and other parts of Henan—arrived on the scene. He captured Yangzhou

---

106. Wei Yuan was residing as a devout widow in a monastery in Chang'an when Huang Chao took the city. Her son, Yang Zhuan 楊篆, described their escape in the epitaph he composed for her a year later: "Last year, rebellious bandits seized Chang'an; everybody—rich and poor—was buffeted [by the turmoil]. I fulfilled [my duties] to wait upon [my mother] and fled with her, hiding out in Wang Valley of Lantian County [in the hills southeast of Chang'an]. For several months, the days were filled with hardship and adversity. At one point, because of the menace of bandits, we braved the threat of enemy troops and crossed the Wei River, reaching the slopes of Pu [in Hezhong]" 去歲逆寇陷長安，士庶波委．余隨侍奔避，潛處于藍田輞谷中．數月之間，終日憂患．竟以寇逼，遂冒賊鋒，越渭[水]，抵蒲坂． Wei succumbed to the hardships of the flight to Hezhong, dying shortly after arriving there, in the fifth month of the year 881. It was only in 883 that her son felt it safe to return to Luoyang to bury her. There are no records of what happened to the son subsequently.

107. Yates, *Washing Silk*, p. 118.
108. For example, *ZZTJ* 254:8248; *ZZTJ* 255:8276.

from Yang Xingmi, holding on to the city until Yang recaptured it in 892.[109] Sima Guang observed that, whereas Yangzhou had been the most prosperous city in the empire, it and its broad surrounding region were "swept clean" 掃地盡 after five years of warfare.[110] In the same five-year period, Sun Ru, Yang Xingmi, and Qian Liu 錢鏐 (852–932)—the future founder of the Wuyue 吳越 Kingdom (902–78)—fought each other for control of the important cities of Runzhou and Changzhou south of the Yangzi. Over four-fifths of the population of these two prefectures may have died in the turmoil.[111] In a few lines of verse, Luo Yin—based in the southeast during the 880s and 890s—described the devastation in this region as well as in Suzhou just to the east:

> Warfare in the two regions reaches the fringes of Yue;
> For several years now, only deer are left alive to inhabit Gusu [west of Suzhou].
> Entire families of exhausted peasants were exterminated under the burden of heavy taxation;
> Over half of the old clans disappeared after the armies came.
>
> 兩地干戈連越絶, 數年麋鹿臥姑蘇.
> 疲甿賦重全家盡, 舊族兵侵太半無.[112]

So heavy was the destruction that, according to Luo, farmland had reverted to pastureland for wild animals.[113]

Although the Wang family maintained control of both Shanguo and Hezhong through the end of the century, this zone too fell into turmoil in the late 880s and 890s. Wang Chongrong was assassinated in 887, and his brother Wang Chongying exacted revenge on his killers and their associates.[114] After Chongying's death in 895, his son and two nephews fought for control of the region, a struggle that turned into a proxy war

---

109. *ZZTJ* 257:8363–65; *ZZTJ* 259:8430.
110. *ZZTJ* 259:8430–31.
111. *ZZTJ* 257:8372.
112. *Luo Yin ji*, p. 135.
113. About the same time, in two lines of verse, Luo Yin pointedly critiqued the imperial court that continued to operate even as it had little authority to deal with the turmoil in the provinces: "The court still performs the music and rituals, while the provinces endure constant warfare" 朝廷猶禮樂, 郡邑忍干戈. See ibid., p. 102.
114. *JTS* 182:4697.

for several regional warlords.¹¹⁵ Over the course of the 890s and the first two decades of the tenth century, Hebei also became the site of increasingly bloody battles between Li Keyong, Zhu Quanzhong, and Liu Rengong 劉仁恭 (d. 914)—governor of Youzhou—with the two other autonomous Hebei provinces caught in the middle and struggling to maintain their autonomy. Violence in Hebei during these decades was extraordinarily brutal.¹¹⁶ Peace was restored only after Li Keyong's successors seized control of all of Hebei on the eve of their reunification of North China. As for Sichuan, it collapsed into turmoil in 887, as Wang Jian 王建 (847–918)—future founder of the Former Shu 前蜀 Kingdom (902–25)—initiated a decadelong series of bloody campaigns to unify the territory under his command and destroy the remnants of a Chengdu-based power structure established by the eunuch Tian Lingzi 田令孜 (d. 893) while the Tang court was in exile there. The population of Chengdu was particularly badly hit during Wang Jian's siege of the city in 890 and 891.¹¹⁷ Finally, Fengxiang was devastated by Zhu Quanzhong's siege of the city in 902 and 903. There were reports of cannibalism as city residents suffered from both starvation and exposure.¹¹⁸ The siege was lifted only after Li Maozhen 李茂貞 (856–924) released the Tang emperor—then under Li's "supervision"—into Zhu's custody.

One way of visualizing the extent of the chaos of the 880s and 890s is to trace the territorial breakdown and the subsequent consolidation of the various post-Tang political entities. Figure 5.1 illustrates the most important regimes of North China and the provinces that they controlled during the period 875 to 920, as reconstructed on the basis of historical chronicles and published reference works. Figure 5.2 depicts the Lower and Middle Yangzi region, with territories defined on the basis of prefectures rather than provinces. Because of the complexities of shifting alliances—so that it is not always clear to what extent a particular province or prefecture was subordinate to an emerging regime—the actual situation may have been even more complicated than suggested on the charts. It is evident, however, that the two decades following

---

115. *ZZTJ* 260:8469; *ZZTJ* 261:8519; *JTS* 182:4697–49. The warlords in question were Zhu Quanzhong, Li Keyong, and Li Maozhen 李茂貞 (856–924).

116. For two examples of particularly violent battles in Hebei, see *ZZTJ* 261:8522–23.

117. Verellen, *Du Guangting*, pp. 141–50.

118. *ZZTJ* 263:8586.

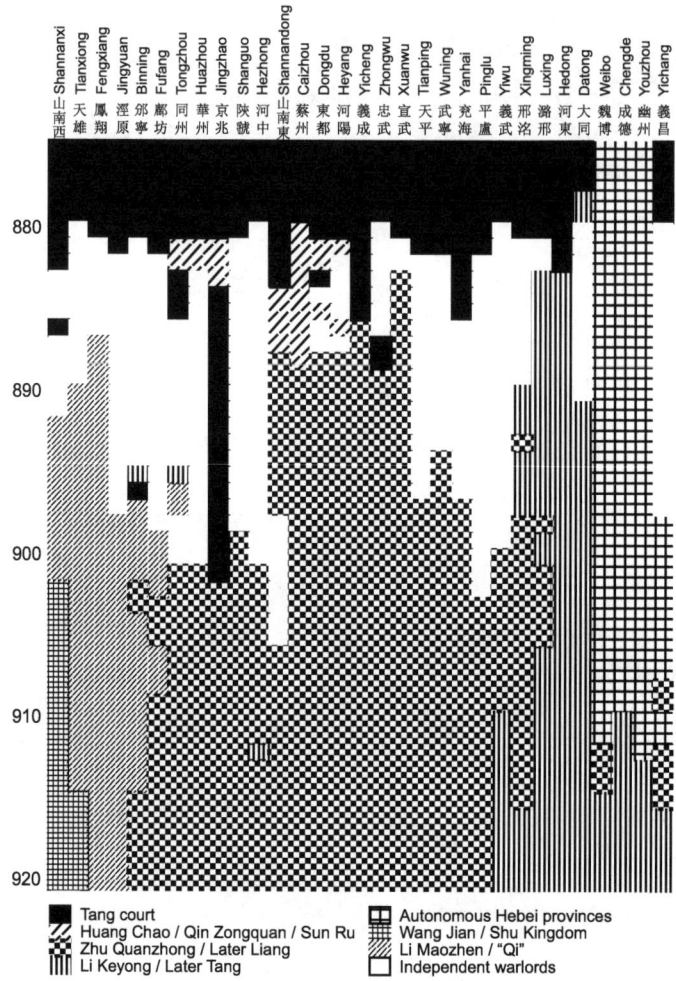

FIGURE 5.1. Consolidation of post-Tang regimes in North China (875–920 CE) (by province and year)

A province is considered part of a regime if the regime leader appointed the provincial governor or if the provincial governor submitted to the regime leader, as assessed primarily through an analysis of Sima Guang, *Zizhi tongjian,* and Yu Xianhao, *Tang cishi kao quan bian*. Because of shifting alliances and the difficulties of unambiguously determining regime affiliations, elements of this diagram remain tentative. The Tang regime is assumed to have been in control of all provinces outside Hebei until the year 880 unless other evidence points to the contrary.

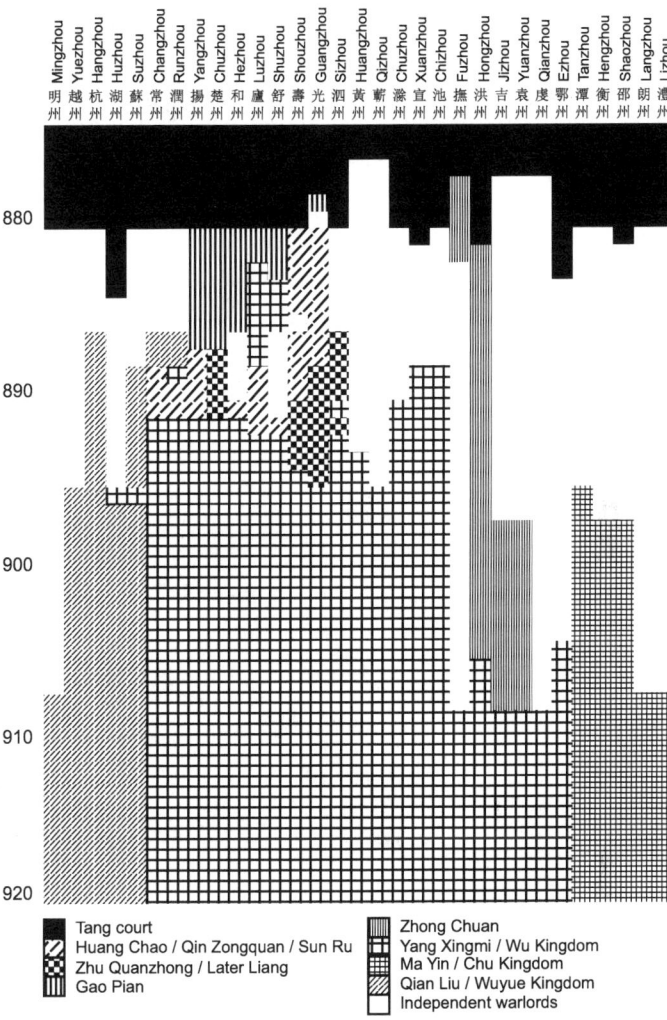

FIGURE 5.2. Consolidation of post-Tang regimes in the Middle/Lower Yangzi (875–920 CE) (by prefecture and year)

A prefecture is considered part of a regime if the regime leader appointed the prefect or if the prefect submitted to the regime leader, as assessed primarily through an analysis of Sima Guang, *Zizhi tongjian*; Yu Xianhao, *Tang cishi kao quanbian*; and Wu Renchen, *Shiguo chunqiu*. Because of shifting alliances and the difficulties of unambiguously determining regime affiliations, elements of this diagram remain tentative. The Tang regime is assumed to have been in control of all prefectures until the year 880 unless other evidence points to the contrary.

Huang Chao constituted the period of greatest anarchy, when many if not most provinces and prefectures were under the control of independent strongmen (marked by white space on the two charts). Much of the violence of the post–Huang Chao period resulted from the attempts by some of these local leaders to acquire neighboring territory in order to establish larger, more viable regimes. It is sometimes suggested that the entire interregnum between the Tang and the Song was a period of unalleviated chaos. In fact, the greatest turmoil occurred in the twenty or thirty years after the Huang Chao uprising. The abdication of the last Tang emperor in 907 actually marked the point at which relative stability had returned to most of the territory of the Chinese heartland. Indeed, it was only by reestablishing order that new regimes acquired the political legitimacy that would allow them to proclaim new dynasties and kingdoms.

The Demise of the Tang Elite

Given the structure of the medieval aristocracy as defined in chapters 2 through 4, it should be evident why the Huang Chao Rebellion was so catastrophic for the great families. Descendants of the dominant political lineages who remained members of the national bureaucratic elite resided overwhelmingly in the two capital cities and the adjoining capital corridor. During the 880s, this region was devastated, its population all but annihilated, invariably decimating most of the great elites who overwhelmingly lived there. Although the total number of people who died will never be known, it is clear that many of the elite residents of Chang'an were unable to escape the city before it fell suddenly to Huang Chao's armies. Several current and former chief ministers—men more likely than nearly anyone else to have had the resources and political connections to arrange their evasions—were trapped and killed before they could flee. Large numbers of other elites who managed to survive the decade—often because they were serving in the provinces when the capital region was overwhelmed—lost their lives in the political purges of the subsequent two decades. Pei Shu 裴樞 (841–905), for example, had held the post of prefect of Shezhou 歙州, south of the Yangzi, until 893, when he was finally forced out by Yang Xingmi.[119] Pei returned to

---

119. *ZZTJ* 259:8447.

the capital to serve as Emperor Zhaozong's (r. 889–904) chief minister but eventually met his death at the Baima post station in 905.[120] The multiple waves of violence spanning nearly an entire generation exacerbated substantially the overall impact of the turmoil on the elite, making it all the more unlikely that a man who was fortunate enough to survive one massacre might survive unscathed through the entire two and a half decades of violence and brutality.

That the violence gradually spread to all major population centers of the empire made the situation all the worse. The colonies of national elites in the provinces, described in chapter 2, were destroyed as well. Moreover, any individual who did survive likely had to flee his home more than once during the 880s and 890s. Although at any given moment there were always pockets of safety in the empire, attaining those havens might be extremely difficult. In a poem titled "Composed on the Road to Hu Pass" 壺關道中作 written in the mid-880s, Wei Zhuang described his flight from the north to the relative safety of the Lower Yangzi region:

> With fighting everywhere, the roads are impassable.
> I retreat north of the mountains in order to get to the Yangzi Delta.
> By dusk, I hope to reach the fort at Hu Pass;
> My lone horse whinnies in the cold amid the wild grass.

處處兵戈路不通, 卻從山北去江東.
黃昏欲到壺關寨; 匹馬寒嘶野草中.[121]

Rather than traveling the most direct way, down the Yellow River to the Bian Canal before heading south, Wei took a route far to the north, through a pass linking Hedong to Hebei near Luzhou. Even along this circuitous route, the poet conveyed the great urgency of his situation, as he rushed to reach the relative safety of the fortress before dark. In a situation where safe routes were few in number, the difficulty of flight was made all the worse by the lack of reliable information following the breakdown of the government courier system. Wei Zhuang described this problem in a poem titled "Ode on Bian Dike" 汴堤行, composed in the vicinity of Luoyang, perhaps in the year 886:

---

120. *ZZTJ* 265:8643.
121. *Wei Zhuang ji jianzhu*, p. 386.

> I want to ascend the Sui era dike, but I plod along too slowly;
> The beacon fires flashing between the clouds announce that the times are not right.
> Finally, I hear that the rebels have been destroyed and the warhorses will rest;
> Then they say there is more fighting far away, that the armies will campaign once more.
> In the morning, I see travelers passing by heading upriver;
> In the evening, I see their corpses floating downriver.
> Across a thousand-mile expanse of green willows, not one bird flies;
> As the sun sets, I vainly seek shelter amid the foundations of an old inn.
>
> 欲上隋堤舉步遲,隔雲烽燧叫非時.
> 纔聞破虜將休馬,又道征遼再出師.
> 朝見西來爲過客,暮看東去作浮屍.
> 綠楊千里無飛鳥,日落空投舊店基.[122]

In this jarring description, Wei illustrates the dangers of depending on rumors as one's source of information. The rumors contradicted each other—had the warfare ended or started up once more?—and refugees who made a wrong decision might easily lose their lives.

The experiences of known survivors give us insight into the various strategies followed in order to stay alive. Often, they relocated more than once, as what was a safe haven one month might dissolve into violence the next. Sikong Tu, whose escape from Chang'an was described above, depended first on a fortuitous encounter with a former servant. He was also fortunate to have a provincial estate in the Zhongtiao 中條 mountains of southern Hedong, a region where Wang Chongrong had managed to hold off Huang Chao's armies. While in Hezhong in early 881, Sikong temporarily took in his erstwhile patron Lu Wo 盧渥 (820–905), the last prerebellion minister of personnel, a man who—like many other elites escaping the capital—probably had no refuge of his own to which he could flee. Sikong maintained good relations with the governing Wang family throughout this period, composing on their behalf the texts of several commemorative inscriptions. He returned to the capital in 885, where he may have participated in the brief regime established after the

---

122. Ibid., p. 184.

Prince of Xiang usurped the throne. During the subsequent purges in 887, he fled back to Hezhong—"on horseback, I return in stealth" 匹馬偷歸, he wrote in a poem composed that year.[123] After Wang Chongrong's assassination, as regional stability declined, he was able to relocate to Huazhou, across the Yellow River and just east of Chang'an, where he remained almost continuously for over a decade. Finally, when Zhu Quanzhong invaded the region in 902, Sikong fled back to his Zhongtiao estate, where he managed to survive until his death of natural causes in 908.[124]

Wei Zhuang was another survivor. Although we do not know how he escaped Chang'an in early 882, it is clear he subsequently relocated numerous times to evade the violence. He spent time in Luoyang; in Runzhou in the south; with the court at Huazhou in the late 890s; and, finally, in Sichuan in the service of Wang Jian, future founder of the Shu Kingdom.[125] It is likely that he would not have survived had he not left Luoyang before Sun Ru's arrival and had he not left the southeast before Gao Pian's assassination. Wei was quite resourceful, often hiding out in vacant homes. "The proprietor wandered west and has not returned" 主人西遊去不歸, he wrote in one poem while staying in the home of a certain "Reminder Lu of Jijian" 吉澗盧拾遺, probably in the outskirts of Luoyang.[126] Perhaps to maintain a low profile, he seems to have traveled alone—"there is nobody with whom I can discuss a dynastic restoration" 無人說得中興事, he observed while seeking shelter on another deserted estate north of the Eastern Capital.[127] In one poem—titled "Sent to the Owner of an Orchard" 寄園林主人—Wei appears not to have known the owner, who remains unnamed:

> At dawn, the orioles warble nonchalantly to themselves,
> As the wandering guest returns in vain at dusk.

---

123. Sikong Tu, *Sikong biaosheng shiwen ji jianjiao*, p. 32.
124. For a meticulous year-by-year reconstruction of Sikong's life after Huang Chao's seizure of the capital, see ibid., pp. 352–82.
125. For a tentative reconstruction of Wei Zhuang's life after the year 880, see Yates, *Washing Silk*, pp. 17–35.
126. *Wei Zhuang ji jianzhu*, p. 136. Although it is not certain that this poem was written in the Luoyang region, based on the approximate dates of other poems in the chapter of Wei Zhuang's collected works in which this poem appears, it is datable roughly to the time Wei was in Luoyang. Moreover, as discussed in chapter 3, most individuals surnamed Lu who held high office lived in the Luoyang region.
127. Ibid., pp. 127–28.

There are still lingering fragrances that remain;
Even now it is worth coming with wine in hand.

曉鶯間自囀, 遊客暮空回.
尚有餘芳在, 猶堪載酒來.[128]

In this case, Wei—the "wandering guest"—probably left the poem behind as a gesture of gratitude. In another era, the chirping birds might have conveyed a sense of hope. But given the horrors of the violence that Wei describes elsewhere in his literary corpus, there is something eerie about these empty houses. One wonders if the owner of the orchard was even still alive.

Most members of the old Tang elite who did survive probably lost all of their worldly possessions. Given how little time people had to flee, especially in the case of Chang'an, few would have managed to take along their belongings. Much of their movable wealth would have been taken by looters. One can get some sense of the quantity of booty seized when Huang Chao's troops were finally chased out of Chang'an. Weighed down by the size of the loot, the rebel soldiers were forced to abandon vast quantities alongside the roadway, to be appropriated in turn by the government soldiers in pursuit.[129] It is unlikely that any of these possessions would have been returned to the original owners. Besides their portable wealth, virtually all of the capital elites would have lost their townhouses in the fires that leveled Chang'an and Luoyang in the 880s.

As the violence spread, those elites based away from the capital also lost everything. For example, Sikong Tu's large library of books and calligraphy was destroyed by fire when troops from Shanguo invaded Hezhong in the late 890s.[130] It is possible that some families had time to bury caches of valuables before fleeing, but even those who survived long enough to return may never have located what they had buried. An account survives of a certain wealthy man Deng Chang 鄧敞, who fled across the Yellow River to Heyang Province just before Huang Chao entered Luoyang. When the violence then spread north of the river, Deng buried his gold and silks in the ground. Unfortunately for Deng,

---

128. Ibid., p. 127. Translation adapted from Yates, *Washing Silk*, p. 95.
129. *ZZTJ* 255:8294; *XTS* 225下:6462.
130. Sikong Tu, *Sikong biaosheng shiwen ji jianjiao*, pp. 220, 329.

it was a band of rebels who discovered the treasure.¹³¹ Indeed, one might imagine that, by the mid-880s, opportunists of all sorts had become quite adept at recognizing freshly filled holes.¹³²

A sense of the financial hardships faced by the survivors among the Tang elite is imparted in Wei Zhuang's poetry. In one poem—titled "My Servant Yang Jin" 僕者楊金—he conveys his own financial decline via the suffering of a bondservant:

> Half a year of hardship rethatching your hovel,
> Not just cold and lonely, but with an empty stomach as well,
> You have exhausted yourself as a farmer.
> In another year, I would seek out a gold fish pendant for you.
>
> 半年辛苦葺荒居, 不獨單寒腹亦虛.
> 努力且爲田舍客, 他年爲爾覓金魚.¹³³

In prerebellion Tang poems discussing a poet's penury, one often has the sense that the poet exaggerates the hardships he faces to arouse the pity of the reader. References to a "hovel," to the cold, and to pangs of hunger are conventional tropes belonging to a long poetic tradition of self-pity. But the claim that a former house domestic must now farm—by shifting the object of pity from the poet, himself, to another man—renders Wei's account all the more authentic. Indeed, in a poem titled "To My Concubine" 贈姬人, Wei makes clear that things could be much worse:

> Do not feel spite because your red skirt is tattered;
> Stop resenting the fact that this white cottage is so rundown.
> Please consider Chang'an and Luoyang:
> Who is there [now] in your former fragrant chambers?
>
> 莫恨紅裙破, 休嫌白屋低.
> 請看京與洛: 誰在舊香閨?¹³⁴

As we have seen, the reference to Chang'an and Luoyang is no exaggeration, and accords well with what we know of the devastation from other

---

131. Li Fang, *Taiping guang ji* 498:4090; *Yu quan zi*, pp. 5–6.
132. For example, the fortunate Daoist Jia Xiang (see above) discovered a cache of 6,000 ounces of silver under the foundations of the vacant house he occupied upon his return to Chang'an. See Du Guangting, *Daojiao lingyan ji* 7.2a.
133. *Wei Zhuang ji jianzhu*, p. 388.
134. Ibid., p. 177.

sources. Most of the elegant court women once dwelling in fragrant chambers were probably dead, their luxurious mansions burned to the ground. Wei is not expressing self-pity here; to the contrary, he is grateful to be alive.

There is no data that allows one to quantify in direct terms the number of elites who died in this period or the total value of the financial loss that they suffered. However, one can assess the impact of the Huang Chao Rebellion and its aftermath on the Tang elite in an indirect way, by measuring changes in epitaph production over time. Figure 5.3 depicts the total number of known epitaphs by decade from two regions of China: the Chang'an-Luoyang region and Hedong and Hebei in the northeast. So as to constitute a relatively random sample of all epitaphs produced in these regions, the figure includes only excavated epitaphs, not epitaphs preserved in literary collections. Both of these regions witnessed dramatic declines in epitaph production during the final decades of the Tang, with no evidence of a resurgence even as late as the 910s. These downturns could have had several causes: the physical elimination of people, large-scale out-migration, or an economic collapse that made elaborate burials unaffordable. In addition, as briefly discussed below, the new elites occupying the capital in the early tenth century brought with them a new burial culture that may not have placed so strong an emphasis on funerary inscriptions.[135] But regardless of its causes, the decline reflected what must have been a catastrophic blow to the old Tang elite in the post-880 period.

A closer examination of figure 5.3 reveals how remarkably the trends it depicts parallel the events of the last four decades of the Tang. The provincial rebellions of the 870s would already have had an impact on the economy of the capitals by—among other things—diminishing in a substantial way the tax revenue that reached the court. Moreover, when individuals died while serving in the provinces in the 870s, it was often unsafe to bring their remains back to the capital for burial. One epitaph for a man from Chang'an who died in the Yangzi Delta region in early 879 noted that "south of the city of Chang'an, the roads are now in turmoil, so [the deceased] could not be returned home for burial" 長安城南方屬道路艱虞, 未克歸祔.[136] Not surprisingly, then, figure 5.3

---

135. Tackett, "Transformation," p. 99.
136. Epitaph of Zhang Zhongli 張中立 (825–79).

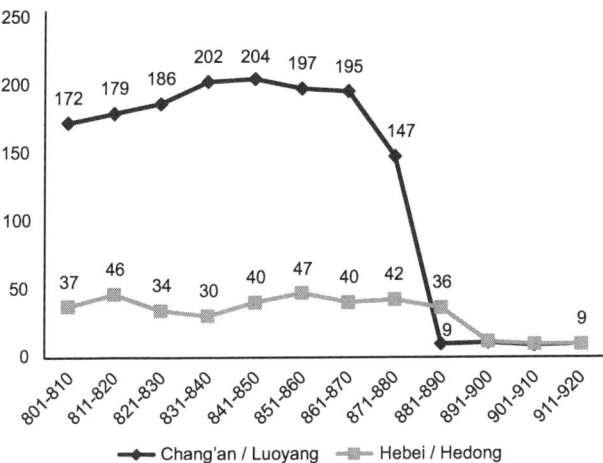

FIGURE 5.3. Number of excavated epitaphs in the capital region and in Hebei/Hedong (by decade) Includes all excavated epitaphs contained in the database. Although it is probably not possible to compare total epitaph production in Hebei/Hedong to total production in Chang'an/Luoyang (because epitaphs are excavated at different rates in different regions), differences in change over time are significant.

reveals a decline in epitaphs from the capital region beginning before the sacking of the capitals. It was only in the 880s, however, that epitaph production truly plummeted. Only nine known epitaphs from the entire capital region were produced in that decade, of which eight are from Luoyang and date to the period before Sun Ru's arrival in the city. Not a single epitaph has ever been found in the Chang'an and Luoyang areas dating to the second half of the 880s. By contrast, epitaph production in the northeast did not decline substantially until the 890s. Indeed, this region, as we have seen, remained relatively stable for several years after the Huang Chao Rebellion.

Figure 5.4 puts the post–Huang Chao decline in epitaph production in the context of the entire Tang dynasty. Although the database compiled for the present monograph does not extend into the seventh and eighth centuries, published compilations of epitaphs from Shaanxi and Henan Provinces provide a representative subsample of all known epitaphs from these provinces. One dramatic trend involved the substantial increase in epitaphs over the course of the early decades of the Tang dynasty, a trend that reached a peak during the Tianbao

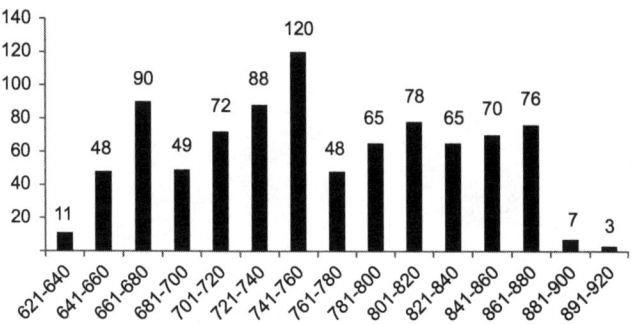

FIGURE 5.4. Number of excavated epitaphs from the capital region (by period)
Includes epitaphs from the following publications: *Xin Zhongguo chutu muzhi: Henan (1)*; *Xin Zhongguo chutu muzhi: Henan (2)*; *Xin Zhongguo chutu muzhi: Henan (3)*; *Xin Zhongguo chutu muzhi: Shaanxi (1)*; *Xin Zhongguo chutu muzhi: Shaanxi (2)*. These publications include all epitaphs from Shaanxi and Henan Provinces—the vast majority of which are from Chang'an, Luoyang, and the capital corridor—excavated since 1949. The sample of epitaphs is probably representative of all epitaphs produced in the capitals and capital corridor during the period 620 to 920.

era (742–56), just before the An Lushan Rebellion. Accounting for this increase would require further research. It could have been the result of the migration of the great clans from their original home bases in the provinces to the capital region, or it might have been a reflection of the great economic prosperity of the Kaiyuan (713–41) and Tianbao eras. After the An Lushan Rebellion, there was a 60 percent decline in epitaph production, indicating the substantial impact of this mid-eighth-century uprising on the capital elites. But epitaph production recovered to early-eighth-century levels within a few decades. The decline in the post–Huang Chao period was substantially more severe and long lasting. Simply put, whereas the capital elites were negatively affected by the An Lushan Rebellion, they were all but annihilated in the aftermath of the late-ninth-century chaos.

It is worth considering at this point why the An Lushan Rebellion was less permanently devastating to the old aristocratic families.[137] At a

---

137. Although traditional historical sources preserve few explicit comparisons between the destructive impact of the Huang Chao Rebellion and the impact of earlier upheavals, the editors of the *New Tang History* do make such a comparison, noting that the Huang Chao Rebellion was far more destructive to the infrastructure of the city of

superficial level, the two rebellions had certain things in common: they involved large rebel armies that first captured Luoyang and then, after a relatively brief skirmish, seized Tongguan pass between the two capital cities, which constituted the last credible defensive position protecting Chang'an. And, in both cases, the rebel armies marched into Chang'an itself with little opposition as the emperors fled southwest to Sichuan. But in three other respects, the two rebellions were fundamentally different. First and foremost, they differed in their basic objectives. As discussed in chapter 4, An Lushan had served the Tang dynasty for many years, understood Chinese political culture, and sought quite rapidly to establish a viable regime. Huang Chao, by contrast, had no ties to the Tang state or the capital elites, and probably very little experience governing. Whereas An proclaimed himself emperor only two months after his rebellion began, Huang wreaked havoc in the provinces for a full four years before acquiring imperial ambitions. Whereas An sought to harness the Tang bureaucratic machinery, Huang (as well as several of the late-ninth-century warlords who followed him) perpetrated a far greater and more systematic slaughter of Tang civil servants. And, whereas An left most of his troops behind in Luoyang and Hebei to avoid overextending himself, and lingered for up to ten days at Tongguan before marching on Chang'an, Huang swept through the pass with his entire army, leaving residents of the capital with very little time to escape.

Second, there were distinctions in both the temporal and the geographic scope of the rebellions. The post-880 disruption both lasted much longer and was far more widespread. The trends are reflected in figure 5.5, which dates and localizes all battles or campaigns noted in Sima Guang's chronicle from 750 through 920 in which reported casualties exceeded ten thousand men. The most violent period of the first upheaval was limited to the two-year period between 756 and 757. Moreover, violence during the first rebellion was concentrated in North China and, more especially, in Hebei and the northeast. The late-ninth-century turmoil, by contrast, affected all major population centers empirewide. Whereas capital elites of the mid-eighth century could flee en masse to the Yangzi Delta region or elsewhere, there were far fewer safe havens for flight in the Tang's final years.

Chang'an than was either the An Lushan Rebellion, the Tibetan attacks on the city, or the revolt orchestrated by Zhu Ci 朱泚 in the early 780s. See *XTS* 225下:6462.

Decade	Decade total	Approximate date	Region	ZZTJ reference
750s	12	756.3	Hebei	217:6959
		756.6	Hebei	218:6964
		756.11	Guanzhong	219:7004
		756.12	Henan	219:7010
		757.1	Hedong	219:7016
		757.1	Henan	219:7016
		757.2	Hedong	219:7019
		757.2	Guanzhong	219:7021
		757.7	Henan	219:7027
		757.9	Guanzhong	220:7034
		758.10	Hebei	220:7063
		758.12	Hebei	220:7064
760s	1	762.10	Henan	222:7134
770s	1	778.1	Hedong	225:7251
780s	7	781.7	Hebei	227:7306
		782.1	Hebei	227:7314
		784.1	Huaixi	229:7394
		784.4	Guanzhong	230:7422
		784.5	Hebei	231:7432
		784.11	Henan	231:7447
		785.3	Hedong	231:7452
790s	0			
800s	0			
810s	1	819.1	Henan	240:7759
820s	1	821.12	Hebei	242:7804
830s	0			
840s	0			
850s	0			
860s	4	869.2	Henan	251:8141
		869.5	Henan	251:8144
		869.7	Henan	251:8147
		869.9	Henan	251:8149
870s	2	878.1	Huainan	253:8195
		878.2	Huainan	253:8199
880s	9	881.2	Guanzhong	254:8247
		882.10	N. Zhejiang	255:8277
		883.2	Guanzhong	255:8288
		885.6	Hebei	256:8322
		887.4	Henan	257:8351

Decade	Decade total	Approximate date	Region	ZZTJ reference
		887.5	Henan	257:8357
		887.8	Henan	257:8361
		888.10	Henan	257:8382
		889.1	Sichuan	258:8385
890s	15	890.9	Henan	258:8403
		890.9	Hedong	258:8405
		891.1	Hebei	258:8411
		891.10	Hebei	258:8420
		892.1	Hebei	259:8424
		892.3	Hebei	259:8428
		893.2	Hebei	259:8439
		894.2	Henan	259:8452
		894.12	Hebei	259:8459
		894.12	Hebei	259:8459
		895.10	Guanzhong	260:8476
		895.12	Sichuan	260:8480
		896.4	Hebei	260:8485
		897.11	Henan	261:8510
		899.3	Hebei	261:8523
900s	8	900.6	Hebei	262:8531
		900.11	Hebei	262:8537
		902.2	Hedong	263:8568
		902.6	Guanzhong	263:8576
		903.6	Henan	264:8611
		903.9	Henan	264:8615
		907.6	Hunan	266:8682
		908.8	Lower Yangzi	267:8703
910s	6	911.1	Hebei	267:8736
		912.3	Hebei	268:8752
		916.10	Sichuan	269:8807
		917.8	Hebei	270:8818
		918.12	Hebei	270:8840
		919.7	Zhejiang	270:8846

FIGURE 5.5. Military battles and campaigns with more than ten thousand reported casualties in the period 750 to 919

Data from Sima Guang, *Zizhi tongjian*. Incidents were identified by searching for the character 萬 (ten thousand) in the digital version of this text, then scanning the results for references to death, and so on. This methodology may have led to the omission of a few incidents. "Casualties" include the dead, the wounded, and, in a few cases, prisoners of war.

Third, the rupture in agricultural production seems to have been greater in magnitude in the 880s and 890s than during the An Lushan Rebellion. As noted above, large areas of Henan could not be farmed for several successive years in the 880s owing to the destruction caused by roving armies. Huge numbers of people seem to have died of starvation. Partly for this reason, city sieges seem to have had an especially great impact on the urban populations. Whereas accounts of cannibalism are extremely rare during the Tang dynasty, there are numerous references to starving urbanites resorting to such practices in the post–Huang Chao period. Cannibalism was reported in Chang'an in 882, in Chenzhou (in central Henan) in 883, in both Jiangling and Xiangzhou in 886, in Yangzhou in 887, in Xuanzhou (south of the Yangzi) in 889, in Pengzhou (in Sichuan) in 894, in Fengxiang in 902, and in Cangzhou (in eastern Hebei) in 906.[138] There were also at least two reported cases of cannibalism perpetrated on the battlefield by starving armies, in 888 in Heyang and in 893 in Hebei.[139] Simply put, compared to earlier periods of upheavals during the Tang, the final quarter century of the dynasty was devastating on a whole different order of magnitude.[140] It was precisely this devastation and its particular concentration in the capital corridor, the home base of the Tang political elites, that led most directly to that elite's demise.

---

138. *ZZTJ* 254:8268, 255:8296, 257:8358, 258:8388, 259:8455, 263:8586, 267:8720; *JTS* 19下:724.

139. In 888, after the warlord in Heyang failed to revive agricultural production, his starving troops resorted to eating human flesh; see *ZZTJ* 257:8375. In 893, after a particularly devastating battle in Hebei, Li Keyong's troops ate some of the war dead; see *ZZTJ* 259:8439.

140. It is worth considering why the idea of the greater severity of the An Lushan Rebellion persists in scholarly literature. According to Steven Pinker, *Better Angels of Our Nature*, pp. 194–95, the An Lushan Rebellion was no less than "the worst atrocity" in world history in terms of overall deaths in relation to the world population of the time (a conclusion he draws by substantially underestimating the degree to which the apparant population collapse post–An Lushan can almost entirely be explained by the empirewide breakdown in census record keeping). One explanation for the persistent exaggeration of the rebellion's impact is simply the influence on scholars of the pervasive references to An Lushan in eighth- and ninth-century literature. By contrast, far fewer poets and prose writers of distinction survived into the tenth century to tell tales of post–Huang Chao devastation.

The Survivors and the New Structure of Power

Some descendants of the old elite did make it through the violence of the post-880 period. Although these individuals had probably lost all that they had once possessed of economic value, they still had their human capital and could find employment among emerging regimes in need of educated and experienced bureaucrats. But these survivors were now on their own. Most had lost numerous friends and family members. The poetry of the period, much of which was composed by scions of the old families, frequently discussed the large-scale deaths of acquaintances. The poet Han Wo 韓偓 (842–923), a native of Chang'an, wrote on this topic in a poem titled "Suffering through the Upheaval" 傷亂:

> In my hometown, warfare has raged now for many years;
> Away from home, all day I see the banners of army troops.
> I've lost touch with my close friends, who grow weak and sick:
> I don't know who now is alive and who is dead.
>
> 故國幾年猶戰鬥, 異鄉終日見旌旗. 交親流落身羸病, 誰在誰亡兩不知.[141]

Wei Zhuang made a similar observation while visiting the town in which he grew up, just east of Chang'an: "Today, there is nobody left to inquire with about my old friends; in the evening light, withered grass covers desolate [grave] tumuli" 今日故人無處問, 夕陽衰草盡荒丘.[142] The act of inquiring about survivors, as seen in this couplet, is a motif that reappeared numerous times in the poetry of the period. When Wei Zhuang encountered a friend in the south, he asked him, "When you left, who was still there in our old ward [in Chang'an]?" 來時舊里人誰在.[143] In a particularly poignant poem dedicated to a hermit who had avoided the "fame" of office by retreating to the mountains, Luo Yin suggested that, for many, inquiring about survivors had become an almost necessary ritual:

> I parted from you fifteen years ago.
> When we parted, the world had not yet fallen into chaos.

---

141. *Han Wo shiji jianzhu*, p. 148.
142. *Wei Zhuang ji jianzhu*, p. 378. For a second poem by Wei expressing a similar sentiment, see Yates, *Washing Silk*, p. 89.
143. Ibid., p. 203.

In this period of upheaval, what joy that we are both still alive!
Can one bear to hear once more about who is living and who is dead?
In this joyous meeting, we pointlessly lament the vestiges of the past:
Among our old friends, who has left us in order to be mourned at a forsaken grave?
I warmly part from you, the Man who has Escaped Fame:
I will think of you as I look to the clouds above Mount Qianqiu.

十五年前即別君, 別時天下未紛紜. 亂罹且喜身俱在, 存沒那堪耳更聞!
良會謾勞悲曩跡, 舊交誰去弔荒墳. 殷懃爲謝逃名客, 想望千秋嶺上雲.[144]

The trauma these poets must have felt at the loss of so many friends and family members is apparent in the near postapocalyptic language common to poems from the 880s and 890s. Dozens of poems from this period seemed to divide up the recent past into the era "before the upheaval" 亂前 and the era "after the upheaval" 亂後.[145] Some writers, like Luo Yin, used such a periodization to discuss the hardships of the new era: "After the upheaval, many a time have my dreams of returning home been thwarted; / Since we parted last, everywhere the roads are obstructed" 亂後幾回鄉夢隔, 別來何處路行難.[146] But more common

---

144. *Luo Yin ji*, p. 107. The poem is titled "Sending Off Scholar Mei Back to Ningguo" 送梅處士歸寧國.

145. Although the expression "after the upheaval" appears in Du Fu's poetry describing the post–An Lushan period as well, self-conscious allusions in the late ninth-century to the great poets of earlier generations are only to be expected in the Chinese poetic tradition. One should not conclude from these allusions that the An Lushan Rebellion was comparable to the Huang Chao Rebellion in severity, which was not the case, as the epitaph data demonstrates.

146. *Luo Yin ji*, p. 137. For a poem by Luo Yin on a very similar theme, titled "Encountering a Friend after the Upheaval" 亂後逢友人, see ibid., p. 86. In a twist on this theme, Du Xunhe 杜荀鶴, who spent much of the final years of the Tang hiding out in the mountains, wrote over a dozen poems praising a life of retreat in the period "after the upheaval." In his poem "Returning to the Mountains after the Upheaval" 亂後歸山, for example, he writes: "In this era of upheaval, I return to a mountain valley, / Where I am joyfully oblivious of the sounds of war drums. / Poetry and calligraphy fill my bookshelves, / And my brother and nephew remain safe from military conscription" 亂世歸山谷, 征鼙喜不聞. 詩書猶滿架, 弟侄未爲軍. See Du Xunhe, *Tangfeng ji* 上:51. For a similar poem, see also 上:41.

were accounts of the disappearance of acquaintances. Wei Zhuang, for example, asserted that, "after the upheaval, my old friends are few in number" 亂後故人少.[147] And several poets, including Tang Yanqian 唐彥謙 and the Buddhist monk Qiji 齊己 (c. 863–c. 937), composed poems about visiting the vacant residences of deceased friends "after the upheaval."[148] In a context where so many members of the elite had vanished, the old social network of capital-based elites—a network that had persisted for several centuries and had survived the An Lushan Rebellion—finally broke down. Survivors who fled the capital faced an entirely new social environment, where they could no longer depend on this network for support. Wei Zhuang sums up the situation in two lines of verse when encountering a friend after escaping North China: "Today, we're at the edge of the world, after each fleeing Qin [i.e., Chang'an].... You and I are both strangers here" (今日天涯各避秦.... 與君俱是異鄉人).[149]

A complete assessment of the impact of the fragmentation of the old capital social network is beyond the scope of the present study. One important effect was that members of the old elite could no longer depend on relatives to obtain posts in government. They were well educated and, to some extent, could still exploit the prestige of their family names to secure offices in the new provincial regimes. But it was now impossible for the same group of families to monopolize the bureaucracy as they once had done. The new regimes were established by a motley group of provincial power holders who appeared on the scene suddenly after Tang political authority evaporated in the year 880. Some had been commanders in the Tang provincial armies; more often than not, however, they were local strongmen with no ties at all to the old Tang power structure.[150] As successful new regimes began to grow by conquering neighboring prefectures and provinces, individuals and their families who had served such a regime since its inception frequently formed the new and very different elites of the tenth century. For example, a disproportionate number of men serving the Wu Kingdom and

---

147. *Wei Zhuang ji jianzhu*, 131.
148. *Quan Tang shi* 672:7687, 845:9564.
149. *Wei Zhuang ji jianzhu*, p. 383.
150. The founders of the Ten Kingdoms, in particular, had no ties to either the regular Tang bureaucracy or the late Tang provincial governments. See Clark, "Scoundrels, Rogues, and Refugees."

its successor, the Southern Tang 南唐 (937–75), were from families who came from Luzhou 盧州, where the Wu founder Yang Xingmi had originated.[151] Although numerous scions of old Tang clans did serve these southern states as well, the core of the new social networks that dominated tenth-century politics would emerge from a very different group of families, largely with provincial origins.

---

151. Tackett, "Transformation," pp. 192–95.

Conclusion

In the ninth century of the Common Era, the bureaucracy of Tang dynasty China was dominated by a circumscribed group of great aristocratic clans that had maintained political influence for centuries. Most of these families had first emerged as provincial elites soon after the fall of the Han dynasty. While still entrenched on provincial estates, they began serving in the governments of a series of dynasties controlling a disunified China. Their positions of political power were solidified over the course of the third and fourth centuries, after bureaucratic recruitment, especially in the north, began to depend increasingly on the official ranking of provincial families.[1] To be sure, the ranked families were large in number, so that, in the long run, they could not all maintain influence at court. Yet many of these families did remain politically significant through the numerous regime changes of the sixth century, through the reunification of China under the Sui, and through the military uprising that established the Tang dynasty.[2]

---

1. Johnson, *Medieval Chinese Oligarchy*, pp. 19–31. So important were the family rankings that one scholar has concluded that the Chinese administration of the era was far from a "bureaucracy" in the Weberian sense; see Grafflin, "Reinventing China." One should be careful, however, not to assume that the Tang great families were as powerful in the earlier period as they would become in the seventh and eighth centuries. With regard to the pre-Tang period, Al Dien has asserted that "the putative 'powerful aristocratic clans' were neither powerful, nor aristocratic, nor even clans." See Dien, "Introduction," p. 1.

2. A careful study of extant epitaphs would substantially clarify how the political elite was affected by the regime changes of the sixth and early seventh centuries. Note that the great families of South China may have been less effective than those of North China at maintaining their political influence into the Tang. See Grafflin, "Great Families." Indeed, the epitaph record seems to corroborate the general absence of descendants of southern clans among the Tang capital elite; see figure 1.5d (in chapter 1).

By the seventh century, the basis of power of this medieval aristocracy had begun to change in fundamental ways. The dismantling under the Sui of the system of ranked families eliminated any juridical protection of their political status. Meanwhile, their decisions to aggregate at the capital over the course of the sixth and seventh centuries led them to lose control of the provincial estates undoubtedly once critical to their long-term survival. They faced a number of additional existential challenges during the Tang dynasty. By the turn of the eighth century, the civil service examination became a regularized—albeit still minor—recruitment tool for the bureaucracy, in principle providing some men of lowly background with an avenue of upward mobility. And, half a century later, new provincial administrations were established that bypassed the central government's recruitment procedures altogether, offering—at least in principle—new opportunities for provincial elites to compete with the old families for political influence. Meanwhile, the breakdown of the equal-field system—which had once mandated the regular redistribution of land—and the deregulation of commerce in the wake of the An Lushan Rebellion of the mid-eighth century created an environment favorable to the development of new landed and commercial elites.

Yet, remarkably, despite political upheaval and despite these fundamental economic and institutional transformations, a great many of the old families managed to adapt to the changing circumstances, retaining their political dominance until the final years of the Tang dynasty. As late as the mid-ninth century, descendants of pre-Tang great clans continued to occupy the lion's share of central government positions, while also monopolizing offices all across the empire, both at the prefectural and county levels, and within the newly established provincial bureaucracies. Yet at the end of the ninth century, after having maintained themselves near the pinnacle of political power for the better part of a millennium—far longer than, for example, most French noble families on the eve of the French Revolution[3]—they disappeared suddenly from the scene. By the founding of the Song dynasty in the second half of the tenth century, they had almost entirely vanished from the historical record.

---

3. Chaussinand-Nogaret, *La noblesse*, pp. 48–49.

The collapse of the medieval aristocracy has long been recognized by historians as a critical component of the changes that utterly transformed China over the course of the "Tang-Song transition." But a comprehensive exploration of the phenomenon has been hampered by a paucity of source materials. The thousands of Tang tomb epitaphs excavated in recent decades, however, hold the promise of revolutionizing our understanding of elite society during this period. On the basis of these funerary biographies in conjunction with a newly compiled biographical database focusing on ninth-century elites, this book has sought to explain both the long-term survival of the great aristocratic clans and their sudden demise.

Making use of the data culled from the epitaphs, this study has proposed a new approach to conceptualizing the Tang elite by treating it primarily in political terms. In the past most historians have focused rather on a particular status elite, namely, those "great clans" identified by surname and choronym—the pre-Tang place of family origin—who based their prestige on descent from illustrious forebears of the distant past. Such great clans were, thus, generally equated with the medieval aristocracy. Indeed, it is clear that an aristocratic mentality linking prestige to ancestry was pervasive under the Tang and that a claim to such descent was a requirement for high status in society. But, by the ninth century, this status group had grown to such a large size that prestigious descent alone was no longer sufficient to maintain a family's position in society. It is clear that the dominant Tang political elite was only a small subgroup among the clans.

In order to identify the members of this subgroup, the present study has proposed two different approaches. First, one can examine the spatial distribution of political power among those families—the economic elite—who could afford the elaborate burials that included tomb epitaphs. By systematically examining the large corpus of extant epitaphs, it was possible to distinguish fundamental differences between capital-based elites and provincial elites. The former tended overwhelmingly to hold offices of national significance generation after generation; the latter rarely held offices, and if they did, they only served locally—usually in lower-tier positions of the provincial administrations. Occasionally, the scions of the capital clans did permanently relocate to the provinces, especially when they had difficulty succeeding in the fiercely competitive environment of the capital. It would have been understood, however, that—with the possible exception of migrants to two or three colonies of national elites that did exist in South China—such outward mobility from the capital led invariably to downward mobility.

A second means of identifying the dominant political elite is to make use of social network analysis, drawing on data from epitaphs and other sources to reconstruct the capital-based kin and marriage networks of politically powerful "patrilines." Most such patrilines can be shown to have held office in nearly every generation since the pre-Tang period. Included among these families were the major subbranches of eminent "marriage-ban clans," as well as the imperial clan, a number of military families, and the families of the most famous ninth-century poetry and prose writers. The marriage network in question included at least three-fifths of known capital elites alive in the ninth century; the substantial majority of ninth-century chief ministers, ministers of personnel, and chief examiners; the majority of provincial governors; and most of the men occupying upper-echelon positions in the provincial bureaucracies. In sum, this highly restricted marriage and kin network essentially defined the dominant political elite of the Tang dynasty.

By defining the political elite on the basis of a marriage network, it becomes more readily apparent how the Tang aristocracy managed to persist for so long. Much past scholarship has tended to assume either an economic or an institutional basis for political power. From this perspective, without provincial lands, the old families lost their ability to assert independence from the state. Their new metropolitan townhouses, their estates in the capital region, and their portable wealth were all more vulnerable to confiscation at the whim of the throne or upon the establishment of a new political regime. Meanwhile, the creation of institutions allowing—in principle—new avenues of upward mobility were said to have dealt such families a further blow. Thus, by the late Tang, the aristocracy supposedly no longer possessed a solid foundation on which to base its authority. The former great families became mere relics, only sustained by the prestige of their clan names. Their downfall was preordained.

What has been neglected in such an analysis is the ability of the elites to transform themselves in order to adapt to changing circumstances. When the clans relocated to the capital cities early in the Tang dynasty, they effectively exchanged their power base in provincial lands for something that was, in fact, even more valuable: integration into a dense, capital-based social network. This network constituted a concrete resource that essentially guaranteed their continued political dominance. Within a culture that placed great emphasis on ties of blood and marriage, the social capital embedded in this network was especially effective. Members of the network rapidly came to dominate the offices that controlled the reproduction of the bureaucracy—notably the offices of chief minister, minister of personnel, chief examiner, and provincial governor. They were thus able to coopt as officeholders successive generations of their own relatives and acquaintances. This network was by no means destined to collapse with the end of the Tang regime. If the transfer of power had consisted of a palace coup or an uprising led by a member of the former regime—as had indeed been the case in the earlier founding of the Sui and Tang dynasties as well as of the abortive regime of An Lushan—a new dynastic founder might well have been expected to harness the previous bureaucratic infrastructure. He would, thus, have depended on a substantial contingent of the capital network to staff his administration. These men would then have brought in their relatives and acquaintances to serve beneath them, and so the old families would have survived yet another change of regime.

However, the Tang did not end with a palace coup but with a series of episodes of such extraordinary violence that nearly the whole capital elite network was itself physically eliminated. The capture of the two capital cities of the Tang dynasty in 880 by the Huang Chao rebels led to a quarter century of endemic violence affecting most parts of the empire. A great many scions of the great clans were killed during the brief occupation of the capitals, where they were concentrated in such large numbers and thereby vulnerable to wholesale slaughter. Those who managed to avoid the massacres at the political center perished in large numbers during the following years in the warfare and violence that gradually spread across most of the empire. With the founding of the numerous post-Tang regimes that ruled over China during the first half of the tenth century, the once all-powerful capital elite network was fragmented and in shambles. The surviving members would have constituted only a small minority in the new courts, where they would no longer have been able to influence state policy or perpetuate their domination over government and society.

Previous historians have tended to see the provincial governments of the post–An Lushan political order as constituting a major destabilizing element for the ninth-century Tang. Data from epitaphs of the period suggests that provincial military forces were indeed led almost entirely by locally based elites, so they did have the potential for threatening dynastic stability. Yet empirical evidence reveals that it was not the local armies who were responsible for the dynastic collapse. In fact, there was a relatively low rate of military mutinies through most of the ninth century. By the mid-ninth century, some kind of consensus had evidently emerged between the Tang regime, the capital-based aristocrats, and the local elites. How this consensus was reached is not entirely certain. But the court was clearly able to appoint capital-based elites to all the top-echelon civilian positions in the provincial administrations—with the one major exception of the autonomous provinces of Hebei. In consequence, as the rebel armies under Huang Chao and his successors marched across the empire, they were as much a threat to local power structures as they were to the dynasty itself. It was only after the rebel armies had sacked the two capitals and the Tang regime had essentially been decapitated that provincial authorities began to act autonomously.[4]

But what, then, prompted the great rebellions that ended the Tang regime? One possibility is that the political consensus at the end of the dynasty was achieved at the expense of the local population. One can imagine that the Tang state—which was structured quite differently from later dynastic states—operated much like a colonial empire. The capital sent out bureaucrats to the provinces, who collaborated with the subaltern elites to extract wealth from the local populations. The big losers in such an arrangement—the local populations—might easily have been motivated to rebel. But there may well have been additional causes for the rebellions. There is, in fact, new climatological evidence that China—and indeed much of the northern hemisphere—was beset by an unusually severe period of droughts during the late 860s and early 870s.[5] The widespread famine created by drastic climate change might

---

4. Even at this point, however, the capital cities of the regional dynasties and kingdoms maintained their preeminence, serving as the site where regional sociopolitical elites aggregated. See Tackett, "Transformation," pp. 181–211.

5. For evidence on the basis of lake sediment analysis of the severity of a global mid- to late-ninth-century drought, see Yancheva et al., "Influence of the Intertropical

have caused the demise of nearly any regime. Regardless of their origins, the great insurrections of the last decades of the ninth century led to the near extermination of the scions of the capital clans, bringing down a political elite that had survived and dominated China for centuries.

There is, however, one further question to consider: why was it that, after the physical elimination of the old aristocratic families, a new aristocracy did not emerge in the subsequent Song dynasty? Much of this book has emphasized what might be termed structural factors—institutional innovations, developments in the organization of the economy, the spatial redistribution of elites, and the reconfiguration of social networks. But certain cultural issues have also been raised. Eulogistic language in the ninth-century epitaphs of capital elites suggests developments in ideology that may, indeed, have accompanied the bureaucratization of the aristocracy, as the scions of the great families came increasingly to value and emphasize the officeholding traditions of their immediate ancestors and relatives by marriage. It was in this manner that they justified the capital-based marriage network that distinguished them from countless other descendants of the old aristocratic clans.

But there is also evidence that the fall of the Tang and the disintegration of the old capital social network entailed the demise of an entire cultural universe. When the capital social network had dominated the bureaucracy and dispatched its representatives to control prefectures and provinces across the empire, it was far easier to impress upon the local elites the capital's manner of configuring the world, underscoring the intrinsic superiority of the capital elite's educational and family backgrounds. But, constituting only a minority in the courts of the tenth-century dynasties and kingdoms, the surviving members of the old capital elite were no longer in a position to impose their views; Tang metropolitan culture lost its hegemony. One such survivor, the late Tang poet Wei Zhuang, articulated the sentiments of irrelevance felt by members of the former political elite, all of whom had been trained to serve as administrators for a bureaucratic state:

> As a [classically educated] *ru* going through a generation of upheaval,

---

Convergence Zone," paying particular attention to the sharp dip evident in figure 3b that the authors date to approximately 860 CE.

Tell me what I am supposed to do!
I'm probably already too old to train in swordsmanship,
And it's also too late now to retreat to the mountains.

爲儒逢世亂，吾道欲何之！學劍已應晚，歸山今又遲.[6]

The irrelevance of the civilian bureaucrats was not a problem that would last, as the various short-lived regimes of the tenth century sought to establish viable states. But that century would also see the emergence of a new ethos that placed far more emphasis on meritocratic values than on the prestige of great clan descent. This ethos developed step by step over the course of the century as provincial elites were brought to the capital to constitute a new capital-based elite at the courts of successive tenth-century regimes. A disproportionate number of these new elites, including the Song imperial clan itself, were descendants of men who had served the autonomous provinces of Hebei, where a distinct regional culture had emerged by late Tang times. This new elite transformed metropolitan culture, while the remnants of the old Tang elite, with an ever diminishing presence at court, lost their ability to impose their value system upon others. This cultural revolution will be the subject of a sequel to this volume.[7]

---

6. *Wei Zhuang ji jianzhu*, p. 168. For another poem by Wei discussing a similar theme, see p. 185.

7. For a general overview of this thesis, see Tackett, "Transformation."

APPENDIX A

Guide to the Accompanying Database

In order to allow readers to examine and use for their own purposes the underlying data on which much of this study is based, a complete database in .mdb (Microsoft Access) format is available for download on the publisher's web site (publications.asiacenter.harvard.edu\tackett 2014) and the author's web site (www.ntackett.com), as is an Excel spreadsheet with basic citation information for the epitaphs.[1] As noted in the conventions at the beginning of the book, many of the database queries used to produce the figures in this volume are available in the .mdb database, as are additional queries cited in the notes. The database also includes basic forms for viewing and searching the data. All epitaphs cited in the monograph can be looked up by epitaph number using the database's "Epitaphs" form in order to obtain full bibliographic information regarding published transcriptions and rubbings, relevant published studies, and excavation reports (when available). The output of some of the queries is designed to be imported into either GIS software (for maps) or a NodeXL Excel template (for network visualization). Below is a description of the data tables and their fields:

1. *People:* This table includes basic prosopographic data on over 30,000 individuals. Included are the subjects of all known ninth-century epitaphs as well as all kinsmen mentioned

---

1. The database is entitled 唐五代人物傳記與社會網絡資料庫(1.0版). The file name is tbdb010.mdb. The Excel spreadsheet is entitled tackettdestruction.xlsx.

in these epitaphs; individuals with *JTS* or *XTS* biographies with ninth-century death dates; ninth-century provincial governors and "top officials" (see below) not mentioned in other data sources; and all individuals mentioned in the genealogical tables of chief ministers, the imperial clan, and provincial dynasts (*XTS* jj. 70–75), excluding most of the distant ancestors mentioned only in the prefaces to these tables. Fields include ID (i.e., the unique person identification number), Surname, Given name, Style (i.e., courtesy name 字), Gender, ClanID, Death year, Age at death, Office (i.e., last office held), Elite type (i.e., MIL for military officer, CIV for civilian bureaucrat, EUN for eunuch, NOH for non-officeholder), XB ("Xiang biao," i.e., whether or not individual appears in the *XTS* table of chief ministers), and References. If a Reference field cites an inscription, one needs to consult the Epitaph form (which links to the MZMs table described below) for full citation information. ClanID is a unique ID number assigned to each reconstructed patriline. ("Patrilines" are defined in chapter 3.) As Microsoft Access does not deal well with recursion, queries involving networks run substantially faster if members of particular kin groups are identified using a static clan ID number (rather than an ID number generated dynamically when the query is run). Clan IDs were initially assigned through an automated process: briefly, the lowest person ID number of each father-son pair was selected to be the clan ID number of both father and son; this procedure was repeated until all father-son pairs had the same clan ID number. Elite type, generally included only for individuals with ninth-century epitaphs, was usually determined based on an evaluation of the individual's career in office—that is, whether all or most offices held by the individual were offices generally held by civilian bureaucrats, by military men, or by eunuchs. Elite type was left blank when the nature of an office held is unclear. In some cases, there is still room for debate regarding an individual's elite type, especially in the case of individuals holding the title of "general," which was sometimes an honorary title given to civilian bureaucrats.

2. *Relations:* This table lists known kinship relationships between individuals in the People table. Fields include SubjectID and TargetID (both of which are references to the unique person identification numbers in the People table), Relationship, Relationship order (sons are numbered in sequence of birth when known), and References. Recognized relationships consist of "daughter of" (D)—in which case the "subject" is the daughter and the "target" is the father—as well as "son of" (S), "wife of" (W), and "son-in-law of" (SiL).

3. *MZMs (*i.e., *muzhiming):* This table includes basic bibliographic information on all inscriptions used in the study, including epitaphs (*muzhiming*) as well as spirit-path inscriptions (*shendaobei*) and a few other minor genres. The genre is identified in the Genre field. The table also incorporates additional biographical data not included in the People table (specifically, data only noted in epitaphs or only exploited in this book in queries involving epitaphs). Fields include PersonID (a reference to the unique person identification numbers in the People table); Excavation reports, Transcriptions, Published rubbings, and Additional scholarship, all of which list relevant bibliographic information; Death prefecture (i.e., Tang era prefecture in which individual died); Death county; Death sub-county (e.g., city ward); Place of death type (i.e., "private residence," etc.); Burial prefecture; Burial county; Modern province (i.e., modern province—as opposed to Tang era province—in which deceased was buried); Number of sons; Number of daughters; Spouse surname (useful for distinguishing women of the same surname); Burial date (i.e., year of burial in case of a tomb epitaph or year of stele erection in case of a *shendaobei*); Choronym; OH (i.e., strength of officeholding tradition, as described in chapter 2 and tabulated in figure 2.4); LOC (i.e., degree to which family officeholding was "local" as opposed to "national," as described in chapter 2

and tabulated in figure 2.5); and # of columns (i.e., number of columns of text on the epitaph stone). Finally, there are a series of true/false fields, including Died where served (i.e., deceased died at the site of a provincial office he or a close relative had held); Temporary burial (i.e., burial identified as 權葬); Ancestral cemetery (useful for identifying individuals buried temporarily but, nevertheless, near their ancestral cemetery); Natal cemetery (for identifying women buried in their patrilineal clan's cemetery); National elite (individuals whose *ancestors* were national elites, thus—as explained in the discussion in chapter 2 regarding figure 2.7—belonging to a pool of people somewhat larger than the pool of national elites defined on the basis of OH and LOC alone); Bieji (i.e., epitaph was preserved in an author's collected works and was never excavated); and No data yet (i.e., epitaph should be excluded from many calculations because the relevant data has not yet been entered into database, usually because the epitaph does not date to the period 800 to 880, because no complete text of the epitaph exists, or because the epitaph was excavated or published only very recently).

4. *Clans:* This table includes basic data on the patrilines. Besides the Clan ID number, fields include Surname, Choronym, Sub-Choronym, Type (i.e., "7" for marriage-ban or "16" for top-16 officeholding clan, as described in chapter 1), CliqueCore (1 = core family of clique A, 2 = core family of clique B, as defined in chapter 3), CliqueFull (i.e., whether or not part of larger network surrounding clique cores), MarriageFull (i.e., whether or not included in marriage network depicted in figure 3.6), and Pre-Tang (1 = can trace ancestry back to Sui, 2 = back to pre-Sui).

5. *Governors:* This table identifies nearly all Tang provincial governors of the post–An Lushan period. Governors who served for substantially less than a year are usually excluded. Fields include PeopleID, Province, sDate (i.e., start date), and eDate (i.e., end date), as well as a few additional fields taken from Wang Shounan's data.

6. *Top Officials (800–880):* This table identifies all known

chief ministers, chief examiners, and ministers and vice ministers of personnel who served during the period from 800 to 880. Fields include PeopleID, Office, sDate, eDate.

7. *Affines:* This table identifies the purported clan background of the affines of the subjects of epitaphs. Fields include linkMZM, Choronym, Surname, Given name, and Relationship to deceased.

8. *Authors:* This table identifies the authors, calligraphers, and carvers of the epitaphs. Fields include linkMZM, Job (distinguishing authors from calligraphers from carvers), Choronym, Surname, Given name, Office, and Agnate (i.e., whether or not author/calligrapher/carver was a clansman of the deceased).

9. *ChorPlace* and *ChorSurnames:* These two tables identify the Tang era prefecture corresponding to particular choronym places as well as the clans (choronym + surname combinations) appearing on the various lists of eminent clans described in chapter 1.

10. *Provinces, Provseats,* and *Counties:* These three tables identify the latitude and longitude coordinates of prefectural and county seats, the seat and subordinate prefectures of each province, and the various regional classifications of prefectures used in the book's tables. See the "Conventions" for the sources of latitude and longitude data.

11. *Wenxigazetteerhedongpeis:* Identifies the Pei clan tombs listed in the Qing-era gazetteer *(Qianlong) Wenxi xian zhi*. See chapter 1, notes 52 and 53.

APPENDIX B

Estimating the Total Size of the Late Tang Capital Elite

Enough epitaphs have been excavated in the Chang'an-Luoyang region to estimate the total capital elite population during the late Tang. Technically speaking, this capital elite is defined as a socioeconomic elite (i.e., individuals from families with the socioeconomic resources to afford an elaborate burial). However, as demonstrated in chapter 2, this capital socioeconomic elite was largely one and the same as the national political power elite. For these calculations, it is necessary to assume that all individuals in the genealogical tables of chief ministers belonged to the wealthier strata of society and received tomb epitaphs at death—even though the majority of their epitaphs have not yet been located.

Having made this assumption, one first needs to determine which of the approximately 17,500 individuals in the *Xin Tang shu* tables lived during the period from 800 to 880. Although the death dates of most are not known, one can estimate those dates by assuming that the difference in years between generations adhered to a standard pattern—thirty-seven years for most elite families and twenty-seven years for the imperial clan. These figures are based on a survey of 265 father-child pairs where the years of birth of both are known and an additional 49 father-child pairs from the imperial clan.[1] It should be noted that the age differential takes into consideration all sons and daughters of a father, not just the firstborn.

---

1. See "Fig6_note1 Age differential (imperial clan)" and "Fig6_note1 Age differential (non-imperial clan)" in database.

After calculating the estimated death dates of all individuals in the *Xin Tang shu* genealogical tables, one comes up with 4,145 individuals who died between 800 and 880. Of these, 3,635 belonged to clans localizable to the capital region, and an additional 300 belonged to clans whose location cannot be determined due to an absence of burial data for any single clan member.[2] These figures include individuals from all clans listed in *XTS* 70上 to *XTS* 75下, excluding only the families of provincial dynasts that appear at the end of *XTS* 75下. To date, excavated epitaphs have surfaced for 94 of these individuals, representing between 2.39 percent and 2.59 percent of the total, depending on whether or not one assumes the 300 clansmen with no location data were in fact based in the capital.[3] The figure 94 includes only excavated epitaphs dating to the period 800–880; excluded are epitaphs preserved in transmitted texts (unless these epitaphs were later excavated) and other types of funerary texts, such as spirit-path inscriptions. When individuals have two epitaphs, the duplicate epitaphs are excluded from this count.

There is no reason to believe that the epitaphs of the clans who produced chief ministers are more likely to have been excavated than the epitaphs for other members of the capital elite. Thus, one can estimate that roughly 2.49 percent of all epitaphs produced at the capital in the ninth century have been excavated so far. Given that there are 934 excavated epitaphs for capital-based adult males (over the age of fifteen) dating to the period from 800 to 880,[4] one can then estimate that the total number of adult males for whom epitaphs were composed is equal to $934 / .0249 = 37{,}510$. On average, the number of these men who would have died per year was approximately $37{,}510 / (880-800) = 469$. According to averages tabulated from extant epitaphs, the life expectancy of elite males living to adulthood was fifty-seven, meaning that the average elite male spent forty-two years as an adult (if one defines adulthood as sixteen *sui* or older). Thus, the approximate number of adult capital elite males alive at any given moment in the ninth century would have been about $469 \times 42 = 19{,}698$, or roughly 19,700. It should be stressed that this is an approximate figure.

---

2. See "Fig 6_note2 n of elites in XB (800-880)" in database.
3. See "Fig 6_note3 n of XB elites with mzm (800-880)" in database.
4. See "Fig 6_note4 n of countable mzm (800-880)" in database.

APPENDIX C

Sources of Ninth-Century Excavated Epitaphs

The texts of some two hundred Tang era funerary biographies survive in the collected works 別集 of late Tang writers, all of which are included in the Qing dynasty collectanea *Quan Tang wen* (Complete Tang prose). Thousands of additional inscriptions have been excavated by archaeologists or tomb robbers, most of which were found in the last few decades, with a dozen or more additional inscriptions unearthed each year. In overall numbers, the bulk of these biographies are tomb epitaphs 墓誌銘, although a certain number of spirit-path steles 神道碑 and other genres of inscriptions also survive. As a result of the popularization of printing during the Song, *transmitted* epitaphs from the Song (preserved in the collected works and literary compilations of the individuals who composed them) greatly outnumber *excavated* epitaphs (defined as epitaphs that were physically unearthed at some point in the past). By contrast, the opposite is true for the pre-Song period: excavated inscriptions greatly outnumber transmitted inscriptions, especially for the period before Huang Chao's capture of the Tang capitals in 880.

Excavated Tang era epitaph stones and/or rubbings of these epitaph stones are available in a wide variety of museums, libraries, and archaeological institutes in China, Taiwan, and a few other locations. One of the major collections of epitaph rubbings, held by the National Library of China in Beijing, has been digitized and is now available online to any citizen of the People's Republic of China. It is important to note, however, that most epitaphs dating to the Tang have been published, either in the form of a transcription or in the form of a reproduction of the rubbing. Moreover, it is my sense that unpublished epitaphs dating to the Tang period (as opposed to those dating to later periods) are almost always published within a decade or so of discovery. Many unpublished epitaphs that I discovered when visiting museums and archaeological institutes during the course of my research have since been published.

The most numerous transcriptions of Tang era epitaphs appear in three large compilations:

1. Zhou Shaoliang 周紹良 and Zhao Chao 趙超, eds., *Tangdai muzhi huibian* 唐代墓誌彙編 (Shanghai: Shanghai guji, 1991); and its follow-up volume, Zhou Shaoliang and Zhao Chao, eds., *Tangdai muzhi huibian xuji* 唐代墓誌彙編續集 (Shanghai: Shanghai guji, 2001).
2. The ten volumes published so far of Wu Gang 吳鋼, ed., *Quan Tang wen buyi* 全唐文補遺 (Xi'an: San Qin chubanshe, 1994–2007).
3. Zhou Shaoliang 周紹良, ed., *Quan Tang wen xinbian* 全唐文新編 (Changchun: Jilin wenshi chubanshe, 2000).

About two-thirds of the excavated epitaphs used in this study were published in one of these sets. More precisely, among 2,231 excavated epitaphs dating to the period 800–880, 1,227 (55 percent) appear in *Tangdai muzhi huibian* or its follow-up volume; and 1,494 (67 percent) appear in one of the ten volumes of *Quan Tang wen buyi*. Of the remaining epitaphs used in this study, many have been published (in the form of both transcriptions and reproductions of the rubbings) in one of the following: the multiple volumes of the *Xin Zhongguo chutu muzhi* 新中國出土墓誌 series; Zhao Junping 趙君平, ed., *Mang Luo beizhi sanbai zhong* 邙洛碑志三百種 (Beijing: Zhonghua shuju, 2004); Zhao Junping and Zhao Wencheng 趙文成, eds., *He Luo muke shiling* 河洛墓刻拾零 (Beijing: Beijing tushuguan chubanshe, 2007); Zhao Liguang 趙力光, ed., *Xi'an beilin bowuguan xincang muzhi huibian* 西安碑林博物館新藏墓誌彙編 (Beijing: Xianzhuang shuju, 2007). Finally, dozens of additional epitaphs have been published in a variety of other monographs, as well as in archaeological journals; many of these epitaphs can be tracked down using the Institute of Archaeology's annual index, *Zhongguo kaoguxue nianjian* 中國考古學年鑒. As of early 2012, only about 10 percent of the epitaphs used in this study had not yet been published. For a complete list of inscriptions with references, see the database described in Appendix A.

Bibliography

ABBREVIATIONS

JTS   Liu Xu 劉昫 et al. *Jiu Tang shu* 舊唐書. Beijing: Zhonghua shuju, 1995.
XTS   Ouyang Xiu 歐陽修 and Song Qi 宋祁. *Xin Tang shu* 新唐書. Beijing: Zhonghua shuju, 1995.
QTW   *Quan Tang wen* 全唐文. Edited by Dong Gao 董誥 et al. Beijing: Zhonghua shuju, 1983.
ZZTJ   Sima Guang 司馬光. *Zizhi tongjian* 資治通鑑. Beijing: Zhonghua shuju, 1956.
SS   Toghtō 脫脫 et al. *Song shi* 宋史. Beijing: Zhonghua shuju, 1995.
WYYH   *Wenyuan yinghua* 文苑英華. Edited by Li Fang 李昉 et al. Beijing: Zhonghua shuju, 1966.

PRE-1900 SOURCES

The bulk of the primary source material used for this study consists of tomb epitaphs and other funerary inscriptions. These are cited by epitaph number in the personal name index, as explained in the Conventions. For full citation information, readers should consult the database. Only the major sources of published epitaphs are listed below.

Bai Juyi 白居易. *Bai Juyi ji jianjiao* 白居易集箋校. Shanghai: Shanghai guji, 1988.

Chen Bangzhan 陳邦瞻. *Songshi jishi benmo* 宋史紀事本末. Beijing: Zhonghua shuju, 1977.

Chen Si 陳思. *Baoke congbian* 寶刻叢編. *Shike shiliao xinbian* 1st ed. Vol. 24. Taipei: Xin wenfeng chuban gongsi, 1979.

Cui Zhiyuan 崔致遠. *Guiyuan bigeng ji jiaozhu* 桂苑筆耕集校注. Beijing: Zhonghua shuju, 2007.

Du Guangting 杜光庭. *Daojiao lingyan ji* 道教靈驗記. *Siku quanshu cunmu congshu* ed. Vol. 258. Jinan: Qi Lu shushe, 1995.

Du Mu 杜牧. *Du Mu ji xinian jiaozhu* 杜牧集繫年校注. Annotated by Wu Zaiqing 吳在慶. Beijing: Zhonghua shuju, 2008.

Du Xunhe 杜荀鶴. *Tangfeng ji*. Beijing: Zhonghua shuju, 1959.

Guanxiu 貫休. *Chan yue ji jiaozhu* 禪月集校注. Annotated by Lu Yongfeng 陸永峰. Chengdu: Sichuan chuban jituan, 2006.

Han Wo 韓偓. *Han Wo shiji jianzhu* 韓偓詩集箋注. Ji'nan: Shandong jiaoyu chubanshe, 2000.

He Luo muke shiling 河洛墓刻拾零. Edited by Zhao Junping 趙君平 and Zhao Wencheng 趙文成. Beijing: Beijing tushuguan chubanshe, 2007.

He Qufei 何去非. *He boshi bei lun* 何博士備論. *Baibu congshu jicheng* 百部叢書集成 ed. Taipei: Yiwen yinshuguan, 1964.

Hong Mai 洪邁. *Rongzhai suibi* 容齋隨筆. Beijing: Zhonghua shuju, 2005.

Hu Ji 胡戟 and Rong Xinjiang 榮新江, eds. *Da Tang xishi bowuguan cang muzhi* 大唐西市博物館藏墓誌. Beijing: Beijing daxue chubanshe, 2012.

Li Fang 李昉, ed. *Taiping guang ji* 太平廣記. Beijing: Zhonghua shuju, 2003.

Li Zuntang 李遵唐, ed. *(Qianlong) Wenxi xian zhi* (乾隆)聞喜縣志. 1766. *Zhongguo difangzhi jicheng* ed. Shanxi, vol. 60. Shanghai: Shanghai shudian, 2005.

Lin Bao 林寶. *Yuanhe xingzuan fu si jiaoji* 元和姓纂附四校記. Edited by Cen Zhongmian 岑仲勉. Beijing: Zhonghua shuju, 1994.

Liu Xu 劉昫 et al. *Jiu Tang shu* 舊唐書. Beijing: Zhonghua shuju, 1995.

Luo Yin 羅隱. *Luo Yin ji* 羅隱集. Edited by Yong Wenhua 雍文華. Beijing: Zhonghua shuju, 1983.

Mang Luo beizhi sanbai zhong 邙洛碑志三百種. Edited by Zhao Junping 趙君平. Beijing: Zhonghua shuju, 2004.

Ouyang Xiu 歐陽修. *Ouyang Xiu quan ji* 歐陽修全集. Beijing: Zhonghua shuju, 2001.
———. *Xin Wudai shi* 新五代史. Beijing: Zhonghua shuju, 1997.

Ouyang Xiu and Song Qi 宋祁. *Xin Tang shu* 新唐書. Beijing: Zhonghua shuju, 1995.

Quan Song wen 全宋文. Edited by Zeng Zaozhuang 曾棗莊 and Liu Lin 劉琳. Chengdu: Ba Shu shu she, 1988.

Quan Tang shi 全唐詩. Beijing: Zhonghua shuju, 1960.

Quan Tang wen buyi 全唐文補遺. Edited by Wu Gang 吳鋼. Xi'an: San Qin chubanshe, 1994–2007.

Quan Tang wen xinbian 全唐文新編. Edited by Zhou Shaoliang 周紹良. Changchun: Jilin wenshi chubanshe, 2000.

Quan Tang wen 全唐文. Edited by Dong Gao 董誥 et al. Beijing: Zhonghua shuju, 1983.

Shen Gua 沈括. *Mengxi bitan jiaozheng* 夢溪筆談校證. Shanghai: Shanghai chuban gongsi, 1956.

Sikong Tu 司空圖. *Sikong Biaosheng shiwen ji jianjiao* 司空表聖詩文集箋校. Edited by Zu Baoquan 祖保泉 and Tao Litian 陶禮天. Hefei: Anhui daxue chubanshe, 2002.

Sima Guang 司馬光. *Zizhi tongjian* 資治通鑑. Beijing: Zhonghua shuju, 1956.

Sun Qi 孫棨. *Beili zhi* 北里志. Shanghai: Gudian wenxue chubanshe, 1957.

Tangdai muzhi huibian 唐代墓誌彙編. Edited by Zhou Shaoliang 周紹良 and Zhao Chao 趙超. Shanghai: Shanghai guji, 1991.

Tangdai muzhi huibian xuji 唐代墓誌彙編續集. Edited by Zhou Shaoliang 周紹良 and Zhao Chao 趙超. Shanghai: Shanghai guji, 2001.

Toghtō 脫脫 et al. *Song shi* 宋史. Beijing: Zhonghua shuju, 1995.

Wang Dingbao 王定保. *Tang zhi yan* 唐摭言. Shanghai: Shanghai shehui kexue yuan chubanshe, 2003.

Wang Zheng 王政 et al., eds. *(Daoguang) Tengxian zhi* (道光)滕縣志. 1846. *Zhongguo difangzhi jicheng* ed. Shandong, vol. 75. Shanghai: Shanghai shudian, 2004.

Wei Zhuang 韋莊. *Wei Zhuang ji jianzhu* 韋莊集箋注. Annotated by Nie Anfu 聶安福. Shanghai: Shanghai guji chubanshe, 2002.

Wenyuan yinghua 文苑英華. Edited by Li Fang 李昉 et al. Beijing: Zhonghua shuju: 1966.

Wu Renchen 吳任臣. *Shiguo chunqiu* 十國春秋. *Wudai shishu huibian* ed. Vols. 7–8. Hangzhou: Hangzhou chubanshe, 2004.

Xi'an beilin bowuguan xincang muzhi huibian 西安碑林博物館新藏墓誌彙編. Edited by Zhao Liguang 趙力光. Beijing: Xianzhuang shuju, 2007.

Xin Zhongguo chu tu muzhi: Beijing (1) 新中國出土墓誌: 北京 (一). Edited by Gao Jingchun 高景春. Beijing: Wenwu chubanshe, 2003.

Xin Zhongguo chu tu muzhi: Chongqing 新中國出土墓誌: 重慶. Edited by Hu Renzhao 胡人朝. Beijing: Wenwu chubanshe, 2002.

Xin Zhongguo chutu muzhi: Hebei (1) 新中國出土墓誌: 河北 (一). Edited by Meng Fanfeng 孟繁峰 and Liu Chaoying 劉超英. Beijing: Wenwu chubanshe, 2004.

Xin Zhongguo chutu muzhi: Henan (1) 新中國出土墓誌: 河南 (一). Edited by Hao Benxing 郝本性 and Li Xiuping 李秀萍. Beijing: Wenwu chubanshe, 1994.

Xin Zhongguo chutu muzhi: Henan (2) 新中國出土墓誌: 河南 (二). Edited by Liu Xiuping 李秀萍. Beijing: Wenwu chubanshe, 2002.

Xin Zhongguo chutu muzhi: Henan (3) 新中國出土墓誌: 河南 (三). Edited by Zhao Genxi 趙跟喜 and Zhang Jianhua 張建華. Beijing: Wenwu chubanshe, 2008.

Xin Zhongguo chutu muzhi: Jiangsu (1) 新中國出土墓誌: 江蘇(一). Edited by Qian Jun 錢浚 and Zhou Gongtai 周公太. Beijing: Wenwu chubanshe, 2006.

Xin Zhongguo chutu muzhi: Shaanxi (1) 新中國出土墓誌: 陝西 (一). Edited by Wu Gang 吳鋼. Beijing: Wenwu chubanshe, 2000.

Xin Zhongguo chutu muzhi: Shaanxi (2) 新中國出土墓誌: 陝西 (二). Edited by Wu Gang 吳鋼. Beijing: Wenwu chubanshe, 2003.

Xin Zhongguo chutu muzhi: Shanghai/Tianjin 新中國出土墓誌: 上海天津. Edited by Song Jian 宋建 et al. Beijing: Wenwu chubanshe, 2009.

Xu Song 徐松. *Dengke jikao buzheng* 登科記考補正. Revised by Meng Erdong 孟二冬. Beijing: Beijing Yanshan chubanshe, 2003.

———. *Zengding Tang liangjing chengfang kao* 增訂唐兩京城坊考. Annotated by Li Jianchao 李健超. Xi'an: San Qin chubanshe, 2006.

Xue Juzheng 薛居正. *Jiu Wudai shi* 舊五代史. Beijing: Zhonghua shuju, 1997.

Yang Chengfu 楊承父 et al., eds. *(Wanli) Tengxian zhi* (萬曆)滕縣志. 1585. *Riben cang Zhongguo hanjian difangzhi congkan* ed. Beijing: Shumu wenxian chubanshe, 1992.

Yu quan zi 玉泉子. Shanghai: Shanghai guji chubanshe, 1953.

Zhao Yi 趙翼. *Nian er shi zha ji* 廿二史劄記. *Baibu congshu jicheng* 百部叢書集成 ed. Taipei: Yiwen yinshuguan, 1964.

Zheng Gu 鄭谷. *Zheng Gu shi ji biannian jiaozhu* 鄭谷詩集編年校注. Shanghai: Huadong shifan daxue chubanshe, 1993.

———. *Zheng Gu shi ji jianzhu* 鄭谷詩集箋注. Shanghai: Shanghai guji chubanshe, 1991.

Zheng Qiao 鄭樵. *Tongzhi* 通志. Taipei: Xinxing shuju, 1959.

POST-1900 SOURCES

Adachi Kiroku 足立喜六. *Chōan shiseki no kenkyū* 長安史蹟の研究. Tokyo: Tōyō Bunko, 1933.

Aubert, Jean-Jacques. *Business Managers in Ancient Rome*. New York: Brill, 1994.

Beckwith, Christopher I. *The Tibetan Empire in Central Asia*. Princeton: Princeton University Press, 1987.

Bol, Peter. *Neo-Confucianism in History*. Cambridge, MA: Harvard University Press, 2008.

———. *"This Culture of Ours": Intellectual Transitions in T'ang and Sung China*. Stanford: Stanford University Press, 1992.

Bossler, Beverly J. *Powerful Relations: Kinship, Status, and the State in Sung China, 960–1279*. Cambridge, MA: Council on East Asian Studies, 1998.

Bourdieu, Pierre. "Le capital social." *Actes de la recherche en sciences sociales* 31.1 (1980): 2–3.

Bray, Francesca. *Technology and Gender: Fabrics of Power in Late Imperial China*. Berkeley: University of California Press, 1997.

Cannon, Aubrey. "The Historical Dimension in Mortuary Expressions of Status and Sentiment." *Current Anthropology* 30.4 (1989): 437–58.

Carr, Christopher. "Mortuary Practices: Their Social, Philosophical-Religious, Circumstantial, and Physical Determinants." *Journal of Archaeological Method and Theory* 2.2 (1995): 105–200.

Chaffee, John. *The Thorny Gates of Learning in Sung China*. New ed. Albany: State University of New York Press, 1995.

Chaussinand-Nogaret, Guy. *La noblesse au XVIIIe siècle: De la féodalité aux lumières*. Paris: Hachette, 1976.

Ch'en Jo-shui 陳若水. "Tangdai Chang'an de huanguan shequn" 唐代長安的宦官社群. *Tang yanjiu* 唐研究 15 (2009): 171–98.

Chen Kang 陳康. "Cong Lun Boyan muzhi tan Tufan mGar shi jiazu de xingshuai" 從論博言墓誌談吐蕃噶爾氏家族的興衰. *Beijing wenbo* 北京文博 1999.4:62–67.

Chen Shuang 陳爽, "Jin ershi nian Zhongguo Dalu diqu Liuchao shizu yanjiu gaiguan" 近二十年中國大陸地區六朝士族研究概觀. *Chūgoku shigaku* 中國史學 11 (2001): 15–26.

Chen Yinke 陳寅恪. *Tangdai zhengzhi shi shulun gao* 唐代政治史述論稿. Shanghai: Shanghai guji chubanshe, 1982.

Cheong Byungjun 鄭炳俊. "Tōdai no kansasshochishi ni tsuite" 唐代の観察処置使について. *Shirin* 史林 77.5 (1994): 40–70.

———. "Tōkō hanki no chihō gyōsei taikei ni tsuite" 唐後半期の地方行政体系について. *Tōyōshi kenkyū* 東洋史研究 51.3 (1992): 72–106.

Cherniack, Susan. "Book Culture and Textual Transmission in Sung China." *Harvard Journal of Asiatic Studies* 54.1 (1994): 5–125.

"CHGIS, Version 4." Cambridge, MA: Harvard-Yenching Institute, January 2007.

Clark, Hugh Roberts. "Consolidation of the South China Frontier: The Development of Ch'üan-Chou, 699–1126." Ph.D. thesis, University of Pennsylvania, 1981.

———. "Scoundrels, Rogues, and Refugees: The Founders of the Ten Kingdoms in the Late Ninth Century." In *Five Dynasties and Ten Kingdoms*, edited by Peter Lorge, pp. 47–77. Hong Kong: The Chinese University of Hong Kong, 2011.

Dalby, Michael T. "Court Politics in Late T'ang Times." In *The Cambridge History of China*, vol. 3: *Sui and T'ang China*, part 1, edited by Denis Twitchett, pp. 561–681. New York: Cambridge University Press, 1979.

Davis, Timothy M. "Entombed Epigraphy in Early Medieval Commemorative Culture and the Rise of Muzhiming as a Literary Genre." Paper presented at the Association for Asian Studies Annual Meeting, 2 April 2011.

———. "Potent Stone: Entombed Epigraphy and Memorial Culture in Early Medieval China." Ph.D. thesis, Columbia University, 2008.

Dewald, Jonathan. *Pont-St-Pierre 1398–1789: Lordship, Community, and Capitalism in Early Modern France*. Berkeley: University of California Press, 1987.

Dien, Albert E. "Introduction." In *State and Society in Early Medieval China*, edited by Albert E. Dien, pp. 1–29. Stanford: Stanford University Press, 1990.

Ebrey, Patricia Buckley. *The Aristocratic Families of Early Imperial China: A Case Study of the Po-ling Ts'ui Family*. New York: Cambridge University Press, 1978.

———. "The Early Stages in the Development of Descent Group Organization." In *Kinship Organization in Late Imperial China, 1000–1940*, edited by Patricia Buckley Ebrey and James L. Watson, pp. 16–61. Berkeley: University of California Press, 1986.

———. *The Inner Quarters: Marriage and the Lives of Chinese Women in the Sung Period*. Berkeley: University of California Press, 1993.

Elvin, Mark. *The Pattern of the Chinese Past*. Stanford: Stanford University Press, 1973.

Esherick, Joseph W., and Mary Backus Rankin. "Introduction." In *Chinese Local Elites and Patterns of Dominance*, edited by Joseph W. Esherick and Mary Backus Rankin, pp. 1–24. Berkeley: University of California Press, 1990.

Fang Chengjun 方成军. "Anhui Sui Tang zhi Song muzang gaishu" 安徽隋唐至宋墓葬概述, *Dongnan wenhua* 東南文化 1998.4:50–55.

Fangshan shijing tiji huibian 房山石經題記彙編. Beijing: Shumu wenxian chubanshe, 1987.

Feng, Linda Rui. "Youthful Displacement: City, Travel, and Narrative Formation in Tang Tales." Ph.D. thesis, Columbia University, 2008.

Gottschalk, Louis, and Margaret Maddox. *Lafayette in the French Revolution: Through the October Days*. Chicago: University of Chicago Press, 1969.

Grafflin, Dennis. "The Great Families in Medieval South China." *Harvard Journal of Asiatic Studies* 41.1 (1981): 65–74.

———. "Reinventing China: Pseudobureaucracy in the Early Southern Dynasties." In *State and Society in Early Medieval China*, edited by Albert E. Dien, pp. 139–70. Stanford: Stanford University Press, 1990.

Guo Peiyu 郭培育 and Guo Peizhi 郭培智, eds. *Luoyang chutu shike shidi ji* 洛陽出土石刻時地記. Zhengzhou: Daxiang chubanshe, 2005.

Hansen, Valerie. *Changing Gods in Medieval China, 1127–1276*. Princeton: Princeton University Press, 1989.

———. *Negotiating Daily Life in Traditional China: How Ordinary People Used Contracts, 600–1400*. New Haven: Yale University Press, 1995.

Hartwell, Robert M. "Demographic, Political, and Social Transformations of China, 750–1550." *Harvard Journal of Asiatic Studies* 42.2 (1982): 365–442.

Herbert, P. A. *Examine the Honest, Appraise the Able: Contemporary Assessments of Civil Service Selection in Early Tang China*. Canberra: Faculty of Asian Studies, 1988.

———. "Perceptions of Provincial Officialdom in Early T'ang China." *Asia Major*, 3rd series 2.1 (1989): 25–57.

Hino Kaisaburō 日野開三郎. *Shina chūsei no gunbatsu* 支那中世の軍閥. Tokyo: Sanseidō, 1942.

Hori Toshikazu 堀敏一. "Hanchin shineigun no kenryoku kōzō" 藩鎮親衛軍の權力構造. *Tōyō bunka kenkyūsho kiyō* 東洋文化研究所紀要 20 (1960): 75–147.

———. "Tōmatsu shohanran no seikaku" 唐末諸叛亂の性格. *Tōyō bunka* 東洋文化 7 (1951): 52–94.

Hua Guorong 華國榮. "Nanjing Liuchao de Wangshi, Xieshi, Gaoshi muzang" 南京六朝的王氏、謝氏、高氏墓葬. In *Between Han and Tang: Visual and Material Culture in a Transformative Period*, pp. 283–93. Beijing: Wenwu chubanshe, 2003.

Huang Ch'ing-lien. "The Recruitment and Assessment of Civil Officials under the T'ang Dynasty." Ph.D. thesis, Princeton University, 1986.

Huang Zhengjian 黃正建. "Han Yu richang shenghuo yanjiu: Tang Zhenyuan Changqing jian wenrenxing guanyuan richang shenghuo yanjiu zhi yi" 韓愈日常生活研究: 唐貞元長慶間文人型官員日常生活研究之一. *Tang yanjiu* 唐研究 4 (1998): 251–73.

Hucker, Charles O. *A Dictionary of Official Titles in Imperial China*. Stanford: Stanford University Press, 1985.

Hymes, Robert P. *Statesmen and Gentlemen: The Elite of Fu-chou, Chiang-hsi, in Northern and Southern Sung*. New York: Cambridge University Press, 1986.

Ikeda On 池田溫. "Tōdai no gunbō hyō" 唐代の郡望表. *Tōyō gakuhō* 東洋學報 42.3 (1959): 57–95, 42.4 (1960): 40–58.

Johnson, David. "The Last Years of a Great Clan: The Li Family of Chao chun in Late T'ang and Early Sung." *Harvard Journal of Asiatic Studies* 37.1 (1977): 5–102.

———. *The Medieval Chinese Oligarchy*. Boulder, CO: Westview Press, 1977.

Kehoe, Dennis P. *Investment, Profit, and Tenancy*. Ann Arbor: University of Michigan Press, 1997.

Lau Nap-yin 柳立言. "He wei 'Tang Song bianqe'" 何謂'唐宋變革'. In *Songdai de jiating he falü* 宋代的家庭和法律, pp. 3–42. Shanghai: Shanghai guji, 2008.

Levy, Howard S. *Biography of Huang Ch'ao*. Berkeley: University of California Press, 1955.

Li Haoyang 李昊陽, ed. *Zhaoling wenshi baodian* 昭陵文史寶典. Xi'an: San Qin chubanshe, 2006.

Li Hongbin 李鴻賓. "Tangchao dui Hebei diqu de jingying ji qi bianhua" 唐朝對河北地區的經營及其變化. *Minzu shi yanjiu* 民族史研究 6 (2003): 96–112.

Li Huarui 李華瑞, "Ershi shiji zhong ri 'Tang Song bianqe' guan yanjiu shuping" 二十世紀中日'唐宋變革'觀研究述評. *Shixue lilun yanjiu* 史學理論研究 2003.4:88–95.

———, ed. *"Tang Song bianqe" lun de youlai yu fazhan* 「唐宋變革」論的由來與發展. Tianjin: Tianjin guji chubanshe, 2010.

Li Xuelai 李學來. "Jiangsu Nanjing shi chutu de Tangdai Langya Wang shi jiazu muzhi" 江蘇南京市出土的唐代琅琊王氏家族墓志. *Kaogu* 考古 2002.5:478–79.

Lin Yeqing 林燁卿. *Huang Chao* 黃巢. Shanghai: Shanghai renmin chubanshe, 1962.

Liu Jianguo 劉建國. "Jiangsu Zhenjiang Tang mu" 江蘇鎮江唐墓. *Kaogu* 考古 1985.2:131–48.

Lu Xiaofan 魯曉帆. "Tang Youzhou zhufang kao" 唐幽州諸坊考. *Beijing wenbo* 北京文博 2005.2:72–79.

Lu Yang 陸揚. "Cong Xichuan he Zhexi shijian lun Yuanhe zhengzhi geju de xingcheng" 從西川和浙西事件論元和政治格局的形成. *Tang yanjiu* 唐研究 8 (2002): 225–56.

———. "Cong xinchu muzhi zai lun 9 shiji chu Jiannan Xichuan Liu Pi shijian ji qi xiangguan wenti" 從新出墓誌再論9世紀初劍南西川劉闢事件及其相關問題. *Tang yanjiu* 唐研究 17 (2011): 331–56.

———. "Dynastic Revival and Political Transformation in Late T'ang China: A Study of Emperor Hsien-Tsung (805–820) and His Reign." Ph.D. thesis, Princeton University, 1999.

Mao Hanguang 毛漢光. "Cong shizu jiguan qianyi kan Tangdai shizu zhi zhongyang hua" 從士族籍貫遷移看唐代士族之中央化. *Zhongyang yanjiuyuan lishi yuyan yanjiusuo jikan* 中央研究院歷史語言研究所集刊 52.3 (1981): 421–510. Republished in *Zhongguo zhonggu shehui shilun* 中國中古社會史論, pp. 235–337. Taipei: Lianjing chuban shiye gongsi, 1988.

———. *Liang Jin Nanbeichao shizu zhengzhi zhi yanjiu* 兩晉南北朝士族政治之研究. Taipei: Taiwan shangwu yinshuguan, 1966.

———. "Tangdai da shizu de jinshi di" 唐代大士族的進士第. *Zhongguo zhonggu shehui shilun* 中國中古社會史論, pp. 339–63. Taipei: Lianjing chubanshe, 1988.

———. "Tangdai tongzhi jieceng shehui biandong: cong guanli jiating beijing kan shehui liudong" 唐代統治階層社會變動:從官吏家庭背景看社會流動. Ph.D. thesis, Guoli zhengzhi daxue zhengzhi yanjiusuo, 1968.

Mao Yangguang 毛陽光. "Xinjian si fang Tangdai Luoyang Mite ren muzhi kao" 新見四方唐代洛陽粟特人墓誌考. *Zhongyuan wenwu* 2009.6:74–80.

McDermott, Joseph P. "Charting Blank Spaces and Disputed Regions: The Problem of Sung Land Tenure." *Journal of Asian Studies* 44.1 (1984): 13–41.

McMullen, David. *State and Scholars in T'ang China*. New York: Cambridge University Press, 1988.

Miyakawa Hisayuki. "An Outline of the Naitō Hypothesis and Its Effects on Japanese Studies of China." *Far Eastern Quarterly* 14.4 (1955): 533–52.

Moore, Oliver. *Rituals of Recruitment in Tang China*. Leiden: Brill, 2004.

Nakasuna Akinori 中砂明德. "Kōki Tōchō no Kōwai shihai" 後期唐朝の江准支配. *Tōyōshi kenkyū* 東洋史研究 47.1 (1988): 30–53.

Nicolet, Claude. *Censeurs et publicains*. Paris: Fayard, 2000.

Ning Xin 寧欣. *Tangdai xuanguan yanjiu* 唐代選官研究. Taipei: Wenjin chubanshe, 1995.

Nugent, Christopher M. B. *Manifest in Words, Written on Paper: Producing and Circulating Poetry in Tang Dynasty China*. Cambridge, MA: Harvard University Asia Center, 2010.

Ōsawa Masaaki 大沢正昭. "Tōmatsu no hanchin to chūō kenryoku" 唐末の藩鎮と中央權力. *Tōyōshi kenkyū* 東洋史研究 32.2 (1973): 141–62.

Otagi Hajime 愛宕元. "Tōdai kōhan ni okeru shakai henshitsu no ichi kōsatsu" 唐代後半における社会変質の一考察. *Tōhō gakuhō* 42 (1971): 91–125.

Owen, Stephen, ed. and trans. *An Anthology of Chinese Literature: Beginnings to 1911*. New York: Norton, 1996.

———. *The Late Tang: Chinese Poetry of the Mid-Ninth Century (827–860)*. Cambridge, MA: Harvard University Asia Center, 2009.

Perry, John Curtis, and Bardwell L. Smith, eds. *Essays on T'ang Society*. Leiden: E. J. Brill, 1976.

Peterson, Charles A[llen]. "The Autonomy of the Northeastern Provinces in the Period Following the An Lu-shan Rebellion." Ph.D. thesis, University of Washington, 1966.

———. "Corruption Unmasked: Yüan Chen's Investigations in Szechwan." *Asia Major*, new series 18 (1973): 34–78.

———. "Court and Province in Mid- and Late T'ang." In *Cambridge History of China*, vol. 3: *Sui and T'ang China*, part 1, edited by Denis Twitchett, pp. 464–560. New York: Cambridge University Press, 1979.

———. "The Restoration Completed: Emperor Hsien-tsung and the Provinces." In *Perspectives on the T'ang*, edited by Arthur F. Wright and Denis Twitchett, pp. 151–91. New Haven: Yale University Press, 1973.

Pinker, Steven. *The Better Angels of Our Nature: Why Violence Has Declined*. New York: Viking, 2011.

Pulleyblank, Edwin G. "The An Lu-shan Rebellion and the Origins of Chronic Militarism in Late T'ang China." In *Essays on T'ang Society*, edited by John Curtis Perry and Bardwell L. Smith, pp. 33–60. Leiden: E. J. Brill, 1976.

Qi Dongfang 齊東方. "The Burial Location and Dating of the Hejia Village Treasures." *Orientations* 34.2 (2003): 20–24.

Reischauer, Edwin O., trans. *Ennin's Diary: The Record of a Pilgrimage to China in Search of the Law*. New York: Ronald Press, 1955.
Rong Xinjiang 榮新江. *Sui Tang Chang'an: xingbie, jiyi ji qita* 隋唐长安：性别，记忆及其他. Shanghai: Fudan daxue chubanshe, 2010.
———, ed. *Tang yanjiu* 唐研究. Vol. 15. Beijing: Beijing daxue chubanshe, 2009.
Roth, Jonathan P. *The Logistics of the Roman Army at War*. Boston: Brill, 1999.
Rudolph, Deborah. "The Power of Places: A Northern Sung Literatus Tours the Southern Suburbs of Ch'ang-An." *Journal of the American Oriental Society* 114.1 (1994): 11–22.

Schafer, Edward H. "The Last Years of Chang'an." *Oriens Extremus* 10–11 (1963–64): 133–79.
Seo Tatsuhiko 妹尾達彥. *Chōan no toshi kekaku* 長安の都市計畫. Tokyo: Kōdansha, 2001.
Shiba Yoshinobu. *Commerce and Society in Sung China*. Trans. Mark Elvin. Ann Arbor: Center for Chinese Studies, 1992.
———. "Sōdai no toshika o kangaeru" 宋代の都市化考える. *Tōhōgaku* 東方學 102 (2001): 1–19.
———. "Urbanization and the Development of Markets in the Lower Yangtze Valley." In *Crisis and Prosperity in Sung China*, edited by John Winthrop Haeger, pp. 13–48. Tucson: University of Arizona Press, 1975.
Skinner, G. William. "Introduction: Urban Development in Imperial China." In *The City in Late Imperial China*, edited by G. William Skinner, pp. 3–31. Stanford: Stanford University Press, 1977.
———. "Regional Urbanization in Nineteenth-Century China." In *The City in Late Imperial China*, edited by G. William Skinner, pp. 211–49. Stanford: Stanford University Press, 1977.
Somers, Robert M. "The End of the T'ang." In *Cambridge History of China*, vol. 3: *Sui and T'ang China*, edited by Denis Twitchett, pp. 682–789. New York: Cambridge University Press, 1979.
Spring, Madeline K. "Fabulous Horses and Worthy Scholars in Ninth-Century China." *T'oung P'ao* 74.4/5 (1988): 173–210.
Sun Guodong 孫國棟. "Tang Song zhi ji shehui mendi zhi xiaorong: Tang Song zhi ji shehui zhuanbian yanjiu zhi yi" 唐宋之際社會門弟之消融：唐宋之際社會轉變研究之一. *Xinya xuebao* 新亞學報 4.1 (1959): 211–304.

Tackett, Nicolas. "Great Clansmen, Bureaucrats, and Local Magnates: The Structure and Circulation of the Elite in Late-Tang China." *Asia Major* 3rd series 21.2 (2008): 101–52.
———. "The Great Wall and Conceptualizations of the Border under the Northern Song." *Journal of Song Yuan Studies* 38 (2008): 99–138.
———. "The Transformation of Medieval Chinese Elites, 850–1000 C.E." Ph.D. thesis, Columbia University, 2006. Available at www.ntackett.com.
Takeda Ryūji 竹田龍兒. "Tōdai shijin no gunbō ni tsuite" 唐代士人の郡望について. *Shigaku* 24.4 (1951): 466–93.

Tan Qixiang 譚其驤. *Zhongguo lishi ditu ji* 中國歷史地圖集. Shanghai: Ditu chubanshe, 1982.

Tang Zhangru 唐長孺. "Menfa de xingcheng ji qi shuailuo" 門閥的形成及其衰落. *Wuhan daxue xuebao (renwen kexue ban)* 武漢大學學報(人文科學版) 1959.8:1–24.

Tonami Mamoru 礪波護. "Chūsei kizokusei no hōkai to hekishōsei" 中世貴族制の崩懷と辟召制. *Tōyōshi kenkyū* 東洋史研究 21.3 (1962): 245–70.

———. "Sōdai shitaifu no seiritsu" 宋代士大夫の成立. In *Chūgoku bunka sōsho* 中國文化叢書, edited by Ogura Yoshihiko 小倉芳彥, vol. 8, pp. 193–210. Tokyo: Taishūkan shoten, 1968.

Treggiari, Susan. "Sentiment and Property: Some Roman Attitudes." In *Theories of Property: Aristotle to the Present*, edited by Anthony Parel and Thomas Flanagan, pp. 53–85. Waterloo, Ontario: Wilfrid Laurier University Press, 1979.

Tsuji Masahiro 辻正博. "Tōchō no tai hanchin seisaku ni tsuite" 唐朝の對藩鎮政策について. *Tōyōshi kenkyū* 東洋史研究 46.2 (1987): 326–55.

Twitchett, Denis, ed. *Cambridge History of China*, vol. 3: *Sui and T'ang China*. Part 1. New York: Cambridge University Press, 1979.

———. "The Composition of the T'ang Ruling Class: New Evidence from Tunhuang." In *Perspectives on the T'ang*, edited by Arthur F. Wright and Denis Twitchett, pp. 47–85. New Haven: Yale University Press, 1973.

———. *Financial Administration under the T'ang Dynasty*. Cambridge: Cambridge University Press, 1963.

———. "The Government of T'ang in the Early Eighth Century." *Bulletin of the School of Oriental and African Studies* 18.2 (1956): 322–30.

———. "Hsüan-tsung." In *Cambridge History of China*, vol. 3: *Sui and T'ang China*, part 1, edited by Denis Twitchett, pp. 333–463.. New York: Cambridge University Press, 1979.

———. "Introduction." In *Cambridge History of China*, vol. 3: *Sui and T'ang China*, part 1, edited by Denis Twitchett, pp. 1–47.. New York: Cambridge University Press, 1979.

———. *Land Tenure and the Social Order in T'ang and Sung China*. London: School of Oriental and African Studies, 1962.

———. "Merchant, Trade, and Government in Late Tang." *Asia Major*, new series 14.1 (1968): 63–95.

———. "Provincial Autonomy and Central Finance in Late T'ang." *Asia Major*, new series 11.2 (1965): 211–32.

———. "The T'ang Market System." *Asia Major*, new series 12.2 (1966): 202–48.

———. "Varied Patterns of Provincial Autonomy in the T'ang Dynasty." In *Essays on T'ang Society*, edited by John Curtis Perry and Bardwell L. Smith, pp. 90–109. Leiden: E. J. Brill, 1976.

Verellen, Franciscus. *Du Guangting (850–933): Taoïste de cour à la fin de la Chine médiévale*. Paris: Collège de France, 1989.

Wang Gungwu. *The Structure of Power in North China during the Five Dynasties*. Stanford: Stanford University Press, 1967.

Wang Shounan 王壽南. *Tangdai fanzhen yu zhongyang guanxi zhi yanjiu* 唐代藩鎮與中央關係之研究. Taipei: Jiaxin shuini gongsi wenhua jijinhui, 1969.

Watanabe Takashi 渡邊孝. "Chū Tō ki ni okeru 'monbatsu' kizoku kanryō no dōkō: Chūō sūyōkanshoku no jinteki kōsei o chūshin ni" 中唐期における「門閥」貴族官僚の動向: 中央樞要官職の人的構成を中心に. In *Yanagida Setsuko sensei koki kinen: Chūgoku no dentō shakai to kazoku* 柳田節子先生古稀記念: 中國の傳統社會と家族, pp. 21–50. Tokyo: Kyūko shoin, 1993.

———. "Chūban Tōki ni okeru kanjin no bakushokukan nyūshi to sono haikei" 中晚唐期における官人の幕職官入仕とその背景. In *Chūtō bungaku no shikaku* 中唐文學の視角, edited by Matsumoto Hajime 松本肇 and Kawai Kōzō 三合康三, pp. 357–92. Tokyo: Sōbunsha, 1998.

———. "Gihaku to Seitoku" 魏博と成德. *Tōyōshi kenkyū* 東洋史研究 54.2 (1995): 96–139.

———. "A Re-Examination of the Recruiting System in 'Military Provinces' in the Late Tang—Focusing on the Composition of the Ancillary Personnel in Huainan and Zhexi." Trans. Jessey J. C. Choo. *Tōyōshi kenkyū* 東洋史研究 64.1 (2005): 1-73.

———. "Tōdai hanshin ni okeru kakyū bakushokukan ni tsuite" 唐代藩鎮における下級幕職官について. *Chūgoku shigaku* 中國史學 11 (2001): 83–107.

———. "Tōkō hanki no hanshin hekishōsei ni tsuite no sai kentō" 唐後半期の藩鎮辟召制についての再檢討. *Tōyōshi kenkyū* 東洋史研究 60.1 (2001): 30–68.

Wechsler, Howard J. "Factionalism in Early T'ang Government." In *Perspectives on the T'ang*, edited by Arthur Wright and Denis Twitchett, pp. 87–120. New Haven: Yale University Press, 1973.

———. "T'ai-tsung the Consolidator." In *The Cambridge History of China*, vol. 3: *Sui and T'ang China*, part 1, edited by Denis Twitchett, pp. 188–241. New York: Cambridge University Press, 1979).

Wickham, Chris. *Framing the Early Middle Ages: Europe and the Mediterranean, 400–800*. New York: Oxford University Press, 2006.

Wittfogel, Karl A. "Public Office in the Liao Dynasty and the Chinese Examination System." *Harvard Journal of Asiatic Studies* 10.1 (1947): 13–40.

Wong, Kwok-yiu. "The White Horse Massacre and Changing Literati Culture in Late Tang and Five Dynasties China." *Asia Major*, 3rd series 23.2 (2010): 33–75.

Wright, Arthur F., and Denis Twitchett, eds. *Perspectives on the T'ang*. New Haven: Yale University Press, 1973.

Wu Hung. *Art of the Yellow Springs: Understanding Chinese Tombs*. Honolulu: University of Hawai`i Press, 2009.

Wu Tingxie 吳廷燮. *Tang fangzhen nianbiao* 唐方鎮年表. Beijing: Zhonghua shuju, 1980.

Xiong, Victor. *Sui-Tang Chang'an: A Study in the Urban History of Medieval China*. Ann Arbor: Center for Chinese Studies, 2000.

Yan Gengwang 嚴耕望. *Tang pu shang cheng lang biao* 唐僕尚丞郎表. Taipei: Lishi yuyan yanjiusuo, 1956.

Yancheva, Gergana, et al. "Influence of the Intertropical Convergence Zone on the East Asian Monsoon." *Nature* 445 (4 January 2007): 74–77.

Yang Baocheng 楊寶成, ed. *Hubei kaogu faxian yu yanjiu* 湖北考古發現與研究. Wuhan: Wuhan daxue chubanshe, 1995.

Yang Jidong. "The Making, Writing, and Testing of Decisions in the Tang Government: A Study of the Role of the 'Pan' in the Literary Bureaucracy of Medieval China." *Chinese Literature: Essays, Articles, Reviews* 29 (2007): 129–67.

Yang Yunru 楊筠如. *Jiupin zhongzheng yu Liuchao menfa* 九品中正與六朝門閥. Shanghai: Shangwu yinshuguan, 1930.

Yang Zihui 楊子慧, ed. *Zhongguo lidai renkou tongji ziliao yanjiu* 中國歷代人口統計資料研究. Beijing: Gaige chubanshe, 1995.

Yanshi Xingyuan Tang mu 偃師杏園唐墓. Beijing: Kexue chubanshe, 2001.

Yao Ping 姚平. *Tangdai funü de shengming licheng* 唐代婦女的生命歷程. Shanghai: Shanghai guji chubanshe, 2004.

Yates, Robin D. S. *Washing Silk: The Life and Selected Poetry of Wei Chuang*. Cambridge, MA: Council on East Asian Studies, Harvard University, 1988.

Ye Wa. "Mortuary Practice in Medieval China: A Study of the Xingyuan Tang Cemetery." Ph.D. thesis, University of California, Los Angeles, 2005.

Yoshioka Makoto 吉岡真. "Hasseiki zenhan ni okeru Tōchō kanryō kikō no jinteki kōsei" 八世紀前半における唐朝官僚機構の人的構成. *Shigaku kenkyū* 153 (1981): 19–43.

———. "Zui Tō zenki ni okeru shihai kaisō" 隋唐前期における支配階層. *Shigaku kenkyū* 155 (1981): 22–39.

Yu Fuwei 余扶危 and Zhang Jian 張劍, eds. *Luoyang chutu muzhi zuzang di ziliao huibian* 洛陽出土墓誌卒葬地資料匯編. Beijing: Beijing tushuguan chubanshe, 2002.

Yu Xianhao 郁賢皓. *Tang cishi kao quanbian* 唐刺史考全編. Hefei: Anhui daxue chubanshe, 2000.

Zhang Guangda 張廣達. "Naitō Kōnan de Tang Song biange shuo ji qi yingxiang" 內藤湖南的唐宋變革及其影響. *Tang yanjiu* 唐研究 11 (2005): 5–71.

Zhang Guogang 張國剛. "Tangdai fanzhen leixing ji qi dongluan tedian" 唐代藩鎮類型及其動亂特點. *Lishi yanjiu* 歷史研究 1983.4:98–110.

———. *Tangdai fanzhen yanjiu* 唐代藩鎮研究. Rev. ed. Beijing: Zhongguo renmin daxue chubanshe, 2009.

Zhang Yun 張蘊. "Guanyu Xi'an nanjiao Biyuan chutu de Wei shi muzhi chukao" 關於西安南郊畢原出土的韋氏墓誌初考. *Kaogu yu wenwu* 考古與文物 2000.1:56–61, 66.

Zhao Chao 趙超. *Gudai muzhi tonglun* 古代墓誌通論. Beijing: Zijincheng chubanshe, 2003.

———. *Xin Tang shu zaixiang shixi biao jijiao* 新唐書宰相世系表集校. Beijing: Zhonghua shuju, 1998.

Zhaoling Tangmu bihua 昭陵唐墓壁畫. Beijing: Wenwu chubanshe, 2006.

Zhongguo wenwu ditu ji: Shaanxi fence 中國文物地圖集: 陝西分冊. Xi'an: Xi'an ditu chubanshe, 1998.

Zhongguo wenwu ditu ji: Shandong fence 中國文物地圖集: 山東分冊. Beijing: Zhongguo ditu chubanshe, 2007.

Personal Name Index

Numbers in brackets are epitaph numbers. If an epitaph (or spirit-path stele) is extant for an individual included in this index, the epitaph number can be used in conjunction with the database (or spreadsheet) to find relevant citations to published transcriptions or rubbings. See Appendix A for more on the database. Page numbers in italics refer to figures and tables.

An (Ms.) 安氏 (800–51), [**3057**], p. 56
An Lushan 安祿山 (c. 703–57), pp. 55n67, 145, 146, 150, 151, 227. *See also* An Lushan Rebellion in General Index

Bai Juyi 白居易 (772–846), pp. 105, 107, 124, 173
Bai Minzhong 白敏中 (792–861), [**85**], pp. 107, 170
Bai Tiao 栢苕 (d. c. 839), [**1223**], p. 130n47
Bi Jiong 畢坰 (751–811), [**3609**], pp. 60n78, 129n40

Cai (Ms.) 蔡氏 (775–850), [**46**], p. 42n38
Cai Zhi 蔡贄 (807–45), [**1507**], p. 23n71
Cao Kui 曹戣, p. 197
Chen (Ms.) 陳氏 (832–56), [**1061**], p. 41n34
Chen Bangzhan 陳邦瞻 (d. 1623), p. 4
Chen Chu 陳楚 (763–823), p. 103
Chen Huan 陳瓛 (780–842), [**3873**], p. 16n38
Chen Shidong 陳士棟 (786–839), [**2000**], p. 79n17
Chen Shishang 陳師上 (779–839), [**2199**], pp. 17n40, 81n23
Chen Si 陳思 (fl. 1225–64), pp. 51, 111–112
Chen Xuanlu 陳宣魯 (808–40), [**2007**], pp. 76–77, 101n47
Cheng An 程安 (761–829), [**3784**], p. 104n60
Cui (Ms.) 崔氏 (742–97), [**4063**], p. 18n46
Cui (Ms.) 崔氏 (770–806), [**2192**], p. 99
Cui (Ms.) 崔氏 (784–858), [**2354**], pp. 17n44, 81n24
Cui (Ms.) 崔氏 (790–826), [**2176**], p. 42n38
Cui (Ms.) 崔氏 (793–843), [**2459**], p. 30
Cui (Ms.) 崔氏 (812–57), [**1236**], p. 81n21
Cui Ang 崔昂 (508–65), [**4259**], pp. 45n49, 145
Cui Bei 崔倍 (747–816), [**2942**], p. 100
Cui Borang 崔伯讓, pp. 56–57
Cui Chengjian 崔成簡 (753–819), [**4006**], p. 19n51
Cui Chui 崔陲 (727–91), [**3839**], p. 140n74

Cui Dashan 崔大善 (571–87), [**4271**], p. 45n49
Cui E 崔鍔 (804–22), [**2444**], p. 80n19
Cui Ezhi 崔諤之 (671–719), [**4241**], p. 100n46
Cui Fangjian 崔方揀 (779–861), [**1488**], pp. 51n59, 56–57
Cui Fu 崔俌 (754–805), [**2984**], p. 74n11
Cui Gan 崔幹 (d. c. 650), [**4270**], p. 45n49
Cui Hang 崔沆 (d. 880), pp. 2n1, 195n29
Cui Hongli 崔弘禮 (766–830), [**2056**], pp. 179–80, 184
Cui Huangzuo 崔黃左 (743–97), [**3305**], p. 100n46
Cui Liang 崔亮 (772–828), [**3129**], p. 80n18
Cui Lifang 崔立方 (787–855), [**1474**], p. 90
Cui Maozao 崔茂藻 (836–75), [**657**], p. 136
Cui Qi 崔芑 (788–851), [**1250**], p. 75n13
Cui Qi 崔琪 (815–60), [**807**], p. 29n4
Cui Qianli 崔千里 (736–97), [**2260**], p. 99
Cui Qiu 崔璆 (d. 883), p. 193
Cui Shao 崔紹 (834–77), [**627**], p. 129n38
Cui Shu 崔鉥 (801–20), [**2443**], p. 79n17
Cui Tai 崔泰 (576–636), [**4260**], p. 45n49
Cui Taizhi 崔泰之 (667–723), [**4198**], p. 100n46
Cui Wu 崔侮 (795–871), [**3025**], p. 21n60
Cui Wujing 崔無競 (631–90), [**4247**], p. 45n49
Cui Xiaochang 崔孝昌 (669–711), [**4266**], p. 100n46
Cui Xinggong 崔行功 (d. 674), pp. 56–57
Cui Xinggui 崔行規 (817–67), [**725**], pp. 42n38, 79n17
Cui Xu 崔昫 (c. 786–c. 834), [**2102**], p. 40n31
Cui Xuanliang 崔玄亮 (608–49), [**4240**], p. 45n49
Cui Xuanliang 崔玄亮 (768–833), [**3842**], p. 105n62
Cui Yan 崔郾 (768–836), p. 140
Cui Yanzhao 崔彥昭 (d. 879), p. 136
Cui Yi 崔倚 (d. c. 812), [**2393**], p. 100n45
Cui Yifu 崔夷甫 (704–56), [**4239**], p. 129n40
Cui Yin 崔胤 (d. 904), p. 204

Cui Yisun 崔貽孫 (859–80), [**189**], pp. 41n35, 211

Cui Yong 崔泳 (746–88), [**4275**], p. 79n17

Cui Yuan 崔圓, p. 100n46

Cui Yuanli 崔元立 (806–26), [**2292**], pp. 19n52, 20

Cui Zhen 崔鎮 (819–75), [**2493**], p. 79n17

Cui Zhi 崔植 (791–856), [**629**], pp. 17n44, 81n24

Cui Zhiyuan 崔致遠 (b. 857), p. 212n104

Cui Zhongfang 崔仲方 (539–614), [**4244**], p. 45n49

Daxi Ge 達奚革 (795–866), [**876**], p. 41n35

Deng Chang 鄧敞, pp. 222–23

Dong Jin 董晉 (724–99), [**4394**], p. 175

Dong Tangzhi 董唐之 (804–58), [**68**], pp. 40, 111n11, 155n32

Dou (Ms.) 竇氏 (d. 879), [**1095**], p. 41

Doulu Zhuan 豆盧瑑 (d. 880), p. 195n29

Du (Ms.) 杜氏 (752–829), [**2044**], p. 19n51

Du (Ms.) 杜氏 (799–835), [**2148**], p. 47n55

Du Fu 杜甫 (712–770), 232n145

Du Guangting 杜光庭 (850–933), pp. 192–93, 196–98

Du Jian 杜兼 (750–809), [**3593**], p. 17n42

Du Mu 杜牧 (803–52), pp. 95–96, 105, 124, 156

Du Qiong 杜瓊 (767–831), [**2068**], p. 93n39

Du Quan 杜詮 (c. 791–c. 850), [**3912**], pp. 95–96

Du Rangneng 杜讓能 (841–93), p. 204

Du Xunhe 杜荀鶴 (846–907), p. 232n146

Du You 杜佑 (735–812), [**2699**], p. 95

Duan Zhang 段章, p. 197

Dugu Yu 獨孤郁 (776–815), [**3656**], pp. 129n37, 134

Emperor Aidi 哀帝 (892–908), pp. 3, 209n87

Emperor Daizong 代宗 (726–79), p. 157

Emperor Dezong 德宗 (742–805), pp. 101n47, 156–58, 160

Emperor Gaozong 高宗 (628–83), p. 35

Emperor Gaozu 高祖 (566–635), pp. 30, 181

Emperor Taizong 太宗 (597–649), pp. 70, 107, 138

Emperor Xianzong 憲宗 (778–820), pp. 179n90, 194n25. See also Xianzong Restoration in General Index

Emperor Xizong 僖宗 (862–88), pp. 2, 187, 189, 195, 200, 204

Emperor Xuanzong 玄宗 (685–762), pp. 120, 135, 146

Emperor Xuanzong 宣宗 (810–59), p. 140

Emperor Yizong 懿宗 (833–73), p. 188

Emperor Zhaozong 昭宗 (867–904), pp. 201, 205, 209, 219

Emperor Zhongzong 中宗 (656–710), pp. 70–71

Empress Wu 武 (623–705), pp. 6, 70, 72n5, 107, 137

Ennin 圓仁 (793–864), 82n25

Fan (Ms.) 范氏 (821–75), [**951**], p. 80

Fan Mengrong 范孟容 (791–831), [**2900**], p. 17n41

Fan Yi 范弈 (739–95), [**2264**], p. 131

Fei Fu 費俯 (856–77), [**1479**], p. 19n53

Feng Shenzhong 馮審中 (810–52), [**1165**], p. 22

Feng Sui 封隨 (778–835), [**1594**], p. 75n12

Fu Cun 傅存 (d. 860), [**814**], pp. 16n37, 23

Fu Lin 符璘 (734–98), [**3777**], p. 103

Fu Yin 傅鈏 (748–813), [**2638**], p. 132n52

Gao Ju 高璩 (d. 865), p. 107

Gao Kai 高鍇 (d. c. 838), p. 139

Gao Lishi 高力士 (690–762), p. 120

Gao Pian 高駢 (d. 887), pp. 189, 212, 213, 217, 221

Gao Ying 高郢 (740–811), p. 140n73

Ge Hong 蓋洪, p. 193

Ge Juyuan 蓋巨源 (811–73), [**1091**], p. 66n91

Geng Zongyi 耿宗倚 (823–81), [**192**], p. 153n24

Gong (Ms.) 龔氏 (744–804), [**3253**], p. 18n47

Gong Zuzhen 龔祖真 (772–847), [**1509**], p. 18n47

Gu Chongxi 顧崇傳 (765–847), [**1510**], p. 23n74

Gu Qian 顧謙 (806–72), [**985**], pp. 41n34, 52–53

Gu Yanwu 顧炎武 (1613–82), pp. 45–46

Guanxiu 貫休 (832–912), pp. 209–10

Guo Liang 郭良 (770–841), [**2197**], p. 21n61

Guo Shun 郭順 (840–88), [**205**], p. 194n26

Guo Wenggui 郭翁歸 (784–845), [**3981**], p. 19n52

Guo Ziyi 郭子儀 (697–781), p. 125

Han Fu 韓復 (783–851), [**3947**], p. 129n37

Han Gongwu 韓公武 (d. 822), p. 74

Han Na 韓拏 (808–19), [**3720**], p. 73n7

Han Qi 韓琦 (1008–75), p. 110n8

Han Shifu 韓師復, p.21n61
Han Shou 韓綬 (821–78), [**625**], p. 174
Han Wo 韓偓 (842–923), p. 231
Han Yu 韓愈 (768–824), pp. 13n34, 17n42, 20n58, 73n7, 98, 124, 132, 137–38, 160
He (Ms.) 何氏 (778–845), [**1962**], p. 53n64
He Fu 何撫 (783–823), [**2434**], p. 74n11
He Fu 何俛 (801–66), [**982**], p. 41n33
He Hongjing 何弘敬 (806–65), [**112**], p. 41n35
He Qufei 何去非 (fl. 1082–90), pp. 148n8, 156n36
He Wenzhe 何文哲 (764–830), [**2397**], p. 43n41
Hong Mai 洪邁 (1123–1202), p. 110
Hou Ji 侯繢 (770–835), [**2149**], p. 75
Hou Luoniang 侯羅娘 (778–852), [**21**], pp. 55, 57n69
Hu Sanxing 胡三省 (1230–1302), p. 111
Hu Xiang 胡珦 (740–818), [**3701**], p. 138n65
Huang Chao 黃巢 (d.884), pp. 2, 167, 182, 188–89, 190n13, 191–96, 199–200, 207. *See also* Huang Chao Rebellion in General Index
Huang Gongjun 黃公俊 (803–78), [**824**], p. 41n33
Huangfu Pi 皇甫鉟 (799–862), [**2482**], pp. 62–64, 175n79
Huangfu Ying 皇甫映 (793–864), [**1695**], p. 130n42

Jia (Mr.) 賈公 (779–817), [**3679**], p. 20n55
Jia Xiang 賈湘, pp. 198, 200, 223n132

Kang Zhida 康志達 (768–821), [**2514**], p. 179n91
Kong Kui 孔戣 (751–824), [**3706**], p. 94n41

Lai Zuoben 來佐本 (d. c. 873), [**672**], p. 19n53
Lei Kuang 雷況 (d. 870), [**1360**], p. 19n52
Li (Mr.) 李公 (764–820), [**2364**], pp. 136, 179n91, 181
Li (Ms.) 李氏 (654–716), [**4282**], p. 72n5
Li (Ms.) 李氏 (720–800), [**3469**], p. 130n47
Li (Ms.) 李氏 (740–815), [**4093**], p. 131
Li (Ms.) 李氏 (d. c. 765), [**3303**], p. 100n46
Li (Ms.) 李氏 (771–822), [**2285**], pp. 17n44, 81n24, 130n47
Li (Ms.) 李氏 (774–839), [**1959**], p. 17n44
Li (Ms.) 李氏 (788–843), [**2461**], p. 130n41
Li (Ms.) 李氏 (804–33), [**2203**], p. 90
Li (Ms.) 李氏 (812–69), [**3027**], p. 23n69
Li (Ms.) 李氏 (813–63), [**787**], pp. 65–66
Li (Ms.) 李氏 (814–62), [**2483**], p. 131n49
Li (Ms.) 李氏 (823–56), [**4090**], p. 23n72
Li (Ms.) 李氏 (828–59), [**2358**], p. 28n2
Li (Ms.) 李氏 (830–55), [**1218**], p. 129n37
Li (Ms.) 李氏 (d. 874), [**1708**], pp. 124, 140n74
Li Baochen 李寶臣 (d. 781), p. 151
Li Bi 李弼 (479–526), [**4645**], p. 45n49
Li Dan 李眈 (d. 857), [**1237**], p. 19n51
Li Dang 李瑞, p. 174
Li Daosu 李道素 (623–39), [**4647**], p. 45n49
Li Daoyin 李道因 (d. 876), [**827**], p. 140n74
Li Desun 李德孫 (815–18), [**3271**], p. 74n10
Li Deyu 李德裕 (787–849), pp. 61, 133, 143n81, 155, 175
Li Di 李迪 (c. 683–c. 747), [**4452**], p. 45n49
Li Duanyou 李端友 (811–53), [**1139**], pp. 129–30
Li Fan 李範 (786–855), [**1580**], pp. 179n91, 184
Li Gao 李皋 (733–92), [**4064**], p. 18n46
Li Gongdu 李公度 (784–852), [**1221**], pp. 17n42, 91
Li Gongfu 李公馥 (c. 830–c. 882), [**4076**], p. 207
Li Guangjin 李光進 (759–815), [**2769**], p. 169
Li Guangyan 李光顏 (762–826), [**2610**], p. 169
Li Hong 李弘 (754–816), [**2935**], pp. 102, 130n42
Li Huai 李懷 (730–801), [**2982**], p. 80n18
Li Huaixian 李懷仙 (d. 768), p. 151
Li Ji 李勣 (594–669), [**3753**], pp. 70–72
Li Ji 李濟 (776–825), [**2527**], pp. 179n91, 181
Li Jiang 李絳 (764–830), p. 135
Li Jing 李荊 (749–821), [**3710**], p. 130n42
Li Jinglue 李景略 (732–86), p. 104
Li Jingrang 李景讓 (c. 789–c. 860), p. 140
Li Jingye 李敬業 (Xu Jingye) (d. 684), p. 70
Li Jiong 李迥 (689–730), [**4619**], p. 45n49
Li Ju 李舉 (750–814), [**2945**], p. 130n42
Li Ju 李璩 (814–71), [**1037**], p. 135
Li Jue 李珏 (785–853), p. 174
Li Junying 李君穎 (540–73), [**4581**], p. 45n49
Li Keyong 李克用 (856–908), pp. 200–201, 208n79, 213, 215, 216, 230n139
Li Liangchen 李良臣 (728–63), [**3461**], p. 169
Li Linfu 李林甫 (683–752), pp. 31, 135, 146
Li Maozhen 李茂貞 (856–924), pp. 215, 216
Li Ning 李寧 (774–856), [**1224**], p. 140n74
Li Ping 李評 (787–831), [**3161**], p. 81n22
Li Pu 李璞 (811–55), [**3132**], p. 82n26

Li Qi 李錡 (d. 807), p. 170
Li Qun 李群 (778–826), [**2529**], p. 81n23
Li Rang 李讓 (793–850), [**1056**], p. 41n33
Li Rui 李蕤 (464–505), [**4633**], p. 45n48
Li Shao'an 李少安 (759–808), [**3552**], pp. 135–36, 184
Li Shihua 李士華 (754–816), [**3844**], pp. 29n3, 29n6
Li Shu 李杼 (802–50), [**1120**], pp. 1n1, 207n77
Li Shu 李述 (814–57), [**1239**], p. 91
Li Wanshun 李婉順 (622–61), [**2705**], p. 176n83
Li Xi 李谿 (d. 895), p. 204
Li Xian 李憲 (c. 480–c. 537), [**4634**], pp. 45n49, 145
Li Xie 李頡 (710–62), [**1924**], p. 98
Li Xie 李澥 (718–60), [**4451**], p. 45n49
Li Xili 李希禮 (511–56), [**4576**], pp. 45n49, 145
Li Xizong 李希宗 (501–40), [**4575**], p. 45n49
Li Xuan 李絢 (558–622), [**4635**], p. 45n48
Li Xun 李巽 (747–809), [**3584**], p. 107
Li Xun 李愻 (d. 788), [**2210**], p. 90
Li Xun 李潯 (803–60), [**3999**], p. 22
Li Yu 李于 (776–823), [**3712**], p. 13n34
Li Yuexiang 李月相 (535–618), [**4646**], p. 45n49
Li Yun 李煜 (d. 886), pp. 204, 220–21
Li Yuzhong 李虞仲 (772–836), p. 131
Li Zaiyi 李載義 (788–837), [**4418**], p. 180n91
Li Zhao 李釗 (826–79), [**2496**], p. 81n22
Li Zhilian 李稚廉 (508–74), [**4578**], p. 45n49
Li Zhongchang 李仲昌 (d. 812), [**2951**], p. 179n91
Li Zumu 李祖牧 (511–69), [**4579**], p. 45n49
Liang Chengzheng 梁承政 (807–70), [**1705**], p. 80n19
Lin Bao 林寶, p. 112
Linghu Huaibin 令狐懷賦 (834–58), [**1154**], p. 97
Linghu Mei 令狐梅 (793–854), [**36**], pp. 43n41, 174
Linghu Zhang 令狐彰 (d. 773), p. 97
Liu Bing 劉冰 (826–68), [**163**], p. 19n51
Liu Bochu 劉伯芻 (755–815), [**4416**], p. 175
Liu Chang 劉敞 (1019–68), p. 172
Liu Congyi 劉從義 (719–805), [**2703**], p. 176n83
Liu Cunxi 劉存希, p. 198
Liu Fang 柳芳, pp. 35, 38–39, 50, 125, *126*
Liu Gongzhi 劉公制 (792–836), [**1935**], p. 18n47

Liu Honggui 劉弘規 (775–826), [**2533**], pp. 79n17, 120
Liu Hui 劉惠 (772–848), [**1230**], pp. 23n69, 40n32
Liu Ji 劉濟 (757–810), [**3599**], p. 161n56
Liu Jurong 劉巨容, p. 189
Liu Lun 劉倫 (d. 782), [**2280**], p. 99
Liu Moran 柳默然 (773–840), [**2011**], p. 99
Liu Neize 柳内則 (749–821), [**2415**], pp. 27–28, 29
Liu Rengong 劉仁恭 (d. 914), p. 215
Liu Ruyuan 劉如元 (724–98), [**3423**], p. 56
Liu Sanfu 劉三復 (d. c. 845), pp. *134*, 168n62, 175–76
Liu Song 柳肇 (751–813), [**3894**], p. 18n46
Liu Tanjing 劉談經 (748–804), [**2999**], p. 80
Liu Yan 劉浣 (727–99), [**3391**], p. 80n18 Liu Yanzhang 柳彦璋, p. 209n88
Liu Ye 劉鄴 (d. 880), pp. *134*, 168n62, 195n29
Liu Yi 劉逸 (776–834), [**1932**], p. 104n61
Liu Yin 劉隱 (873–911), p. 168
Liu Yingdao 劉應道 (613–80), [**2706**], p. 176n83
Liu Yuan 劉媛 (794–818), [**2704**], p. 176n83
Liu Zizheng 劉自政 (782–851), [**14**], p. 104
Liu Zongyuan 柳宗元 (773–819), pp. 27, 124
Liu Zunli 劉遵禮 (816–68), [**131**], p. 79n17
Lu (Ms.) 盧氏 (750–805), [**3228**], p. 28n2
Lu (Ms.) 路氏 (751–804), [**2967**], p. 42n38
Lu (Ms.) 盧氏 (767–812), [**3641**], p. 29n3
Lu (Ms.) 盧氏 (767–818), [**2940**], p. 130n42
Lu (Ms.) 盧氏 (795–860), [**806**], p. 80n18
Lu (Ms.) 盧氏 (811–58), [**1118**], p. 129n39
Lu (Ms.) 盧氏 (818–81), [**1119, 1121**], pp. 1–2, 28n2, 195n27, 207n77
Lu Boqing 盧伯卿 (774–840), [**2015**], p. 42n38
Lu Chisong 盧赤松 (569–625), [**4618**], p. 2n1
Lu Chong 盧重 (792–847), [**2335**], p. 184n97
Lu Chu 盧初 (732–75), [**2043**], pp. 20, 29n5, 62
Lu Chuyue 盧處約 (780–834), [**2449**], p. 136
Lu Congya 盧從雅 (767–834), [**2312**], p. 74
Lu Dongmei 盧東美 (734–87), [**3542**], p. 98n42
Lu Fan 盧璠 (750–819), [**3257**], p. 175n79
Lu Fang 盧方 (768–830), [**2547**], p. 79n17
Lu Guang 盧廣 (c. 738–c. 775), [**2278**], pp. 65, 130n47
Lu Hongxuan 盧弘宣 (c. 774–c. 850), p. 175
Lu Houde 盧厚德 (d. c. 844), [**2462**], p. 130n41

Lu Jian 盧緘 (804–61), [**2479**], p. 81n21
Lu Jifang 盧季方 (782–848), [**1700**], p. 80n18
Lu Jiu 盧就 (794–851), [**1251**], pp. 174–75
Lu Leniang 盧樂娘 (858–78), [**630**], p. 79n17
Lu Lü 盧侶 (c. 758–c. 814), [**3644**], p. 179n91
Lu Pan 盧槃 (d. 879), [**1370**], pp. 20n56, 81n22
Lu Pu 盧溥 (786–850), [**2341**], p. 136–37
Lu Pude 盧普德 (611–80), [**4604**], p. 45n49
Lu Qi 盧綺 (792–850), [**3436**], p. 130n42
Lu Qu 盧衢 (815–57), [**2351**], p. 130n41, 131n48, 138
Lu Quanjiao 路全交 (c. 797–c. 854), [**31**], p. 130n42
Lu Shigong 盧士羣 (745–821), [**2419**], p. 137n62
Lu Shiying 盧士瑛, p. 136
Lu Shou 盧綬 (751–810), [**2605**], p. 136
Lu Wengou 盧文構, p. 45n49
Lu Wo 盧渥 (820–905), p. 220
Lu Xian 盧涀 (714–801), [**2975**], p. 131n48
Lu Xian 盧峴 (720–74), [**4574**], p. 64
Lu Xiang 盧湘 (d. 787), [**3001**], p. 136
Lu Xie 盧攜 (d. 880), p. 195
Lu Yan 盧沇 (712–74), [**3225**], p. 98
Lu Zhan 盧占 (d. 866), [**1368**], p. 20n56
Lu Zhi 盧直 (771–823), [**2377**], p. 79n17
Lu Zhizong 盧知宗 (816–74), [**668**], p. 124
Lu Zixian 盧子獻 (842–69), [**1703**], p. 80
Lu Zonghe 盧宗和 (789–832), [**3166**], p. 79n17
Lü (Ms.) 呂氏 (764–816), [**3680**], p. 20n55
Lü Cangyuan 呂藏元 (669–736), [**2772**], p. 111n10
Lü Dejun 呂德俊 (697–762), [**4744**], p. 110n10
Lü Jianchu 呂建初 (826–69), [**142**], p. 19
Lü Xiaqing 呂夏卿 (j.s. 1042), pp. 109–110
Lü Yin 呂諲 (715–65), p. 110n10
Lun Boyan 論博言 (805–65), [**1289**], pp. 152n21, 153n24
Luo (Ms.) 駱氏 (746–808), [**1816**], p. 17n43
Luo Qian 駱潛 (848–84), [**199**], pp. 41n34, 52n63
Luo Quansi 駱全嗣, pp. 192–93
Luo Xian 駱暹 (737–85), [**2960**], p. 102n50
Luo Xiang 羅珦 (736–809), [**3591**], p. 52n63
Luo Yin 羅隱 (833–910), pp. 196, 208, 214, 231–32

Ma Jing 馬儆 (d. 832), [**2063**], p. 20n57
Ma Liang 馬良 (810–83), [**597**], p. 41n33
Ma Qian 馬倩 (743–812), [**3636**], p. 102
Ma Wan 馬琬 (835–58), [**1689**], p. 130n42
Ma Yin 馬殷 (854–931), p. 217
Ma Zhiling 馬直令 (831–74), [**4304**], pp. 21n60, 56
Ma Zong 馬總 (d. 823), p. 160
Meng Jiao 孟郊 (751–814), [**3649**], p. 23n69
Miao Hongben 苗弘本 (797–855), [**1217**], p. 111n12
Miao Zhen 苗縝 (786–844), [**1949**], p. 21n60
Niu Sengru 牛僧孺 (780–848), [**913**], pp. 133, 138, 152n22
Niu Yanzong 牛延宗 (834–77), [**646**], p. 18n47

Ouyang Chen 歐陽諶, p. 110
Ouyang Wei 歐陽琟 (697–761), [**4399**], p. 110
Ouyang Xiu 歐陽修 (1007–72), pp. 109–110, 171–72, 173

Pan Kejian 潘克儉 (782–842), [**3980**], p. 94
Pei (Ms.) 裴氏 (792–821), [**2516**], pp. 129n37, 129n39
Pei (Ms.) 裴氏 (852–77), [**4530**], p. 19n51
Pei Che 裴澈, p. 194n24
Pei Daosheng 裴道生 (780–84), [**2980**], p. 91
Pei Du 裴度 (765–839), pp. 160, 161, 170, 173n75
Pei Gao 裴誥 (801–50), [**1697**], p. 174n78
Pei Ji 裴垍 (d. 811), p. 158
Pei Ji 裴佶 (d. 813), p. 175n79
Pei Jian 裴兼 (763–810), [**2953**], p. 90
Pei Shu 裴樞 (841–905), pp. 218–19
Pei Tian 裴腆, p. 136
Pei Wu 裴武 (d. 826), p. 175n79
Pei Wu 裴渥, pp. 193–94
Pei Xu 裴諝, p. 136
Pei Zha 裴札 (728–84), [**2995**], pp. 42n38, 91, 174
Peng (Mr.) 彭公 (c. 780–c. 831), [**2424**], p. 75

Qian Liu 錢鏐 (852–932), pp. 214, 217
Qiao Shixi 喬師錫 (785–848), [**3955**], p. 23n72
Qiji 齊己 (c. 863–c. 937), p. 233
Qin Zongquan 秦宗權 (d. 889), pp. 207–8, 212, 216–217
Qing Zhixia 青陟霞 (760–852), [**3084**], p. 132
Qiu Zhicheng 仇志誠 (775–839), [**2572**], p. 104n58
Quan Deyu 權德輿 (759–818), [**3723**], pp. 101, 134

Quan Gao 權皋 (723–68), [**3874**], p. 101n48
Quan Jun 權均 (720–51), [**4311**], p. 101n48

Ren Xuan 任玄 (812–68), [**136**], p. 41n34

Shang Rang 尚讓, pp. 193, 199
Shangguan Zheng 上官政 (765–829), [**2439**], p. 8n23
Shen Chuanshi 沈傳師 (769–827), [**4316**], p. 94n40
Shen Gua 沈括 (1031–95), p. 5n10
Shen Jiji 沈既濟 (fl. 780s), p. 140
Shen Xian 申憲 (d. c. 850), [**2247**], p. 18n47
Shi (Ms.) 石氏 (774–853), [**1253**], p. 18n47
Shi Hong 石洪 (771–812), [**3625**], p. 20n58
Shi Shimian 施士丐 (734–802), [**3490**], p. 19n52
Shi Siming 史思明 (703–761), p.55n67
Shi Xiaozhang 史孝章 (800–38), [**3575**], p. 28n2
Sikong Tu 司空圖 (837–908), pp. 191, 197, 213, 220–21, 222
Sima Guang 司馬光 (1019–86), pp. 187–88, 189–90, 196, 214
Song (Ms.) 宋氏 (759–819), [**2391**], p. 19n53
Song Ti 宋遏 (735–85), [**4668**], p. 40n30
Song Zaichu 宋再初 (777–858), [**69**], p. 40n30
Su (Ms.) 蘇氏 (824–78), [**638**], p. 20n55
Sun (Ms.) 孫氏 (794–850), [**849**], p. 52n63
Sun Bei 孫備 (832–70), [**1772**], p. 20
Sun Dang 孫讜 (809–68), [**134**], pp. 72–73, 81n23
Sun Gongyi 孫公乂 (772–851), [**1149**], pp. 85–86
Sun Jiazhi 孫嘉之 (657–739), [**4310**], p. 79n17
Sun Jingyu 孫景裕 (d. 870), [**1036**], p. 81n23
Sun Ju 孫筥 (788–860), [**817**], p. 80n20
Sun Qi 孫榮 (fl. 889), p. 140
Sun Ru 孫儒 (d. 892), pp. 208, 213–14, *216–17*, 221, 225
Sun Sui 孫綏 (798–878), [**180**], p. 39n28
Sun Ying 孫嬰 (745–801), [**3215**], p. 79n17

Tang Yanqian 唐彥謙, p. 233
Tao Daiqian 陶待虔 (d. 849), [**1083**], p. 41n35
Tao Ying 陶英 (737–801), [**2261**], pp. 81n23, 130n45
Tian Chengsi 田承嗣 (704–78), pp. 125, 151, 162
Tian Hongzheng 田弘正 (764–821), p. 180

Tian Lingzi 田令孜 (d. 893), pp. 187, 215
Tong Guozheng 同國政 (787–851), [**1135**], p. 21

Wang (Mr.) 王公 (780–829), [**2546**], p. 80n19
Wang (Ms.) 王氏 (c. 771–c. 804), [**2981**], p. 131n51
Wang (Ms.) 王氏 (824–70), [**149**], pp. 40, 111n11
Wang (Ms.) 王氏 (836–49), [**2512**], p. 23n70
Wang Bin 王斌, p. 203
Wang Chengyuan 王承元 (801–833), p. 104
Wang Chongrong 王重榮 (d. 887), pp. 212, 214, 220–21
Wang Chongying 王重盈 (d. 895), pp. 212, 214
Wang Chucun 王處存 (831–95), p. 167
Wang Chuzhi 王處直 (863–923), p. 167
Wang Dajian 王大劍 (743–809), [**3198**], p. 22n67
Wang E 王鍔 (740–815), p. 175
Wang Gong 王珙, pp. 212n105, 214
Wang Gongshu 王公淑 (780–848), [**1296**], p. 153n24
Wang Gui 王珪 (571–639), p. 107
Wang Jian 王建 (847–918), pp. 215, *216*, 221
Wang Jin 王瑾 (826–47), [**4084**], p. 81n23
Wang Jinpo 王金婆 (829–62), [**1584**], p. 132n52
Wang Ke 王珂, pp. 212n105, 214
Wang Nixiu 王逆修 (c. 773–c. 823), [**2624**], p. 104
Wang Qi 王岐 (747–803), [**3236**], p. 16n37
Wang Rui 王睿 (810–72), [**1590**], p. 55
Wang Shi 王適 (771–814), [**3715**], p. 75n13
Wang Shiyong 王時邕 (799–845), [**1943**], p. 23
Wang Taizhen 王太真 (840–62), [**97**], pp. 18n49, 82n25
Wang Tan 王譚 (813–64), [**776**], p. 107n1
Wang Tingcou 王庭湊 (d. 834), p. 151
Wang Wan 王綰 (d. 797), [**3165**], p. 76n15
Wang Wujun 王武俊 (735–801), p. 125
Wang Xianzhi 王仙芝 (d. 878), pp. 188, 207, 209, 211
Wang Xiting 王希庭 (762–841), [**2524**], p. 18n47
Wang Xiuben 王修本 (d. 837), [**1728**], p. 61
Wang Xuanqi 王玄起 (649–96), [**2715**], p. 61n82
Wang Xun 王訓 (727–67), [**4094**], p. 75n13
Wang Xun 王詢 (c. 808–77), [**3024**], p. 23n72

Personal Name Index

Wang Ying 王郢, p. 209n88
Wang Yuanzhen 王元貞 (c. 781–c. 860), [**3070**], p. 132
Wang Yun 王惲 (789–845), [**1972**], p. 19n51
Wang Zhaocheng 王照乘 (795–856), [**1687**], p. 84
Wang Zhen 王振 (768–833), [**2099**], p. 17n40
Wang Zhengyan 王正言 (755–818), [**2127**], p. 28n2
Wang Zhi 王晊 (c. 802–c. 882), [**194**], p. 195n28
Wang Zhiyong 王志用 (787–837), [**2570**], p. 80n19
Wei (Ms.) 韋氏 (771–802), [**2259**], p. 132
Wei (Ms.) 韋氏 (802–57), [**219**], pp. 61n83, 130n46
Wei (Ms.) 衛氏 (844–86), [**200**], p. 41n34
Wei Anshi 韋安石 (651–714), p. 107
Wei Bin 韋斌 (d. c. 793), [**4407**], p. 107n1
Wei Bing 韋冰 (774–827), [**2531**], p. 82n25
Wei Chengsu 韋承素 (788–847), [**191**], p. 107n1
Wei Chou 魏儔 (819–65), [**761**], p. 79n17
Wei Dushi 韋都師 (d. 856), [**1233**], p. 80
Wei Fang 韋方 (800–30), [**3964**], p. 81n23
Wei Feng 韋渢 (735–810), [**3351**], p. 107
Wei Guohua 衛國華 (777–830), [**3788**], p. 104
Wei Jinghong 衛景弘 (812–55), [**1686**], pp. 22, 130
Wei Miao 魏邈 (760–814), [**3312**], p. 94
Wei Ting 韋挺 (770–825), [**2528**], p. 111n12
Wei Wendu 韋文度 (789–844), [**2586**], p. 81n23
Wei Xiang 韋祥 (d. 812), [**2297**], p. 80
Wei Xingsu 韋行素 (793–827), [**2027**], p. 130n44
Wei Yu 韋翰 (d. 859), [**3986**], p. 17n43
Wei Yuan 韋媛 (810–81), [**598**], pp. 42n38, 50n56, 213
Wei Zhaodu 韋昭度 (d. 895), p. 204
Wei Zhi 韋陟 (696–760), p. 107
Wei Zhongfu 魏仲俛 (782–825), [**2163**], p. 79n17
Wei Zhonglian 魏仲連 (780–848), [**1760**], p. 79n17
Wei Zhouji 魏舟濟 (790–849), [**2906**], p. 20n57
Wei Zhuang 韋莊 (847–910), pp. 191, 196, 198–203 passim, 206–207, 219–23 passim, 231, 233, 241–42

Wen Lingshou 溫令綬 (806–74), [**667**], pp. 41n35, 153n24
Wu Chongyin 烏重胤 (761–827), p. 174
Wu Qindai 武欽戴 (665–79), [**4284**], p. 72n5

Xiao Fang 蕭放 (742–83), [**2300**], p. 174
Xie Guan 謝觀 (793–865), [**738**], pp. 102n50, 179n91
Xie Shaoqing 解少卿 (770–835), [**1890**], p. 42n38
Xu (Mr.) 許公 (d. 867), [**130**], pp. 39, 59n77
Xu Ji 徐及 (751–834), [**1933**], p. 22n65
Xu Jingye 徐敬業. *See* Li Jingye
Xu Taiqing 許太清 (770–857), [**1650**], p. 18n47
Xu Yin 徐寅 (j.s. 892), p. 208
Xu Zhi 許贄 (809–52), [**20**], p. 41n34
Xue (Ms.) 薛氏 (805–48), [**3969**], p. 24n76
Xue Baoji 薛寶積, [**2782**], *cover photo*, p. 51
Xue Daoshi 薛道實, [**2781**], p. 51
Xue Jian 薛蹇 (749–815), [**3838**], p. 51n58
Xue Ping 薛苹 (746–819), [**4446**], p. 51n58
Xue Ping 薛平 (757–836), [**1158**], pp. 51n58, 174
Xue Song 薛嵩 (d. 772), p. 174
Xue Yiju 薛貽矩 (850–912), [**4825**], p. 51n58
Xue Zan 薛贊 (762–840), [**2014**], p. 93
Xun (Ms.) 荀氏 (809–54), [**30**], p. 20n55

Yan Haowen 閻好問 (810–73), [**677**], pp. 41, 153n24
Yan Moudao 顏謀道 (642–721), [**2707**], p. 97
Yan Youming 顏幼明 (785–866), [**119**], p. 97
Yan Yuanzhen 顏元貞 (d. c. 745), [**2129**], p. 75n12
Yang (Ms.) 楊氏 (d. 757), [**3676**], p. 101n48
Yang Guozhong 楊國忠 (d. 756), p.135n60
Yang Hangong 楊漢公 (785–861), [**967**], pp. 42n38, 107
Yang Hao 楊晧 (840–58), [**800**], pp. 38n24, 79n17
Yang Jian 楊釗 (833–79), [**1375**], p. 19n53
Yang Ning 楊寧 (744–817), [**2927**], p. 79n17
Yang Ning 楊凝 (773–803), [**3896**], p. 24n76
Yang Qianguang 楊乾光 (794–853), [**1219**], p. 174
Yang Shan 楊贍 (789–826), [**2172**], p. 104
Yang Sili 楊思立 (d. 875), [**626**], pp. 38n24, 79n17
Yang Tong 楊彤, p. 76

Yang Xiaozhi 楊孝直 (751–835), **[2113]**, p. 104
Yang Xigu 楊希古, p. 193
Yang Xingmi 楊行密 (852–905), pp. 213–14, 217, 218, 234
Yang Xishi 楊希適, p. 23
Yang Zhuan 楊篆, p. 213n106
Yao Jixian 姚季仙 (787–863), **[103]**, p. 41n34
Yao You 姚侑 (747–802), **[2972]**, pp. 79n17, 81n23
Yu (Ms.) 于氏 (840–71), **[2911]**, p. 82n26
Yu Chenghuan 庾承歡 (767–820), **[2228]**, p. 140n74
Yu Chengxuan 庾承宣 (d. 835), p. 140
Yu Cong 于琮 (d. 880), p. 195n29
Yu Ruxi 于汝錫 (791–847), **[3974]**, pp. 17n44, 81n24
Yu Yan 于偃 (710–50), **[4174]**, p. 23n72
Yu Youfang 庾游方 (c. 818–c. 859), **[1612]**, p. 140n74
Yuan (Ms.) 源氏 (735–96), **[2251]**, p. 101n47
Yuan (Ms.) 元氏 (770–804), **[3529]**, p. 90
Yuan Gun 元袞 (758–809), **[3354]**, p. 22n66
Yuan Shengjin 元昇進 (770–845), **[2477]**, p. 87
Yuan Wei 源蔚, p. 20n56
Yuan Weicheng 袁惟承 (753–814), **[2947]**, p. 130n43
Yuan Xian 苑咸 (710–58), **[2985]**, p. 75
Yuan Zhen 元稹 (779–831), p. 124
Yue Bangsui 樂邦穗 (827–77), **[193]**, pp. 41n34, 153, 179

Zhai (Ms.) 翟氏 (d. 819), **[3705]**, p. 74
Zhang (Mr.) 張公 (789–859), **[1260]**, p. 22n65
Zhang (Ms.) 張氏 (751–824), **[2167]**, p. 131n50
Zhang (Ms.) 張氏 (759–820), **[2508]**, p. 56
Zhang (Ms.) 張氏 (761–817), **[2005]**, pp. 22, 131
Zhang (Ms.) 張氏 (795–855), **[1231]**, pp. 19n53, 41n35
Zhang (Ms.) 張氏 (807–69), **[4082]**, p. 30n7
Zhang Chan 張嬋 (816–40), **[2008]**, p. 101n47
Zhang Guan 張觀 (803–63), **[788]**, pp. 17n44, 81n24
Zhang Hong 張翃 (709–78), **[3294]**, p. 101n47
Zhang Jianzhang 張建章 (806–66), **[121]**, p. 152
Zhang Jing 張婧 (825–66), **[4078]**, p. 21n60
Zhang Jirong 張季戎 (790–851), **[972]**, p. 103n56
Zhang Jiuling 張九齡 (678–740), p. 119

Zhang Liangfu 張良輔 (754–814), **[3645]**, p. 103
Zhang Liuke 張留客 (842–71), **[223]**, p. 80n20
Zhang Maozhao 張茂昭 (762–811), p. 103
Zhang Qiqiu 張齊丘 (656–91), **[4312]**, p. 101n47
Zhang Quanyi 張全義 (852–926), p. 208–9
Zhang Shiji 張仕濟 (789–810), **[1926]**, p. 55
Zhang Shiling 張士陵 (763–816), **[3282]**, p. 100
Zhang Shiyu 張時譽 (688–733), **[4313]**, p. 101n47
Zhang Shuzun 張叔遵 (810–71), **[152]**, p. 103n53
Zhang Wengui 張文規, p. 137
Zhang Wu 張武 (826–83), **[892]**, pp. 39–40
Zhang Xiang 張翔 (724–79), **[3293]**, p. 101n47
Zhang Xiaozhong 張孝忠 (730–91), p. 125
Zhang Xin 張信 (782–850), **[1146]**, p. 17n44
Zhang Xun 張曛 (747–813), **[3324]**, p. 68n93
Zhang Ying 張嬰 (834–55), **[42]**, p. 101n47
Zhang Zhifang 張直方 (d. 880), pp. 194, 195, 196
Zhang Zhongli 張中立 (825–79), **[826]**, p. 224n136
Zhao (Ms.) 趙氏 (d. 819), **[2384]**, p. 19n52
Zhao Cong 趙琮 (d. 875), **[651]**, p. 39
Zhao Congyi 趙從一 (792–868), **[1092]**, p. 41n34
Zhao Gongliang 趙公亮 (842–84), **[594]**, p. 23
Zhao Gui 趙珪 (806–47), **[1748]**, p. 99
Zhao Huang 趙璜 (804–62), **[91]**, p. 99
Zhao Junzhi 趙君旨 (776–834), **[2110]**, p. 74
Zhao Teng 趙藤 (756–810), **[4083]**, p. 79n17
Zhao Tu 趙途 (811–70), **[4047]**, p. 79n17
Zhao Wenxin 趙文信 (763–845), **[2585]**, p. 19n51
Zhao Yi 趙翼 (1727–1814), pp. 148n8, 156n36
Zhao Zhang 趙璋, p. 193
Zheng (Ms.) 鄭氏 (762–803), **[2966]**, p. 130n45
Zheng (Ms.) 鄭氏 (780–838), **[2318]**, p. 18n46
Zheng (Ms.) 鄭氏 (784–833), **[2098]**, pp. 80n19, 82n26
Zheng (Ms.) 鄭氏 (808–64), **[1701]**, p. 80n18
Zheng (Ms.) 鄭氏 (d. 808), **[3176]**, p. 95
Zheng (Ms.) 鄭氏 (827–58), **[63]**, p. 140n74
Zheng (Ms.) 鄭氏 (d. 871), **[652]**, p. 75n13
Zheng Cong 鄭漴 (747–93), **[3185]**, p. 179n91
Zheng Congdang 鄭從讜 (d. 887), p. 173n75
Zheng Fang 鄭魴 (777–834), **[3028]**, p. 130n47

Personal Name Index

Zheng Gao 鄭高 (745–805), **[3516]**, p. 99
Zheng Gu 鄭谷 (c. 851–c. 910), pp. 201–2, 211
Zheng Guan 鄭瑄 (791–854), **[1300]**, p. 91
Zheng Guang 鄭光 (d. 857), p. 194n25
Zheng Gun 鄭緄 (796–820), **[2383]**, p. 95
Zheng Hanzhang 鄭漢璋, p. 194n25
Zheng Hao 鄭顥 (d. c. 860), p. 140
Zheng Jinsi 鄭進思 (626–75), **[4058]**, p. 99
Zheng Juan 鄭涓 (821–65), **[763]**, p. 42n38
Zheng Juzhong 鄭居中 (784–837), **[2426]**, p. 131n50
Zheng Lu 鄭魯 (c. 768–c. 824), **[2929]**, pp. 94–95, 96
Zheng Qiao 鄭樵 (1104–62), p. 5
Zheng Sanqing 鄭三清 (844–52), **[956]**, p. 132n52
Zheng Shaofang 鄭紹方 (768–809), **[1822]**, p. 131n48
Zheng Shuyi 鄭恕己 (d. 851), **[852]**, p. 19
Zheng Xingzhe 鄭行者 (805–8), **[2037]**, p. 74n10
Zheng Xiushi 鄭秀實 (784–856), **[1107]**, p. 66n91
Zheng Xuan 鄭絢 (722–86), **[2936]**, p. 131n51
Zheng Zizhang 鄭子章 (831–53), **[34]**, p. 82n25
Zhi Mo 支謨 (829–79), **[2646]**, p. 136
Zhi Song 支詠, pp. 101–2
Zhi Zhijian 支志堅 (812–61), **[793]**, p. 111n11
Zhong Chuan 鍾傳 (d. 906), p. *217*
Zhou (Ms.) 周氏 (764–839), **[2001]**, p. 103n56
Zhou Bao 周寶 (d. 887), pp. 212, 213
Zhou Yu 周璵 (787–856), **[53]**, pp. 41n35, 153, 179
Zhu Ci 朱泚 (742–84), p. 227n137
Zhu Quanzhong 朱全忠 (852–912), pp. 3, 204, 205, 209, 212, 215, *216–217*, 221
Zhu Shan 朱贍 (809–65), **[128]**, pp. 87, 178
Zhu Siniang 朱四娘 (d. 850), **[1272]**, p. 23n70
Zhu Wen 朱溫. *See* Zhu Quanzhong
Zhu Zhongliang 朱忠亮 (d. 813), p. 104

General Index

Page numbers in italics refer to figures and tables

affinal kin: as authors or calligraphers of epitaphs, 20, 131; and family prestige, 27–29, 37–38, 65–66; and funeral arrangements, 22, 76–77, 131–32; as political patrons, 133–34, 135–37, 174–75; sources of data on, 13–16, 32, 38n25, 65–66, 108–9, 112, 245, 247; and the support of orphans and widows, 130–31. *See also* endogamy; marriage network of Late Tang elites

agnatic kin: as authors or calligraphers of epitaphs, 20, 130; and family prestige, 65; and funeral arrangements, 22, 73–76, 129–30; as political patrons, 135–37, 139, 142; sources of data on, 13–16, 65, 108–9, 245; and the support of orphans and widows, 94–95, 111, 129. *See also* patrilines; pedigree

An Lushan Rebellion, 146; and the aristocracy, 145; and the autonomous Hebei provinces, 55n67, 97; compared to the Huang Chao Rebellion, 26, 186, 226–30, 232n145, 239; historiography of, 6–7, 147, 148n8, 155–56, 230n140; long-term impact, 6–7, 26, 122n26, 147–48, 150–51, 185, 236; and migration, 55, 58, 98–101, 136, 181; war heroes, 125, 144. *See also* An Lushan in Personal Name Index

ancestral sacrifices, 74–75, 77, 113, 129n38. *See also* burials; rituals for

Anding Huangfu clan, 62–64

aristocracy: adaptability of, 69, 142, 148, 186, 236, 238–39; as a capital elite, 25–26, 71–72, 84–87, 105–6, 119–21, 123–24; Chinese as compared to European and Roman, 9n24, 11–12, 58–60, 68, 236; demographics of, 42–43, 121–22, 248–49; destruction of, 2–3, 5–8, 147–48, 190–91, 218–34, 239–42; hereditary rights of, 6, 12; long-term survival of, 1, 7, 124, 142–45, 185–86, 235–36; and officeholding, 7, 26, 61–68, 123–24, 168, 176–78, 236; and marriage endogamy, 5, 12, 27–29, 30, 61–66 passim, 129; provincial colonies, 88–98, 102, 211, 213, 219, 237–38; as a subset of the great clans, 25, 29, 105, 142, 237. *See also* great clans; marriage network of Late Tang elites; national elites

aristocratic ethos, 3, 5, 12, 27–29, 61–66, 67–68, 143, 237

army supervisors, 75, 158

autonomous Hebei provinces, xv, 10; and capital elites, 136, *166*, 169, 176–77, 178–81, 184; character of provincial elites, 85–86; and the great clans, 36–40 passim, *47*, 51n59; origins of, 147, 151; as place of origin of post-Tang elites, 190n14, 242; and post-Huang Chao violence, 213, 215, *216*, 224–25; relationship to court, 151–55, 157, 161–67, 240; unique culture, 183–84. *See also* Chengde Province; Weibo Province; Youzhou

Baima Massacre, 204, 219
Baoke congbian, 111–12, 116, 118
Beizhou, 30, 154–55, 184
Binzhou, 104, 136, 194
Blon clan, 112, 152n21
blood relatives. *See* agnatic kin
Bohai Gao clan, 36n23
Boling Cui clan, 35n20, 45, 56–57, 99–100, 119, 145n83. *See also* marriage-ban clans
Bozhou, 97
Buddhism, 23, 29n6, 100, 102, 132, 154, 207
bureaucratic appointments: to central government posts, 84–85, 159, 172–73; formal selection procedures, 132–35; informal procedures, 135–37, 171; monopolization by aristocracy, 133–37, 141; to provincial posts, 72–73, 84–87, 178–79, 182. *See also* selection examination
bureaucratic recruitment. *See* civil service examination; *yin* (protection) privilege
burials: costs of, 17–25, 130; land for, 18, 21–22, 23, 76–77, 101n47, 132; and place of residence, 36, 73–82; preparations for, 16–23, 129–30, 131–32; rituals for, 18–19, 22, 81n24, 82n25, 130; secondary, 18, 22, 75, 76, 99–102; sumptuary laws regarding, 24; temporary, 75–76, 81–82, 99, 113, 246. *See also* clan cemeteries; tombs

Caizhou, 207, *216*
calligraphy, 19–21, 83, 133, 176, 222, 232n146. *See also* epitaphs, calligraphers for
Cangzhou, 179n90, 230
cannibalism, 33n16, 199, 208, 212, 215, 230
capital cities: cost of living, 21–22, 93–95; and the great clans, 1, 44–47, 67, 236; as home base of aristocracy, 25–26, 71–72, 84–87, 105–6, 119–21, 123–24; urban wards, 79n17, 102, 197, 245. *See also* Chang'an; Luoyang
capital elites. *See under* aristocracy
capital corridor, 10, 46–47, 50–51, 82, 88, 98, 116, 120–21. *See also* geographic variations, capital vs. provinces
carvers, 19, 21, 24n76, 247
Chang'an: compared to Luoyang, 50, 119–21, 125, 133–34, 139, 144–45; flight from city during rebellions, 192–93, 197–98, 201, 227; food supply, 59, 196, 199; and the Huang Chao Rebellion, 2, 26, 189, 191–200; massacres in, 2, 195–99, 201, 203–5; physical destruction of, 200–203, 205–6; residency patterns, 127–29; walls and gates of, 192–93, 196–97, 201–2, 206n73. *See also* capital cities
Changzhou, *54*, 214, *217*
Chengde Province, *xv*, *162*, *216*; and capital elites, 104, 125, 179, 181; relationship to court, 104, 151, 152n21. *See also* autonomous Hebei provinces
Chenjun Xie clan, 35n21, 52, *54*. *See also* émigré clans
Chenjun Yin clan, *54*. *See also* émigré clans
Chenjun Yuan clan, 35n21, 52, *54*. *See also* émigré clans
Chenzhou, 87, 104, 178, 230
chief examiners, 133–34, 139–40, 144, 238, 239, 246–47
chief ministers: and capital elite marriage network, 124, *134*, 144, 238, 239; in database, 246–47; geographic origins of, 119–21, 133, *134*; and great clans, 7; as political patrons, 132, 134, 135, 143, 174–75; prestige of, 20, 65–66; and provincial governments, 173; serving Huang Chao's regime, 193, 198; and post-Huang Chao violence, 195, 204, 218, 219
children: adoption of, 42n40, 94–95, 111, 120, 129–31; burial of, 23, 73–74, 131–32; of concubines, 12n32, 41, 42n38, 124–25; education of, 1, 28–29, 60, 131, 138; marriage of, 1, 90, 129, 130, 131, 138; naming, 111n11; number per family, 42–43; sources of data on, 16, 42n37, 245

Chinese Biographical Database (CBDB), 11
Chinese Historical Geographic Information System (CHGIS), xiv, 11
Chu Kingdom, *217*
choronyms, 30–35, 40–41, 47–50, 66–67, 73, 245–47 passim. *See also* great clans
cinnabar, 13n34
civil service examination: as mid-Tang institutional innovation, 137, 142, 236; as method of bureaucratic recruitment, 132, 236; monopolization by aristocracy, 138–41, 142; prefectural candidates, 140, 159; suspicions about fairness, 139, 142–43; and social mobility, 6, 137–41, 142, 236. *See also* chief examiners
clan cemeteries, 17, 46–47, 52n63, 53, 73–77, 96, 113–18, 246
clan genealogies, 5, 12, 41, 63n87, 64, 109–10, 112
clans. *See* great clans; imperial clan; *and individual clans by name*
class struggle, 8, 10, 190n13, 196
climate change, 240–41
cliques. *See under* marriage network of Late Tang elites
colonialism: and cultural hegemony of the capital, 182–83, 241; and exploitation of local populations, 188, 240; and subaltern elite, 183, 240; Tang dynasty as structurally different from later dynastic states, 25, 240
commercialization, 4, 6–7, 147, 154, 171, 236
commissioners, 7, 149–50, 170–71. *See also* governors
concubinage, 12, 25, 41, 42n36, 43–44, 67, 124–5, 223
core vs. periphery. *See under* geographic variation
corruption and nepotism, 59–60, 68, 94n41, 139, 143, 174n77
country villas. *See under* land and property
courtesy names (styles), 62, 111, 112, 244
cultural change, 3, 11, 183–84, 224, 241–42
cultural isolation, 10, 183–84

Daoism, 65, 99, 140, 197–98
digital methodologies, xiii, 10–11, 112–3; potential problems with, 11
disease and illness, 2, 189, 199
distant genealogies, 62–64, 67
divination, 17, 75, 100
Dunhuang manuscripts, 31, 67

General Index

Eastern Jin Dynasty, 35n21, 51–52, 57
education: of children, 1, 60, 131, 138; and family prestige, 5, 12, 28; as human capital, 231, 233, 241–42
émigré clans, 35n21, 51–52, 54–55, 57–58
endogamy, 5, 12, 27–29, 30, 61–66 passim, 129. *See also* marriage-ban clans; marriage network of Late Tang elites
enfeoffments, 56
epitaphs, 13–25; authors of, 19–21, 66, 130, 247; calligraphers for, 19–21, 66, 247; compared to dynastic history biographies, 9, 24, 71n4, 73n8, 110–11; content of, 13–17, 32, 65–66, 73, 108–9; cost to produce, 19–21, 23; decline in production post-Huang Chao, 190, 191, 224–26; as a historical source, xiii, 9, 13–17, 110, 245–47, 250–52; as indicators of wealth, 16, 24–25, 32, 47, 57, 82–83; production of, 19–21, 23; reading aloud of, 19n51; Tang vs. Song, 250; transmitted vs. excavated, 13, 24, 25, 224, 246, 250; as "veritable records," 17. *See also* spirit-path steles
equal field system, 6, 60, 236
eunuchs: in database, 244; geographic distribution within capital region, *121*, *127*, *128*; marriage network, 127; political influence, 104n60, 187, 215; political purges, 204–5; recruitment, 102–103; as social pariahs, 133; and epitaphs, 9, 120–21; wealth, 21–22, 103; wives and children, 120, 127. *See also* army supervisors
examinations. *See* civil service examination; selection examination
Ezhou, 80, *217*

family trees, 113–18
famines, 188, 199–200, 206–7, 213, 215, 230, 240–41. *See also* cannibalism
Fangshan stone classics, 154
Fanyang Lu clan, 1, 35n20, 45, 64, 116–18. *See also* marriage-ban clans
Fengxiang, 104, 162, 200, 201, 213, 215, 216, 230
Five Dynasties and Ten Kingdoms: and the aristocracy, 3, 231, 233–34, 239; consolidation of new regimes, *216–17*, *218*; and late Tang provincial governments, 156, 158, 185
foreign trade, 102, 154
Former Shu Kingdom, 215, 216, 221
Fuchun Sun clan, 33n19, 52n63
Fufang Province, *162*, *169*n63, 216
Fufeng Dou clan, 35n21, 41

Fufeng Ma clan, 56
Fuzhou, 210, 217

Gaoyang Xu clan, *54*. *See also* émigré clans
genealogical tables in *Xin Tang shu*, 109–11, 136, 244, 248–49
genealogies. *See* clan genealogies
geographic variation, 10, 16, 24n77, 69; capital vs. provinces, 10, 25, 71–72, 82–88, 237–38; Chang'an vs. Luoyang, 50, 119–21, 125, 133–34, 139, 144–45; core vs. periphery, 53–55, 57–58; North China vs. South China, 10, 156, 161, *163–66*. *See also* autonomous Hebei provinces
geology, 16
geomancy, 17–18
government apartments, 78–79, 80
governors: accession to office, 149, 151, 157, 161, 163, 167; and accusations of corruption, 60n78, 94n41; and capital elite marriage network, 125, 160, *165–66*, *168–69*, 238, 239; in database, 246; military vs. civilian, 150–51, 160, 161, 164, 167–68; need for charisma, 182n92; as patrons, 22, 141, 143, 173–75; prestige of, 65n88; retinues, 22, 103–4, 172–73. *See also* autonomous Hebei provinces; provincial governments
Grand Canal, 54, 57, 59, 102
grave goods, 13, 18, 24n75, 71, 83n27. *See also* burials; tombs
great clans, 27–68; claims of descent from, 32, 34–35, 36–44, 108; classification of, 29–36, 38–39, 175; demographic expansion of, 41–44, 67; geographic dispersal, 44–61; lists of, 31–35, 44, 67; relocation to the capital, 1, 44–47, 67, 236; as a status elite, 8, 25, 105, 237; still at place of clan origin, 45–47, 50–55, 57. *See also* émigré clans; marriage-ban clans; *and individual clans by name*
Guangping Song clan, 40n30
Guangzhou, 210, 211, 217

Han dynasty, 1, 62, 63, 235
Hangzhou, *54*, 76, 101, 178n88, 209, 217
Hanoi. *See* Jiaozhi
Hebei. *See* autonomous Hebei provinces
"Hebei custom," 151, 184
Hedong Liu clan, 35n21
Hedong Pei clan, 35n21, 36n23, 40, 46–47, 50, 116, 247
Hedong Province, 46, 104, *162*, 173n75, *216*

Hedong Xue clan, 35n21, 50–51, *115*, 116
Hedong Wei clan, *54*. See also émigré clans
Hejian Liu clan, 40n32
Henan Changsun clan, 35n21
Henan Lu clan, 35n21
Henan Yan clan, 41
Henan Yu clan, 35n21, 114
Henan Yuan clan, 35n21, 50
Henan Yuwen clan, 35n21
hereditary titles, 12, 132n53
Heyang Province, *162*, 208, *216*, 222, 230
Hezhong, 116, 162, 212–13, 214–15, 216, 220–21, 222
Hezhou, 210, 217
home base. See place of residence
Hongnong Liu clan, 40n32
Hongnong Yang clan, 35n21, 36n23, 38n24, 115
Hongzhou, 82n26, 90, 91, 174, 217
Huang Chao Rebellion, 2–3, 187–234; as apocalyptic, 202, 231–33; in Chang'an, 2, 189, 191–200; compared to An Lushan Rebellion, 26, 186, 226–30, 232n145, 239; as evidence of peasantry's revolutionary potential, 190n13; eyewitness accounts of, 191, 192–215 *passim*, 219–24 passim, 231–33 passim; and the destruction of the aristocracy, 2–3, 26, 106, 190–91, 200–204, 209, 218–34, 239; impact on agricultural productivity, 199, 202–3, 206–7, 208, 230; impact on Hebei and Hedong, 213, 215, *216–17*, 225; in Luoyang, 2, 189, 192, 194–95, 206–8; origins of, 187–90; in South China, 2, 188–89, 209–12, 219, 224–25; and subsequent chaos, 2–3, 167–68, 200–201, 204–6, 207–9, 212–18, 227–29, 239; violence of rebellion and its aftermath, 2, 8, 190–91, 195–205, 207–15, 218–20, 227–29, 239. See also Huang Chao in Personal Name Index
Huazhou, 94, 107, *115*, 200, 216, 221
Huzhou, 53, 54, 217

imperial clan (of the Song), 184, 242
imperial clan (of the Tang): and capital marriage network, 25–26, 119, 124, 125, 134, 144–45, 238; claim to great clan descent, 38n24; and post-Huang Chao violence, 194, 205; and provincial governors, 162, 169; years between generations, 248
inbreeding, 124–25
Inner Mongolia, 56, 85

Jiannan Xichuan Province, 157, *162*
Jiaozhi (Hanoi), xv, 85, 103n53
Jiangling, 88, 95, 98, 104, 211–12, 230
Jiangzhou, 116
Jin Dynasty, 70, 105n64
Jingzhao Du clan, 35n21, 50
Jingzhao Wei clan, 35n21, 36n23, 50, *114*, *115*
Jingzhou. See Jiangling
jinshi degree. See civil service examination
Jiyang Jiang clan, *54*. See also émigré clans

Khitans, 125, 152, 183n93
kinship. See affinal kin; agnatic kin
Korea, 70, 212
Kuaiji Luo clan, 52n63

"Lament of the Lady of Qin," 31n12, 191, 196, 202, 206, 213
land and property: as basis of power and influence, 8, 12, 45–46, 58, 68, 238; for burials, 18, 21–22, 23, 76–77, 101n47, 132; contracts, 18; deregulation of, 6–7, 147, 236; government grants of, 103n57, 138; in or near the capital, 26, 77–79, 94, 99, 103n57, 138, 238; in the provinces, 58–61, 82n26, 88–91, 94–96, 136, 220–21, 235–36; laws regarding, 60; loss, destruction, or seizure of, 60, 191, 200–201, 202–4, 222, 231; mulberry land, 23n71, 39n29, 60n78, 203; price of, 21–22, 94; private residences, 77–80, 88–91, 95, 96, 127; purchase of, 18, 21–22, 76, 94, 101n47; rental of, 23, 59, *78*; as unsafe investment, 60–61
landed elites, 9, 39, 45–46, 58–61, 68, 88, 94–96
Langya Wang clan, 35n21, 36n23, 52, *54*, 57. See also émigré clans
Lanling Xiao clan, 35n21, 133. See also émigré clans
Later Liang Dynasty, 205, *216–17*
Later Tang Dynasty, *216*
Le'an Sun clan, 33n19, 39n28, 52n63, *114*, 140n76
libraries, 60, 138, 222
Lingnan Province, 94n41, *162*, 168
Liuzhou, 82n26
localism, 72, 87–88, 105, 182
Longxi Dong clan, 40
Longxi Li clan, 35n20, 38n24, 45, 65, *114*. See also imperial clan; marriage-ban clans
Longzhou, 87

General Index

Lower Yangzi region: and capital elites, 93, 97–102, 178; and the great clans, 36–40 passim, 47, 51–55, 57–58, 67; land, 18, 22; local elites, 83–86 passim; and post-Huang Chao violence, 212, 213–14, 217, 219, *229*. *See also relevant prefecture names*
Lujiang He clan, *54*. *See also* émigré clans
Luoyang: compared to Chang'an, 50, 119–21, 125, 133–34, 139, 144–45; and the Eastern Capital Command, 103, 120, 150; as home base of marriage-ban clans, 1, 44–45, 50, 119–20, 125–26, 142, 144–45; and the Huang Chao Rebellion, 2, 26, 189, 194–95, 206–8; massacres in, 208; physical destruction of, 208–9; reconstruction of, 209; and selection and civil service examinations, 132, 139. *See also* capital cities
Luzhou 潞州, 18n45, *49*, *53*, 56, 83n29, 87, 104, 219
Luzhou 廬州, *217*, *234*

marriage. *See* affinal kin; endogamy
marriage-ban clans, 35, 38–40 passim, 50, 51n59, 64, 66, 119, 125, *126*, 238, 246
marriage network of Late Tang elites, 25–26, 122–45; cliques, 25–26, *123*, 125–29, *134*, 144–45, 246; and cultural hegemony, 182–84, 241–42; destruction of, 106, 191, 231–34, 241–42; geographic concentration in capital, 119–21, 123–24; geographic distribution within capital region, 125–29, 142; prestige of, 66, 67; and provincial governors, *166*, 168–69; and social capital, 10–11, 133–37, 139–41, 144–45, 148, 238–39; as a sub-culture, 11, 241–42. *See also* affinal kin; agnatic kin; patronage
Mengzhou, *53*, 75, 103, *115*, 117
merchants, 7, 9, 39, 88, 102, 154
meritocratic ethos, 3, 5, 7, 10, 172, 242
metropolitan culture, 133, 183–84, 241–42
mGar clan. *See* Blon clan
migration (of elites): to capital, 44–45, 76–77, 99–102, 105, 106, 119, 226; and clan cemeteries, 76–77, 99–102; of great clan descendants, 44–58, 105, 226; of non-officeholders, 102–3; of military men, 103–4; and officeholding, 55–57, 86–87, 90–93; to provinces, 86–87, 105, 237–38; and social mobility, 96–98, 105–6, 237–38; to South China, 98–101; and warfare, 55, 98–101, 219–22

militia system, 149
military elites: and capital elite social network, 87, 124, 125, *126*, 144, 238; in Chang'an, 103, 120; in database, 244; number of offspring, 42–43; and provincial governments, 103–4, 151, 157, 161, 167–68
military valor, 12
ministers of personnel, 132–35, 144, 238, 239, 246–47
Ming Dynasty, 59n73, 63n87, 206n73
Mingzhou, *53*, *217*
mutinies, 151, 158, 167–168, 182, 240
muzhiming. *See* epitaphs

Naitō thesis, 3n4. *See also* Tang-Song transition
Nanjing, 52n61, *54*, 55, 57
Nanyang Zhang clan, 36n23
Nanzhao, 152n21
national elites, 84–98, 102, 168, 182, 211, 213, 237–38. *See also* aristocracy
native tribes, 103n53, 212
near genealogies, 62, 63, 64, 67
"newly risen" elites, 6–7, 9–10, 137, 171
non-officeholders, 39–40, 84, *85*, 97, 102, 244, 245. *See also* landed elites; merchants
Northern Wei Dynasty, 30, 35n21
Northern Zhejiang, 52n63, 84, *85*, 178, *228–229*

officeholding traditions (of elite families), 61–64, 84–86, 122–24, 165, 168, 237, 245

Palace Armies, 158
Parhae, 152
patrilines: and claims of prestigious descent, *37*, 38; empirical reconstruction, 108–13, 123, 244, 246; geographic distribution, 119–21; vs. great clans, 108; localizing, 113–18; of provincial governors, *162*, *165–66*, 168; of top officials, 133, *134*, 139–40. *See also* marriage network of Late Tang elites
Pei Du precedent, 160, 161, 170
Pengcheng Liu clan, 36n23, 40n32, 56
Pengzhou, 230
Pinglu Province, 104n61, 157, *162*, 174, *216*
place of residence. *See under* burials
polo, 187
primogeniture, 41
private residences. *See under* land and property
poetry, as a historical source, 191
political patrons. *See under* affinal kin; agnatic kin

political power, 8, 11, 12, 29, 36, 71–72
political factionalism and purges, 6, 10, 70, 195, 204–5, 218–19, 221
posthumous offices, 62, 111
provincial elites: vs. capital elites, 25, 71–72, 82–88, 237–38; and civil service examination, 140–41; claims to great clan descent, 36–40, 44; collaboration with court and capital elites, 185, 240; and metropolitan culture, 133, 182–84, 241; migration to capital, 102–3; and officeholding, 84, 86–87, 119–21 passim, 133–34, 172–73, 177–78; and post-Tang order, 185, 240.
provincial governments, 147–78, 247; and capital social network, *166*, 168–69, 173–75, 178; classification of subordinate offices, 176–77; and decentralization, 26, 151–56, 167–68; domination of by aristocracy, 26, *165–66*, 168–69, 170, 172–78, 240; and local elites, 87, 103–4, 177–78, 182–83, 185; and informal recruitment system, 171, 236; as mid-Tang institutional innovation, 137, 142, 147, 170–71, 236; origins of, 149–50, 170–71; and promotion to high office, 103–4, 172–73, 174–75; and recentralization, 157–70, 185, 240; and social mobility, 7, 26, 142, 147–48, 170–78, 236; and tenth-century regimes, 156, 158, 185; as tools of central government control, 26, 159–60. *See also* autonomous Hebei provinces; governors; *and the various provinces by name*

Qi Dynasty (of Huang Chao), 193–94
Qi Kingdom (of Li Maozhen), *216*
Qinghe Cui clan, 30, 35n20, 100, *114*, 119, 133. *See also* marriage-ban clans
Qinghe Zhang clan, 36n23, 55, 56
Qingzhou, 39, 53, 87, 105n61
Quanzhou, 88n33, 94n41, 178n88

relatives by marriage. *See* affinal kin
rumors, 139, 192, 211, 220
Runan Zhou clan, 52. *See also* émigré clans
Runzhou, *54*, 212, 214, *217*, 221
Ruzhou, 91, 117, 189

selection examination, 132–33, 135, 138, 141, 143; southern selection, 133n54. *See also* bureaucratic appointments
Shanguo Province, *162*, 212, 214, *216*, 222
Shaozhou, 91, 119, *217*

Shence Army, 103, 169
Shezhou, 218
Sichuan: and the An Lushan Rebellion, 146, 227; central government control over, 131, 157; and the Huang Chao Rebellion, 2, 195, 207, 227; in the post-Huang Chao period, 213, 215, 221, *229*, 230
silk production, 154, 203
social capital, 11, 26, 60, 129–41, 144, 239
social mobility: and civil service examination, 6, 137–41, 142, 236; downward mobility, 29, 33, 44, 142, 238; and intermarriage with imperial clan, 144; and migration from capital, 97–98, 105, 238; and migration to capital, 103, 106; and provincial governments, 7, 26, 142, 147–48, 170–78, 236
social networks. *See* marriage network of Late Tang elites
Sogdians, 102n52
Song dynasty. *See* localism; Tang-Song transition
Song perspective on the Tang, 5, 148n8, 156n36, 171–73, 187–88, 189–90
Songzhou, 90, 104n60
souls, 18, 22, 73–74, 75n14, 76–77
South Sea trade, 94n41
Southern Han Kingdom, 168
Southern Tang Kingdom, 234
spirit-path steles, *cover photo*, 13, 24n76, 51, 110, 113, 116n19, 245
status and prestige: of choronyms, 32, 34–36, 66–67; and cultural hegemony of capital elites, 182–184, 204, 233, 241–42; of great clan descent, 27–29, 34–35, 44, 64, 67, 237; of land ownership, 59–60; of marriage relations, 29, 62, 65–66; of "near genealogy," 64–65, 67; of officeholding pedigrees, 12, 61–68; relationship to wealth and power, 8, 9, 29, 71–72; vs. social capital, 11, 108, 141
Sui dynasty, 6, *123*, 124, *165*, 235–36, 239, 246
survivors of Late Tang violence, 220–24, 231–34, 239, 241–42
Suzhou, 35n21, 47–50, 52–53, *54*, 214, *217*. *See also* Lower Yangzi

Taiyuan Wang clan, 35n20, 39, 55. *See also* marriage-ban clans
talent, 5, 7, 64, 68, 142–43, 172, 173
Tang-Song transition, 3–5, 60, 68, 143, 147, 190, 236–37
Tanzhou, 210, *217*

tax revenue, 59, 60, 147, 153–55, 158, 188, 212, 224
temples, 78–79
Tianping Province, 107, *162*, 174, 216
Tianshui Zhao clan, 36n23, 39, 40
Tibetans, 112, 147, 152n21, 185n99, 227n137
tomb robbers, 13, 118, 250
tombs, 13, 16–18, 23–25, 70–71, 73–77, 118. *See also* burials; clan cemeteries; epitaphs; grave goods
Tongguan pass, 189, 227
Tongzhou, 90, *216*
transport costs, 19, 22, 53, 59, 61, 75, 82
travel inns, 78–79, 127
Turks, 71n3, 200, 213

Uighurs, 147, 185n99

warlordism. *See* Huang Chao Rebellion, and subsequent chaos
Warring States Period, 155
wealth: portable wealth, 60, 198, 200, 222–23, 231, 238; relationship to status and power, 8, 71–72. *See also* land and property; epitaphs, as indicators of wealth
Weibo Province, xv, *162, 216*; and capital elites, 125, 162, 179–81, 184; composition of local elite society, 84–85, 97, 151; relationship to court, 152, 167, 195. *See also* autonomous Hebei provinces
Weizhou, 155
women: empresses, 132n53, 193; epitaphs for, 23, 93n39; imperial princesses, 111n13, 122n27; natal clan cemeteries, 52n63, 81, 246; natal clans, 123, 129; palace women, 106; principal wives, 12n32, 27, 41, 42n38, 81, 124; sources of data on, 9, 16, 245–46; widows, 1, 22, 95, 129–31, 213; wives of eunuchs, 120. *See also* concubinage; *and names of individual women in Personal Name Index*
Wu Kingdom, 213, 217, 233–34
Wujun Gu clan, 35n21, 53
Wujun Lu clan, 35n21, 53
Wujun Zhang clan, 35n21, 53
Wujun Zhu clan, 35n21, 178
Wuxing Yao clan, 53
Wuyue Kingdom, 214, *217*

Xi (state), 152
Xiangzhou, 89–93 passim, 98, 104, 211–12, 230
Xianzong Restoration, 155–61, 167, 168–69, 185
Xingyang Zheng clan, 35n20, 50, 124, 133. *See also* marriage-ban clans
Xuanzhou, *217*, 230
Xuzhou 徐州, 102
Xuzhou 許州, 207

Yan dynasty, 146
Yangzhou, 22, *53*, 89–92 passim, 98–102 passim, 214, *217*, 230. *See also* Lower Yangzi region
Yicheng Province, 104, *162*, 174, *216*
yin (protection) privilege, 68, 132, 136, 137, 141, 143
Yingchuan Xu clan, 39
Yingchuan Xun clan, *54. See also* émigré clans
Yingchuan Yu clan, 52
Yiwu Province, 103, 125, *162*, 167, 175, 184n96, 216
Yongji Canal, 154–55
Youzhou, xv, *162, 216*; and great clans, *48, 53*; as highly centralized independent state, 84, 151–54, 179; political instability in, 151, 167. *See also* autonomous Hebei provinces
Yuanhe xingzuan, 110, 112
Yuezhou, 52n63, *217*

Zhaojun Li clan, 35n20, 45, 119, 145n83. *See also* marriage-ban clans
Zhaoling, 70–71
Zhaoyi Province, 36–40 passim, *47*, 84, 85, *162*. *See also* Luzhou; Mingzhou
Zhengzhou, 50, 52, 53, 81n22, 115, 117, 208
Zhenjiang, 24, 54
Zhexi Province, 52, 150, *162*, 170
Zhongwu Province, 87, *162*, 178, *216*
Zizhi tongjian, 187–88, 189–90

Harvard-Yenching Institute Monograph Series
(titles now in print)

24. *Population, Disease, and Land in Early Japan, 645–900*, by William Wayne Farris
25. *Shikitei Sanba and the Comic Tradition in Edo Fiction*, by Robert W. Leutner
26. *Washing Silk: The Life and Selected Poetry of Wei Chuang (834?–910)*, by Robin D. S. Yates
28. *Tang Transformation Texts: A Study of the Buddhist Contribution to the Rise of Vernacular Fiction and Drama in China*, by Victor H. Mair
30. *Readings in Chinese Literary Thought*, by Stephen Owen
31. *Remembering Paradise: Nativism and Nostalgia in Eighteenth-Century Japan*, by Peter Nosco
33. *Escape from the Wasteland: Romanticism and Realism in the Fiction of Mishima Yukio and Oe Kenzaburo*, by Susan Jolliffe Napier
34. *Inside a Service Trade: Studies in Contemporary Chinese Prose*, by Rudolf G. Wagner
35. *The Willow in Autumn: Ryutei Tanehiko, 1783–1842*, by Andrew Lawrence Markus
36. *The Confucian Transformation of Korea: A Study of Society and Ideology*, by Martina Deuchler
37. *The Korean Singer of Tales*, by Marshall R. Pihl
38. *Praying for Power: Buddhism and the Formation of Gentry Society in Late-Ming China*, by Timothy Brook
39. *Word, Image, and Deed in the Life of Su Shi*, by Ronald C. Egan
41. *Studies in the Comic Spirit in Modern Japanese Fiction*, by Joel R. Cohn
42. *Wind Against the Mountain: The Crisis of Politics and Culture in Thirteenth-Century China*, by Richard L. Davis
43. *Powerful Relations: Kinship, Status, and the State in Sung China (960–1279)*, by Beverly Bossler
44. *Limited Views: Essays on Ideas and Letters*, by Qian Zhongshu; selected and translated by Ronald Egan
45. *Sugar and Society in China: Peasants, Technology, and the World Market*, by Sucheta Mazumdar
49. *Precious Volumes: An Introduction to Chinese Sectarian Scriptures from the Sixteenth and Seventeenth Centuries*, by Daniel L. Overmyer
50. *Poetry and Painting in Song China: The Subtle Art of Dissent*, by Alfreda Murck
51. *Evil and/or/as the Good: Omnicentrism, Intersubjectivity, and Value Paradox in Tiantai Buddhist Thought*, by Brook Ziporyn
53. *Articulated Ladies: Gender and the Male Community in Early Chinese Texts*, by Paul Rouzer

55. *Allegories of Desire: Esoteric Literary Commentaries of Medieval Japan*, by Susan Blakeley Klein
56. *Printing for Profit: The Commercial Publishers of Jianyang, Fujian (11th-17th Centuries)*, by Lucille Chia
57. *To Become a God: Cosmology, Sacrifice, and Self-Divinization in Early China*, by Michael J. Puett
58. *Writing and Materiality in China: Essays in Honor of Patrick Hanan*, edited by Judith T. Zeitlin and Lydia H. Liu
59. *Rulin waishi and Cultural Transformation in Late Imperial China*, by Shang Wei
60. *Words Well Put: Visions of Poetic Competence in the Chinese Tradition*, by Graham Sanders
61. *Householders: The Reizei Family in Japanese History*, by Steven D. Carter
62. *The Divine Nature of Power: Chinese Ritual Architecture at the Sacred Site of Jinci*, by Tracy Miller
63. *Beacon Fire and Shooting Star: The Literary Culture of the Liang (502–557)*, by Xiaofei Tian
64. *Lost Soul: "Confucianism" in Contemporary Chinese Academic Discourse*, by John Makeham
65. *The Sage Learning of Liu Zhi: Islamic Thought in Confucian Terms*, by Sachiko Murata, William C. Chittick, and Tu Weiming
66. *Through a Forest of Chancellors: Fugitive Histories in Liu Yuan's* Lingyan ge, *an Illustrated Book from Seventeenth-Century Suzhou*, by Anne Burkus-Chasson
67. *Empire of Texts in Motion: Chinese, Korean, and Taiwanese Transculturations of Japanese Literature*, by Karen Laura Thornber
68. *Empire's Twilight: Northeast Asia Under the Mongols*, by David M. Robinson
69. *Ancestors, Virgins, and Friars: Christianity as a Local Religion in Late Imperial China*, by Eugenio Menegon
70. *Manifest in Words, Written on Paper: Producing and Circulating Poetry in Tang Dynasty China*, by Christopher M. B. Nugent
71. *The Poetics of Sovereignty: On Emperor Taizong of the Tang Dynasty*, by Jack W. Chen
72. *Ancestral Memory in Early China*, by K. E. Brashier
73. *'Dividing the Realm in Order to Govern': The Spatial Organization of the Song State*, by Ruth Mostern
74. *The Dynamics of Masters Literature: Early Chinese Thought from Confucius to Han Feizi*, by Wiebke Denecke
75. *Songs of Contentment and Transgression: Discharged Officials and Literati Communities in Sixteenth-Century North China*, by Tian Yuan Tan
76. *Ten Thousand Scrolls: Reading and Writing in the Poetics of Huang Tingjian and the Late Northern Song*, by Yugen Wang

77. *A Northern Alternative: Xue Xuan (1389-1464) and the Hedong School*, by Khee Heong Koh
78. *Visionary Journeys: Travel Writings from Early Medieval and Nineteenth-Century China*, by Xiaofei Tian
79. *Making Personas: Transnational Film Stardom in Modern Japan*, by Hideaki Fujiki
80. *Strange Eventful Histories: Identity, Performance, and Xu Wei's* Four Cries of a Gibbon, by Shiamin Kwa
81. *Critics and Commentators: The* Book of Poems *as Classic and Literature*, by Bruce Rusk
82. *Home and the World: Editing the Glorious Ming in Woodblock-Printed Books of the Sixteenth and Seventeenth Centuries*, by Yuming He
83. *Courtesans, Concubines, and the Cult of Female Fidelity*, by Beverly Bossler
84. *Chinese History: A New Manual*, by Endymion Wilkinson
85. *A Comprehensive Manchu-English Dictionary*, by Jerry Norman
86. *Drifting among Rivers and Lakes: Southern Song Dynasty Poetry and the Problem of Literary History*, by Michael Fuller
87. *Martial Spectacles of the Ming Court*, by David M. Robinson
88. *Modern Archaics: Continuity and Innovation in the Chinese Lyric Tradition, 1900-1937*, by Shengqing Wu
89. *Cherishing Antiquity: The Cultural Construction of an Ancient Chinese Kingdom*, by Olivia Milburn
90. *The Burden of Female Talent: The Poet Li Qingzhao and Her History in China*, by Ronald Egan
91. *Public Memory in Early China*, by K. E. Brashier
92. *Women and National Trauma in Late Imperial Chinese Literature*, by Wai-yee Li
93. *The Destruction of the Medieval Chinese Aristocracy*, by Nicolas Tackett